# C. H. SPURGEON'S
# SERMON NOTES

## GENESIS TO REVELATION

193 Sermon Outlines
Edited and Condensed

BY

## DAVID OTIS FULLER, D.D.

*Pastor, Wealthy Street Baptist Church*
*Grand Rapids, Michigan*

**Four Volumes in One**

ZONDERVAN PUBLISHING HOUSE

GRAND RAPIDS                    MICHIGAN

SPURGEON'S SERMON NOTES
Copyright 1941, 1969 by
Zondervan Publishing House
Grand Rapids, Michigan

Second printing....1969

*Printed in the United States of America*

# PREFACE

The more one reads and studies Spurgeon, the more one is filled with wonder at this remarkably gifted "preacher of the ages." Dr. Richard Ellsworth Day, in his admirable biography, "The Shadow of the Broad Brim," gives us a wealth of intimate glimpses into this life of one of God's spiritual giants.

Before his death Spurgeon read Pilgrim's Progress a hundred times. His entire literary style was powerfully shaped by John Bunyan. He had but one purpose and passion in life, to preach Christ in all His glory and power. He made short shrift of the "pink tea" variety of minister when he said, "Beware of running about from this meeting to that, contributing your share to the general blowing up of windbags. Your pulpit preparations are your first business."

Mr. Spurgeon was a master of the spoken and the written word. Listen to this sentence from Metropolitan pulpit, "When this great universe lay in the mind of God like unborn forests in the acorn's cup." It was Dwight L. Moody who frankly confessed that his fires came from the Bible *and* Spurgeon—"Everything he ever said, I read. My eyes just feast on him. If God can use Mr. Spurgeon why should He not use the rest of us."

This volume of Spurgeon's Sermon Notes has been condensed from four original volumes of about 1500 pages, covering the entire Bible. It is filled brimful and running over with nearly *two hundred* sermon outlines and nearly *five hundred* choice illustrations. These are not for the lazy preacher who scorns or neglects thorough preparation, but rather they are intended for those ministers, missionaries, Bible teachers who need a spark now and then to make the fire burn and glow with new heat and power.

It is the earnest hope and prayer of the editor of this condensed volume of sermon notes, that every one who puts it to use will think of the Lord Jesus Christ in the same way as did the great preacher of London when he wrote:

> What the hand is to the lute,
> What the breath is to the flute,
> What is fragrance to the smell,
> What the spring is to the well,
> What the flower is to the bee,
> That is Jesus Christ to me.
>
> What's the mother to the child,
> What the guide in pathless wild,
> What is oil to troubled wave,
> What is ransom to the slave,
> What is water to the sea,
> That is Jesus Christ to me.

*Grand Rapids, Mich.*                                    DAVID OTIS FULLER.

# CONDENSED PREFACE

On several occasions the question has been put to me, "Could you not help us with some outlines of discourses?" To which I have replied that there were many works of that kind on the market. The reply has been that they would like something plainer and less rhetorical. I felt encouraged by their request to try what could be done in the direction indicated.

I have prepared these frameworks not to encourage indolence, but to help bewildered industry; and I hope that I have not written so much as to enable any man to preach without thought, nor so little as to leave a weary mind without help.

The preachers who can entirely dispense with notes must be few; but, if their preaching is up to the mark, they are happy men. Some go on crutches, and read almost all the sermon; this, as a rule, must be a lame business. The most of us need to carry a staff, even if we do not often lean upon it. The perfectly able man requires nothing of the kind. I am not one of these first class brethren; "with my staff have I crossed this Jordan," and I hereby lend it to any who feel that they can pursue their journey by its aid.

As we pour a little water down a pump to help it to draw up a stream from below, so may these sermon notes refresh many a jaded mind, and then set it working so as to develop its own resources. May the Holy Spirit use these outlines for the help of His busy servants. To Him shall be all the praise, and to His Church the profit. What are we without Him? What is impossible to us when He is with us? May those brethren who use this small selection of topics enjoy the Lord's presence in so doing.

\* \* \* \* \*

I hope to lend a handful of chips and shavings, or if you will, a bundle of firewood, to a brother, with which he may kindle a fire on his own hearth, and prepare food for his people. Possibly a lazy brother may boil his own pot with my sticks, but even that I shall not deplore so long as the food is well cooked.

Should I be so unfortunate as to be a helper to the utterly idle man, by tempting him to gather no fuel of his own, I shall not even then view the matter with despair, for perhaps the idler may burn his fingers in the operation; and I shall fall back upon the consideration that he would have taken wood from some other pile if he had not met with mine. A man will do no great harm with my faggots if he will use holy fire; the truths which are contained in these Notes will injure no man if they be honestly allowed to speak for themselves.

\* \* \* \* \*

I hope and believe that these Notes will not be of much use to persons who fail to think for themselves. For such talkers I have no sort of compassion. My outlines are meant to be aids to preparation, and nothing more. . . . In all these outlines evangelical truth is set forth as clearly as I am able to do it. This will injure my work in the estimation of those whose admiration I do not covet; but this will cause me no alarm, for the weight of their censure is not great.

Whatever the times may be, there shall be no doubt as to where the writer of these outlines took up his standing in the hour of controversy. I know nothing but the doctrines of grace, the teaching of the Cross, the Gospel of Salvation; and I write only that these things may be the more widely published. If those who believe these truths will honor me by using my Notes, I shall rejoice, and shall trust that the blessing of God will go with their discourses. It is no small pleasure to be helping brethren in the faith to sow beside all waters the living seed of the Word of God.

\* \* \* \* \*

It was never my design to help men to deliver a message which is not their own. It is ill when prophets steal their prophecies from one another, for then they are likely—all of them—to become false prophets. But as the young prophet borrowed an axe of a friend, and was not censured for it so long as the strokes he gave with it were his own, so may we refrain from condemning those who find a theme suggested to them, and a line of thought laid before them, and with all their hearts use them in speaking to the people.

This should not be their custom; every man should have an axe of his own, and have no need to cry, "Alas, master! it was borrowed"; but there are times of special pressure, bodily sickness, or mental weariness, wherein a man is glad of brotherly help, and may use it without question. For such occasions I have tried to provide.

Oh, that I may help some of my brethren so to preach as to win souls for Jesus! Warm, personal testimony is greatly useful in this direction and, therefore, I trust that, by adding his own hearty witness to the truths which I have here outlined, many a believer may speak successfully for the Lord. I commend my humble labors to Him Whom I desire to serve by them. Without the Holy Spirit, there is nothing here but a valley of dry bones; but if the breath shall come from the four winds, every line will become instinct with life.

Your brother in Christ Jesus,

*Westwood, March, 1886*                                          C. H. SPURGEON.

# TABLE OF CONTENTS

11

# CHAPTER 1

# HASTENING LOT

*"When the morning arose, then the angels hastened Lot"* (Gen. 19:15).

Were these personages angels, or divine appearances? It matters not: they were messengers sent from God to save. In any case they teach us how to deal with men if we are to arouse and bless them. Picture the two angels with all their four hands occupied in leading out Lot and his wife and his two daughters.

I. THE RIGHTEOUS NEED TO BE HASTENED.

1. *In what?* In matters of obedience to their Lord.
   In coming out from the world. (Verse 26).
   In seeking the good of their families. (Verse 12).
2. *Why?* The flesh is weak. Lot was an old man, too much tinctured with worldliness.
   Sodom has a sluggish influence.
3. *By what means?* By reminding them of their obligations, their opportunities.
   By leading them to consider the flight of time and brevity of life.
   By warning them of sure ruin.

II. THE SINNERS NEED TO BE HASTENED.

1. *Sinners are very slow and apt to linger.*
   They have settled down in the Sodom of sin.
   They do not believe our warning. (Verse 14).
   Delay is Satan's grand device for their ruin.
2. *Our business is to hasten them.*
   We must be in earnest ourselves as these angels were.
   We must also be patient and repeat our pleadings.
   We must be resolute, and lay hold on their hands.
3. *We have many arguments with which to hasten them.*
   Their imminent danger while lingering.
   The sin of loitering when God commands.
   The supreme necessity of immediate decision.

When a young man made an open profession of the gospel, his father, greatly offended, gave him this advice: "James, you should first get yourself established in a good trade, and then think of the matter of religion." "Father," said the son, "Jesus Christ advises me differently; He says, 'SEEK YE FIRST THE KINGDOM OF GOD.'"

"Brother," said a dying man, "Why have you not been more pressing with me about my soul?" "Dear James," replied the brother, "I have spoken to you several times." "Yes," was the answer, "you are not to blame; but you were always so quiet over it; I wish you had gone on your knees to me, or had taken me by the neck and shaken me, for I have been careless, and have nearly slept myself into hell."

## CHAPTER 2

## POWER WITH GOD

*"As a prince hast thou power with God."* (Gen. 32:28).

When Jacob had prevailed with God he had no reason to fear Esau. It was the power of a single individual, exhibited in a time of deep distress: how much more power will be found where two or three agree in prayer!

I. WHAT THIS POWER CANNOT BE.

> Cannot be magical. Some seem to fancy that prayers are charms, but this is idle. (Matt. 6:7).
> Cannot be meritorious.
> Cannot be independent. It must be given by the Lord.

II. WHENCE THIS POWER PROCEEDS.

1. It arises from the Lord's nature: His goodness and tenderness are excited by the sight of our sorrow and weakness. A soldier about to kill a child put aside his weapon when the little one cried out, "Don't kill me, I am so little."

2. It comes out of God's promise. In His covenant, in the gospel, and in the Word, the Lord puts Himself under bonds to those who know how to plead His truth and faithfulness.

3. It springs out of the relationships of grace. A father will surely hear his own children.

4. It grows out of the Lord's previous acts. His election of His people is a power with Him since He is unchanging in His purposes.

III. How Can It Be Exercised.

1. There must be a deep sense of weakness. (II Cor. 12:10).
2. There must be simple faith in the goodness of the Lord. (John 14:12).

> "Faith treads on the world, and on hell;
>   It vanquishes death and despair:
> And, what is still stranger to tell,
>   It overcomes heaven by prayer."

3. There must be earnest obedience to His will. (John 9:31).
4. The whole heart must be poured out. (Hos. 12:4).

IV. To What Use This Power May Be Turned.

1. For ourselves.
   For our own deliverance from special trial.
   Our future comfort, strength, and growth, when, like Jacob, we are called to successive trials.
2. For others.
   Jacob's wives and children were preserved, and Esau's heart was softened.
   In other instances, Abraham, Job, Moses, Samuel, Paul, etc., exercised power with God for the good of others.
   How terrible to have no power with God, but to be fighting against Him with our puny arm!

Jacob, though a man, a single man, a travelling man, a tired man, yea, though a worm, that is easily crushed and trodden under foot, and no man (Is. 41:14), yet in private prayer he is so potent, that he overcomes the Omnipotent God; he is so mighty, that he overcomes the Almighty.—Thomas Brooks.

How often have I seen a little child throw its arms around its father's neck, and win, by kisses and importunities and tears, what had else been refused. Who has not yielded to importunity, even when a dumb animal looked up in our face with suppliant eyes for food? Is God less pitiful than we?—Dr. Guthrie.

This is the key that has opened and again shut heaven. It hath vanquished mighty armies, and unlocked such secrets as passed the skill of the very Devil himself to find out. It hath strangled desperate plots in the very womb wherein they were conceived; and made those engines of cruelty prepared against the saints recoil upon the inventors of them; so that they have inherited the gallows which they did set up for others. At the knock of prayer prison-doors have opened, the grave hath delivered up its dead; and the sea's leviathan, not able to digest his prey, hath been made to vomit it up again. W. Gurnall.

CHAPTER 3

"I HAVE ENOUGH"

*"Esau said, I have enough." "Jacob said, I have enough."*
(Gen. 33:9, 11).

It is as rare as it is pleasing to meet with a man who has enough; the great majority are craving for more. Here we see two persons who were content. Two brothers of dissimilar disposition, each saying "I have enough." Where shall we find two brothers like them?

I. HERE IS AN UNGODLY MAN WHO HAS ENOUGH.

Because Esau has other faults, there is no necessity that he should be discontented and grasping: contentment is a moral excellence as much as a spiritual grace.

1. Yet it has its evil side.
   It tends to breed a contempt for spiritual riches.
   It may thus be a sign of having one's portion in this life.

II. HERE IS A GODLY MAN WHO HAS ENOUGH.

1. It is a pity that this is not true of every Christian man. Some appear to be eager after the world though they profess to be separated from it.
2. It is delightful to have enough. Contentment surpasses riches.
3. It is pleasant to have somewhat to spare for the poor; and this should be the aim of our labor. (Eph. 4:28).
4. It is best of all to have all things. In the margin we read that Jacob said, "I have all things." "All things are yours." (I Cor. 3:22).

A poor Christian woman, who was breaking her fast upon a crust and a cup of water, exclaimed, "What! All this and Christ too!"

A Puritan preacher asking a blessing on a herring and potatoes, said, "Lord, we thank thee that thou hast ransacked sea and land to find food for thy children"—*Maxims for Meditation.*

Is not the bee as well contented with feeding on the dew, or sucking from a flower, as the ox that grazeth on the mountains? . . . Discontent robs a man of the power to enjoy what he possesses. A drop or two of vinegar will sour a whole glass of wine.

## Chapter 4

# JOSEPH OPENING THE STOREHOUSES

*"Joseph opened all the storehouses."* (Gen. 41:56).

Remark the bounty of providence in raising up Joseph to save the house of Israel, yea, and the whole world, from famishing. Then note the greatness of sovereign grace in raising up Jesus to save His people, and to be God's salvation to the ends of the earth.

Joseph had beforehand filled the vast storehouses, and our text shows us how he used the store—"Joseph opened all the storehouses." How much more has been done by Jesus! Oh, to be partakers of His grace!

I. JOSEPH OPENED THE STOREHOUSES BY ROYAL AUTHORITY.
1. The King was only to be approached through Joseph. (Verse 55). So with Jesus. (John 14:6).
2. The king commanded that Joseph should be obeyed. (Verse 55). (John 5:23).
3. In all the land no other could open a storehouse save Joseph. (John 3:35).

II. JOSEPH WAS A FIT PERSON TO OPEN THE STOREHOUSES.
1. He planned the storehouses, and was justly appointed to control them. See verses 33 to 36 and 38. (Heb. 1:1-3).
2. He did it on a noble scale. (Verse 49).
3. He had wisdom to distribute well.
   The parallel is easily drawn, for our Lord Jesus is that Housekeeper, one of a thousand, who has provided for our soul's famine. (Col. 1:19; John 1:16).

III. JOSEPH ACTUALLY OPENED THE STOREHOUSES.
1. For this purpose he filled them. Grace is meant to be used.
2. He opened them at a fit time. (Verses 55, 56).
3. He kept them open while the famine lasted. They were never closed while a hungering applicant drew near.

IV. JOSEPH OPENED THE STOREHOUSES TO ALL COMERS.
1. Many people came from far for food. (Verse 57).
2. We read of none being sent empty away.
   Yet Joseph did but sell while Jesus gives without money. Will you not come to Him for heavenly bread?

*William Bridge* says: "There is enough in Jesus Christ to serve us all. If two, or six, or twenty men be athirst, and they go to drink out of a bottle, while one is drinking, the other envies, because he thinks there will not be enough for him too: but if a hundred be athirst, and go to the river, while one is drinking, the other envies not, because there is enough to serve them all."

"All the spiritual blessings wherewith the Church is enriched are in and by Christ. The apostle instances some of the choicest: Eph. 1:3. Our election is by Him (verse 4). Our adoption is by Him (verse 5). Our redemption and remission of sins are both through Him. All the gracious transactions between God and His people are through Christ. God loves us through Christ; He hears our prayers through Christ; He forgives us all our sins through Christ.

"Through Christ He justifies us; through Christ He sanctifies us; through Christ He upholds us; through Christ He perfects us. All His relations to us are through Christ; all we have is from Christ; all we expect to have hangs upon Him. He is the golden hinge upon which all our salvation turns."—RALPH ROBINSON.

## CHAPTER 5

## TOO LITTLE FOR THE LAMB

*"They shall take to them every man a lamb, according to the house of their fathers, a lamb for an house: and if the household be too little for the lamb, let him and his neighbor next unto his house take it according to the number of the souls; every man according to his eating shall make your count for the lamb."* (Ex. 12:3, 4).

The lamb was to be eaten, all eaten, eaten by all, and eaten at once. The Lord Jesus is to be received into the soul as its food, and this is to be done with a whole Christ, by each one of His people, and done just now.

I. THE TEXT REMINDS US OF A PRIMARY PRIVILEGE.

1. That each man of Israel ate the passover *for himself;* "every man according to his eating." So do we feed upon Jesus, each one as his appetite, capacity, and strength enable him to do.

2. But this same delicious fare should be enjoyed by *all the family:* "a lamb for an house."
   Let not these two favors be despised. Let no man be content without personal salvation, nor without the salvation of his whole house. We have both promised in that famous text, Acts 16:31.

## II. The Text Mentions A Possibility, And Provides For It.

There may be a want of persons to feed upon the Lamb, though there can be no lack of food for them to feed upon. The last thing that was supplied to the great marriage feast was guests. The oxen and the fatlings were killed, and all things were ready, long before "the wedding was furnished with guests."

1. One family is certainly too small a reward for Jesus—too little for the lamb.

2. One family is too little to render Him all the praise, worship, service, and love which He deserves.

3. One family is too little to do all the work of proclaiming the Lamb of God, maintaining the truth, visiting the church, winning the world. Therefore let us call in the neighbor next unto our house.

   If our neighbor does not come when invited, we are not responsible; but if he perished because we did not invite him, blood-guiltiness would be upon us. "If thou dost not speak . . . his blood will I require at thine hand" (Ezek. 33:8).

## III. The Whole Subject Suggests Thoughts Upon Neighborly Fellowship in the Gospel.

1. It is good for individuals and families to grow out of selfishness, and to seek the good of a wide circle.

2. It is a blessed thing when the center of our society is "the Lamb."

3. Innumerable blessings already flow to us from the friendships which have sprung out of our union in Jesus. Church fellowship has been fruitful in this direction.

A little boy asked his mother which of the characters in "The Pilgrim's Progress" she liked best. She replied, "Christian, of course; he is the hero of the whole story." Her son said, "I don't, mother; I like Christiana best; for when Christian went on his pilgrimage he started alone, but when Christiana went she took the children with her."

A man was going to his work one morning, when he was told that the river had burst its banks, and was sweeping down the valley, carrying death and destruction wherever it went. His informant did not seem much concerned about the matter, but the brave workman immediately rushed off down to the lower part of the valley, shouting, "If that's so, somebody has got to let the people know." By his timely warning he saved the lives of many people.

CHAPTER 6

# UNSEASONABLE PRAYER

*"Wherefore criest thou unto me?"* (Ex. 14:15).

There may come a time when this question needs to be asked even of a Moses. There is a period when crying should give place to action; when prayer is heard and the Red Sea is dividing, it would be shameful disobedience to remain trembling and praying.

I. SOMETIMES THE ANSWER WILL BE VERY UNSATISFACTORY.

1. Because I was brought up to do so. Some have perpetrated gross hypocrisy through repeating forms of prayer which they learned in childhood.

2. It is a part of my religion. These pray as a Dervish dances or a Fakir holds his arm aloft; but they know nothing of the spiritual reality of prayer. (Matt. 6:7).

3. I feel easier in my mind after it. Ought you to feel easier? May not your formal prayers be a mockery of God, and so an increase of sin? (Isa. 1:12, 15; Ezek. 20:31).

II. SOMETIMES THE ANSWER WILL BETRAY IGNORANCE.

1. When it hinders immediate repentance. Instead of quitting sin and mourning over it, some men talk of praying. "To obey is better than sacrifice," and better than supplication.

2. When it keeps from faith in Jesus. The gospel is not "pray and be saved"; but "believe on the Lord Jesus Christ and thou shalt be saved." (Matt. 7:21; John 6:47).

3. When we suppose that it fits us for Jesus. We must come to Him as sinners, and not set up our prayers as a sort of righteousness. (Luke 18:11, 12).

III. SOMETIMES THE ANSWER WILL BE QUITE CORRECT.

1. Because I must. I am in trouble, and must pray or perish. Sighs and cries are not made to order, they are the irresistible outbursts of the heart. (Ps. 42:1; Rom. 8:26).

2. Because I know I shall be heard, and therefore I feel a strong desire to deal with God in supplication. "Because he hath inclined his ear unto me, therefore will I call upon him" (Ps. 116:2).

3. Because I delight in it; it brings rest to my mind, and hope to my heart. It is a sweet means of communion with my God. "It is good for me to draw near to God" (Ps. 73:28).

4. Where must those be who depend upon their own **prayers?**
   What are those who live without prayer?
   What are those who can give no reason for praying, but
   superstitiously repeat words without heart?

An anxious inquirer to whom I had plainly put the great gospel
command, "Believe in the Lord Jesus," constantly baffled my
attempts to lead her out of self to Christ.  At last she cried out,
"Pray for me! pray for me!"  She seemed greatly shocked when I
replied, "I will do nothing of the kind.  I have prayed for you
before; but if you refuse to believe the word of the Lord, I do not
see what I can pray for.  The Lord bids you believe His Son, and
if you will not do so, but persist in making God a liar, you will
perish, and you richly deserve it."  This brought her to her bearings.
She begged me again to tell her the way of salvation; she quietly
received it as a little child, her frame quivered, her face brightened,
and she cried, "Sir, I can believe, I do believe, and I am saved.
Thank you for refusing to comfort me in my unbelief."  Then she
said very softly, "Will you not pray for me now?"  Assuredly I
did, and we rejoiced together that we could offer the prayer of
faith.

In a great thaw on one of the American rivers, there was a man
on one of the cakes of ice, which was not yet actually separated
from the unbroken mass.  In his terror, however, he did not see
this, but knelt down and began to pray aloud for God to deliver him.
The spectators on the shore cried loudly to him: "Man, stop praying, and run for the shore."  So I would say to some of you, "Rest
not in praying, but believe in Jesus."—*Quoted in the "Christian." 1874.*

On one occasion, when Bunyan was endeavoring to pray, the
tempter suggested "that neither the mercy of God, nor yet the
blood of Christ, at all concerned him, nor could they help him by
reason of his sin; therefore it was vain to pray."  Yet he thought
with himself, "I will pray."  "But," said the tempter, "your sin is
unpardonable."  "Well," said he, "I will pray."  "It is to no
boot," said the adversary.  And still he answered, "I will pray."
And so he began his prayer: "Lord, Satan tells me that neither thy
mercy nor Christ's blood is sufficient to save my soul.  Lord, shall
I honor Thee most by believing Thou wilt and canst? or him, by
believing Thou neither wilt nor canst? Lord, I would fain honor
Thee by believing that Thou canst and wilt."  And while he was thus
speaking, "as if some one had clapped him on the back," that Scripture fastened on his mind, "Oh, man, great is thy faith."

CHAPTER 7

## WHO IS ON THE LORD'S SIDE?

*"Then Moses stood in the gate of the camp, and said, Who is on the Lord's side? Let him come unto me. And all the sons of Levi gathered themselves together unto him."* (Ex. 32:26).

Decision is that which the Lord looks for in His ministers, and when He sees it He will reward it.

All true men ought to be decided, for a dreadful conflict is going on at this present day, and a curse will fall on neutrals.

I. THE LORD'S FRIENDS AND WHAT THEY MUST DO.

They must own their allegiance openly. "Consecrate yourselves today to the Lord" (verse 29).

They should come out and rally to the standard: "Who is on the Lord's side? let him come unto me." We do this by open union with the church, by boldly rebuking sin, by testifying for truth, by not conforming to the world, and by conforming to Christ our Lord. (II Cor. 8:5).

They must be willing to be in a minority: one tribe against eleven, if need be.

They must become aggressive. "Put every man his sword by his side" (verse 27).

II. THE LORD'S HOST AND ITS ENCOURAGEMENTS.

Their cause is that of right and truth. A good cause is a firm foundation and a powerful stimulus of valor. "Thrice armed is he whose cause is just. Fear not. Fight on. Truth will prevail." Christ Himself is our Captain. Who can hesitate with such a Chieftain? "A leader and commander for the people" (Is. 45:4).

It is the side of conscience, and of a clean heart.

It is that side of the warfare which ends in heaven and victory, world without end. (Rev. 19:14).

III. PROPOSALS FOR ENLISTMENT.

Put on the colors—by confessing Christ openly in baptism.

Submit to drill—be willing to learn, and yield to discipline.

Put on the regimentals—wear the garments of holiness, the livery of love, the whole armor of God. (Eph. 6:13, 18).

Enter on civil war first. Wage war within your own soul. Slay sin, conquer self, cast down high looks, etc.

March to the field. Fight with falsehood, superstition, cruelty, oppression, drunkenness, uncleanness, and sin of every sort, anywhere and everywhere.

Guizot, in his life of St. Louis of France, says that the latter had many vassals who were also vassals of the King of England, and that many subtle and difficult questions arose as to the extent of the service which they owed to these kings. At length the French king commanded all those nobles who held lands in English territory to appear before him, and then he said to them: "As it is impossible for any man living in my kingdom and having possessions in England rightly to serve two masters, you must either attach yourselves altogether to me, or inseparably to the King of England." After saying this, he gave them a certain day by which to make their choice.

A dear friend of mine, the head of a family of grown-up sons and daughters, lately passed away very suddenly. The day before he died all the members of the household were with him, including one who had recently, like the rest, experienced the power of saving grace. The father's joy was great, as he put his hand upon one after another of his offspring, saying with an overflowing heart, "And *this one* on the Lord's side! and *this one* on the Lord's side!" How would it be with our hearer should he have to stand at the death-bed of a godly parent? Would that parent rejoice over him because he is on the Lord's side?

## Chapter 8

# LAYING THE HAND ON THE SACRIFICE

*"He shall lay his hand upon the head of the sin offering."*
(Lev. 4:29).

The question with many souls is how to obtain an interest in Christ so as to be saved by Him. Never could a weightier question be asked.

It is certain that this is absolutely needful; but alas, it has been fearfully neglected by many. In vain did Christ die if He is not believed in.

The text gives us a pictorial answer to the question: How can Christ's sacrifice become available for me?

I. THE INTENT OF THE SYMBOL.

1. It *was a confession of sin:* else no need of a sin offering.
   To this was added a confession of the desert of punishment, or why should the victim be slain?
   There was also an abandonment of all other methods of remov-

ing sin. The hands were empty, and laid alone upon the sin offering.

Do this at the cross; for there alone is sin put away.

2. *It was a consent to the plan of substitution.*
Some raise questions as to the justice and certainty of this method of salvation; but he who is to be saved does not so, for he sees that God Himself is the best judge of its rightness, and if He is content *we* may assuredly be so.
There is no other plan which meets the case, or even fairly looks at it. Man's sense of guilt is not met by other proposals.

3. *It was a dependence—leaning on the victim.*
Is there not a most sure stay in Jesus for the leaning heart? Consider the nature of the suffering and death by which the atonement was made, and you will rest in it.
Consider the dignity and worth of the sacrifice by whom the death was endured. The glory of Christ's person enhances the value of His atonement. (Heb. 10:5-10).
Remember that none of the saints now in heaven have had any other atoning sacrifice. "Jesus only" has been the motto of all justified ones. "He offered one sacrifice for sins forever" (Heb. 10:12).
Those of us who are saved are resting there alone; why should not *you*, and every anxious one?

## II. THE SIMPLICITY OF THE SYMBOL.

1. There were no antecedent rites. The victim was there, and hands were laid on it: nothing more. We add neither preface nor appendix to Christ; He is Alpha and Omega.

2. The offerer came in all his sin. "Just as I am." It was to have his sin removed that the offerer brought the sacrifice; not because he had himself removed it.

3. There was nothing in his hand of merit, or price.

4. There was nothing on his hand. No gold ring to indicate wealth; no signet of power; no jewel of rank. The offerer came as a man, and not as learned, rich, or honorable.

When Christmas Evans was about to die, several ministers were standing around his bed. He said to them: "Preach Christ to the people, brethren. Look at me; in myself I am nothing but ruin. But look at me in Christ; I am heaven and salvation."

It is not the quantity of thy faith that shall save thee. A drop of water is as true water as the whole ocean. So a little faith is as true faith as the greatest. A child eight days old is as really a man as one of sixty years; a spark of fire is as true fire as a great flame;

a sickly man is as truly living as a healthy man. So it is not the measure of thy faith that saves thee—*it is the blood that it grips to that saves thee.*

As the weak hand of a child, that leads the spoon to the mouth, will feed it as well as the strong arm of a man; for it is not the hand that feeds thee—albeit, it puts the meat into thy mouth, but it is the meat carried into thy stomach that feeds thee. So if thou canst grip Christ ever so weakly, He will not let thee perish . . . The weakest hands can take a gift as well as the strongest. Now, Christ is this gift, and weak faith may grip Him as well as strong faith, and Christ is as truly thine when thou hast weak faith, as when thou hast come to those triumphant joys through the strength of faith.—WELSH.

# CHAPTER 9

## AGAINST MURMURING

> *"And when the people complained, it displeased the Lord: and the Lord heard it; and His anger was kindled; and the fire of the Lord burnt among them, and consumed them that were in the uttermost parts of the camp"* (Num. 11:1).

Observe how the mischief began in the outskirts among the mixed multitude, and how the fire of the Lord burned in the uttermost parts of the camp. The great danger of the Church lies in her camp-followers or hangers-on; they infect the true Israel.

I. A DISSATISFIED SPIRIT CAUSES DISPLEASURE TO THE LORD.

 1. This we might infer from our own feelings, when dependents, children, servants, or receivers of alms are always grumbling. We grow weary of them, and angry with them.
 2. In the case of men toward God it is much worse for them to murmur, since they deserve no good at His hands, but the very reverse. "Wherefore doth a living man complain, a man for the punishment of his sins?" (Lam. 3:39; Ps. 103:10).

II. A DISSATISFIED SPIRIT FANCIES IT WOULD FIND PLEASURE IN THINGS DENIED IT.

Israel had manna, but sighed for fish, cucumbers, melons, onions, etc.

1. It is injurious to ourselves, for it prevents our enjoying what
   we already have. It leads men to slander angels' food and
   call it "this light bread." It led Haman to think nothing of
   his prosperity because a single person refused him reverence.
   (Esther 5:13).
2. Is slanderous toward God, and ungrateful to Him.
3. Leads to rebellion, falsehood, envy, and all manner of sins.

III. A DISSATISFIED SPIRIT SHOWS THAT THE MIND NEEDS REGU-
LATING.

Grace would put our desires in order, and keep our thoughts and
affections in their proper places, thus:

1. Content with such things as we have. (Heb. 13:5).
2. Toward other things moderate in desire. "Give me neither
   poverty nor riches" (Prov. 30:8).
3. Concerning earthly things which may be lacking, fully re-
   signed. "Not as I will, but as thou wilt" (Matt. 26:39).
4. First, and most eagerly, desiring God. "My soul thirsteth for
   God" etc. (Ps. 42:2).
5. Next, coveting earnestly the best gifts. (I Cor. 12:31).
6. Following ever in love the more excellent way. (I Cor. 12:31).

I have read of Caesar, that, having prepared a great feast for his
nobles and friends, it fell out that the day appointed was so
extremely foul that nothing could be done to the honor of their
meeting; whereupon he was so displeased and enraged, that he
commanded all them that had bows to shoot up their arrows at
Jupiter, their chief god, as in defiance of him for that rainy weather;
which, when they did, their arrows fell short of heaven, and fell
upon their own heads, so that many of them were very sorely
wounded.

So all our mutterings and murmurings, which are so many arrows
shot at God Himself, will return upon our own pates, or hearts;
they reach not Him, but they will hit us; they hurt not Him, but
they will wound us; therefore, it is better to be mute than to
murmur; it is dangerous to contend with One Who is a consuming
fire. (Heb. 12:29).—THOMAS BROOKS.

The Israelites are called in the same text "murmurers" and
"rebels" (Num. 17:10); and is not rebellion as the sin of witchcraft? (I Sam. 15:23). Thou that art a murmurer art in the account
of God as a witch, a sorcerer, as one that deals with the devil. This
is a sin of the first magnitude. Murmuring often ends in cursing;
Micah's mother fell to cursing when the talents of silver were taken
away. (Judges 17:2). So doth the murmurer when a part of his

estate is taken away. Our murmuring is the devil's music; **this is** that sin which God cannot bear.—T. WATSON.

I dare no more fret than curse or swear.—JOHN WESLEY.

A child was crying in passion, and I heard its mother say: "If you cry for nothing, I will soon give you something to cry for." From the sound of her hand, I gathered the moral that those who cry about nothing are making a rod for their own backs, and will probably be made to smart under it.

## CHAPTER 10

## MAN'S EXTREMITY GOD'S OPPORTUNITY

> *"For the Lord shall judge His people, and repent Himself for His servants, when He seeth that their power is gone, and there is none shut up or left"* (Deut. 32:36).

To ungodly men the time of their fall is fatal; there is no rising again for them. They mount higher and higher upon the ladder of riches; but at last they can climb no higher, their feet slide, and all is over.

But it is not so with three characters of whom we will now speak; they are judged in this world that they may not be condemned hereafter. (I Cor. 11:32).

I. THE LORD'S OWN CHURCH.

1.  A church may be sorely tried—"power gone, none left." Through the lack of a faithful ministry, there may be no increase; and those who remain may grow feeble and dispirited. By general falling off of hearers, members, etc., a church may be sorely distressed. Various circumstances may scatter a people, such as internal dissension, pestilent heresy, and lack of spiritual life. Where there is no spiritual food hungry souls find no home. (Job 15:23).

2.  The Trial is permitted:
    To find out His servants and drive out hypocrites. (Is. 33:14).
    To test the faith of sincere saints, and to strengthen it.
    To manifest His own grace by supporting them under the trying times, and by visiting them with future blessing.
    To secure to Himself the glory when the happier days are granted.

## II. THE TRIED BELIEVER.

1. His power may be gone. Personally he becomes helpless.
   Bodily health fails, prudence is baffled, skill is taken away,
   courage sinks, even spiritual force departs. (Lam. 3:17, 18).
2. His earthly help may fail. "There is none shut up or left."
   A man without a friend moves the compassion of God.
3. He may be assailed by doubts and fears, and hardly know
   what to do with himself. (Job 3:23-26). In all this there
   may be chastisement for sin. It is so described in the context.

## III. THE CONVINCED SINNER.

He is cleaned out of all that wherein he prided himself.

1. His self-righteousness is gone. (Job 9:30-31).
2. His ability to perform acceptable works is gone. (Eph. 2:1).
3. His proud romantic dreams are gone. (Is. 29:8).
4. His worldly delights, his bold defiance, his unbelief, his big
   talk, his carelessness, his vain confidence, are all gone.
5. Nothing is left but the pity of God. (Ps. 103:13).
   When the tide has ebbed out to the very uttermost, it turns.
   The prodigal has spent all before he returned.
   Man's extremity is God's opportunity.
   Extremities are a warrant for importunities.

A man at his wit's end is not at his faith's end.—MATTHEW HENRY.

Grandly did the old Scottish believer, of whom Dr. Brown tells
us in his *Horæ Subsecivæ*, respond to the challenge of her pastor,
regarding the ground of her faith. "Janet," said the minister, "what
would you say if, after all He has done for you, God should let you
drop into hell?" "E'en's (even as) He likes," answered Janet; "if
He does, He'll lose mair than I'll do"—meaning that He would lose
His honor for truth and goodness. Therefore, the Lord cannot leave
His people in the hour of their need.

A person who could not swim had fallen into the water. A man
who could swim sprang in to save him. Instead, however, of at once
taking hold of the struggling man, he kept at some distance from
him until he had ceased struggling; he then laid hold of him, and
pulled him ashore. Upon the people on the pier asking him why he
did not at once take hold of the drowning person, he replied, "I
could not attempt to save a man so long as he could try to save
himself." The Lord acts thus toward sinners; they must cease from
themselves, and then He will display the power of His grace upon
them.

So long as a sinner has a mouldy crust of his own he will not feed
upon heavenly manna. They say that half a loaf is better than no
bread, but this is not true; for on half a loaf men lead a starvation

existence; but when they have no bread they fly to Jesus for the food which comes down from heaven. As long as a soul has a farthing to bless itself with, it will foolishly refuse the free forgiveness of its debts; but absolute penury drives it to the true riches.

CHAPTER 11

MORAL INABILITY

*"And Joshua said unto the people, Ye cannot serve the Lord"* (Joshua 24:19).

In answer to Joshua's challenge, the people had said, "We will serve the Lord, for He is our God." But Joshua knew them too well to trust them, and reminded them that they were undertaking what they could not perform. They did not believe him, but cried, "Nay, but we will serve the Lord"; but their after history proved the truth of Joshua's warning. God's word knows us better than we know ourselves. God's Omniscience sees each part of our being as an anatomist sees the various portions of the body, and He therefore knows our moral and spiritual nature most thoroughly. A watchmaker is the best judge of a watch; and He Who made man has the best knowledge of his condition and capacity. Let us dwell upon His verdict as to human ability.

I. THE CERTAINTY OF THE TRUTH THAT UNRENEWED MEN CANNOT SERVE GOD.

It is not a physical but a moral inability, and this is not in their nature, but in their fallen nature; not of God, but of sin.

1. The nature of God renders perfect service impossible to depraved man. (See context, vs. 19).

2. The best they could render as unrenewed men would lack heart and intent, and therefore must be unacceptable. (Is. 1:15).

3. The law of God is perfect, who can hope to fulfil it? If a look may commit adultery, who shall in all points keep the law? (Matt. 5:28).

4. The carnal mind is inclined to self-will, self-seeking, lust, enmity, pride, and all other evils. (Rom. 8:7).

## II. THE DISCOURAGEMENT WHICH ARISES FROM THIS TRUTH.

It is alleged that this will drive men to despair, and our reply is that the kind of despair to which it drives men is most desirable and salutary.

1. It discourages men from an impossible task.
   They might as well hope to invent perpetual motion as to present a perfect obedience of their own, having already sinned. If a man should try to hold up a ladder with his own hand, and at the same time climb to the top of it, he would have less difficulty than in causing his evil nature to attain to holiness.

2. It discourages from a ruinous course.
   Self-righteousness is a deadly thing; it is a proud refusal of mercy, and a rebellion against grace. Self-confidence of any sort is the enemy of the Savior.

3. It discourages reliance upon ceremonies or any other outward religiousness, by assuring men that these cannot suffice.

4. It discourages from every other way of self-salvation, and thus shuts men up to faith in the Lord Jesus. Nothing better can befall them. (Gal. 2:22, 23).

## III. THE NECESSITIES OF WHICH WE ARE REMINDED BY THIS TRUTH.

Unregenerate men, before you can serve God you need:
A new nature, which only the Spirit of God can create in you.
Reconciliation. How shall an enemy serve his king?
Acceptance. Till you are accepted, your service cannot please God.
Continued aid. This you must have to keep you in the way when once you are in it. (I Sam. 2:9; Jude 24:25).

No wasp will make honey; before it will do that it must be transformed into a bee. A sow will not sit up to wash its face like the cat before the fire; neither will a debauched person take delight in holiness. No devil could praise the Lord as angels do, and no unregenerate man can offer acceptable service as the saints do.—GEORGE BUSH, *in "Notes on Joshua."*

The existence of sin within us entails on us certain consequences which we have no more power to evade than the idiot has power to change his look of idiocy; or the palsied hand has power to free itself from its torpor.—B. W. NEWTON.

"Man cannot be saved by perfect obedience, for he cannot render it; he cannot be saved by imperfect obedience, for God will not accept it."—BRITISH EVANGELIST.

> "Run, run, and work, the law commands,
> But gives me neither feet nor hands;
> But sweeter sounds the gospel brings,
> It bids me fly, and gives me wings."

## CHAPTER 12

# THE FAITHFUL OLIVE-TREE

*"But the olive tree said unto them, Should I leave my
fatness, wherewith by me they honor God and man, and
go to be promoted over the trees?"* (Judges 9:9).

The trees were under God's government and wanted no king; but
in this fable they "went forth," and so quitted their true place. Then
they sought to be like men, forgetting that God had not made them
to be conformed to a fallen race. Revolting themselves, they strove
to win over those better trees which had remained faithful.

I. APPARENT PROMOTIONS ARE NOT TO BE SNATCHED AT.

The question is to be asked, *Should I?*

Emphasis is to be laid on the *I.* Should I? If God has given me
peculiar gifts or special grace, does it become *me* to trifle with
these endowments? Should I give them up to gain honor for
myself? (Neh. 6:11).

A higher position may seem desirable, but would it be right to
gain it by such cost? (Jer. 45:5).

Can I expect God's blessing upon such strange work. Put the
question in the case of wealth, honor, power, which are set before
us. Should we grasp at them at the risk of being less at peace,
less holy, less prayerful, less useful?

II. ACTUAL ADVANTAGES ARE NOT TO BE TRIFLED WITH.

It is the greatest advantage in life to be useful both to God and
man. "By me they honor God and man." We ought heartily to
prize this high privilege.

We may also meet the temptations by the reflection:

That the prospect is startling. "Shall I leave my fatness?" For
an olive to do this would be unnatural: for a believer to leave
holy living would be worse. (John 6:68).

That the retrospect would be terrible—"leave my fatness." What
must it be to have left grace, and truth and holiness, and Christ?
Remember Judas.

That it would all end in disappointment; for nothing could com-
pensate for leaving the Lord. All else is death. (Jer. 17:13).

III. TEMPTATION SHOULD BE TURNED TO ACCOUNT.

Let us take deeper root. The mere proposal to leave our fatness
should make us hold the faster to it.

Let us feel the more content, and speak the more lovingly of our
gracious state, that none may dare to entice us. When Satan
sees us happily established he will have the less hope of over-
throwing us.

Many to obtain a higher wage have left holy companionships and sacred opportunities for hearing the word and growing in grace. Such persons are as foolish as the poor Indians who gave the Spaniards gold in exchange for paltry beads. Riches procured by impoverishing the soul are always a curse. To increase your business so that you cannot attend week-night services is to become really poorer; to give up heavenly pleasure and receive earthly cares in exchange is a sorry sort of barter.—GEORGE HERBERT.

CHAPTER 13

## RUTH DECIDING FOR GOD

*"And Ruth said, Intreat me not to leave thee, or to return from following after thee: for whither thou goest I will go; and where thou lodgest, I will lodge: thy people shall be my people, and thy God my God"* (Ruth 1:16).

This is a brave, outspoken confession of faith, and it is made by a woman, a young woman, a poor woman, a widow woman, a foreigner.

I.  AFFECTION FOR THE GODLY SHOULD INFLUENCE US TO GODLINESS. Many forces combine to effect this:

1. There is the influence of companionship. We ought to be affected by godly people more than we are by the wicked, since we should lend ourselves to their influence.

2. The influence of admiration. Imitation is the most sincere praise; what we favor we follow. Let us therefore copy the saints.

3. The influence of fear of separation. It will be an awful thing to be eternally divided from the dear ones who seek our salvation; it is even painful to have to leave them at the Lord's Table, when they partake and we do not.

II.  RESOLVES TO GODLINESS WILL BE TESTED.

1. By counting the cost. You yourself will have to come out from your friends, as Ruth did. You will have to share the lot of God's people, as Ruth shared with Naomi. (Heb. 11:24, 26).

2. By the duties involved in religion. Ruth must work in the fields. Some proud people will not submit to the rules of Christ's house, nor to the regulations which govern the daily lives of believers.

3. By the apparent coldness of believers. Naomi does not persuade her to keep with her, but the reverse. She was a prudent woman, and did not wish Ruth to come with her by persuasion, but by conviction.

III. SUCH GODLINESS MUST MAINLY LIE IN THE CHOICE OF GOD.

1. This is the believer's distinguishing possession. "Thy God shall be my God."

2. His great article of belief. "I believe in God."

3. His trust and stay. (See Ruth 2:12). "This God is our God forever and ever, He will be our guide even unto death" (Ps. 48:14).

IV. BUT IT SHOULD INVOLVE THE CHOICE OF HIS PEOPLE.

A near Kinsman is among them. The true Boaz is willing to take us to Himself, and to redeem our inheritance.

Let us make deliberate, humble, firm, joyful, immediate choice for God and His saints; accepting their lodging in this world, and going with them whither they are going.

The converted freedman gave happy expression to his decided adhesion to Christ when he said, "I have got safe past de *go-back corner*. I'm goin' all de journey home. And if you don't see me at de first of them twelve gates up dere, just look on to de next one, for I'm bound to be dere." Alas! for thousands, in all our congregations; they never get by the "go-back corner"—DR. CUYLER.

The power of Christian character shining forth from the face, form, and through the speech of a Christian man, is finely illustrated in the following incident: An Afghan once spent an hour in the company of Dr. William Marsh, of England. When he heard that Dr. Marsh was dead, he said, "His religion shall now be my religion; his God shall be my God; for I must go where he is, and see his face again."

I know his sackcloth and ashes are better than the fool's laughter. RUTHERFORD.

If God's people will not be ashamed of us we need not be ashamed of them. I should not like to go into public assembly disguised in the dress of a thief; I prefer my own clothes, and I cannot understand how Christians can bear themselves in the array of worldlings.

CHAPTER 14

## THE BATTLE IS THE LORD'S

*"And all this assembly shall know that the Lord saveth
not with sword and spear: for the battle is the Lord's,
and He will give you into our hands"* (I Samuel 17:47).

There are always two ways of handling the same doctrine. The
truth in the text may be used as a narcotic or as a stimulant. Some
are so wicked as to say that if it be the Lord's battle, we are excused
from fighting; as if, seeing the harvest is the Lord's, we might justly
refuse to sow or reap. We see how David used this truth; it fired
his soul and nerved his arm. We are all battling on one side or the
other, and the worst of all are those who boast their neutrality. To
the Christian man these words are so true that he may emblazon
them on his banner, and write them as the headline of "the book
of the wars of the Lord."

I. THE GREAT FACT: "The battle is the Lord's."

1. Inasmuch as it is for truth, right, holiness, love, and all those
things which the Lord loves, the battle is the Lord's (Ps. 45:4).

2. His name and glory are the object of it. It is His honor to
see righteousness established in the earth. The gospel greatly
glorifies God; men strike at the divine honor when they oppose
it, and the Lord will vindicate His own name; thus our conflict becomes God's battle. (Is. 40:5).

3. We fight only by His power. The Holy Ghost is our strength;
we can do nothing without the Lord; hence the battle is His
in the highest degree. (II Chron. 13:12; 20:12).

4. He has bidden us fight. At our monarch's bidding we go upon
this warfare. We are not free-lances on our own account,
but warriors under His command. (I Tim. 6:12).

II. ITS INFLUENCE ON OUR MINDS.

1. We make light of opposition. Who can stand against the
Lord?

2. We are not cowed by our weakness. "When I am weak then
am I strong." The Lord will make us mighty in His own
fight.

3. We throw ourselves into the work heartily. We owe so much
to the Lord Jesus that we must fight for Him. (I Cor. 16:13).

4. We choose the best weapons. We dare not fire the Lord's
cannons with the devil's powder. Love, truth, zeal, prayer, and
patience should be at their best in God's battle. (II Cor. 10:4).

5. We are confident of victory. Can the Lord be defeated? He vanquished Pharaoh, and He will do the same with Satan in due season. (I Cor. 15:25).

III. LESSONS IN CONNECTION WITH IT.

*Make it God's cause.* Never let it sink into a selfish matter.
By your motive. Aim at His glory only. Keep clear of all sinister designs.
By your method. Contend for the faith as Jesus would have contended, and not in a way which the Lord would disapprove.
By your faith. Can you trust God to fight His own battles?

Mr. Oncken told me that he was summoned before the burgomaster of Hamburg, who bade him cease from holding religious meetings. "Do you see that little finger?" cried he. "As long as I can move that finger I will put down the Baptists." "Yes," said Oncken, "I see your little finger, and I also see a great arm which *you* cannot see. As long as the great arm of God is lifted on our behalf, your little finger will have no terror for us."—DAVID GRACEY *in "The Sword and the Trowel."*

It is not the will of God that His people should be a timorous people.—MATTHEW HENRY.

It has been said of the persecuted Quakers, that, looking steadfastly at the strength of their Almighty leader, they

> "Said not, who am I? but rather,
> Whose am I, that I should fear?"
> *—Annals of the Early Friends.*

Luther's strength lay in the way in which he laid the burden of the Reformation upon the Lord. Continually in prayer he pleaded, "Lord, this is Thy cause, not mine. Therefore, do Thine own work; for if this gospel do not prosper, it will not be Luther alone who will be a loser, but Thine own name will be dishonored."

Queen Elizabeth requested a merchant to go abroad on her service, and when he mentioned that his own business would be ruined, she replied, "You mind my business and I will mind yours." If it be but the Lord's battle, we may be sure that He will see us through with it.

## CHAPTER 15

## DAVID'S SPOIL

*"This is David's spoil"* (I Samuel 30:'20).

We see in David a type of the Lord Jesus, in His conflicts and victories, and as in a thousand things beside, so also in the spoil To him as a warrior against evil the spoils of war belong.

I. ALL THE GOOD THAT WE ENJOY COMES TO US THROUGH JESUS.

All that we held under the law the spoiler has taken.

By our own efforts we can never gain what we have lost.

Our great Leader has made us share the spoil.

1. It was for David's sake that God gave success to the hosts of Israel.

2. It was under David's leadership that they won the battle.
   Even thus is Jesus the Captain of our salvation. (Heb. 2:10). Within us He has wrought a great deliverance. He has overcome the strong man, taken from him all his armor, and divided his spoils. (Luke 11:22). He can say with Job, "I plucked the spoil out of his teeth" (Job 29:17).
   Our eternal heritage was forfeited; He has redeemed it (Eph. 1:14).
   The prey is taken from the mighty. "David recovered all."

II. THAT WHICH IS OVER AND ABOVE WHAT WE LOST BY SIN COMES BY JESUS. (verse 20).

As Jesus has made us more safe than we were before the fall, so has He also made us more rich.

1. The exaltation of humanity to kinship with God. This was not ours at the first, but it is acquired for us by the Lord Jesus. Election, sonship, heirship, spiritual life, union to Christ, espousal to Jesus, fellowship with God, and the glory of the future wedding-feast—all these are choice spoils.

2. The fact that we are redeemed creatures, for whom the Creator suffered, is an honor belonging to none but men, and not to men except through Jesus Christ. (Heb. 2:16).

3. Our resurrection, which is a gem not found in the crown of seraphs, comes by our risen Lord. (II Cor. 4:14).

4. Our manifestation of the full glory of the Lord. Our experience will declare to all intelligent beings the choicest wisdom, love, power, and faithfulness of God. (Eph. 3:10).

III. THAT WHICH WE WILLINGLY GIVE TO JESUS MAY BE CALLED HIS SPOIL.

1. Our hearts are His alone forever. Hence, all that we have and are belongs to Him. "This is David's spoil"—the love and gratitude of our lives. (I John 4:19).

2. Our special gifts. Our tithes and dedicated things are for Him. Let us give plentifully. (Mal. 3:10). Abraham gave Melchizedek the tenth of the spoil. (Gen. 14:20).

3. Yield to Jesus now, and find in Him your safety, your heaven.
   What say you? Are you David's spoil?
   If not, sin and Satan are spoiling you every day.

1. Sin contracts no guilt that grace does not more than remove.
2. Sin deforms no beauty that grace does not more than renew. 3.
Sin loses no blessedness that grace does not more than restore.—
*Outline of Sermon on Rom. 5:20, by the late Charles Vince.*

We all remember the poem of "The Man of Ross." Every good
thing in the place came from him. Ask who did this or that,
  " 'Tis the man of Ross,' each lisping babe replies."

Even so, as we survey each blessing of our happy estate, and ask
whence it came, the only answer is, "This is Jesus' spoil. The
crucified hand has won this for us."

# CHAPTER 16

## PRAYER FOUND IN THE HEART

*"For Thou, O Lord of hosts, God of Israel, has revealed
to Thy servant, saying, I will build thee an house: therefore hath Thy servant found in his heart to pray this
prayer unto Thee"* (II Samuel 7:27).

How often God does for His servants what they desire to do for
Him! David desired to build the Lord a house, and the Lord built
him a house.

I. HOW DID HE COME BY HIS PRAYER? He "found in his heart
to pray this prayer."

He found it, which is a sign he looked for it. Those who pray at
random will never be accepted; we must carefully seek out our
prayers. (Job 13:4).

In his heart—not in a book, nor in his memory, nor in his head,
nor in his imagination, nor only on his tongue. (Ps. 84:2).

It is proof that he had a heart, knew where it was, could look into
it, and did often search it. (Ps. 67:6).

It must have been a living heart, or a living prayer would not have
been within it.

It must have been a believing heart, or he would not have found
"this prayer" in it.

It must have been a serious heart, not flippant, forgetful, cold,
indifferent, or he would have found a thousand vanities in it, but
no prayer. Question: Would prayer be found in your heart at this
time? (Hosea 7:11).

## II. How Did This Prayer Come To Be In His Heart?

1. The Lord's own Spirit instructed him how to pray. By giving him a sense of need. Great blessings teach us our necessity, as in David's case.

2. The Lord inclined him to pray.
   It has been said that an absolute promise would render prayer needless; whereas the first influence of such a promise is to suggest prayer. The Lord inclined David's heart:
   By warming his heart. Prayer does not grow in an ice-well.

## III. How May You Find Prayer In Your Hearts?

Look into your heart, and make diligent search.
Think of your own need, and this will suggest petitions.
Think of your ill-desert, and you will humbly cry to the Lord.
Think of the promises, the precepts, and the doctrines of truth, and each one of these will summon you to your knees.
Have Christ in your heart, and prayer will follow. (Acts 9:11).
Live near to God, and then you will often speak to Him.
Do you find prayers and other holy things in your heart? Or is it full of vanity, worldliness, ambition, and ungodliness?
Remember that you are what your heart is. (Prov. 23:7).
"A great part of my time," said M'Cheyne, "is spent in getting my heart in tune for prayer."

It is not the gilded paper and good writing of a petition that prevails with a king, but the moving sense of it. And to that King who discerns the heart, heart-sense is the sense of all, and that which he only regards; he listens to hear what that speaks, and takes all as nothing where that is silent. All other excellence in prayer is but the outside and fashion of it; this is the life of it.—LEIGHTON.

I asked a young friend, "Did you pray before conversion?" She answered that she did after a sort. I then inquired, "What is the difference between your present prayers and those before you knew the Lord?" Her answer was, "Then I said my prayers, but now I *mean* them. Then I said the prayers which other people taught me, but now I find them in my heart."

There is good reason to cry "Eureka!" when we find prayer in our heart. Holy Bradford would never cease praying or praising till he found his heart thoroughly engaged in the holy exercise. If it be not in my heart to pray, I must pray till it is. But oh, the delight of pleading with God when the heart casts forth mighty jets of supplication, like a geyser in full action! How mighty is supplication when the whole soul becomes one living, hungering, expecting desire!

Remember, God respecteth not the arithmetic of our prayers, how many they are; nor the rhetoric of our prayers, how long they are; nor the music of our prayers, how methodical they are; but the divinity of our prayers, how heart-sprung they are. Not gifts, but graces, prevail in prayer.—TRAPP.

## CHAPTER 17

## CLINGING TO THE ALTAR

> *"Joab fled unto the tabernacle of the Lord, and caught hold on the horns of the altar.*
> *"And Benaiah came to the tabernacle of the Lord, and said unto him, Thus saith the king, come forth. And he said, Nay; but I will die here"* (I Kings 2:28, 30).

Joab had little enough of religion, yet he flies to the altar when the sword pursues him.

Many are for running to the use of external religion when death threatens them. Then they go to greater lengths than Scripture prescribes; they not only go to the tabernacle of the Lord but they must needs cling to the altar.

I. AN OUTWARD RESORT TO ORDINANCES AVAILS NOT FOR SALVATION.

If a man will rest in external rites he will die there.

Sacraments, in health or in sickness, are unavailing as means of salvation. They are intended only for those saved already, and will be injurious to others. (I Cor. 11:29).

Ministers. These are looked upon by some dying persons with foolish reverence. In the hour of death resort is made to their prayers at the bedside. Importance is attached to funeral sermons and ceremonials. What superstition!

Feelings. Dread, delight, dreaminess, despondency; these have, each in its turn, been relied upon as grounds of hope; but they are all futile.

What an awful thing to perish with your hand on the altar of God!

II. A SPIRITUAL RESORT TO THE TRUE ALTAR AVAILS FOR SALVATION.

We will use Joab's case as an illustration.

1. His act; he "caught hold on the horns of the altar."
   We do this spiritually by flying from the sword of justice to the person of Jesus.

And by taking hold upon His great atoning work, and thus through faith uniting ourselves to His propitiation.

2. The fierce demand of His adversary. "Thus saith the king, Come forth!" This is the demand of unbelieving Pharisees who teach salvation by works.
   Accusing conscience within the man.
   Satan, quoting Holy Scripture falsely.

3. The desperate resolve of Joab. "Nay, but I will die here." This is a wise resolution, for we:
   Must perish elsewhere.
   Cannot make our case worse by clinging to Christ.
   Have nowhere else to cling. No other righteousness or sacrifice.
   Cannot be dragged away if we cling to Jesus.
   Receive hope from the fact that none have perished here.

4. The assured security. "He that believeth on the Son hath everlasting life." (John 3:36). If you perished trusting in Jesus your ruin would:
   Defeat God.
   Dishonor Christ.
   Dishearten sinners from coming to Jesus.
   Discourage saints, making them doubt all the promises.
   Distress the glorified, who have rejoiced over penitents, and would now see that they were mistaken.

Come, then, at once to the Lord Jesus, and lay hold on eternal life.
You may come; He invites you.
You should come; He commands you.
You should come now; for now is the accepted time.

When a man goes thirsty to the well, his thirst is not allayed merely by going there. On the contrary, it is increased by every step he goes. It is by what he draws out of the well that his thirst is satisfied. Just so it is not by the mere bodily exercise of waiting upon ordinances that you will ever come to peace, but by tasting of Jesus in the ordinances, whose flesh is meat indeed, and His blood drink indeed.—M'CHEYNE.

A pilot loves to get the helm in his hand, a physician delights to be trusted with hard cases, an advocate is glad to get his brief; even so is Jesus happy to be used. Jesus longs to bless, and therefore He says to every sinner, as He did to the woman at the well, "Give Me to drink." Oh, to think that you can refresh your Redeemer! Poor sinner, haste to do it.

CHAPTER 18

# HEART-COMMUNING

*"And she came to Jerusalem with a very great train, with camels that bare spices, and very much gold, and precious stones: and when she was come to Solomon, she communed with him of all that was in her heart"* (I Kings 10:2).

It is not generally a wise thing to tell out all your heart. Samson reached the climax of folly when he did this to Delilah. Yet if we could meet with a Solomon who could solve all our difficulties, we might wisely do so.

We have a greater than Solomon in Jesus, who is incarnate Wisdom. The mischief is, that with Him we are too silent, and with worldly friends too communicative. This evil should be rectified.

I. WE OUGHT TO COMMUNE WITH HIM OF ALL THAT IS IN OUR HEART.

1. Neglect of intercourse with Jesus is very unkind; for He invites us to talk with Him. Shall our heavenly Bridegroom be deprived of the fellowship of our souls?

2. To conceal anything from so true a Friend betrays the sad fact that there is something wrong to be concealed.

3. Reticence toward Jesus is greatly aggravated by our usual eagerness to tell our troubles to others. Will we make a confidant of man, and hide the matter from our God?

II. WE NEED NOT CEASE COMMUNING FOR WANT OF TOPICS.

1. Our sorrows. He knows what they are, will comfort us under them, help us to profit by them, and in due time remove them.

2. Our joys. He will sober and salt them. Joy without Jesus is the sun without light, the essence of it is gone. Joy without Jesus would be as evil as the golden calf which provoked the Lord to jealousy.

3. Our successes and failures should be reported at headquarters. The disciples of the martyred John took up the body, and went and told Jesus. (Matthew 14:12). Our Lord's own evangelists returned and told what had been done. (Luke 9:10).

4. Our fears; fears of falling, needing, failing, fainting, dying. To mention these to Jesus is to end them.

III. Nor Should We Cease Communing For Want of Reasons.

1. How ennobling and elevating is intercourse with the Son of God!

2. How consoling and encouraging is fellowship with Him Who has overcome the world!

3. How safe and healthy is a daily walk with the ever-blessed Son of man!

4. How proper and natural for disciples to talk with their Teacher, and saints with their Savior!

A workman in time of need would part with everything before his tools; for to lose them would be to lose all. Reading the Word of God and prayer are the tools of the Christian's craft; without them he is helpless. How is it, then, that when time presses, he so often foregoes these, or shortens them? What is this but to sell his tools?

If there be anything I do, if there be anything I leave undone, let me be perfect in prayer.—Henry Martyn.

Lack of holy communion is a very grievous thing. True love is communicative; it cannot bear to keep its secrets from its Beloved, nor to be restrained in its converse with him. The stronger faith is, the more wants it tells, and the more fully it tells them. Do you want anything of which you cannot tell your Lord? It argues either no real need, or else little faith. (Eph. 3:12). "In whom we have boldness." The word translated boldness is *"telling all."*—Thomas Boston.

## Chapter 19

## ELIJAH FAINTING

*"But he himself went a day's journey into the wilderness, and came and sat down under a juniper tree: and he requested for himself that he might die; and said, It is enough; now, O Lord, take away my life; for I am not better than my fathers"* (I Kings 19:4).

We may learn much from the lives of others. Elijah himself is not only a prophet but a prophecy. His experience is our instruction. Sometimes we enter into a strange and mysterious state of depression, and it is well to learn from Scripture that another has been in that Valley of Deathshade. Weary, and sick at heart, sorely tried ones are apt to faint. At such a time they imagine that some strange thing has happened unto them; but, indeed, it is not so. Looking down upon the sands of time they may see the print of a man's foot, and it ought to comfort them when they learn that he was no mean man, but a mighty servant of the Lord.   Let us study:

## I.   ELIJAH'S WEAKNESS.

1.   He was a man of like passions with us. (James 5:17).
He failed in the point wherein he was strongest, as many other saints have done.   Abraham, Job, Moses, Peter, etc.

2.   He suffered from a terrible reaction. Those who go up, go down. The depth of depression is equal to the height of rapture.

3.   He was sadly weary with the excitement of Carmel, and the unwonted run by the side of Ahab's chariot.

4.   His wish was folly.   "O Lord, take away my life."
He fled from death.   If he wished to die, Jezebel would have obliged him, and he needed not to have fled.
He was more needed than ever to maintain the good cause.
Strange that he who was to escape death should cry, "Take away my life!"
How unwise are our prayers when our spirits sink!

## II.   GOD'S TENDERNESS TO HIM.

1.   He allowed him to sleep; this was better than medicine, or inward rebuke.

2.   He fed him with food convenient.

3.   He allowed him to tell his grief (see verse 10); this is often the readiest relief.   He stated his case, and in so doing eased his mind.

4.   He revealed Himself and His ways. The wind, earthquake, fire, and still small voice were voices from God.   When we know what God is we are less troubled about other matters.

5.   He told him good news.   "Yet I have left Me seven thousand in Israel" (verse 18).   His sense of loneliness was thus removed.

6.   He gave him more to do—to anoint others by whom the Lord's purposes of chastisement and instruction should be carried on.
Let us learn some useful lessons.
It is seldom right to pray to die; that matter is best left with God; we may not destroy our own lives, nor ask the Lord to do so. Three saints in Scripture prayed to die, Elijah, Moses, Jonah. All three prayers unanswered.
To the sinner it is never right to seek to die; for death to him is hell.   The wilful suicide seals his own sure condemnation.
What is this we hear?   Elijah fainting and giving up! that heroical spirit dejected and prostrate!   He that durst say to Ahab's face, "It is thou and thy father's house that trouble Israel"; he that could

raise the dead, open and shut the heavens, fetch down both fire and water with his prayers; he that durst chide and contest with all Israel; that durst kill the four hundred and fifty Baalites with the sword—doth he shrink at the frowns and threats of a woman? Doth he wish to be rid of his life, because he feared to lose it? Who can expect an undaunted constancy from flesh and blood when Elijah fails?

The strongest and holiest saint upon earth is subject to some qualms of fear and infirmity; to be always and unchangeably good is proper only to the glorious spirits in heaven. Thus the wise and holy God will have His power perfected in our weakness. It is in vain for us, while we carry this flesh about us, to hope for so exact health as not to be cast down sometimes with fits of spiritual distemper. It is no new thing for holy men to wish for death; who can either marvel at or blame the desire of advantage? For the weary traveller to long for rest, the prisoner for liberty, the banished for home, it is so natural, that the contrary disposition were monstrous. The benefit of the change is a just motive to our appetition; but to call for death out of a satiety of life, out of an impatience of suffering, is a weakness unbeseeming a saint. It is not enough, O Elijah! God hath more work yet for thee; thy God hath more honored thee than thy fathers, and thou shalt live to honor Him.—BISHOP HALL.

Elijah "arose and went for his life." But better he had stood to his task as a prophet, and answered as Chrysostom did when Eudoxia the empress threatened him. "Go tell her," said he, "I fear nothing but sin"; or as Basil did, when Valens, the Arian emperor, sent him word that he would be the death of him: "I would he would," said he; "I shall but go to heaven the sooner."

Luther had his fits of fear, though ordinarily he could say, "I care neither for the Pope's favor nor fury." Gregory doubted not to say that because Elijah began to be tickled with high conceits of himself for the great acts which he had done, he was suffered thus to fear, and to fall beneath himself, for his humiliation. The like we see in Peter, scared by a silly wench; to show us how weak, even as water, we are, when left a little to ourselves.—JOHN TRAPP.

Who told Elijah it was "enough"? God did not; He knew what was enough for Elijah to do and to suffer. It was not enough. God had more to teach him, and had more work for him to do. If the Lord had taken him at his word, and had also said "it is enough," Elijah's history would have wanted its crowning glory.—KITTO.

I. *The cause of Elijah's despondency.* 1. Relaxation of physical strength. 2. Second cause—want of sympathy. "I, even I only, am left." Lay he stress on *only*. The loneliness of his position was shocking to Elijah. 3. Want of occupation. As long as Elijah had prophet's work to do, severe as that work was, all went on healthily; but his occupation was gone. Tomorrow and the day after, what has he left on earth to do? The misery of having nothing to do proceeds from causes voluntary or involuntary in their nature.

4. Fourth cause—disappointment in his expectations of success On Carmel the great object for which Elijah had lived seemed on the point of being realized. Baal's prophets were slain—Jehovah acknowledged with one voice; false worship put down. Elijah's life-aim—the transformation of Israel into a kingdom of God, was all but accomplished. In a single day all this bright picture was annihilated.

II. *God's treatment of it.* 1. First, he recruited His servant's exhausted strength. Read the history. Miraculous meals are given—then Elijah sleeps, wakes, and eats; on the strength of that, he goes forty days' journey. 2. Next, Jehovah calmed his stormy mind by the healing influences of nature. He commanded the hurricane to sweep the sky, and the earthquake to shake the ground. He lighted up the heavens till they were one mass of fire. All this expressed and reflected Elijah's feelings.

The mode in which nature soothes us is by finding meeter and nobler utterances for our feelings than we can find in words—by expressing and exalting them. In expression there is relief. 3. Besides, God made him feel the earnestness of life. What *doest* thou here, Elijah? Life is for doing. A prophet's life for nobler doing —and the prophet was not doing, but moaning. Such a voice repeats itself to all of us, rousing us from our lethargy, or our despondency, or our protracted leisure, "What doest thou here?" here in this short life. 4. He completed the cure by the assurance of victory. "Yet have I left Me seven thousand in Israel who have not bowed the knee to Baal." So, then, Elijah's life had no failure after all.—F. W. ROBERTSON.

## CHAPTER 20

## WHERE IS THE GOD OF ELIJAH?

> *"And he took the mantle of Elijah that fell from him, and smote the waters, and said, Where is the Lord God of Elijah?"* (II Kings 2:14).

The great object to be desired is God, Jehovah, Elijah's God. With Him all things flourish. His absence is our decline and death.

Those entering on any holy work should seek for the God who was with their predecessors. What a mercy that the God of Elijah is also the God of Elisha! He will also be with us, for "this God is our God, forever and ever, He will be our guide even unto death" (Ps. 48:14).

Still we do not need antiquities from the past, nor novelties of the present, nor marvels for the future; we only want the Triune God, Father, Son, and Holy Spirit, and we shall then see among us wonders equal to those of Elijah's age. "Where is the Lord God of Elijah?" The old mantle, used with faith in the same God, parted the waters hither and thither. The power is where it used to be.

### I. THE QUESTION TURNED INTO PRAYER.

At this day our one need is Elijah's God.

1. The God Who kept him faithful must make us stand firm should we be left alone in the truth. (I Cor. 1:8).

2. The God Who raised the dead by Him must cause us to bring men up from their death in sin. (I Kings 17:22).

3. The God Who gave him food for a long journey must fit us for the pilgrimage of life, and preserve us to the end. (I Kings 19:8).

4. The God Who divided Jordan for the prophet will not fail us when we are crossing into our Canaan. (II Kings 2:8).

### II. THE QUESTION ANSWERED. The Lord God of Elijah is not dead, nor sleeping, nor on a journey.

1. He is still in heaven regarding His own reserved ones.
   They may be hidden in caves, but the Lord knoweth them that are His.

2. He is still to be moved by prayer to bless a thirsty land.

3. He is still able to keep us faithful in the midst of a faithless generation, so that we shall not bow the knee to Baal.

4. He is coming in vengeance. Hear ye not His chariot wheels? He will bear away His people.
   Oh, to have that presence, so as to be girded with His strength!
   Oh, to live so as never more to ask this question!

"God of Queen Clotilda," cried out the infidel Clovis I of France, when in trouble on the field of battle; "God of Queen Clotilda! grant me the victory!" Why did he not call upon his own god? Saunderson, who was a great admirer of Sir Isaac Newton's talents, and who made light of his religion in health, was, nevertheless, heard to say in dismal accents on a dying-bed, "God of Sir Isaac Newton, have mercy on me!" Why this changing of gods in a dying hour? —*"Addresses to Young Men," by* REV. DANIEL BAKER.

*The God of Elijah gave him the experience of the sweet fruits of dependence on the Lord,* and of a little going far, with His blessing. (I Kings 17:16). . . . But where is the God of Elijah at this day, when what we have seems to be blown upon, that it goes in effect for nothing? Our table is plentifully covered, yet our souls are starved; our goodness sometimes looks as a morning cloud, it blackens the face of the heavens, and promises a heavy shower, but quickly proves as a little cloud, like unto a man's hand, which is ready to go for nothing; yea, this generation is blinded by the means that have a natural tendency to give light. Ah! "Where is the Lord God of Elijah?"

*The God of Elijah gave him the experience of a gracious boldness to face the most daring wickedness* of the generation he lived in, though it was one of the worst. This eminently appeared in his encounter with Ahab. (I Kings 18:1) . . . But where is the God of Elijah now, while the iniquities of our day meet with such faint resistance, while a brave brow for the cause of God, a tongue to speak for Him, and a heart to act, are so much wanting? The wicked of the world, though they have an ill cause in hand, yet they pursue it boldly; but, alas! the people of God shame their honest cause by their cowardice and faint appearing in it. If God give us not another spirit, more fitted for such a day, we shall betray our trust, and bring the curse of the succeeding generation on us.

*The God of Elijah gave him the experience of being enabled to go far upon a meal.* (I Kings 19:8). But where now are such experiences, while there is so little strength in the spiritual meals to which we now sit down? This is a time wherein there is much need of such an experience; the Lord seems to be saying to His people, "Rise and eat, for the journey is long"; and what a hard journey some may have, ere they get another meal, who knows? Oh, for more feeding power in the doctrine preached among us!

*The God of Elijah gave him the experience of the Lord's removing difficulties out of his way, when he himself could do nothing at them:* Jordan divided. So Peter had the iron gate opened to him of its own accord; for when the Lord takes the work in hand, were it never so desperate as to us, it will succeed well with him.—THOMAS BOSTON.

Chapter 21

EYES OPENED

> *"And Elisha prayed, and said, Lord, I pray thee, open his eyes, that he may see. And the Lord opened the eyes of the young man; and he saw: and, behold, the mountain was full of horses and chariots of fire round about Elisha"* (II Kings 6:17).

I. The Natural Eye Is Blind To Heavenly Things.

God is everywhere; yet sin-blinded eyes see Him not.

Men themselves are evil, guilty, fallen; yet they see not their own wounds, and bruises, and putrefying sores.

This want of spiritual discernment makes man ignoble.

Samson blinded is a sorry spectacle; from a judge in Israel he sinks to a slave in Philistia.

This keeps a man content with the world; he does not see how poor a thing it is, for which he sweats, and smarts, and sins, and sacrifices heaven.

This places men in danger. "If the blind lead the blind, both shall fall into the ditch" (Matt. 15:14).

II. God Alone Can Open Man's Eyes.

We can lead the blind, but we cannot make them see; we can put truth before them, but we cannot open their eyes; that work remains with God alone.

Some use artificial eyes, others try spectacles, telescopes, colored glasses, etc., but all in vain, while the eyes are blind. The cure is of the Lord alone.

1. To give sight is the same wonder as creation. Who can make an eye? In the sinner the faculty of spiritual vision is gone.

2. The man is born blind. His darkness is part of himself. (John 9:32).

   Satan counterfeited this in the garden when he said, "Your eyes shall be opened, and ye shall be as gods" (Gen. 3:5).

III. We May Pray Him To Open Men's Eyes. We ought to cry, "Lord, I pray thee, open his eyes, that he may see."

1. When we hear them inquiring, we should inquire of the Lord for them. Their prayer should call up ours.

2. The prayers of others availed for us, and therefore we ought to repay the blessing to the prayer-treasury of the church.

3. It will glorify God to open their eyes; let us pray with great expectancy, believing that He will honor His Son.

IV. GOD DOES OPEN MEN'S EYES.

1. He has done it in a moment. Notice the many miracles performed by our Lord on blind men.

2. He can open *your* eyes. Many are the forms of blindness, but they are all comprehended in that grand statement, "The Lord openeth the eyes of the blind" (Ps. 146:8).

V. EVEN THOSE WHO SEE NEED MORE SIGHT.

1. In the Scriptures more is to be seen. "Open Thou mine eyes, that I may behold wondrous things out of Thy law" (Ps. 119:18).

2. In the great doctrines of the gospel there is much latent light.

3. In Christ Jesus Himself there are hidden glories. "Sir, we would see Jesus." (John 12:21; Heb. 2:9).

One of the saddest conditions of a human creature is to read God's Word with a veil upon the heart, to pass blindfolded through all the wondrous testimonies of redeeming love and grace which the Scriptures contain. And it is sad, also, if not actually censurable, to pass blindfolded through the works of God, to live in a world of flowers, and stars and sunsets, and a thousand glorious objects of nature, and never to have a passing interest awakened by any of them.—DEAN GOULBOURN.

# CHAPTER 22

# HALF-BREEDS

*"They feared not the Lord."*
*"They feared the Lord, and served their own gods."*
*"Unto this day . . . they fear not the Lord"* (II Kings 17: 25, 33, 34).

It is as needful to warn you against the false as to urge you to the true. Conversion, which is a divine change, is imitated, and the spurious palmed off as genuine. This answers the devil's purpose in several ways: it eases the conscience of the double-minded, adulterates the church, injures its testimony, and dishonors true religion.

I. THEIR FIRST ESTATE. "They feared not the Lord."

1. They had little or no religion of any sort.

2. But they were near a God-fearing people, and near to king Hezekiah, under whom there had been a great revival. Such influence creates a great deal of religiousness.

II.   THEIR SHAM CONVERSION.  "They feared the Lord."

1.  They were wrought upon by fear only; the "lions" were their evangelists, and their teeth were cutting arguments.

2.  They were instructed by an unfaithful priest; one of those who had practised calf-worship, and now failed to rebuke their love of false gods.  Such persons have much to answer for.

3.  But their conversion was radically defective; for:
    There was no repentance.
    No expiatory sacrifice was offered on God's one altar.
    The false gods were not put away (verse 29).  While sin reigns grace is absent.
    They rendered no obedience to Him.  Even their worship was will-worship.  "They feared the Lord, and *served* their own gods;" a very significant distinction.
    The religious drunkard.  See him weep!  Hear him talk!  He has a dread of God, but he serves Bacchus.
    The saintly skinflint.  He has "a saving faith" in the worst sense.

III.  THEIR REAL ESTATE.  "They fear not the Lord."

1.  They own Him not as God alone.

2.  They act so as to prove that they are not His.  See the future history of these Samaritans in the book of Nehemiah.

In real conversion there must be:
    Idol-breaking.  Sin and self must be abandoned.
    Concentration.  Our only God must be adored and served.

## CHAPTER 23

## THE LESSON OF UZZA

*"And David and all Israel played before God with all their might"* (I Chron. 13:8).
*"And David was afraid of God"* (I Chron. 13:12).
*"So David . . . went to bring . . . the ark of the covenant . . . with joy"* (I Chron 15:25).

Right things must be done in a right manner, or they will fail.  In this case the failure was sad and signal, for Uzza died, and the ark turned aside to the house of Obed-edom.

I.   THE FAILURE.  First Text.  I Chron. 13:8.

Here were multitudes.  Crowds do not insure blessing.
Here was pomp-singing, harps, trumpets, etc., yet it ended in mourning.  Gorgeous ceremonial is no guarantee of grace.

Here was energy: "they played before God with all their might."
This was no dull and sleepy worship, but a bright, lively service,
and yet the matter fell through.

There was no sacrifice. This was a fatal flaw; for how can we
serve the Lord apart from sacrifice?

II. THE FEAR. Second Text. I Chron. 13:12.

The terrible death of Uzza caused great fear. Thus the Lord slew
Nadab and Abihu for offering strange fire; and the men of Beth-
shemesh for looking into the ark.

His own sense of unworthiness for such holy work made him cry,
"How shall I bring the ark of God home to me?"

Some make the holiness of God and the strictness of His rule an
excuse for wicked neglect.

Others are overwhelmed with holy fear; and therefore pause a
while, till they are better prepared for the holy service.

III. THE JOY. Third Text. I Chron. 15:25.

1. God blessed Obed-edom. Thus may humble souls dwell with
   God and die not.
2. Preparation was made and thought exercised by David.
3. The mind of the Lord was considered (verse 15).
4. The priests were in their places. Men and methods must both
   be ruled by God (verse 14).
5. Sacrifices were offered (verse 26). The great and perfect
   sacrifice must ever be to the front.

*The doing of a duty in a wrong manner alters the nature of it, and
makes it sin.* Hence "the ploughing of the wicked is sin" (Prov. 21:
4). Hence prayer is accounted a howling upon their beds (Hosea
7:14). Unworthy communicating is not counted as eating the Lord's
supper (I Cor. 11:20). If a house be built of ever so strong timber
and good stones, yet if it be not well founded, and rightly built,
the inhabitant may curse the day he came under the roof of it.

*Duties not performed according to the right order are but the half
of the service we owe to God, and the worst half too.*—THOMAS BOSTON.

## CHAPTER 24

## REHOBOAM THE UNREADY

*"And he did evil, because he prepared not his heart to
seek the Lord"* (II Chron. 12:14).

This is the summing up of Rehoboam's life: he was not so bad as
some, but he did evil in various ways, not so much from design as
from neglect.

The evil effects of the father's sin and the mother's idolatry were seen in their son, yet there was another cause—namely, a want of heart-preparation.

I. HE DID NOT BEGIN LIFE WITH SEEKING THE LORD.

1. II Chron. 10:1. That which commences without God will end in failure.
2. II Chron. 10:8. Those who reject divine wisdom generally refuse all other wisdom.
3. II Chron. 10:13, 14. He had none of his father's wisdom. How can they act prudently and prosperously who are not guided of the Lord?

II. HE WAS NOT FIXED AND PERSEVERING IN HIS SEEKING THE LORD.

1. For three years his loyalty to his God made him prosper, by bringing into Judah all the better sort of people who fled from Jeroboam's calf-worship (II Chron. 11:13, 17), yet he forsook the Lord who had prospered him.
2. He grew proud, and God handed him over to Shishak (verse 5).
3. He humbled himself and was pardoned, yet he stripped the Lord's house to buy off the king of Egypt.
4. He wrought no great reforms and celebrated no great passover, yet he owned, "the Lord is righteous" (verse 6).

III. HE HAD NO CARE TO SEEK THE LORD THOROUGHLY.

Yet no man is good by accident; no one goes right who has not intended to do so. Without heart, religion must die.

The kind of preparation required by me, in order to be diligent and acceptable seeking of the Lord, my God, is somewhat after this fashion:

To feel and confess my need of God in the whole of my life.

To cry unto Him for help and wisdom.

To yield to His guidance, and not to follow the counsel of vain persons, nor to bluster at those around me.

To be anxious to be right in everything, searching the Scriptures, and seeking by prayer, to know what I should do.

To serve the Lord carefully and earnestly, leaving nothing to chance, passion, fashion, or whim.

Oh, for the confirming power of the Holy Ghost!

Oh, for vital union with the Lord Jesus!

The preacher studies his discourse carefully, though it will only occupy part of an hour; and is our life-sermon worthy of no care and consideration? A saintly life is a work of far higher art than the most valuable painting or precious statue, yet neither of these can be produced without thought. A man must be at his best to produce an immortal poem, yet a few hundred lines will sum it all up. Let us not dream that the far greater poem of a holy life can be made to flow forth like impromptu verse.

## CHAPTER 25

## HELP ASKED AND PRAISE RENDERED

*"And Judah gathered themselves together, to ask help of the Lord: even out of all the cities of Judah they came to seek the Lord"* (II Chron. 20:4).

The sudden news of a great invasion came to Jehoshaphat, and, like a true man of God, he set himself to seek the Lord, and proclaimed a fast. The people came together with all speed, and the whole nation earnestly cried to the Lord for His aid.

I. HOW THEY ASKED HELP.
They expressed their confidence (verse 6).
They pleaded His past acts (verse 7).
They confessed their condition; They had:
No power. "We have no might against this great company."
No plan. "Neither know we what to do" (verse 12).
Then they lifted their souls to God. "Our eyes are upon Thee."
Where could they look with more certainty?

II. HOW THEY RECEIVED IT.
By renewed assurance. "The Lord will be with you" (verse 17).
By the calming of their fears. "Be not afraid."
By urging them to greater faith (verse 20).
By distinct direction (verse 16).

III. HOW THEY ACTED BY THIS HELP.
They worshipped. With every sign of reverence, the king and his people bowed before Jehovah (verse 18). Worship girds us for warfare.
They praised. Before they received the mercy. Read verse 21.
They saw the promise fulfilled (verse 24).
They blessed the Lord (verse 26).
They had rest (verse 30).
Is there not a cause for our assembling even now to plead against the Moabites, Ammonites, and Edomites of superstition, worldliness, and infidelity?
This chapter, which begins with danger, fear and trouble all around, ends with joy, praise, quiet and rest. Two words seem to stand out in this chapter—PRAISE AND PRAYER—twin sisters which should always go together  One word links them here—FAITH.

## CHAPTER 25-A

# ESTHER'S EXALTATION; OR, WHO KNOWETH?

*"And who knoweth whether thou art come to the kingdom for such a time as this?"* (ESTHER 4:14).

Do not waste time in generalities but come down to personalities. We might properly say of any Christian church or individual that they have their own appointed place in the purpose of Divine mercy. If the candle is lighted, even though it be set upon a golden candlestick, it is not lighted for itself, but that it may give light to all that are in the house.

## I.   THE FIRST WORD IS "HEARKEN"

1. *Hearken to* a question. Will you separate your interests from those of your people and your God? Do you mean to say, "I shall look to my own salvation, but I cannot be supposed to take an interest in saving others"? In such a spirit as that I do not say you *will* be lost, but I say you *are* lost already.

   O professed servant of God, minister, deacon, or private church member, thou shalt perish if once thou beginnest to live to thyself.

2. *Hearken, God* can do without you. Enlargement and deliverance will arise to His people from another place if it come not by us. The Great Owner of the vineyard will have fruit at the end of the year, and if yonder tree does not bear it, He will cut it down.

## II.   THE CALL IS NOW, "CONSIDER"

1. *Consider* why the Lord has brought you where you are. Has He done it for your own sake? Does He intend all this merely that you may practice self-indulgence?

   We are members of one body, and God acts towards us with that fact in view. He does not bless the hand for the hand's sake, but for the sake of the whole body. You are saved—that you may save; you are taught—that you may teach.

2. *Consider* with what talents you are endowed for the Lord's work. You are endowed with special capacity for a certain work, so that no one is so fitted for it as yourself; you are a key to a lock which no other key will fit so well.

   Let each one of you feel that he has come to his own little kingdom for such a time as this. You and your work fit each other; God has joined you together, let no man put you asunder.

### III.  THE WORD IS NOW, "ASPIRE"

Rise to the utmost possible height.  Fulfill your calling to its loftiest degree.  Not only do all you are sure you can do, but aim at something which as yet is high up among the questions.  Say to yourself, "Who knoweth?"

1. *No one knows the limit* of his possibilities for God.
   Though you be no better than a mere cipher, yet the Lord can make something of you.  Set one before a cipher and it is ten directly.  Let two or three noughts combine to serve the Lord, and if the Lord Jesus heads them these nothings become tens of thousands.

   In dark times God makes lamps with which to remove the gloom. Martin Luther is sitting by his father's hearth in the forest when the Pope is selling his wicked indulgences; he will come out soon, and stop the crowing of the cock of the Romish Christ-denying Peter.  John Calvin is quietly studying when false doctrine is most rife, and he will be heard of at Geneva.

When Louis Napoleon was shut up in the fortress of Ham, and everybody ridiculed his foolish attempts upon France, yet he said to himself, "Who knows?  I am the nephew of my uncle, and may yet sit upon the imperial throne."  And he did so before many years passed.  Who knows?  Does anybody know what God may do by and through you?  Does anybody know what capacities slumber within your bosom?

Load your cannon with rough bits of rocks or stones from the road if nothing better comes to hand; ram them in with plenty of power; and apply the fire.  When you have nothing else to hurl at the foe, place yourself in the gun.

There was a man who strove in the House of Commons for what he thought would be a great boon to seamen, but he could not prevail. At last he broke through all the rules of the house and acted like a fanatic, and when everybody saw that the man was so in earnest that he was ready to faint and die, they said, "We must do something," and it was done.

An enthusiasm that overpowers yourself is likely to overpower others.  Do not fail from want of fervor.  Never mind if men think you crazy.  When you are overwhelmed yourself the flood of zeal will bear all opposition before it.  When you become so fanatically insane as to be absorbed by a passion for the glory of God, the salvation of men, the spread of truth, and the reclaiming of the fallen masses, there shall be about you the truest sanity and the mightiest force.

CHAPTER 26

# GOOD CAUSE FOR GREAT ZEAL

*"Now because we have maintenance from the king's pal-
ace, and it was not meet for us to see the king's dishonor,
therefore have we sent and certified the king"* (Ezra 4:14).

In the land were certain half-and-half persons, half breeds. They
wanted to join in building Jerusalem. The Jews refused. Angry,
they wrote the king. They called the Jews a troublesome people
and told Artaxerxes they were moved by gratitude to write him.

It was false; but hypocrites often use the best of words to cover
their deceit. Take these words out of those black mouths and put
them in your mouth and mine. They will suit us well if we turn
them to the great King of kings.

I. A FACT ACKNOWLEDGED.

"We have maintenance from the King's palace."
We have a new life and therefore new wants and new hunger and
a new thirst and God has maintained us out of His own palace.
1. We have an unfailing portion.
   Times of need have come, but the needed supply has come too.
2. We have a soul-satisfying portion.
A soul that gets what God gives him has quite as much as he can
hold, and as much as he can ever want. There is nothing in the
worldling's estate to envy. The more he has the worse it will be
for him to leave it.

II. A DUTY RECOGNIZED.

"It was not meet for us to see the King's dishonor." Good reasoning and it comes home to us. What are the things that may dishonor
God in our lives?
1. Ourselves. Art thou doing anything that dishonors thy God,
   professor—at home, in thy business, social life?
2. Our loved ones. Parents must not tolerate anything in those
   over whom they have control that would bring dishonor to
   God. Remember Eli.
3. Mutilating, misrepresenting His Word. We must always bear
   our protest against false doctrine.

III. A COURSE OF ACTION PURSUED.

"Therefore have we sent and certified the king."
How shall we do that? It is a holy exercise of the saints to report
to the Lord the sins and sorrows they observe among the people,
the blasphemies, the false teaching, the foul sophistry.

After those people had certified the king, they took care *to plead* with him. That praying is poor shift that is not made up of pleading. John Knox cried again and again in prayer "Give me Scotland or I die!"

---

I remember the remark of a Unitarian doctor, which I thought eminently correct. He said of a certain Calvinist, who was accused of speaking sharply against Unitarians. "Quite right; and so he ought, because if the Calvinist be right the Unitarian is not a Christian at all, but if the Unitarian be right the Calvinist is an idolater, because he worships one who is a man and is not the Son of God."

"We cannot impart to our children new hearts, but we can see to it that there shall be nothing within our gates that is derogatory to the Gospel of the Jesus Christ. I charge you see to it. But you cannot control your children, you say. Then the Lord have mercy upon you! It is your business to do it and you must do it, or else you will soon find they will control you."

CHAPTER 27

## THOSE WHO DESIRE

*"O Lord, I beseech Thee, let now Thine ear be attentive to the prayer of Thy servant, and to the prayer of Thy servants, who desire to fear Thy name"* (Nehemiah 1:11).

Nehemiah believed that there were others praying besides himself. He was not so gloomy, so self-opinionated, so uncharitable as to think that he alone loved the house of the Lord, and prayed for it. He believed that the Lord had many praying servants besides himself. In this he was more hopeful than Elijah. (I Kings 19:10, 18).

I. THIS INCLUDES ALL WHO HAVE ANY TRUE RELIGION.
  1. True godliness is always a matter of desire.
    Not of custom, fashion, habit, excitement, passion, or chance.
  2. Every part of it is a matter of desire.
    Repentance, faith, love, etc. None of these can be found in a man unless he desires to have them.
    Prayer, praise, service, alms, and all good deeds are matters of the heart's desire. Oh, to abound in them!
    The same may be said of heaven, of resurrection, and of the future glories of Christ's reign on earth.
    Good men are like Daniel, men of desires (Daniel 9:23, margin).

Desire is the life-blood of piety, the egg of holiness, the dawn of grace, the promise of perfection.

II. THIS INCLUDES MANY GRADES OF GRACE.

1. Those who earnestly and heartily long to be right with God, though afraid to think themselves saved. These are always desiring.

2. Those who know that they fear God, but desire to fear Him more. Some of the best of men are of this order.

3. Those who delight in the ways of God, and long to abide in them all their days. No man perseveres in holiness unless he desires to do so. Tender desires breed watchful walking, and, by God's Spirit, lead to consistent living.

Now all these people can pray acceptably; indeed, they are always praying, for desires are true prayers.

We need the prayers of all these people, as well as of advanced saints. The rank and file are the main part of the army. If none but eminent believers prayed, our treasury of supplication would be scantily furnished.

Lastly LET US PRAY NOW—all of us, great and small. In the Holy Ghost let us pray, and thereby support our ministers, missionaries, and other workers, who, like Nehemiah, lead the way in holy service.

When Napoleon returned from Elba, a man at work in a garden recognized the emperor, and at once followed him. Napoleon welcomed him cheerfully, saying, "Here we have our first recruit." When even one person begins to pray for us, however feeble his prayers, we ought to welcome him. He who prays for me enriches me.

Grains of sand and drops of rain combine for the greatest of purposes, and achieve them. There may be more real prayer in a little gathering of obscure desirers than in the great assembly where everything is done with ability rather than with agony of desire.

Never let your pastor lose his prayer-book. It should be written in the hearts of his people. If you cannot preach, or give largely, or become a church-officer, you can, at least, pray without ceasing.

CHAPTER 28

## THE SORROWFUL MAN'S QUESTION

*"Why is light given to a man whose way is hid, and whom God hath hedged in?"* (Job 3:23).

Job's case was such that life itself became irksome. He wondered why he should be kept alive to suffer. Could not mercy have per-

mitted him to die out of hand?    Light is most precious, yet we may
come to ask why it is given.

I.   THE CASE WHICH RAISES THE QUESTION.

   1.   He walks in deep trouble, so deep that he cannot see the
        bottom of it.   He cannot see any ground for comfort either
        in God or in man.   "His way is hid."

   2.   He can see no cause for it.   No special sin has been com-
        mitted.   No possible good appears to be coming out of it.

   3.   He cannot tell what to do in it.   Patience is hard, wisdom is
        difficult, confidence scarce, and joy out of reach, while the
        mind is in deep gloom.   Mystery brings misery.

   4.   He cannot see the way out of it.   (Ex. 14:3).

II.   THE QUESTION ITSELF: "Why is light given?" etc.

   1.   It is an unsafe one.   It is an undue exaltation of human judg-
        ment.   Ignorance should shun arrogance.

   2.   It reflects upon God.   It insinuates that His ways need ex-
        planation, and are either unreasonable, unjust, unwise, or
        unkind.

III.   ANSWERS WHICH MAY BE GIVEN TO THE QUESTION.

   1.   To an ungodly man sufficient answers are at hand.
        It is mercy which, by prolonging the light of life, keeps you
        from worse suffering.   For you to desire death is to be eager
        for hell.   Be not so foolish.
        It is love which calls you to repent.   Every sorrow is intended
        to whip you Godward.

   2.   To the godly man there are yet more apparent reasons.
        Your trials are sent:
        To let you see all that is in you.   In deep soul-trouble we dis-
        cover what we are made of.
        To bring you nearer to God.   The hedges shut you up to God;
        the darkness makes you cling close to Him.   Life is continued
        that grace may be increased.
        To make you an example to others.   Some are chosen to be
        monuments of the Lord's special dealings; a sort of lighthouse
        to other mariners.
        To magnify the grace of God.   If our way were always bright
        we could not so well exhibit the sustaining, consoling, and
        delivering power of the Lord.

At the same time that men often desire death, and feel that it
would be a relief, it might be to them the greatest possible calamity.
They may be wholly unprepared for it.   For a sinner, the grave

contains no rest; the eternal world furnishes no repose. One design
of God in such sorrows may be to show to the wicked how intolerable
will be future pain, and how important it is for them to be ready
to die. If they cannot bear the pains and sorrows of a few hours
in this short life, how can they endure eternal sufferings? If it is
so desirable to be released from the sorrows of the body here—if
it is felt that the grave, with all that is repulsive in it, would be a
place of repose, how important is it to find some way to be secured
from everlasting pains!

The true place of release from suffering, for a sinner, is not the
grave; it is in the pardoning mercy of God, and in that pure heaven
to which he is invited through the Blood of the cross. In that holy
heaven is the only real repose from suffering and from sin; and
heaven will be all the sweeter in proportion to the extremity of
pain which is endured on earth.—BARNES.

CHAPTER 29

# THE SINNER'S SURRENDER TO HIS PRESERVER

*"I have sinned; what shall I do unto Thee, O Thou pre-
server of men?"* (Job 7:20).

Job could defend himself before men, but he used another tone
when bowing before the Lord; there he cried, "I have sinned." The
words would suit any afflicted saint; for, indeed, they were uttered
by such an one; but they may also be used by the penitent sinner,
and we will on this occasion direct them to that use.

I.  A CONFESSION. "I have sinned."

In words this is no more than a hypocrite, nay, a Judas, a Saul, a
Balaam, might say. Do not many call themselves "miserable
sinners" who are indeed despicable mockers? Yet seeing Job's
heart was right his confession was accepted.

1. It was personal. I have sinned, whatever others may have
   done.

2. It was to the Lord. He addresses the confession not to his
   fellow-man but to the Preserver of men.

3. It was a confession wrought by the Spirit. See verse 18, where
   he ascribes his grief to the visitation of God.

4. It was feeling. He was cut to the quick by it. Read the
   whole chapter. This one fact, "I have sinned," is enough to
   brand the soul with the mark of Cain, and burn it with the
   flames of hell.

5. It was a believing confession. Mingled with much unbelief Job still had faith in God's power to pardon. An unbelieving confession may increase sin.

## II. AN INQUIRY. "WHAT SHALL I DO UNTO THEE."

In this question we see:

1. His willingness to do anything, whatever the Lord might demand, thus proving his earnestness.

2. His bewilderment; he could not tell what to offer, or where to turn; yet something must be done.

3. His surrender at discretion. He makes no conditions, he only begs to know the Lord's terms.

## III. A TITLE. "O THOU PRESERVER OF MEN!"

*Observer* of men, therefore aware of my case, my misery, my confession, my desire for pardon, my utter helplessness.

*Preserver* of men.

By His infinite long-suffering refraining from punishment.

By daily bounties of supply, keeping the ungrateful alive.

By the plan of salvation, delivering men from going down into the pit, snatching the brands from the burning.

No sooner had Job confessed his sin but he is desirous to know a remedy. Reprobates can cry, "Peccavi," I have sinned; but then they proceed not to say as here, "What shall I do?" They open their wound, but lay not on a plaster, and so the wounds made by sin are more putrefied, and grow more dangerous. Job would be directed what to do for remedy; he would have pardoning grace and prevailing grace upon any terms.—TRAPP.

Job was one of those whom Scripture describes as "perfect," yet he cried, "I have sinned." Noah was perfect in his generation, but no drunkard will allow us to forget that he had his fault. Abraham received the command, "Walk before me and be thou perfect," but he was not absolutely sinless. Zacharias and Elizabeth were blameless, and yet there was enough unbelief in Zacharias to make him dumb for nine months.

The doctrine of sinless perfection in the flesh is not of God, and he who makes his boast of possessing such perfection has at once declared his own ignorance of himself and of the law of the Lord. Nothing discovers an evil heart more surely than a glorying in its own goodness. He that proclaimeth his own praise publisheth his own shame.

Man is in himself so feeble a creature, that it is a great wonder that he has not long ago been crushed by the elements, exterminated by wild beasts, or extirpated by disease. Omnipotence has bowed itself to his preservation, and compelled all visible things to form the Body-guard of Man. We believe that the same Preserver of men Who has thus guarded the race watches with equal assiduity over every individual.

The unconditional surrender implied in the question, "What shall I do unto Thee?" is absolutely essential from every man who hopes to be saved. God will never raise the siege until we hand out the keys of the city, open every gate, and bid the Conqueror ride through every street, and take possession of the citadel. The traitor must deliver up himself and trust the prince's clemency. Till this is done the battle will continue; for the first requisite for peace with God is complete submission.

## CHAPTER 30

## JOB'S SURE KNOWLEDGE

*"For I know that my redeemer liveth"* (Job 19:25).

Difficulties of translation very great. We prefer a candid reading to one which might be obtained by pious fraud. It would seem that Job, driven to desperation, fell back upon the truth and justice of God. We may use the words in the most complete evangelical sense, and not be guilty of straining them; indeed, no other sense will fairly set forth the patriarch's meaning. From what other hope could he obtain consolation but from that of future life and glory?

I. JOB HAD A TRUE FRIEND AMID CRUEL FRIENDS. He calls Him his Redeemer, and looks to Him in his trouble.

The Hebrew word will bear three renderings, as follows:
1. His Kinsman.

    Nearest akin of all. No kinsman is so near as Jesus. None so kinned, and none so kind.

    Voluntarily so. Not forced to be a brother, but so in heart, and by His own choice of our nature; therefore more than brother. Not ashamed to own it. "He is not ashamed to call them brethren." (Heb. 2:11). Even when they had forsaken Him He called them "my brethren." (Matt. 28:10).

    Eternally so. Who shall separate us? (Rom. 8:35).
2. His Vindicator.

    From every false charge; by pleading the causes of our soul. From every jibe and jest; for he that believeth in Him shall not be ashamed or confounded.

    From true charges, too; by bearing our sin Himself and becoming our righteousness, thus justifying us.

From accusations of Satan. "The Lord rebuke thee, O Satan!" (Zech. 3:2). "The accuser of our brethren is cast down" (Rev. 12:10).

3. His Redeemer.
Of his person from bondage.
Of his lost estates, privileges and joys, from the hand of the enemy.
Redeeming both by price and by power.

## II. Job Had Real Property Amid Absolute Poverty. He speaks of "my Redeemer," as much as to say, "Everything else is gone, but my Redeemer is still my own, and lives for me."

He means:
1. I accept Him as such, leaving myself in His hands.
2. I have felt somewhat of His power already, and I am confident that all is well with me even now, since He is my Protector.
3. I will cling to Him forever. He shall be my only hope in life and death. I may lose all else, but never the Redemption of my God, the kinship of my Savior.

## III. Job Had A Living Kinsman Amid A Dying Family. "My Redeemer liveth."

He owned the great Lord as ever living:
What have we to do with the dead Christ of the Church of Rome? *Our* Redeemer lives.
What with the departed Christ of Unitarians? Our divine Vindicator abides in the power of an endless life.

## IV. Job Had Absolute Certainty Amid Uncertain Affairs.

"I know." He had no sort of doubt upon that matter. Everything else was questionable, but this was certain.
His faith made him certain. Faith brings sure evidence; it substantiates what it receives, and makes us *know*.
His trials could not make him doubt. Why should they? They touched not the relationship of his God, or the heart of his Redeemer, or the life of his Vindicator.
Have you this great knowledge?
Do you act in accordance with such an assurance?
Will you not at this hour devoutly adore your loving Kinsman?
In times of sharp trials believers are (1) driven out of themselves to look to their God, their Redeemer. (2) Driven to look within themselves for a knowledge sure and unquestioning—"I know." (3) Driven to hold by personal faith to that which is set forth in the covenant of grace—"my Redeemer." (4) Driven to live much upon the unseen—the living Redeemer, and his advent in the latter day.

Tried saints, when greatly in the dark, have been led to great discoveries of comfortable truth. "Necessity is the mother of invention." Here Job found an argument from the justice of God for his own comfort. God could not leave His sincere servant under slander; therefore if he died undefended, and years passed away so that the worms consumed his body, yet a Vindicator would arise, and the maligned and injured Job would be cleared.

Thus the Spirit revealed to the afflicted patriarch a future state, a living Next-of-Kin, a future judgment, a resurrection, and an eternal justification of saints. Great light came in through a narrow window, and Job was an infinite gainer by his temporary losses.

A weak faith is glad to look off from all difficulties, for it shrinks back at them; as Martha, considering Lazarus was four days dead, and begun to putrefy, her faith began to fail her; it was too late now to remove the gravestone. But Faith in its strength considers all these, urges these impossibilities, and yet overcomes them; as Elijah, in his dispute with Baal's priests, took all the disadvantages to himself. "Pour on water," said he; and again, "Pour on more water"; faith shall fetch fire from heaven to inflame the sacrifice.

"So," saith Job, "let me die, and rot, and putrefy in the grave— nay, let the fire burn my body, or the sea swallow it, or wild beasts devour it, yet it shall be restored to me; death shall be *praedae suae custos*, like the lion that killed the prophet, and then stood by his body, and did not consume it." Job's faith laughs at impossibilities, is ashamed to talk of difficulties; with Abraham, considers not his own dead body, but believes above and against hope; knew God would restore it.—R. BROWNRIG.

Faith is, or should be, strongly persuaded of what it believeth. It is an evidence, not a conjecture; not a surmise, but a firm assurance. We should certainly know what we believe: "We know that Thou art a Teacher come from God" (John 3:2). "We believe, and are sure, that Thou art that Christ, the Son of the living God" (John 6:69). "We know that we have a building of God" (II Cor. 5:1). "We know that we shall see Him as He is" (I John 3:2). "Be ye steadfast, unmoveable, always abounding in the work of the Lord, for as much as ye know that your labor is not in vain in the Lord" (I Cor. 15:58).

Believers of old shame us, who live in the clear sunshine of the gospel. Job lived long before the gospel was revealed; the redemption of souls was at that time a great mystery, being sparingly revealed to a few; only one of a thousand could bring this message to a condemned sinner, that God had found a ransom. (Job 33:23).— MANTON.

## CHAPTER 31

# REBELLING AGAINST THE LIGHT

*"They are of those that rebel against the light"* (Job 24:13).

These evidently had the light, and this should be esteemed as no small privilege, since to wander on the dark mountains is a terrible curse. Yet this privilege may turn into an occasion of evil.

Light has a sovereignty in it, so that to resist it is to rebel against it. God has given it to be a display of Himself, for God is light; and He has clothed it with a measure of His majesty and power of judgment.

Rebellion against light has in it a high degree of sin. It might be virtue to rebel against darkness, but what shall be said of those who withstand the light? resisting truth, holiness and knowledge?

## I. DETECT THE REBELS.

Well-instructed persons, who have been accustomed to teach others, and yet turn aside to evil; these are grievous traitors. Children of Christian parents who sin against their early training; upon whom prayer and entreaty, precept and example are thrown away. Hearers of the word, who quench convictions deliberately, frequently, and with violence.

## II. DESCRIBE THE FORMS OF THIS REBELLION.

Some refuse light, being unwilling to know more than would be convenient; therefore they deny themselves time for thought, absent themselves from sermons, neglect godly reading, shun pious company, avoid reproof, etc.

Others scoff and fight against it, calling light darkness, and darkness light. Infidelity, ribaldry, persecution, and such like, become their resort and shelter.

Many darken it for others, hindering its operations among men, hiding their own light under a bushel, ridiculing the efforts of others, etc.

## III. DECLARE THE FOLLY OF THIS REBELLION.

Light is our best friend, and it is wisdom to obey it; to resist it is to rebel against our own interest.

Light triumphs still. Owls hoot, but the moon shines. Opposition to truth and righteousness is useless; it may even promote that which it aims to prevent.

Light would lead to more light. Consent to it, for it will be beneficial to your own soul.

Light would lead to heaven, which is the center of light.

Off the coast of New Zealand a captain lost his vessel by steering in the face of the warning light, till he dashed upon the rock immediately beneath the lighthouse. He said that he was asleep; but this did not restore the wreck, nor save him from condemnation. It is a terrible thing for rays of gospel light to guide a man to his doom.

It cannot be denied that the wicked sin knowingly; but the godly have a light beyond other men, such a divine, penetrating light as no hypocrite can attain to. They have better eyes to see sin than others; and for them to meddle with sin, and embrace this dunghill, must needs provoke God, and make the fury rise up in His face. Oh, therefore, you that are the people of God, flee from sin; your sins are more enhanced, and have worse aggravation in them, than the sins of the unregenerate.—THOMAS. WATSON.

## CHAPTER 32

## THE HYPOCRITE DISCOVERED

*"Will he always call upon God?"* (Job 27:10).

A hypocrite may be a very neat imitation of a Christian. He professes to know God, to converse with Him, to be dedicated to His service, and to invoke His protection; he even practises prayer or at least feigns it. Yet the cleverest counterfeit fails somewhere, and may be discovered by certain signs. The test is here, "Will he always call upon God?"

I. WILL HE PRAY AT ALL SEASONS OF PRAYER?

Will he pray in private? Or is he dependent upon the human eye and the applause of men?
Will he pray if forbidden? Daniel did so. Will he?
Will he pray in business? Will he practise ejaculatory prayer? Will he look for hourly guidance?
Will he pray in pleasure? Will he have a holy fear of offending with his tongue? Or will company make him forget his God?
Will he pray in darkness of soul? Or will he sulk in silence?

II. WILL HE PRAY IMPORTUNATELY?

If no answer comes, will he persevere? Is he like the brave horse who will pull at a post at his master's bidding?
If a rough answer comes, will he plead on? Does he know how to wrestle with the angel, and give tug for tug?
If no one else prays, will he be singular, and plead on against wind and tide?

If God answer him by disappointment and defeat, will he feel that delays are not denials, and still pray?

III. WILL HE CONTINUE TO PRAY THROUGHOUT THE WHOLE OF LIFE?

The hypocrite soon gives up prayer under certain circumstances. If he is in trouble, he will not pray, but will run to human helpers. If he gets out of trouble, he will not pray, but quite forget his vows.

If men laugh at him, he will not dare to pray.

If men smile on him, he will not care to pray.

1. He grows weary. He can make a spurt, but he cannot keep it up. Short prayers are sweet to him.

2. He grows secure. Things go well and he sees no need of prayer; or he is too holy to pray.

We have heard of a child who said her prayers, and then added, "Good-by, God; we are all going to Saratoga, and pa and ma won't go to meeting, or pray any more till we come back again." We fear that many who go to the seaside, or other holiday resorts, give God the go-by in much the same manner.—GUTHRIE.

Ahaz will not ask a sign, even when God bids him, lest he should tempt the Lord (Is. 7:10, 12); a great piece of modesty in show, but a sure symptom of infidelity. He would not ask a sign because he could not believe the thing; not to avoid troubling of God, but himself. He seems very mannerly, but shows himself very malapert.

Thus, this hypocrite will serve God only by fits and starts, when he himself lists. He never troubles God unless God troubles him. In health, wealth, peace, he can comfort himself. He never prays but in trouble; in his affliction he will seek God early. (Hosea 5:15). God is fain to go away, and return to His place, else this man would never look after Him. When God hath touched him, he acquaints God with his misery, but when times grow better with him, he excludes God from his mirth.—SAMUEL CROOK.

## CHAPTER 33

## RAIN AND GRACE: A COMPARISON

*"Who hath divided a watercourse for the overflowing of waters, or a way for the lightning of thunder; to cause it to rain on the earth, where no man is; on the wilderness, wherein there is no man; to satisfy the desolate and waste ground; and to cause the bud of the tender herb to spring forth?"* (Job 38:25-27).

God challengeth man to compare with his Maker even in the one matter of the rain. Can he create it? Can he send a shower upon the desert, to water the lone herbs which else would perish in the burning heat? No, he would not even think of doing such a thing. That generous act cometh of the Lord alone.

We shall work out a parallel between grace and rain.

## I. GOD ALONE GIVETH RAIN, AND THE SAME IS TRUE OF GRACE.

He directs each drop, and gives each blade of grass its own drop of dew—to every believer his portion of grace.

He moderates the force, so that it does not beat down or drown the tender herb. Grace comes in its own gentle way. Conviction, enlightenment, etc., are sent in due measure.

He holds it in His power. Absolutely at His own will does God bestow either rain for the earth or grace for the soul.

## II. RAIN FALLS IRRESPECTIVE OF MEN, AND SO DOES GRACE.

Grace waits not man's observation. As the rain falls where no man is, so grace courts not publicity.

Nor his co-operation. It "tarrieth not for man, nor waiteth for the sons of men" (Micah 5:7).

Nor his prayers. Grass calls not for rain, yet it comes. "I am found of them that sought me not" (Is. 65:1).

## III. RAIN FALLS WHERE WE MIGHT LEAST HAVE EXPECTED IT.

It falls where there is no trace of former showers, even upon the desolate wilderness; so does grace enter hearts which had hitherto been unblessed, where great need was the only plea which rose to heaven (Is. 35:7).

It falls where there seems nothing to repay the boon. Many hearts are naturally as barren as the desert (Is. 35:6).

It falls where the need seems insatiable; "to satisfy the desolate." Some cases seem to demand an ocean of grace; but the Lord meets the need, and His grace falls where the joy and glory are all directed to God by grateful hearts. Twice we are told that the rain falls "where no man is." When conversion is wrought of the Lord no man is seen; the Lord alone is exalted.

## IV. THIS RAIN IS MOST VALUED BY LIFE.

The rain gives joy to seeds and plants in which there is life. Budding life knows of it; the tenderest herb rejoices in it; so is it with those who begin to repent, who feebly believe, and thus are just alive.

The rain causes development. Grace also perfects grace. Buds of hope grow into strong faith. Buds of feeling expand into love. Buds of desire rise to resolve. Buds of confession come to open avowal. Buds of usefulness swell into fruit.

The rain causes health and vigor of life. Is it not so with grace? The rain creates the flower with its color and perfume, and God is pleased. The full outgrowth of renewed nature cometh of grace, and the Lord is well pleased therewith.

Let us acknowledge the sovereignty of God as to grace.

Let us cry to Him for grace.

Let us expect Him to send it, though we may feel sadly barren, and quite out of the way of the usual means of grace.

Oh, how pleasant are the effects of rain to languishing plants, to make them green and beautiful, lively and strong, fragrant and delightful! So the effect of Christ's influences are most desirable to drooping souls, for enlightening and enlivening them, for confirming and strengthening them, for comforting and enlarging them, for appetizing and satisfying them, transforming and beautifying them. —JOHN WILLISON.

Be not to me as a cloud without rain, lest I be to Thee like a tree without fruit.—SPURSTOWE.

The grass springs up; the bud opens; the leaf extends; the flowers breathe forth their fragrance as if they were under the most careful cultivation. All this must be the work of God, since it cannot even be pretended that *man* is there to produce these effects. Perhaps one would be more deeply impressed with a sense of the presence of God in the pathless desert or on the boundless prairie, where no man is, than in the most splendid park or the most tastefully cultivated garden which man could make. In the one case, the hand of God alone is seen; in the other, we are constantly admiring the skill of man.—BARNES.

## CHAPTER 34

## GOOD CHEER FOR THE NEEDY

*"For the needy shall not always be forgotten: the expectation of the poor shall not perish forever"* (Psalm 9:18).

The practical value of a text very much depends upon the man to whom it comes. The song of the troubadour was charming to Richard Coeur de Lion because he knew the responsive verses. The trail is full of meaning to the Indian, for his quick eye knows how to follow it; it would not mean a tithe as much to a white man. The sight of the lighthouse is cheering to the mariner, for from it he gathers his whereabouts. So will those who are spiritually poor and needy eagerly lay hold on this promise, prize it, and live upon it with content.

## I. Two Bitter Experiences Ended.

1. "The needy shall not always be forgotten." You have been forgotten:
   By former friends and admirers.
   In arrangements made and plans projected.
   In judgments formed and in praises distributed.
   In help estimated and reliance expressed.

In fact, you have not been a factor in the calculation; you have been forgotten as a dead man out of mind. This has wounded you deeply, for there was a time when you were consulted among the first.

This will not be so always.

2. "The expectation of the poor shall not perish forever."
   You have been disappointed:
   In your natural expectation from justice, gratitude, relationship, age, sympathy, charity, etc.
   In your confidence in man.
   In your judgment of yourself.
   In your expectations of providence.

This disappointment shall only be temporary. Your expectation shall not perish forever; you shall yet receive more than you expected.

## II. Two Sad Fears Removed. Fears Which Are Naturally Suggested By What You Have Already Experienced.

1. Not forever shall you be forgotten:
   You shall not meet with final forgetfulness.
   In the day of severe trouble.
   In the night of grief and alarm for sin.
   In the hour of death.

2. Nor shall your expectation perish:
   Your weakness shall not frustrate the power of God.
   Your sin shall not dry up the grace of God.
   Your constitutional infirmities shall not cause your overthrow.
   Your future trials shall not be too much for you.

## III. Two Sweet Promises Given.

1. "Not always be forgotten"; you shall not be overlooked:
   At the mercy-seat, when you are pleading.
   From the pulpit, and in the Word, when your soul is hungering.
   In your sufferings and service, when to be thought of by the Lord will be your main consolation.

2. "Expectation shall not perish forever." You shall not be disappointed:

Peace shall visit your heart.

Sin shall be vanquished without and within.

Let the poor man hope in God.

Let him feast on the future if he find the present to be scant.

Above all, let him rest in the promise of a faithful God.

An aged Christian, lying on his death-bed in a state of such extreme weakness that he was often entirely unconscious of all around him, was asked the cause of his perfect peace. He replied, "When I am able to think, I think of Jesus; and when I am unable to think of Him, I know He is thinking of me."

Thirty years ago, before the Lord caused me to wander from my father's house and from my native place, I put my mark upon this passage in Isaiah: "Thou shalt know that I am the Lord," etc. (chap. 49:23). Of the many books I now possess, the Bible that bears this mark is the only one that belonged to me at that time. It now lies before me, and I find that, although the hair which then was dark as night has mean-while become sable silvered, the ink which marked this text has grown into intensity of blackness as the time advanced, corresponding with, and in fact recording, the growing intensity of the conviction that "they shall not be ashamed" who wait for thee. I believed it then, but I know it now, and I can write "Probatum est" with my whole heart over against the symbol which that mark is to me of my ancient faith. . . . Under many perilous circumstances, in many most trying scenes, amid faintings within and fears without, and under tortures that rend the heart, and troubles that crush it down, I have waited for Thee, and lo! I stand this day as one not ashamed.—DR. JOHN KITTO.

## CHAPTER 35

## SALUS JEHOVAE

*"But the salvation of the righteous is of the Lord"*
(Psalm 37:39).

Salvation is a very large term, and describes the whole life of true believers—their whole experience, from their first consciousness of the ruin of the fall to their entrance into Glory. They feel their need of being perpetually saved from self, sin, Satan, and the world. They trust in God for preservation, and their end is peace (verse 37).

I. THIS IS THE ESSENCE OF SOUND DOCTRINE.

The salvation of the righteous is of the Lord, **even of the** Triune Jehovah, Father, Son and Holy Ghost in:

1. The planning.
2. The providing.
3. The beginning.
4. The carrying on.
5. The completion.

II. THIS IS A NECESSARY FACT. The saints recognize it, for:

1. Their inward conflicts make them know that God alone must work salvation. They are too fickle and feeble to save themselves.
2. Their outward temptations drive them to the same conclusion. They are well kept whom God keeps, but none else.
3. The world's hate drives them away from all hope in that quarter. God is greater than a world in arms.

III. THIS IS A REASON FOR HUMILITY.

1. It strips the righteous of all pride in the fact of their being saved.
2. Of all exultation in self because they continue in their integrity.
3. Of all undue censure of the fallen; for they, themselves, would have failed had not the Lord upheld them.
4. Of all self-confidence as to the future, since their weakness is inherent and abiding.
5. Of all self-glorying, even in heaven, since in all things they are debtors to sovereign grace.

IV. THIS IS A FRUITFUL GROUND OF HOPE.

1. In reference to our own difficulties; God can give us deliverance.
2. In reference to our tried brethren; the Lord can sustain, sanctify, and deliver them.
3. In reference to sinners; they cannot be too degraded, obstinate, ignorant, or false; God can work salvation even in the worst.

"Salvation is of the Lord." This is the sum of Jonah's discourse; one word for all; the very moral of his history. The mariners might have written upon their ship, instead of Castor and Pollux, or the like device, *Salvation is the Lord's;* the Ninevites in the next chapter might have written upon their gates, *Salvation is the Lord's;* and all mankind, whose cause is pitted and pleaded by God against the hardness of Jonah's heart, might have written in the palms of their hands, *Salvation is the Lord's*. It is the argument of both the Testaments, the staff and support of heaven and earth. They would both sink, and all their joints be severed, if the salvation of the Lord were not.—KING *on Jonah.*

Thus the saints hold heaven. Not by conquest, but by heritage. Won by another arm than their own, it presents the strongest imaginable contrast to the spectacle in England's palace that day when the king demanded to know of his assembled nobles by what title they held their lands? What title! At the rash question a hundred swords leaped from their scabbards. Advancing on the alarmed monarch—"By these," they said, "we won, and by these will keep them."

How different the scene which heaven presents! All eyes are turned on Jesus with looks of love; gratitude glows in every bosom, and swells every song; now with golden harps they sound His praise; and now, descending from their thrones to do Him homage, they cast their crowns in one glittering heap at the feet which were nailed on Calvary. From this scene, learn in whose name to seek salvation, and through whose merits to hope for it; and with a faith in harmony with the worship of the skies, be this your language—"Not unto us, O Lord, not unto us, but unto Thy name give glory."—DR. GUTHRIE.

"This brook will soon run dry," said one. "Nay," quoth his fellow, "it flows from a living spring, which was never known to fail in summer or in winter." A man was reputed to be very rich by those who saw his expensive houses, and horses, and charges; but there were others who judged that his name would soon be in the *Gazette*, for he had no capital. "There is nothing at the back of it," said one, and the saying meant much. Now, the believer has the eternal deep for his spring of supply, and the all-sufficiency of God as the substance of his wealth. What cause has he to fear?

If salvation were partly of God and partly of man it would be as sorry an affair as that image of Nebuchadnezzar's dream, which was partly of iron and partly of clay. It would end in a break-down. If our dependence were upon Jesus in a measure, and our own works in some degree, our foundation would be partly on the rock and partly on the sand, and the whole structure would fall. Oh, to know the full meaning of the words, *"Salvation is of the Lord"*;

Experience alone can beat this truth into men's minds. A man will lie broken at the foot of the precipice, every bone dislocated by the fall, and yet hope to save himself. Piles of sin will fall upon him and bury him, and yet his self-trust will live. Mountains of actual transgression will overwhelm him, and yet he will stir himself to self-confident effort, working like the Cyclops which Etna heaped upon them. Crushed to atoms, every particle of our nature reeks with conceit. Ground to powder, our very dust is pungent with pride. Only the Holy Ghost can make a man receive that humbling sentence, *"Salvation is of the Lord."*

## CHAPTER 36

## SPARROWS AND SWALLOWS

> *"Yea, the sparrow hath found an house, and the swallow a nest for herself, where she may lay her young, even Thine altars, O Lord of hosts, my king, and my God"* (Psalm 84:3).

David, as an exile, envied the birds which dwelt around the house of the Lord. So the Christian, when debarred the assembly of the saints, or under spiritual desertion, will pine to be once more at home with God.

These birds found in the sanctuary what we would find in God.

I. HOUSES FOR THEMSELVES.

    1. Consider what they were. Sparrows.
    Worthless creatures. Five for two farthings.
    Needy creatures, requiring both nests, food, and everything else.
    Numerous creatures; but none were driven away.
    2. Consider what they enjoyed?
    Safety.

| | |
|---|---|
| Rest. | All this in the house of God, hard by |
| Abode. | His altars. Thus do believers find all |
| Delight. | *in Christ Jesus.* |

    Society.
    Nearness.

It is not every bird that does this. The eagle is too ambitious. The vulture too foul. The cormorant too greedy. The hawk too war-like. The ostrich too wild. The barn-door fowl too dependent upon man. The owl too fond of darkness.

These sparrows were little and loving.

II. NESTS FOR THEIR YOUNG.

Children should be housed in the house of God. The sanctuary of God should be the nursery of the young.

    1. They will be safe there, and free there. The swallow, the "bird of liberty," is satisfied to find a nest for herself near the

altars of God. She is not afraid of bondage there either for herself or her young.

2. They will be joyful there. We should try to make our little ones happy in God, and in His holy worship.

3. They are likely to return to the nest, as the swallows do; even as the young salmon return to the rivulet where they were hatched. Young folks remember their first impressions.

4. Children truly brought to Christ have every blessing in that fact.
They are rich; they dwell in God's palace.
They are educated; they abide in the Lord's Temple.
They are safe for time and eternity.

Are you sighing after Christ for yourself and your children?

Are you content without Christ? Then you are not likely to care about your children.

Do you already possess a home in Jesus? Rest not till all yours are housed in the same place.

Sir Thomas More used to attend the parish church at Chelsea, and there putting on a surplice, he would sing with the choristers at matins and high mass. It happened, one day, that the Duke of Norfold coming to Chelsea to dine with him, found him at church thus engaged. As they walked home together arm in arm, after service, the duke exclaimed. "My Lord Chancellor a parish clerk! A parish clerk! you dishonor the king and his office!" "Nay," he replied, smiling, "your Grace cannot suppose that the king, our master, will be offended with me for serving his Master, or thereby account his office dishonored."

"God fails not," as one has beautifully said, "to find a house for the most *worthless*, and the nest for the most *restless* of birds." What confidence this should give us! How we should rest!—*Things New and Old.*

As a rule, the children of godly parents are godly. In cases where this is not the case there is a reason. I have carefully observed and detected the absence of family prayer, gross inconsistency, harshness, indulgence, or neglect of admonition. If trained in God's ways, they do not depart from them.

CHAPTER 37

# ANGELIC PROTECTION IN APPOINTED WAYS

*"For He shall give His angels charge over thee, to keep thee in all thy ways"* (Psalm 91:11).

We are pilgrims on our way to Canaan. He who set us free by the passover deliverance also provides for our journey to the land which floweth with milk and honey. All the way to the promised land is covered by this divine safe-conduct.

I. THERE ARE WAYS WHICH ARE NOT IN THE PROMISE.

"All thy ways" are mentioned; but some tracks are not to be followed by children of God, and are not their ways.

1. Ways of presumption. In these men court danger, and, as it were defy God. "Cast thyself down," said Satan to our Lord, and then urged this promise. (Matt. 4:6).

2. Ways of sin, dishonesty, lying, vice, worldly conformity, etc. We have no permit to bow in the house of Rimmon. (Eph. 5:12).

3. Ways of worldliness, selfishness, greed, ambition. The ways by which men seek personal aggrandizement are usually dark and crooked and are not of God. (Prov. 28:22; I Tim. 6:9).

4. Ways of will worship, wilfulness, obstinacy, fancy, daydreaming, absurd impulse, etc. (Jer. 2:18).

5. Ways of erroneous doctrine, novel practice, fashionable ceremonial, flattering delusion, etc. (II Tim. 3:5).

II. THERE ARE WAYS IN WHICH SAFETY IS GUARANTEED.
1. The way of humble faith in the Lord Jesus.
2. The way of obedience to divine precepts.
3. The way of childlike trust in providential guidance.
4. The way of strict principle and stern integrity.
5. The way of consecrated service and seeking God's glory.
6. The way of holy separation and walking with God.

III. THESE WAYS LEAD US INTO VARIED CONDITIONS.
1. They are changeful and varied; "all thy ways."
2. They are sometimes stony with difficulty; "foot against a stone."
3. They may be terrible with temptation.
4. They may be mysteriously trying. Devils may throng the path—only to be met by holy angels.
5. They are essentially safe, while the smooth and easy roads are perilous.

IV. BUT WHILE WALKING IN THEM ALL BELIEVERS ARE SECURE.

1. The Lord Himself concerns Himself about them. "He shall give His angels charge over thee." He will personally command those holy beings to have an eye to His children. David charged his troops to spare Absalom, but his bidding was disregarded. It is not so with God.

2. Each one is personally watched over. "Charge over *thee* to keep *thee*." (Is. 42:6; Gen. 28:15).

3. That watchfulness is perpetual—"All thy ways." (Ps. 121:3, 4).

4. All this comes to them by Jesus, Whose the angels are, and Whom they serve. (Is. 43:4).

   How cheerfully we should watch over others! How vigorously should we hold them up whenever it is in our power! To cast off a stumbling brother is not angelic, but the reverse.

While King William, at a battle in Flanders, was giving orders in the thickest of the fight, he saw, to his surprise, among his staff one Michael Godfrey, a merchant of London, and Deputy Governor of the Bank of England, who had thus exposed himself in order to gratify his curiosity. The king, riding up to him, said, "Sir, you ought not to run these hazards; you are not a soldier, you can be of no use here." "Sire," answered Godfrey, "I run no more hazard than your Majesty." "Not so," said William; "I am here where it is my duty to be, and I may, without presumption, commit my life to God's keeping; but you—" The sentence needed no completion, for at that very moment a cannon ball laid Godfrey lifeless at the king's feet. He had been wise had he restricted himself to the ways of his calling and duty.

A dying saint asked that his name should be put upon his tombstone, with the dates of his birth and death, and the one word, *"Kept."*

No angel will give in his account with sorrow, saying, "I could not keep him; the stones were too many, his feet too feeble, the way too long." No, we shall be kept to the end; for in addition to angels, we have the safeguard of their Lord; He keepeth the feet of His saints (II Sam. 2:9).

## CHAPTER 38

## LIVING PRAISE

*"The dead praise not the Lord, neither any that go down into silence. But we will bless the Lord from this time forth and for evermore. Praise the Lord"* (Psalm 115: 17, 18).

The living God should be adored by a living people. A blessing God should be blessed by a blessing people. Whatever others do, we ought to bless Jehovah. When we bless Him we should not rest till others do the same; we should cry to them, "Praise the Lord." Our example and our persuasion should rouse them to praise.

I. A MOURNFUL MEMORY. "The dead praise not the Lord, neither any that go down into silence." This reminds us:
  1. Of silenced voices in the choirs of Zion. Good men and true who neither sing nor speak among us any longer.
  2. Of our own speedy silence; so far as this world is concerned we shall soon be among the dead and silent ones.
  3. Of the ungodly around us, who are already spiritually dead, and can no more praise the Lord than if they were dumb.

II. A HAPPY RESOLUTION. "But we will bless the Lord."
  In the heart, song, testimony, action, we are resolved to give the Lord our loving praise; because:
  1. We are blessed of the Lord; shall we not bless Him?
  2. He will bless us. More and more will He reveal His love to us; let us praise Him more and more. Be this our steadfast vow, that we will bless the Lord, come what may.

III. AN APPROPRIATE COMMENCEMENT. "We will bless the Lord from this time forth."
  1. When spiritually renewed and comforted. When the four times repeated words, "He will bless," have come true in our experience. (verses 12-14).
  2. When led to confess Christ. Then should we begin the never-ending life-psalm. Service and song should go together.
  3. When years end and begin—New-Year's days, birthdays, etc., let us bless God for:
  Sin of the year forgiven.
  Need of the year supplied.
  Mercy of the year enjoyed.

IV. AN EVERLASTING CONTINUANCE. "From this time forth and forevermore."
  1. Weariness shall not suspend it. We will renew our strength as we bless the Lord.
  2. Final falling shall not end it; the Lord will keep our soul in His way, and make us praise Him all our days.
  3. Nor shall death so much as interrupt our songs, but raise them to a purer and fuller strain.
  4. Nor shall any supposable calamity deprive the Lord of our gratitude. "The Lord gave, and the Lord hath taken away; blessed be the name of the Lord" (Job 1:21).

Praise is the highest function that any creature can discharge. The rabbis have a beautiful bit of teaching buried among their rubbish about angels. They say that there are two kinds of angels, the angels of service and the angels of praise, of which two orders the latter is the higher, and that no angel in it praises God twice; but having lifted up his voice in the psalm of heaven, then ceases to be. He has perfected his being, he has reached the height of his greatness, he has done what he was made for; let him fade away. The garb of legend is mean enough, but the thought it embodies is that ever true and solemn one, without which life is naught: "Man's chief end is to glorify God."—DR. MACLAREN.

When we bless God for mercies we prolong them, and when we bless Him for miseries we usually end them. When we reach to praise we have compassed the design of a dispensation, and have reaped the harvest of it. Praise is a soul in flower, and a secret, hearty blessing of the Lord is the soul fruit-bearing. Praise is the honey of life, which a devout heart sucks from every bloom of providence and grace. As well be dead as be without praise; it is the crown of life.

## CHAPTER 39

## WHAT IS YOUR COMFORT?

*"This is my comfort in my affliction: for Thy word hath quickened me"* (Psalm 119:50).

In some respects the same event happens to us all; to good men, to great men, to well-instructed men, as well as to the wicked, the obscure, and the ignorant. Each of these can speak of "my affliction." "The heart knoweth his own bitterness" (Prov. 14:10).

It is a grand matter when "my affliction" is in each case balanced by "my comfort." It was so in David's case, and he is a fair representative of all believers. How is it with each one of our hearers?

I. BELIEVERS HAVE THEIR PECULIAR COMFORT.

1. *This*, as different from others. Worldly men get their drops of comfort from such sources as they prefer; but the godly man looks to his experience of the Word, and says, "This is my comfort" (Ps. 4:6).

2. *This*, as having it near at hand. He does not say *that*, as if he pointed it out in the distance; but *this*, as grasping it.

II. THAT COMFORT COMES FROM A PECULIAR SOURCE. "Thy word hath quickened me."

1. In part it is outward.

The Word of God, full of promises, is our comfort. (Rom. 15:4).

The Word of God, full of records of His goodness, is the confirmation of our confidence. (Ps. 77:5-10).

2. In part it is inward.

In past experience he had felt the power of the word in raising him:

Into life from death (Ps. 116:8).

Into higher life from lower (Ps. 119:67).

In present experience he was then feeling its power in making:

His mind less worldly.

His heart more prayerful.

His spirit more tender.

His faith more simple.

III. THAT THE FORM OF OUR COMFORT IS A TEST OF CHARACTER.

1. Some look to wealth; when their corn and their wine are increased, they say, "This is my comfort." They mind the main chance; they are worldly (Luke 12:19).

2. Some seek to dreams and visions, omens and fancies, impressions and presentiments; they are superstitious.

3. Some run to sin, drink, gaming, worldly company, dissipation, opium; they are wicked.

4. Some resort to their fellow-men for advice and assistance; they are unwise, and will be disappointed (Jer. 17:5).

What is your comfort?

Has this blessed volume quickened you?

If so, look to it under all trials, for it will never fail you.

The Rev. E. Paxton Hood says: "When I visited one day, as he was dying, my beloved friend Benjamin Parsons, I said, 'How are you today, sir?' He said, 'My head is resting very sweetly on three pillows—infinite power, infinite love, and infinite wisdom.'"

"Speak to me now in Scripture language alone," said a dying Christian. "I can trust the words of God; but when they are the words of man, it costs me an effort to think whether I may trust to them." —RALPH ERSKINE.

I was questioning my spiritual life, I who have so long been a preacher to others. I entered a little rustic assembly. An unlettered man preached the gospel; he preached it heartily; my tears began to flow; my soul leaped at the very sound of the Word of the Lord. What a comfort it was to me! How frequently have I thought of it since! The Word did revive me; my heart was not dead to its influence; I was one of those happy people who know the joyful sound. Assurance was bright in my soul—the Word had quickened me.

What energy a text will breathe into a man! There is more in one divine sentence than in huge folios of human composition. There are tinctures of which one drop is more powerful than large doses of the common dilutions. The Bible is the essence of truth; it is the mind of God, the wisdom of the Eternal. By every word of God men are made to live, and are kept in life.

## CHAPTER 40

## FLIGHT TO GOD

*"I flee unto Thee to hide me"* (Psalm 143:9).

What a mercy it is for us all that David was not an untried man! We have all been enriched by his painful experience. He was

"A man so various that he seemed to be
Not one, but all mankind's epitome."

May it not be a blessing to others that we also are tried? If so, ought we not to be right glad to contribute our quota to the benefit of the redeemed family?

David may be our example; let us flee unto God as he did. We shall profit by our foes if we imitate this prudent warrior in his habitual way of escaping from his enemies.

The great point is, however, not only to see what David did, but to do the like promptly, and constantly. What, then, is essential in order to our copying the man of God?

I. A PERCEPTION OF DANGER. No man will flee if he is not afraid; there must be a knowledge and apprehension of danger, or there will be no flight.

1. Men perish in many instances because they have no sense of danger. The noxious air is not observed, the sunken reef is not seen, the train rushes to collision unwarned. Ignorance of danger makes the danger inevitable.
   Men will dare to die without fear of hell.

2. Every man is really in danger. The sinner is asleep on the top of a mast.

3. Some dangers are slowly perceived. Those connected with sweet sin.

II. A SENSE OF WEAKNESS. No man will flee for hiding if he feels able to fight the matter through in his own strength.

1. We are all weak and unable to cope with sin.
2. Some think themselves mighty men of valor, but these are among the very weakest of the weak.
3. Past failure should teach us not to trust our own strength.
4. In a deep sense of weakness we are made strong; in fancied strength lies the worst form of weakness.

III. A PRUDENT FORESIGHT. "I flee unto Thee to hide me."

1. He would not venture into the danger or wait till it overtook him; but he took time by the forelock and fled. Often this is the highest form of courage.
2. Escape through *fear* is admirable prudence. It is not a mean motive; for Noah, "moved by fear, prepared an ark."
3. While we *can* flee we should; for time may come when we shall be unable. David says, "I flee"; he means—"I am fleeing, I always do flee unto Thee, my God."

A man should not live like a beast, who sees no further than the meadow in which he feeds. He should foresee evil and hide himself; for this is common prudence (Prov. 22:3).

IV. A SOLID CONFIDENCE. "To Thee to hide me." He was sure:

1. That there was safety in God.
2. That he might flee to God.
3. That he might flee there and then.

V. AN ACTIVE FAITH. He did not lie passive, but aroused himself. This may be clearly seen:

In his fleeing to God. Directness, speed, eagerness.

From some sins there is no safety but in flight. Our French school book represented Mentor as saying to his pupil in the court of Calypso, "Fly, Telemaque; there remains no other mode of conquest but by flight!" "Flee youthful lusts"; they are not to be wrestled with, but fled from.

God's people often find by experience that the places of their protection are places of destruction. Well, when all other places fail, Christ will not fail. See how it was with David. (Ps. 142:4, 5). But when his hiding place at Ziklag was gone, yet his Saviour was not gone; "He encouraged himself in the Lord his God" (I Sam. 30:6). It is a mighty encouragement to believers that Christ is a hiding-place. 1. He is a safe and strong hiding-place (Is. 33:16); 2. He is a large hiding-place. 3. He is a hiding-place to the soul as well as to the body. 4. He hath undertaken to hide us; God hath committed all His elect to Christ, that He should hide them.—RALPH ROBINSON.

Under the influence of great fear the most timid creatures have sometimes fled to men for security. We have heard of a dove flying into a lady's bosom to escape from a hawk, and even of a hare running to a man for shelter. The confidence of the feeble secures the guardianship of the strong. He would be brutal indeed who would refuse protection to such simple reliance. Surely, if in our need we fly into the bosom of our God, we may be sure that love and majesty will unitedly smile upon us.

CHAPTER 41

## "THINGS ARE NOT WHAT THEY SEEM"

*"All the ways of a man are clean in his own eyes; but the Lord weigheth the spirits"* (Prov. 16:2).

Occasionally in seasons of collapse and disaster great discoveries are made concerning those who appeared to be commercially sound but turn out to be rotten. All looked solid and substantial until the inevitable crash came, and then no man felt that he could trust his neighbor. No doubt these schemers thought their ways "clean," but the event discovered their dirty hands.

Spiritual failures of like kind occur in the church. Great reputations explode, high professions dissolve. Men readily cajole themselves into the belief that they are right, and are doing right. A weighing time comes and their professions are exposed.

I. THE WAYS OF THE OPENLY WICKED. Many of these are "clean" in their own eyes.

To effect this self-deception:

They give pretty names to sin.

They think ill of others, making them out to be much worse than themselves, and finding in this an excuse for themselves.

II. THE WAYS OF THE OUTWARD RELIGIONIST. These seem "clean."

His observance of ceremonies.

His regular attendance at worship.

His open profession of religion.

His generosity to the cause, and general interest in good things. Thus ministers, deacons, members, etc., may boast, and yet when the Lord weighs their spirits they may be castaways.

III. THE WAYS OF THE WORLDLY PROFESSOR. He thinks himself "clean." Let him honestly consider whether he is "clean":

In his secret life? In his private and hidden indulgences?
In his pleasures and amusements?
In his company and conversation?
In his forsaken closet, forgotten Bible, lukewarm religion, etc.
What a revelation when the weighing of his spirit comes!

IV. THE WAYS OF THE SECURE BACKSLIDER. He dreams that his way is "clean," when a little observation will show him many miry places:

Decline in private prayer (Job 15:4).
Sin gradually getting the upper hand (Jer. 15:10).
Conversation scantily spiritual (Eph. 5:4).
Scriptures little read (Hos. 8:12).
Heart growing hard (Heb. 3:13).

How beautiful all things look when winter has bleached them! What a royal bed is to be seen in yonder corner! The coverlet is whiter than any fuller on earth could white it! Here might an angel take his rest, and rise as pure as when he reclined upon it. Pshaw! it is a dunghill, and nothing more.

All the ships that came into the harbor were claimed by one person in the city. He walked the quay with a right royal air, talked largely about owning a navy, and swaggered quite sufficiently had it been so. How came he to be so wealthy? Listen, he is a madman. He has persuaded himself into this folly, but in truth he has not a tub to call his own. What absurdity! Are not many the victims of even worse self-deception? They are rich and increased in goods according to their own notion; yet they are naked, and poor, and miserable.

"This must be the right way, see how smooth it is! How many feet have trodden it!" Alas! that is precisely the mark of the broad road which leadeth to destruction.

"But see how it winds about, and what a variety of directions it takes! It is no bigot's unbending line." Just so; therein it proves itself to be the wrong road; for truth is one and unchanging.

"But I like it so much." This also is suspicious; for what an unrenewed man is so fond of is probably an evil thing. Hearts go after that which is like themselves, and graceless men love graceless ways.

"Would you have me go that narrow and rough road?" Yes, we would; for it leadeth unto life; and though few there be that find it, yet those who do so declare that it is a way of pleasantness. It is better to follow a rough road to heaven than a smooth road to hell.

CHAPTER 42

# PONDERING HEARTS

*"The Lord pondereth the hearts"* (Prov. 21:2).

The Lord's tests are thorough and exact. The shekel of the sanctuary was double that which was used for common weighings, so at least the Rabbis tell us; those who profess to be saints are expected to do more than others. The sanctuary shekel was the standard to which all common weights ought to be conformed. The law of the Lord is the standard of morals. The balances of God are always in order, always true and exact.

I. THE WEIGHING OF HEARTS.

1. God has already performed it. Every man's purpose, thought, word, and action is put upon the scale at the first moment of its existence. God is not at any instant deceived.

2. Trials form an important order of tests. Impatience, rebellion, despair, backsliding, apostasy, have followed upon severe affliction or persecution.

3. Prosperity, honor, ease, success, are scales in which many are found wanting. Praise arouses pride, riches create worldliness, and a man's deficiencies are found out. (Prov. 27:21).

4. Great crises in our own lives, in families, in religious thought, in public affairs, etc., are weights and scales. A man's heart can hardly be guessed at when all goes on steadily.

5. Truth is ever heart-searching. Some left Jesus when He preached a certain doctrine. Hearts are weighed by their treatment of the truth. When they refused God's Word that word condemned them.

II. THE HEARTS WHICH ARE WEIGHED.

They greatly vary, but they may be divided roughly into three classes, upon which we will dwell, hoping that our hearers will judge themselves.

1. *Hearts which are found wanting at once.*
   The natural heart. (Jer. 17:9; I Cor. 2:14).
   The double heart. (Hosea 10:2).
   The heartless heart. No decision, energy, or seriousness. (Hosea 7:7).
   The perverse heart. Rebellious, wilful, sinful.

2. *Hearts which turn out to be wanting on further weighing.*
   "Another heart," such as Saul had. A new phase of feeling, but not a new nature.

A humbled heart, like that of Ahab when Elijah had prophesied his ruin. Humbled, but not humble; turned, but not turned from iniquity.

3. *Hearts which are of good weight.*

The trembling heart: penitent, afraid of sin, etc.
The tender heart: sensitive, affectionate, longing.
The broken heart: mourning, pining, humble, lowly.
The pure heart: loving only that which is good and clean, mourning sin in itself and others, sighing for holiness.
The fixed heart: resting firmly, abiding steadfastly, etc. Is your heart ready for the weighing? Have you no fear of the final trial? Is this confidence well founded?

Heaven's Sovereign saves all beings, but Himself,
That hideous sight, a naked human heart.

—Young.

In the mythology of the heathen, Momus, the god of fault-finding, is represented as blaming Vulcan, because in the human form, which he had made of clay, he had not placed a window in the breast, by which whatever was done or thought there might easily be brought to light. We do not agree with Momus, neither are we of his mind who desired to have a window in his breast that all men might see his heart. If we had such a window we should pray for shutters, and should keep them closed.

## Chapter 43

## TO HEAVENLY MERCHANTMEN

*"Buy the truth, and sell it not"* (Prov. 23:23).

When describing the pilgrims passing through Vanity Fair, Mr. Bunyan says:

"That which did not a little amuse the merchandisers was, that these pilgrims set very light by all their wares; they cared not so much as to look upon them; and if they called upon them to buy, they would put their fingers in their ears and cry, 'Turn away mine eyes from beholding vanity'; and look upward, signifying that their traffic was in heaven.

"One chanced, mockingly, beholding the carriage of the men, to say unto them, 'What will ye buy?' But they, looking gravely upon him, said, 'We buy the truth.'"

I. THE COMMODITY: "the truth."

1. Doctrinal truth. The gospel. The three R's—ruin, redemption, and regeneration. The doctrines of grace.
   A gospel buyer must learn to discriminate, so as to reject
   Salvation without Christ as God.
   Pardon without an atoning sacrifice.
   Life without the new birth.
   Regeneration without faith.
   Faith without works.
   Safety without perseverance in holiness.

2. Experimental truth. The new birth and the heavenly life are real gems. But of these there are base imitations.
   Discriminate between true religion and
   Faith without repentance.
   Talk without feeling.
   Life without struggles.
   Confidence without examination.
   Perfection without humility.

II. THE PURCHASE: "buy the truth." Here let us at once

1. Correct an error. Strictly speaking, truth and grace cannot be either bought or sold. Yet Scripture says, "Buy wine and milk without money and without price."

2. Expound the word. It is fitly chosen; for in order to be saved we should be ready to buy truth if it were to be bought.

3. Paraphrase the sentence.
   Buy what is *truly the truth*.
   Buy *all* the truth.
   Buy *only* the truth.
   Buy the truth *at any price*.
   Buy *now* the truth.

4. Give reasons for the purchase
   It is in itself most precious.
   You need it at this moment for a thousand useful purposes.
   You will need it in time and in eternity.

5. Direct you to the market.
   "Buy of me," saith Christ.
   The market-day is now on, "Come, buy."

III. THE PROHIBITION: "Sell it not."
Some sell it for a livelihood; for respectability; for repute of being scientific and thoughtful; to gratify a friend; for the pleasure of sin; for nothing at all but mere wantonness; but you must hold to it as for life itself.
Buy it at any price and sell it at no price.
You are lost without it. Sell it not!

It is a legacy which our forefathers have bought with their blood, which should make us willing to lay down anything, and to lay out anything, that we may, with the wise merchant in the gospel (Matt. 13:45), purchase the precious pearl, which is of more worth than heaven and earth, and which will make a man live happy, die comfortably, and reign eternally.—THOMAS BROOKS.

Now, as I said, the way to the Celestial City lies just through this town where this lusty fair is kept; and he that would go to the city, and yet not go through this town, must needs go out of the world. The Prince of princes Himself, when here, went through this town to His own country, and that upon a fair-day too.

Yea, and as I think, it was Beelzebub, the chief lord of this fair, that invited Him to buy of its vanities; yea, would have made Him lord of the fair, would He but have done him reverence as He went through the town; yea, because He was such a person of honor, Beelzebub had Him from street to street, and showed Him all the kingdoms of the world in a little time, that he might, if possible, allure that blessed One to cheapen and buy some of his vanities; but He had no mind to the merchandise, and therefore left the town without laying out so much as one farthing upon these vanities. This fair, therefore, is an ancient thing, of long standing, and a very great fair.—BUNYAN.

## CHAPTER 44

## GOD'S GLORY IN HIDING SIN

*"It is the glory of God to conceal a thing: but the honor of kings is to search out a matter"* (Prov. 25:2).

When justice is baffled, hood-winked by bribes, or misled by prejudice, or puzzled by falsehood, it is to a king's damage and dishonor, and he is bound to search the matter to the bottom. A magistrate's honor lies in the discovery of crime, but the glory of God lies in His graciously and justly hiding guilt from view.

With God no search is needful, for He sees all; His glory is to cover that which is plain enough to His eye, to cover it justly and effectually.

I.  THAT IT IS GOD'S GLORY TO COVER SIN.

1. The guilt, aggravations, motives, and deceits of a life, the Lord is able to remove forever by the atoning blood.
2. Sin which is known and confessed, He yet can cover so that it shall not be mentioned against us any more forever.
3. He can do this justly through the work of Jesus.

4. He can do this without compensation from the offender himself, because of what the Substitute has done.

5. He can do this without any ill effect on others; no man will think that God connives at sin, seeing He has laid its punishment on Jesus.

II. THIS SHOULD BE A GREAT ENCOURAGEMENT TO SEEKING SOULS.

1. Not to attempt to cover their own sin, since it is God's work to hide their iniquities, and they may leave it with Him.

2. To give God glory by believing in His power to conceal sin, even their own crimson sin.

3. To believe that He is willing to do it at this moment for them.

III. THIS SHOULD BE A MIGHTY STIMULUS TO SAINTS.

1. To glorify God in covering their sin. Let them talk of pardon with exultation, and tell how the Lord casts sin behind His back, casts it into the depths of the sea, blots it out, and puts it where if it be sought for it cannot be found. Jesus "made an end of sin."

2. To aim at the covering of the sins of others by leading them to Jesus that their souls may be saved from death.

3. To imitate the Lord in forgetting the sins of those who repent. We are to put away forever any wrong done to ourselves, and to treat converts as if they had not disgraced themselves aforetime. When we see a prodigal let us "bring forth the best robe and put it on him," that all his nakedness may be concealed and his rags forgotten.

Come and lay bare your sin that the Lord may conceal it at once.

*Mrs. Elizabeth Fry's* labors among the female prisoners at Newgate owed much of their success to her tenderness in dealing with them. "I never ask their crimes, for we have all come short," was her quiet reproof to some one curious about a prisoner's offence.

German rationalists, discussing the sins of the patriarchs, were designated by *Dr. Duncan:* "Those Ham-like writers!" He often said, "Let us speak tenderly of the faults of the Old Testament saints."

# CHAPTER 45
# GOOD NEWS

*"As cold waters to a thirsty soul, so is good news from a far country"* (Prov. 25:25).

It is only on hot summer days that *we* can appreciate the illustration here employed; for we dwell in a well-watered country where thirst is readily assuaged. Yet we can imagine ourselves in the condition of Hagar, Ishmael, and Samson; or of a caravan in the desert; or of poor sailors in a boat upon the salt sea dying for a draught of water.

I. GOOD NEWS FOR SINNERS FROM GOD.

Sin put men into a far country, but here is the good news:
1. God remembers you with pity.
2. He has made a way for your return.
3. He has sent a messenger to invite you home.
4. Many have already returned, and are now rejoicing.
5. He has provided all means for bringing you home.
6. You may return at once. "All things are ready."

If this good news be received it will be exceedingly refreshing to thirsty souls. To others it will be commonplace.

II. GOOD NEWS FOR SAINTS FROM HEAVEN.

1. News does come from heaven. By the Spirit's application of the Word, and by the sweet whispers of Jesus' love.
2. If for a while suspended, the renewal is sweeter than ever, even as cold water is doubly refreshing to a specially thirsty soul.

III. GOOD NEWS FOR HEAVEN FROM EARTH.

It gives joy to the home circle to hear that:
1. Sinners are repenting.
2. Saints are running their race with holy diligence.
3. Churches are being built up and the gospel is spreading.
4. More saints are ripening and going home.

The Hawaiian notions of a future state, where any existed, were peculiarly vague and dismal, and Mr. Ellis says that the greater part of the people seemed to regard the tidings of *ora loa ia Jesu* (endless life by Jesus) as the most joyful news they had ever heard, "breaking upon them," to use their own phrase, "like light in the morning." "Will my spirit never die? and can this poor weak body live again?" an old chieftain exclaimed, and this delighted surprise seemed the general feeling of the natives.—*From "Six Months in the Sandwich Islands," by* MISS BIRD.

*Dr. Field,* in his "Journey Through the Desert," speaks of being upon Mount Sinai, and writes: "Here in a pass between rocks under a huge granite boulder is a spring of water, which the Arabs say never fails. It was very grateful in the heat of the day, especially as we found snow in a cleft of the rocks, which, added to the natural coldness of the spring, gave us ice-water on Mount Sinai."

CHAPTER 46

# THE HONORED SERVANT

*"Whoso keepeth the fig tree shall eat the fruit thereof: so he that waiteth on his master shall be honored"* (Prov. 27:18).

I. CHRIST IS OUR MASTER.

1. Our sole Master. We serve others, that we may serve Him; we do not divide our service. "One is your Master, even Christ."

2. Our choice Master. There is not such another in the universe.

3. Our chosen Master. We cheerfully take His yoke; to serve Him is to us a kingdom. "I love my Master." (Ex. 21:5).

4. Our gracious Master; bearing with our faults, cheering us when faint, aiding us when weary, tending us in sickness, instructing us with patience, promising a great reward, etc.

5. Our life Master. Our ear is bored to His door-post; we are His to all eternity.

II. OUR BUSINESS IS TO SERVE HIM.

1. Expressed by the sense of *"keeping the fig tree."* We are to see to our Lord as a good body-servant watches over his master. Remaining with Him. Never quitting His side, or getting out of communion with Him.
Defending Him. Allowing none to speak against Him or to injure His honor while we have a tongue in our heads.
Striving for His objects. Consecrating ourselves to carry out the grand purposes of our Lord, and laying aside everything which would hinder us in this one pursuit.

2. Expressed by the words, *"waiteth on his master."*
Waiting His word. "Speak Lord; for Thy servant heareth." (I Sam. 3:9; Ps. 85:8).
Seeking His smile. "Make Thy face to shine upon Thy servant" (Ps. 31:16).
Depending upon Him for strength. "Give Thy strength unto Thy servant" (Ps. 86:16).
Expecting the fulfilment of His promises. "Remember the word unto Thy servant, upon which Thou hast caused me to hope" (Ps. 119:49).
Consecrated to His service—"body, soul, and spirit."
Having no private ends. (I Chron. 12:18).

Acquiescent in His will.  Ready either to suffer or to labor as He may appoint. (Luke 17:7-10).
The contrary of this is:
Self seeking.  Lusting after honor, wealth, ease, pleasure.
Self-guiding; doing your own will, and yet pretending to serve the Lord.
Self-applauding; robbing our Lord of the glory which belongs to Him alone.

III.  OUR SERVICE WILL BRING HONOR.

1.  Among your fellow-servants here below.
2.  Even among enemies, who will be forced to admire sincerity and fidelity.
3.  From our Lord, who will give us a sweet sense of acceptance even here below.
4.  At the judgment day, before the assembled universe.
5.  Throughout eternity, among angels and glorified spirits.
    Let us grieve that we have not served Him better.
    Let us repent if we have not served Him at all.
    Let us pray Him to receive us into His service this day.

"Two aged ministers met one Saturday at a station in Wales as they were going to preach in their respective places on Sunday.  'I hope,' said Mr. Harris, of Merthyr, to Mr. Powell, of Cardiff—'I hope the Great Master will give His face tomorrow.'  'Well, if He does not,' replied Mr. Powell, 'I will speak well of Him behind His back.' "

*Rutherford,* speaking of how his Lord encouraged him with great fellowship while he was serving Him, says in his quaint way, "When my Master sends me on His errands, He often gives me a bawbee for myself;" by which he meant that as sure as ever God employed him He gave him a penny for reward, as we do to boys who go upon our errands.

A dog which follows anybody and everybody belongs to no one, and no one cares for it.  The more it shows its devotion to its master the greater is the man's attachment to it.  In domestic service we should not care to keep a body-servant who spent half his time in waiting upon another employer.

Old and faithful servants grow to look upon all their master's property as their own.  One such said, "Here comes our carriage, and there are our dear children coming home from school!"  Our Lord Jesus loves to see us feel a fellowship—a community of interests with Himself.  He makes such service to be its own reward, and adds heaven besides.  He will not cast off His old servants, but He will grant them to be with Him in His glory, as they have been with Him in His humiliation.

## CHAPTER 47

# FEAR OF MAN DESTROYED BY TRUST IN GOD

*"The fear of man bringeth a snare: but whoso putteth his trust in the Lord shall be safe"* (Prov. 29:25).

We have here a double proverb; each half is true by itself; and, put together, the whole is forcible and full of teaching. He who fears man is in great danger from that very fact; he who trusts in the Lord is in no danger of any sort; trusting in the Lord is the great antidote against the fear of man.

I. HERE IS A VERY COMMON EVIL. "The fear of man bringeth a snare."

1. It leads men into great sins at times, snaring them, and holding them like birds taken by a fowler. Aaron yielded to popular clamor and made the calf. Saul cared more to be honored among the people than to please the Lord. Pilate feared that a charge would reach Caesar, and so he violated his conscience. Peter denied his Master for fear of a silly maid.

2. It keeps many from conversion; their companions would ridicule, their friends would be annoyed, they might be persecuted, and so they are numbered with the "fearful and unbelieving."

3. It prevents others avowing their faith. They try to go to heaven through a back door. Remember—"With the mouth confession is made unto salvation" (Rom. 10:10).

4. It lowers the dignity of good men. David was a poor creature before Achish, and even Father Abraham made but a poor figure when he denied his wife.

5. It hinders many in duties which require courage. Jonah will not go to Nineveh because he may be thought a false prophet if God forgives that city. Galatian preachers went aside to false doctrine to be considered wise, etc.

II. HERE IS A VERY PRECIOUS SAFEGUARD. "Whoso putteth his trust in the Lord shall be safe."

Not slavish fear of man, but childlike trust in the Lord will be the protection of the believer.

1. The truster is safe from fear of man.
   God is with us, therefore we are strong, and need not fear.
   We are determined, and will not fear.
   We pray, and lose our fear.
   We prepare for the worst, and fear vanishes.

2. After all, what is there to fear?  What can man do unto us?
   God being with us, our safety is perfect, continuous, eternal,
   even though the whole human race should besiege us.  (Rom.
   8:31).

III.  HERE IS A VERY GLORIOUS DOCTRINE.  We may take in the
widest sense the doctrine of the second sentence,

"Whoso putteth his trust in the Lord shall be safe":
From the damning and conquering power of sin.
From the overcoming force of temptation.
From the deadening effect of sorrow.
From the destroying force of Satan.
From death, and hell, and every evil.
From all injury which men can inflict.
Will you fear a worm, or trust your God?
Break the snare in which fear has entangled you.
Enter the palace of safety by the door of trust.

The soul that cannot entirely trust God, whether man be pleased
or displeased, can never long be true to Him; for while you are
eyeing man you are losing God, and stabbing Christianity at the
very heart.—MANTON.

"Fear of man."  Grim idol—bloody-mouthed—many souls he has
devoured and trampled down into hell!  His eyes are full of hatred
to Christ's disciples.  Scoffs and jeers lurk in his face.  The laugh
of the scorner growls in his throat.  Cast down this idol.  This keeps
some of you from secret prayer, from worshipping God in your family, from going to lay your case before ministers, from openly confessing Christ.  You that have felt God's love and Spirit dash this
idol to pieces.  Who art thou, that thou should'st be afraid of a man
that shall die?"  "Fear not, thou worm, Jacob."  "What have I to do
any more with idols?"—M'CHEYNE.

One fire puts out another.  Nothing so effectually kills the fear
of man as abundance of the fear of God.  Faith is an armor to the
soul, and, clothed with it, men enter the thick of the battle without
fear of wounds.  Fear of man deadens conscience, distracts meditation, hinders holy activity, stops the mouth of testimony, and
paralyzes the Christian's power.  It is a cunning snare which some
do not perceive, though they are already taken in it.

CHAPTER 48

# THE WORD OF A KING

*"Where the word of a king is, there is power"* (Eccles. 8:4).

God alone is rightfully sovereign without limit. He is King in the most absolute sense; and so it should be; for He is supremely good, wise, just, holy, etc.

As He is Maker of all, dominion over His creatures is a matter of natural right.

He has infinite power wherewith to carry out His royal will.

Even in His least word there is Omnipotence.

Let us consider this,—

## I. TO EXCITE OUR AWE.

Let us carefully think of—

1. His creating word, by which all things arose out of nothing.

2. His preserving word, by which all things abide.

3. His destroying word, by which He will shake earth and heaven.

Who can stand before any of these without trembling adoration? Power attends them to the fullest degree, for each one is the word of a King.

## II. TO ENSURE OUR OBEDIENCE.

1. Each precept is to be obeyed at once, heartily, to the full, by every one, since the King commands.

2. His service must not be shunned, for that were to rebel against our Sovereign. Jonah did not find this successful: for the Lord will not be trifled with, and will make runaways know that His arm is long.

3. Disobedience is to be repented of. If we have fallen into sin, let the King's word have a gracious power to subdue us to hearty grief.

## III. TO INSPIRE OUR CONFIDENCE.

1. That He is able to give to the penitent, pardon; for he has promised in His Word to do so.

2. That he will give to the believing, power to renew their lives. "He sent His word, and healed them," is true, spiritually.

3. That He will give to the tempted, power to overcome temptation. God ensures the believer's victory over every assault of Satan through the word. This weapon Jesus used in the wilderness.

4. That He will give to the suffering, power to endure with patience, and to gather profit from the trial.

5. That He will give to the dying, hope, peace, beatific vision, etc. One word from the Lord of life robs death of its sting.

## IV. TO DIRECT OUR CHRISTIAN EFFORT.

1. We must look nowhere else for power. Education, oratory, music, wealth, ceremonialism, are weakness itself, if depended on.

2. We must rely upon the word of our King as the instrument of power whenever we seek to do works in His name. Preach it: for nothing else will break hard hearts, comfort the despairing, beget faith, or produce holiness. Plead it in prayer: for the Lord will surely keep His own promises, and put forth His power to make them good. Practise it: for none can gainsay a life which is ordered according to the precepts of the Lord. An obedient life is full of a power before which men and devils do homage.

Read much the royal Word.

Speak more than ever the King's word, which is the gospel of peace.

Believe in the word of King Jesus, and be bold to defend it.

Bow before it, and be patient and happy.

No language ever stirs the deeps of my nature like the Word of God; and none produces such a profound calm within my spirit. As no other voice can, it melts me to tears, it humbles me in the dust, it fires me with enthusiasm, it fills me with felicity, it elevates me to holiness. Every faculty of my being owns the power of the sacred Word: it sweetens my memory, it brightens my hope, it stimulates my imagination, it directs my judgment, it commands my will, and it cheers my heart.

The word of man charms me for the time; but I outlive and outgrow its power; it is altogether the reverse with the Word of the King of kings: it rules me more sovereignly, more practically, more habitually, more completely every day. Its power is for all seasons: for sickness and for health, for solitude and for company, for personal emergencies and for public assemblies. I had sooner have the Word of God at my back than all the armies and navies of all the great powers; ay, than all the forces of nature; for the Word of the Lord is the source of all the power in the universe, and within it there is an infinite supply in reserve.

CHAPTER 49

# THE ROSE AND THE LILY

*"I am the rose of Sharon and the lily of the valleys"*
(Song of Solomon 2:1).

Here we have the Bridegroom praising Himself, and this is a thing to be considered with careful attention.

This self-praise is not tainted with pride: such a fault could not find a place in the lowly Jesus. His ego-ism is not egotism. He does not commend Himself for His own sake, but for our sakes. He sets himself forth in glowing terms because:

In condescension He desires our love. What a poor thing it is for Him to care about! Yet He thirsts after it.

In wisdom He uses the best way to win our love.

In tenderness He deigns to describe Himself that we may be encouraged by His familiarity in praising Himself to us.

This is one of the most effectual proofs of lowliness.

Of necessity He describes Himself, for who else can describe Him? "No man knoweth the Son, but the Father:" (Matt. 11:27).

I. THE EXCEEDING DELIGHTFULNESS OF OUR LORD.

He compares Himself, not only, as in other places, to needful bread, and refreshing water, but to lovely flowers. In Jesus there are all delights as well as all necessaries.

1. He is now all that He ever was, for His "I am" runs through all eternity in unabated force.

2. He is delightful to the eye of faith, even as flowers are to the bodily sight. What more beautiful than roses and lilies?

3. He is delightful in the savor which comes of Him. In Him is a delicious, varied, abiding fragrance.

Yet blind men see no color, and men without scent perceive no odor in the sweetest flowers; and carnal men see no delights in Jesus. Roses and lilies require eyes and light ere they can be appreciated, and to know Jesus we must have grace and gracious dispositions. He says, "I am the Rose of Sharon"; and so He is essentially; but the grave question is, "is He this to you?" Yes, or no.

II. THE SWEET VARIETY OF HIS DELIGHTFULNESS.

1. Of the rose, majesty; of the lily, love.

2. Of the rose, suffering; of the lily, purity.

3. Of both, a great variety; all the roses and all the lilies, all the beauties of heaven and earth meet in Jesus.

III. THE EXCEEDING FREENESS OF HIS DELIGHTFULNESS.

1. Meant to be plucked and enjoyed as roses and lilies are.

2. Abundant as a common flower. He is not as a rare orchid, but as the anemones which covered Sharon's plains, and as the lilies which abounded in all the valleys of Palestine.

3. Abiding in a common place, as roses in Sharon and lilies in the valleys, where every passer-by was free to gather according to his own sweet will. Not found on inaccessible steeps, or within guarded enclosures, Jesus is out in the open: a flower of the common. This is a leading idea of the text. Those who desire Christ may have Him.

4. Scattering fragrance, not over a room or a house, but far and wide, perfuming every wandering wind.

5. Yet roses and lilies fail to set forth our Beloved for His is unfading virtue. They are soon withered, but "He dieth no more."

"I am the Rose of Sharon, and the Lily of the Valleys"; words most seemly in the lips of the Lord Jesus Christ, in whom it is not robbery from others, but condescension and grace, to commend Himself to the sons of men. "I am meek and lowly," would be the utterance of pride in Gabriel, but it is humility in Jesus, Who has stooped that He might become meek and lowly. "I am the true Vine," "I am the good Shepherd," etc., are the expressions alike of truth and grace, and so here.—A. MOODY STUART.

Not to flowers which only the rich and great can possess, but to those easily obtainable, does He liken Himself; for always did He stoop to the lowliest, and the common people ever heard Him gladly.—H. K. WOOD, *in "The Heavenly Bridegroom and his Bride."*

CHAPTER 50

## CONSTRAINING THE BELOVED

*"I found him. I held him. I brought him"* (Song of Solomon 3:4).

I. "I FOUND HIM": OR, LOVE IN FELLOWSHIP.

1. I was enquiring for Him.

2. I had got beyond all men and means, and could not be content with any but Himself.

3. I beheld His person. He drew near in His Word and ordinances. I perceived Him by the Spirit. Faith saw Him clearly.

4. I was filled with content. I looked for no one else, for in finding Him I had found my all for earth and heaven.

## II. "I HELD HIM": OR, LOVE IN POSSESSION.

1. By my heart's resolve, determining never to lose Him again.

2. By my tearful pleas, entreating Him not to make me wretched by withdrawing.

3. By making Him my all in all. He stays where He is prized and I set Him on a high throne in my spirit.

4. By renouncing all other loves, sins, idols, etc. He is jealous, and I kept myself altogether for Him.

## III. "I BROUGHT HIM": OR, LOVE IN COMMUNICATION.

1. By our own spirit: communing with Jesus before we go to public worship, and going there with Him in our company.

2. By our words: we should so speak as to set forth Jesus, and promote fellowship with Him. Alas, how many speak controversially, or without savor, or with carnal oratory.

Wherein is no room for the Beloved! Oh, for a crucified style of speech!

See what the church needs!—Christ in her midst.

See how He is likely to come!—He must be brought.

See what must first be done!—He must be held.

See who alone can do this!—those who have found Him.

Yet see, also, who may find Him!—all who love Him, and seek Him. Are we among the number?

Hold Him by not offending Him. First, by sloth. When the soul turns sleepy or careless, Christ goes away. Secondly, by idols. You cannot hold two objects. Thirdly, by being unwilling to be sanctified. Fourthly, by an unholy house. "I brought Him into my mother's house." Remember to take Christ home with you, and let Him rule in your house. If you walk with Christ abroad but never take Him home, you will soon part company forever.—MCCHEYNE.

"I found Him"; I, a man, found the Lord of Glory; I, a slave to sin, found the great Deliverer; I, the child of darkness, found the Light of life; I, the uttermost of the lost, found my Savior and my God; I, widowed and desolate, found my Friend, my Beloved, my Husband. Go and do likewise, sons and daughters of Zion, and He will be found of you; for "then shall ye find when ye search with all your heart."

CHAPTER 51

# INVITATION TO A CONFERENCE

*"Come now, and let us reason together, saith the Lord: though your sins be as scarlet, they shall be as white as snow; though they be red like crimson, they shall be as wool"* (Isaiah 1:18).

The sinful condition of men is terrible in the extreme. This is set forth vividly in previous verses of the chapter. They are altogether alienated from their God.

I. AN INVITATION TO A CONFERENCE.

Sinful men do not care to think, consider, and look matters in the face; yet to this distasteful duty they are urged.

If they reason, they rather reason against God than together with Him; but here the proposal is not to discuss, but to treat with a view to reconciliation. This also ungodly hearts decline.

1. They prefer to attend to ceremonial observances. Outward performances are easier, and do not require thought.
2. Yet the matter is one which demands most serious discussion, and deserves it; for God, the soul, heaven, and hell are involved in it. Never was wise counsel more desirable.
3. It is most gracious on the Lord's part to suggest a conference. Kings do not often invite criminals to reason with them.
4. The invitation is a pledge that He desires peace, is willing to forgive, and anxious to set us right.

II. A SPECIMEN OF THE REASONING ON GOD'S PART.

1. The one main ground of difference is honestly mentioned,— "though your sins be as scarlet." God calls the most glaring sinners to come to Him, knowing them to be such.
2. This ground of difference God Himself will remove,—"they shall be as white as snow." He will forgive, and so end the quarrel.
3. He will remove the offence perfectly,—"as snow—as wool."
   He will remove forever the guilt of sin.
   He will discharge the penalty of sin.
   He will destroy the dominion of sin.
   He will prevent the return of sin.

III. THIS SPECIMEN REASONING IS AN ABSTRACT OF THE WHOLE ARGUMENT.

Each special objection is anticipated.

1. The singular greatness of your sins,—"red like crimson." This is met by a great atonement, which cleanses from all sin.

2. The long continuance of your sins. Cloth dyed scarlet has lain long in the dye-vat. The blood of Jesus cleanses at once.
3. The light against which your sins were committed. This puts a glaring color upon them. But "all manner of sin and blasphemy shall be forgiven unto men."
4. The despair which your sins create: they are so glaring that they are ever before you, yet they shall be washed out by the blood of the Lamb of God, which taketh away the sin of the world.

Certain scarlet cloth is first dyed in the grain, and then dyed in the piece; it is thus double-dyed. And so are we with regard to the guilt of sin; we are double-dyed for we are all sinners by birth, and sinners by practice. Our sins are like scarlet, yet by faith in Christ they shall be as white as snow: by an interest in Christ's atonement, though our offences be red like crimson, they shall be as wool; that is, they shall be as white as the undyed wool.—*"Friendly Greetings."*

When a man has taken up sin into him, till it is as much himself as his black skin is part and parcel of the Ethiopian, yet the Lord can put the sin away as thoroughly as if the negro became a fair Caucasian. He takes the spots out of human tigers, and leaves not one of them.

Consider how the Tyrian scarlet was dyed; not superficially dipped, but thoroughly drenched in the liquor that colored it, as thy soul in custom of sinning. Then was it taken out for a time and dried, put in again, soaked and sodden the second time in the vat; called therefore twice-dyed; as thou complainest thou hast been by relapsing into the same sin. Yea, the color so incorporated into the cloth, not drawn over, but diving into the very heart of the wool, that, rub a scarlet rag on what is white, and it will bestow a reddish tincture upon it; as perchance, thy sinful practice and precedent have also infected those which were formerly good, by thy badness. Yet such scarlet sins, so solemnly and substantially colored, are easily washed white in the blood of our Saviour.—THOMAS FULLER.

## CHAPTER 52

## NO RAIN

*"I will also command the clouds that they rain no rain upon it"* (Isaiah 5:6).

Rain essential for growth of seed and fruit, and its withdrawal for a length of time a terrible temporal judgment, especially in hot climates.

Especially is it a mark of anger for clouds to be overhead, and
yet to drop no rain: to have the means of grace, but no grace with
the means.

Let us consider:

## I. WHAT IT MEANS.

1. Ministers allowed to preach, but without power.
2. The Word read, but with no application to the heart.
3. Formality of prayer kept up, but no pleading with God.

The clouds, ordained to rain, are commanded not to do so; commanded by God Himself, with Whom is the key of the rain; commanded altogether to withhold their refreshing showers. There is no necessary connection between outward ordinances and grace; we may have clouds of the first, and no drops of the second.

## II. WHAT IT INVOLVES.

1. No conversions, for these are by the Spirit.
2. No restorations of backsliders. Withered plants are not revived when there is no rain.
3. No refreshing of the weary: comfort and strength come not except by the dew of heaven.
4. No spiritual activities. Lukewarmness reigns through routine unto death. The workers move like persons walking in their sleep.

## III. HOW IT MANIFESTS ITSELF.

A parched season spiritually has its own signs in the individual.
1. The man feels glutted with the gospel, and wearied with it.
2. He begins to criticise, carp, cavil, and despise the Word.
3. Soon he is apt to neglect the hearing of it.
4. Or he hears and perverts the Word, either to boasting, to ridicule, to controversy, or to ill-living.

It is a horrible thing when that which should be a savor of life unto life becomes a savor of death unto death, when even the clouds refuse to rain.

Is it so with any one of us?

## IV. HOW IT CAN BE PREVENTED.

Let us humbly use the means without putting our trust in them, and then let us,—
1. Confess our ill-desert. The Lord might justly have withheld His grace from us.
2. Acknowledge our dependence upon the heavenly showers of spiritual influence.
3. Pray incessantly, till, like Elias, we bring down the rain.
4. Look alone to Jesus. "He shall come down like rain."

5. Value the least sign of grace, watching for it as the prophet did from the top of Carmel, till he saw the little cloud arise from the sea.

6. Use the blessing more diligently when it returns, bringing forth fruit unto God.

God's grace can save souls without any preaching; but all the preaching in the world cannot save souls without God's grace.— BENJAMIN BEDDOME.

The hearer sometimes complains that there is no food for his soul; when the truth is that there is no soul for the food.—JOSEPH PARKER.

Every preacher must have felt that in certain places his labor is in vain. For some cause unknown to him, there is no response to his appeals, no fruit of his teaching. I knew a place from which Mr. Whitefield was chased away, and it was said of it that ever since there appeared to be a blight upon it; and indeed it seemed so. I have seen churches acting wrongly, and becoming withered from that time.

On the other hand, we feel when there is dew about, and we know when there is a sound of abundance of rain. I have preached at times with the absolute certainty of success because a grace-shower was on saint and sinner, on preacher and people.

In a newspaper we met with the following:—

"There was an old turnpike-man, on a quiet country road, whose habit was to shut his gate at night, and take his nap. One dark, wet midnight I knocked at his door, calling, 'Gate, gate!' 'Coming,' said the voice of the old man. Then I knocked again, and once more the voice replied, 'Coming.' This went on for some time, till at length I grew quite angry, and jumping off my horse, opened the door, and demanded why he cried 'Coming' for twenty minutes, and never came. 'Who is there?' said the old man, in a quiet, sleepy voice, rubbing his eyes. 'What d'ye want, sir?' Then awakening, 'Bless yer, sir, and ax yer pardon I was asleep; I gets so used to hearing 'em knock, that I answer "coming" in my sleep, and take no more notice about it.' "

Thus may the ministry accomplish nothing because the habitual hearer remains in a deep sleep, out of which the Spirit of God alone can awaken him. When the secret influence from heaven ceases to speak to the heart, the best speaking to the ear avails little.

CHAPTER 53

# ENQUIRERS ANSWERED

*"What shall one then answer the messengers of the nation? That the Lord hath founded Zion, and the poor of His people shall trust in it"* (Isaiah 14:32).

It is clear that Zion attracts attention. The messengers of the nations enquire concerning her.

The Church excites attention by—
The peculiarity of her people.
The specialty of her teaching.
The singularity of her claims.
The greatness of her privileges.

I. WHAT DO THE MESSENGERS ASK?
Concerning Zion, or the church, they ask:—
1. What is her origin? (Ps. 78:68-69).
2. What is her history? (Ps. 87:3).
3. Who is her King? (Ps. 99:2).
4. What is her charter? (Gal. 4:26).
5. What are her laws? (Ezek. 43:12).
6. What is her Treasure? (Ps. 147:12-14, Rev. 21:21).
7. What is her present security? (Ps. 48:13).
8. What is her future destiny? (Ps. 102:16).

II. WHY DO THEY ASK?
1. Some from mere contempt. Perhaps when they know more their contempt will evaporate.
2. Some from idle curiosity. Yet many who come to us from that poor motive are led to Christ. Zaccheus came down from his tree as he did not go up.
3. Some from a desire to become citizens. How can they be initiated? What is the price of her franchise? What will be required of her burgesses? Is there room for more citizens?

III. WHY SHOULD THEY BE ANSWERED?
1. It may silence their cavils.
2. It may win them to God.
3. It will do us good to give a reason for the hope that is in us.
4. It will glorify God to tell of what His grace has done for His church and of what it is prepared to do.

IV. WHAT SHOULD BE THE ANSWER?
1. That her origin is from Him. "The Lord hath founded Zion."
2. That His people are poor in themselves, and rely upon another. It is a city to which the poor flee for refuge, as many fled to the cave of Adullam who were in debt and discontented.

3. That their trust is in the foundation which the Lord hath laid.

Visiting a vaulted passage in the palace of Nero, at Rome we were shown certain frescoes upon the roof.  To exhibit these a candle was lifted up upon a telescopic rod, and then moved along from picture to picture.  Let the candle stand for the believer, and let him be willing to be so elevated in life as to shine upon those high mysteries of our holy faith which else had never been perceived by other men.  Eminent saints in the past have served such a purpose; their lives have cast a light upon priceless truths, which else had been forgotten.

A young Kaffir, who was brought to England to be educated for mission-work, in his own country, when taken to St. Paul's Cathedral, gazed up into the dome for some time as if lost in wonder, and when at length he broke silence, it was to ask, "Did man make this?"  Those who obtain a view of the grandeur and glory of the spiritual temple may ask a similar question.  We can tell them that its "Builder and Maker is God."

Enquirers should be answered.  It is never well to be dumb to attentive ears.  As some one has wisely said, "we shall have to give an account of idle silence, as well as of idle speech."

Our testimony should be bright and cheerful.  The dismal tale some tell of trials and temptations is not likely to fetch home the prodigal from the far country: such lean and discontented followers will never make anybody say, "How many hired servants of my Father have bread enough, and to spare!"—MARK GUY PEARSE.

## CHAPTER 54

## OUR HIDING-PLACE

*"A man shall be as an hiding-place from the wind, and a covert from the tempest"* (Isaiah 32:28).

Immense boons have come to nations by Kings like David, prophets like Samuel, deliverers like Gideon, lawgivers like Moses.

But what are all good men put together compared with THE MAN Christ Jesus?

Let us consider that,—

I. THIS LIFE IS LIABLE TO STORMS.

1. Mysterious hurricanes within, which cause the most dreadful confusion of mind.
2. Overwhelming tempests of spiritual distress on account of sin.

3. Wild attacks from human enemies, who taunt, slander, threaten, etc.

4. Trying gales of temporal losses, bereavements, and other afflictions.

## II. FROM THESE STORMS THE MAN CHRIST JESUS IS OUR HIDING-PLACE.

1. As truly Man. Sympathizing with us.

2. As more than Man, ruling every tempest.

3. As Substitutionary Man.

In Him we are delivered from divine wrath.

In Him we are covered from Satan's blasts.

In Him we dwell above trial by happy fellowship with Him.

In Him we are victors over death.

4. As the Coming Man. We dread no political catastrophes, or social disruptions, for "He must reign." The end is secured. "Behold, He cometh with clouds" (Rev. 1:7).

## III. LET US SEE TO IT THAT WE TAKE SHELTER IN THE MAN.

1. Let Him stand before us, interposing between us and the punishment of sin. Hide behind Him by faith.

2. Let Him daily cover us from all evil, as our Shield and Protector (Ps. 119:114).

O you that are out of Christ, the tempest is lowering! Come to this covert; hasten to this hiding-place!

He is a capacious hiding-place: "Yet there is room." As in Adullum all David's army could hide, so is Jesus able to receive hosts of sinners.

I creep under my Lord's wings in the great shower, and the waters cannot reach me. Let fools laugh the fools' laughter, and scorn Christ, and bid the weeping captives in Babylon to sing them one of the songs of Zion. We may sing, even in our winter's storm, in the expectation of a summer's sun at the turn of the year. No created powers in hell, or out of hell, can mar our Lord's work, or spoil our song of joy. Let us then, be glad and rejoice in the salvation of our Lord, for faith had never yet cause to have tearful eyes, or a saddened brow, or to droop or die.—SAMUEL RUTHERFORD.

A shelter is nothing if we stand in front of it. The main thought with many a would-be Christian is his own works, feelings, and attainments: this is to stand on the windy side of the wall by putting self before Jesus. Our safety lies in getting behind Christ, and letting Him stand in the wind's eye. We must be altogether hidden, or Christ cannot be our hiding-place.

Foolish religionists hear about the hiding-place, but never get into it. How great is the folly of such conduct. It makes Jesus to be of no value or effect. What is a roof to a man who lies in the open, or a boat to one who sinks in the sea? Even the Man Christ Jesus, though ordained of God to be a covert from the tempest, can cover none but those who are in Him. Come then, poor sinner, enter where you may; hide in Him Who was evidently meant to hide you, for He was ordained to be a hiding-place, and must be used as such, or the very aim of His life and death would be missed.

## CHAPTER 55

## THE LIFE-LOOK

*"Look unto Me, and be ye saved, all the ends of the earth: for I am God, and there is none else"* (Isaiah 45:22).

The nations have been looking to their idols for all these centuries, but in vain.

Many of them are looking to their boasted philosophies and still in vain.

False religions, politics, alliances, theories, organizations, men— all will be in vain to save the nations. They must look to God.

I. WHAT MEANS THE WORD "LOOK" IN REFERENCE TO GOD?

1. Admit His reality by looking to Him. Consider that there is a God, and enthrone Him in your mind as a real Person, the true God, and your Lord.

2. Address yourself to Him by prayer.

3. Acknowledge that from Him only salvation can come.

4. Abide alone in HIM for salvation. Keep your eyes fixed on Him, as the Morning Star of your day.

II. FOR WHAT PART OF SALVATION ARE WE THUS TO LOOK?

For every part of it from beginning to end.

1. Pardon. This must be God's act, and it can only come through the atonement which He has provided in Christ Jesus.

2. Preparation for pardon, namely, life, repentance, faith. Grace must prepare us for more grace.

3. Renewal of heart is the Holy Ghost's work: look to Him for it. Regeneration must be of the Lord alone.

4. Sustenance in spiritual life is of the Lord alone. All growth, strength, fruit, must be looked for from Him.

### III.  What Is Our Encouragement To Look?

1. His command.  He bids us look, and therefore we may look.
2. His promise.  He says, "Look, and be saved," and He will never run back from His own word.
3. His Godhead.  "For I am God."  All things are possible to Him: His mercy is equal to our salvation, His glory will be manifest thereby.

Who will refuse so simple an act as to look.

### IV.  What Is the Best Time In Which To Look?

Look now, at this very moment.

1. The command is in the present tense: "Look unto Me."
2. The promise is in the same tense: "and be ye saved."  It is a fiat, like "light be."  It takes immediate effect.
3. Your need of salvation is urgent: you are already lost.
4. The present time is yours, no other time is yours to use; for the past is gone, and the future will be present when it comes.
5. Your time may soon end.  Death comes suddenly.  Age creeps on us.  The longest life is short.
6. It is the time which God chooses: it is ours to accept it.

To this text, under God, I owe my own deliverance from despair. An explanation of the work of Jesus, given by a humble, unlettered lay preacher, was followed by a direct appeal to me.  "Young man, you are miserable, and you will never be happy unless you obey this message.  Look!  Look!"  I did look, and in that instant lost my crushing load of guilt.  It was all clear to me.  Jesus had taken the sins of all believers.  I believed, and knew that He had taken mine, and therefore I was clear.  The matchless truth of the substitution of the divine Lord for me was light and liberty to my soul.  A look saved me, and for my present salvation I have no other resort but still to look.  "Looking unto Jesus," is a motto both for penitent and preacher, for sinner and saint.  C. H. S.

There is an affecting story of a celebrated literary man.  Heinrich Heine, who was prematurely disabled by disease, and utterly heart-sick and weary.  In one of the art-palaces of Paris there is the famous statue called the Venus of Milo, the bewitching goddess of pleasure, which, by the rude accident of time, has lost both her arms, but still preserves much of her supreme, enchanting beauty.  At the feet of this statue Heine cast himself down in remorse and despair, and, to use his own words, "There I lay a long time, and wept so passionately that a stone must have had compassion on me.  The goddess looked down compassionately upon me, but she was help-less to console me.  She looked as if she would say 'See you not that I have no arms, and that therefore I can give you no help?'"

So, vain and useless is it to look to any for spiritual help and comfort, except to Him of Whom it is declared, "Behold, the Lord's hand is not shortened, that it cannot save."

Some divines would need a week in which to tell you what you are to do to be saved: but the Holy Ghost only uses four letters to do it. Four letters, and two of them alike—"Look!"

Be not like the man in the interpreter's house, whose eyes were fixed on the ground where he was raking together straws and dust, and who would not look up to him who was offering him a celestial crown. Look up! Look up!

CHAPTER 56

# THE REDEEMER DESCRIBED BY HIMSELF

(Isaiah 50:2-6)

There was no one to take up the divine challenge: no one to answer for guilty man. To the call of God for one who could save, there was no answer but the echo of his voice.

I. BEHOLD THE MESSIAH AS GOD!

1. He comes in fulness of power. "Is My hand shortened at all?"
2. His power to save is equal to that with which He destroys. Let Egypt be the instance: "I dry up the sea," etc.
3. His power is that which produces the phenomena of nature. "I clothe the heavens with blackness."
4. This should excite deep gratitude, that He Who rebukes the sea was Himself rebuked; He Who clothes the heavens with blackness was Himself in darkness for our sake.

II. BEHOLD HIM AS THE APPOINTED TEACHER.

1. Instructed and endowed: "the Lord hath given me the tongue of the learned." He knows, and He imparts knowledge.
2. Condescending to the needy: "to him that is weary."

III. BEHOLD HIM AS THE SERVANT OF THE LORD!

1. Obedient in all things: "I was not rebellious." In no point did Jesus refuse the Father's will, not even in Gethsemane.
2. Persevering through all trials: "neither turned away back." He did not relinquish the hard task, but set His face as a flint to carry it through.
3. Courageous in it all: as we see in the verse following our text.

What a model for our service! Consider Him, and copy Him.

IV. BEHOLD HIM AS THE PEERLESS SUFFERER!

1. His entire submission; His back, His cheeks, His hair, His face.
2. His willing submission: "I gave my back to the smiters." "I hid not my face."
3. His lowly submission, bearing the felon's scourge, and the utmost of scorn: "shame and spitting."
4. His patient submission. Not a word of reproach, or resentment.

Place the first and the last together: *the God and the Sufferer.* What condescension! what ability to save!

Place the two middle names together: *the Teacher and the Servant,* and see how sweetly He serves by teaching, and teaches by serving.

I imagine myself placed in the world at the time when the Christ was expected, commissioned to announce to it that God was about to send His own Son, having endowed Him with the "tongue of the learned." What excitement in all the schools of philosophy! What gatherings of the sages of the earth!

But this Divine person shall speak for Himself to the assembled throng of philosophers and sages. "Yes, the Lord God hath given Me the tongue of the learned; and I have descended that I might speak with that tongue to every nation of the earth. But He hath not given me the tongue that I might tell how stars and planets roll, or settle the disputes of the wise."

He hath not given me the tongue that I should know how to speak a word to you, ye disputers of this world; but simply that I should know how to speak a word in season to him that is weary. Oh, how fallen are the expectant countenances of philosophers and sages! "Is this all?" they exclaim. "Was it only for this that the tongue of the learned was bestowed? Does this require, or can this employ the tongue of the learned?"

Nay, men of science, turn not angrily away. With all your wisdom you have never been able to do this. The weary have sought to you in vain. They have found no "word in season," no word of comfort and sustainment; and why then should you be indignant at the province here assigned to "the tongue of the learned"?—*Condensed from* HENRY MELVILL.

CHAPTER 57

# THE REDEEMER'S FACE SET LIKE A FLINT

*"For the Lord God will help me; therefore shall I not be confounded: therefore have I set my face like a flint, and I know that I shall not be ashamed"* (Isaiah 50:7).

There was no flint in the heart of Jesus, but there was much in His face. He was as resolute as He was submissive. Read verse 6

and this verse together—"I hid not My face from shame and spitting
. . . I have set My face like a flint." Gentleness and resolve are
married.

In Luke 9:51, we read, "He steadfastly set his face to go to
Jerusalem." In our Lord there was no turning aside, though none
helped Him, and every one hindered Him. He was neither confounded by thoughts within His own soul, nor rendered ashamed by
the scorn of others.

I. His Steadfast Resolve Tested.

1. By the offers of the world. They would make Him a king.
2. By the persuasions of friends. Peter rebuked Him. All the
   disciples marvelled at His determination. His relatives sought
   a very different career for Him.
3. By the unworthiness of His clients.
   He that ate bread with Him betrayed Him.
   His disciples forsook Him and fled.
   The whole race conspired to put Him to death.
4. By the bitterness which He tasted at His entrance upon His
   great work.
5. By the ease with which He could have relinquished the
   enterprise.
   Pilate would have released Him had Jesus pleaded.
   Legions of angels would have come to His rescue.
   He might Himself have come down from the cross.
6. By the taunts of those that scoffed.
   The people, the priests, the thieves: "Let us see whether Elias
   will come to save Him."
7. By the full stress of the death-agony.
   The pain, thirst, fever, fainting, desertion, death: none of
   these moved Him from His invincible resolve.

II. His Steadfast Resolve Imitated.

1. Our purpose must be God's glory, as His was.
2. Our education must be God's teaching, as His was.
3. Our life must combine active and passive obedience, as His
   did. (See verses 5 and 6).
4. Our strength must lie in God, as His did.
5. Our path must be one of faith, as His was. Note verse 10,
   and its remarkable connection with the whole subject.
6. Our resolve must be carefully made, and steadily carried out
   till we can say, "It is finished," in our manner and degree.

A secret divine support was rendered to the human nature of our
Redeemer; for the great work in which He was engaged required
abundant strength. One has well said that "it would have broken

the hearts, backs, and necks of all the glorious angels in heaven, and all the mighty men upon earth, had they engaged in it." Upon the Father's aid the Lord Jesus relied, according to our text; and this enabled Him to contemplate the tremendous woes of the passion with a resolve of the most steadfast kind.

Faith in God is the best foundation for a firm resolution and a firm resolution is the best preparative for a great undertaking. There is nothing so hard but that it can be cut by that which is harder: against his hard labor our Lord set His harder determination. His face was as a flint; you could not turn Him to leave His work, nor melt Him to pity himself. He was set upon it: He must die because He must save His people; and He must save His people because He loved them better than Himself.

The saints endeavor to imitate the strong resolve of their Lord to yield themselves up. For instance, a Scottish peasant, dying as a martyr on the scaffold, said, "I came here to die for Christ, and if I had as many lives in my hand as I have hairs on my head, I would lay them all down for Christ."

Oh, what a sea of blood, a sea of wrath, of sin, of sorrow and misery, did the Lord Jesus wade through for your internal and eternal good! Christ did not plead, "This cross is too heavy for Me to bear; this wrath is too great for Me to lie under; this cup, which hath in it all the ingredients of divine displeasure, is too bitter for Me to sup of, how much more to drink the very dregs of it!" No, Christ stands not upon this; He pleads not the difficulty of the service, but resolutely and bravely wades through all, as the prophet shows. Christ makes nothing of His Father's wrath, the burden of your sins, the malice of Satan, and the rage of the world, but sweetly and triumphantly passes through all.

Ah, souls, if this consideration will not raise up your spirits above all the discouragements that you meet with, to own Christ and His service, and to stick and cleave to Christ and His service, I am afraid nothing will! A soul not stirred by this, not raised and lifted up by this, to be resolute and brave in the service of God, notwithstanding all dangers and difficulties, is a soul left of God to much blindness and hardness.—THOMAS BROOKS.

## CHAPTER 58

## CHRISTOPATHY

*"With His stripes we are healed"* (Isaiah 53:5).

What a chapter! A Bible in miniature. The Gospel in its essence. When our subject brings us near to the passion of our Lord, our feelings should be deeply solemn, our attention intensely earnest.

Hark, the scourge is falling! Forget everything but "His stripes."

We have each one a part in the flagellation: we wounded Him, for certain; is it as certain that "with His stripes we are healed"? Observe with deep attention,—

## I. THAT GOD HERE TREATS SIN AS A DISEASE.

Sin is a great deal more than a disease, it is a wilful crime; but the mercy of our God leads Him to consider it under that aspect, in order that He may deal with it in grace.

1. It is not an essential part of man as he was created: it is abnormal, disturbing, and destructive.

2. It puts the faculties out of gear, and breaks the equilibrium of the life-forces, just as disease disturbs the bodily functions.

3. It weakens the moral energy, as disease weakens the body.

4. It either causes pain, or deadens sensibility, as the case may be.

5. It frequently produces visible pollution. Some sins are as defiling as the leprosy of old.

6. It tends to increase in the man, and it will prove fatal before long.

Sin is a disease which is hereditary, universal, contagious, defiling, incurable, mortal. No human physician can deal with it. Death, which ends all bodily pain, cannot cure this disease: it displays its utmost power in eternity, after the seal of perpetuity has been set upon it by the mandate: "He that is filthy, let him be filthy still."

## II. THAT GOD HERE DECLARES THE REMEDY WHICH HE HAS PROVIDED.

Jesus is His Son, whom He freely delivered up for us all.

1. Behold the heavenly medicine: The stripes of Jesus in body and in soul. Singular surgery, the Healer is Himself wounded, and this is the means of our cure!

2. Remember that these stripes were vicarious: He suffered in our stead.

3. Accept this atonement, and you are saved by it.
   Prayer begs for the divine surgery.
   Belief is the linen cloth which binds on the plaster.
   Trust is the hand which secures it to the wound.
   Repentance is the first symptom of healing.

4. Let nothing of your own interfere with the one medicine. You see the proper places of prayer, faith, and repentance; do not misuse them, and make them rivals of the "stripes."
   By the stripes of Jesus we are healed and by these alone.

One remedy, and only one, is set forth by God. Why seek another?

III. **That This Divine Remedy Is Immediately Effective.**

1. Our conscience is healed of its smart: eased but not deadened.
2. Our heart is healed of its love of sin. We hate the evil which scourged our Well-Beloved.
3. Our life is healed of its rebellion. We are zealous of good works.

If you are healed, behave accordingly.

Quit diseased company.

Do a healthy man's work.

Praise the Physician, and His singular surgery.

Publish abroad His praises.

The Balsam-tree sheds its balm to heal the wounds of those that cut it; and did not our blessed Savior do the like? They mock Him, and He prays for them; they shed His blood and He makes it a medicine for their healing; they pierce His heart, and He opens therein a fountain for their sin and uncleanness. Was it ever heard, before or since, that a physician should bleed, and thus heal his patient or that an offended prince should die to expiate the treasons of his rebellious subjects?

Our heavenly Balsam is a cure for all diseases. If you complain that no sins are like yours, remember that there is no salvation like Christ's. If you have run the complete round of sin, remember that the blood of Jesus Christ cleanseth from all. No man ever perished for being a great sinner, unless he was also an unbelieving sinner. Never did a patient fail of a cure who accepted from the great Physician the balm of His atoning blood.

See how Christ, Whose death was so bitter to Himself, becomes sweetness itself to us. Rejection was His, but acceptance is ours; the wounding was His, but the healing is ours; the blood was His, but the balm is ours; the thorns were His, but the crown is ours; the death was His, but the life is ours; the price was His, but the purchase is ours. There is more power in Christ's blood to save than in your sin to destroy. Do but believe in the Lord Jesus and thy cure is wrought.—*Modernized from* Spurstow's *"Spiritual Chymist."*

You who live by this medicine, speak well of it. Tell to others, as you have opportunity, what a Saviour you have found. If all the persons who have felt the efficacy of a dying Saviour's wounds, apprehended by faith, were to publish their cases, how greatly would His power and grace be displayed!—John Newton.

He cures the mind of its blindness, the heart of its hardness, the nature of its perseverance, the will of its backwardness, the memory of its slipperiness, the conscience of its benumbness, and the affections of their disorder, all according to His gracious promises (Ezek. 36: 26-27).—John Willison.

Dr. Cheyne was an eminent as well as a pious physician; but he was supposed to be severe in his regimen. When he had prescribed, and the patient began to object to the treatment, he would say, "I see you are not bad enough for me yet."

Some are not bad enough for Christ yet—we mean in their own apprehension; but when they find and feel that they are entirely lost, and have no other help or hope, they will cordially acquiesce in His recommendations, however mysterious, however humbling, however trying.—JAY.

CHAPTER 59

# REPENTANCE

*"Let the wicked forsake his way, and the unrighteous man his thoughts: and let him return unto the Lord, and He will have mercy upon him"* (Isaiah 55:7).

This is the great chapter of gospel invitation. How free! How full! How plain and pressing are the calls to receive grace!

I. THE NECESSITY OF CONVERSION.

The text makes this clear, but it may also be inferred from—

1. The nature of God. How can a holy God wink at sin, and pardon sinners who continue in their wickedness?

2. The nature of the gospel. It is not a proclamation of tolerance for sin, but of deliverance from it. It contains no single promise of forgiveness to the man who goes on in his iniquity.

3. The facts of the past. No instance has occurred of pardon given to a man while obstinately persisting in his evil way. Conversion always goes with salvation.

4. The well-being of the sinner himself requires that he should quit his sin, or feel its penalty. To be favored with a sense of divine pardon, while obstinately abiding in sin, would confirm the man in sin; and sin itself is a worse evil than its penalty.

II. THE NATURE OF CONVERSION.

1. It deals with the life and conduct. The man's "way." His natural way; that into which he runs when left to himself.

His habitual way; to which he is accustomed.

His beloved way; wherein his pleasures lie.

The general way; the broad road in which the many run.

This, our text says, he must "forsake." He must have done
with sin, or he will be undone. It will not suffice for him to—
Own that it is wrong;
Profess to be sorry for following it;
Resolve to leave it, and end in resolve, or
Move more cautiously in it.
No, he must forsake it altogether, at once, and forever.
2. It deals with the "thoughts." A man must forsake—
His unscriptural opinions, and self-formed notions—
About God, His law, His gospel, His people.
About sin, punishment, Christ, self, etc.
3. It deals with the man in reference to God. "Let him return
unto the Lord."
It bids him cease from pride, neglect, opposition, distrust, dis-
obedience, and all other forms of alienation from the Lord.
He must turn and return: wandering no further, but coming
home.

### III. The Gospel of Conversion.
1. A sure promise is made to it. "He will have mercy upon him."
2. The pardon which comes with it is the result of a full atonement, which renders the pardon abundant, just, safe, and easy
of belief to the awakened conscience.

Oh, that the sinner would consider the need of a total change of
thought within, and way without! It must be thorough and radical
or it will be useless.

Total and terrible ruin must ensue if you continue in evil.

May this hour see the turning-point in your life's course! God
saith, "Let him return." What doth hinder you?

William Burns was preaching one evening in the open air, to a
vast multitude. He had just finished, when a man came timidly up
to him, and said, "O Sir! will you come and see my dying wife?"
Burns consented; but the man immediately said, "Oh! I am afraid
when you know where she is you won't come." "I will go wherever
she is," he replied.

The man then tremblingly told him that he was the keeper of the
lowest public-house in one of the most wretched districts of the
town. "It does not matter," said the missionary, "come away." As
they went, the man, looking up in the face of God's servant, said
earnestly, "O Sir! I am going to give it up at the term." Burns
replied, "There are no terms with God." However much the poor
trembling publican tried to get Burns to converse with him about
the state of his soul, and the way of salvation, he was unable to
draw another word from him than these—"There are no terms with
God."

The shop was at last reached. They passed through it in order to reach the chamber of death. After a little conversation with the dying woman, the servant of the Lord engaged in prayer, and while he was praying the publican left the room, and soon a loud noise was heard, something like a rapid succession of determined knocks with a great hammer. Was this not a most unseemly noise to make on such a solemn occasion as this? Is the man mad? No.

When Burns reached the street, he beheld the wreck of the publican's sign-board strewn in splinters upon the pavement. The business was given up for good and all. The man had in earnest turned his back on his low public-house, and returned to the Lord, who had mercy upon him, and unto our God, who abundantly pardoned all his sins. Nothing transpired in his after-life to discredit the reality of his conversion.—WILLIAM BROWN, *in "Joyful Sound."*

## CHAPTER 60

## ABUNDANT PARDON

*"Let him return unto the Lord, and He will have mercy upon him: and to our God, for He will abundantly pardon"* (Isaiah 55:7).

I. LET US CONTEMPLATE THE ABUNDANCE OF DIVINE PARDON.

1. The abundance of the objects of the pardon. Since the days of Adam and even until now God has pardoned multitudes among all nations, classes, and ages.
   We quickly lose patience when many offend, but it is not so with our God. "Thou hast forgiven this people from Egypt even until now" (Num. 14:19).

2. The abundant sins which are pardoned. Who can count the thoughts, words, and deeds which are pardoned! These repeated ad nauseam. (Is. 43:24; Rev. 3:16).

3. The abundant means of pardon.
   The atonement of His Son, and His righteousness.
   The infinite merit of the ever-living Advocate.
   The Holy Spirit ever present to apply gospel provisions.

4. The abundant ease of the terms of pardon.
   No hard conditions of penance or purgatory.
   Only ask and have; repent and trust.
   Even the repentance and faith required are also given.

5. The abundant fullness of the pardon.
   It covers all sin, past, present, and to come

6. The abundant blessings which attend it.

Freedom from the reigning power of inbred sin.
Adoption into the heavenly family.
Acceptance so full that we may challenge accusers.
Communion with the thrice-holy God.
Ultimate admission into glory itself with the perfect ones.

## II. LET US CONSIDER ITS PROPER INFERENCES.

1. Then there is no room for despair. If the Lord only pardoned now and then, it were well to seek His favor even on the bare chance of obtaining it; but now let us return unto Him in sure and certain hope of pardon.

2. Here is a special call to the greatest sinners, since abundant mercy is most appropriate to their case: and no less should the less guilty come, since there must be room for them.

3. If such mercy be slighted, we may be sure it will entail great wrath.

That sin which is not too great to be forsaken, is not too great to be forgiven.

What is a little sparkle of fire, if it fall into the main sea? The same are the sins of a penitent person when dealt with by the mercy of God.—THOMAS HORTON.

One of the captive followers of the Duke of Monmouth was brought before James the Second. "You know it is in my power," said the king, "to pardon you." "Yes," said the man, who well knew his cruel character, "but it is not in your nature." However unwise this answer was, its truth was soon seen. Happily, we know that God has not only the power but the disposition to show mercy. "Also, unto Thee, O Lord, belongeth mercy."

Lord, before I commit a sin, it seems to me so shallow that I may wade through it dry-shod from any guiltiness; but when I have committed it, it often seems so deep that I cannot escape without drowning. Thus I am always in extremities: either my sins are so small that they need not any repentance, or so great that they cannot obtain Thy pardon. Lend me, O Lord, a reed out of Thy sanctuary, truly to measure the dimension of my offences. But O! as Thou revealest to me more of my misery, reveal also more of Thy mercy; lest, if my wounds, in my apprehension, gape wider than Thy tents (plugs of lint), my soul run out at them. If my badness seem bigger than Thy goodness but one hair's breadth, but one moment, that is room and time enough for me to run to eternal despair.—THOMAS FULLER.

## CHAPTER 61

# RETURN! RETURN!

*"Return thou backsliding Israel, saith the Lord." "Turn, O backsliding children, saith the Lord." "Return, ye backsliding children, and I will heal your backsliding"* (Jeremiah 3:12, 14, 22).

It is a fearful thing that a believer should backslide.

Such mercy has been shown to him.

Such love has been enjoyed by him.

Such prospects lie before him.

Such comfort is sacrificed by his backsliding.

I. WONDER AWAKENED BY THE CALL.

There would seem to be many reasons why the Lord should not invite the backslider to return. We will follow the guidance of the chapter, which will richly repay a careful exposition.

1. The usual jealousy of love. Note the terrible imagery of verse 1. A wanton adulteress is allowed to return to her husband.

2. The abundance of the sin: "Thou hast polluted the land" (verse 2). The very earth felt the leprosy of the idolatry.

3. The perversion of mercy. God did not reserve His anger forever, and they sinned the more because of His long-suffering (verse 5).

II. MEMORIES AROUSED BY THE CALL.

Does it not remind you of other days?

1. When you first came to Jesus?

2. When you were happy with other believers.

3. When you could teach and warn others.

4. When you began to go aside, a little.

III. DIRECTIONS GIVEN TO MAKE OBEDIENCE TO THE CALL EASY.

1. "Only acknowledge thine iniquity" (verse 13). What a simple matter!

2. Lament the evil: "Weeping and supplications" (verse 21). Do you not mourn your sin even now?

3. Heartily renew allegiance: "Behold, we come unto Thee; for Thou art the Lord our God" (verse 22).

IV. PROMISES MADE TO THOSE ANSWERING TO THE CALL.

Such shall obtain—

1. Special guidance: "I will bring you to Zion" (verse 14).

2. Suitable food: "Feed you with knowledge" (verse 15).

3. Spiritual insight. (See verses 16 and 17).

Upon the conscious backslider the threefold call should be pressed, "Return!" "Turn!" "Return!"

I was weary of a cold heart towards Christ, and His sacrifice, and the work of His Spirit—of a cold heart in the pulpit, in secret prayer, and in study. For fifteen years previously I had felt my heart burning within, as if going to Emmaus with Jesus.

On a day ever to be remembered by me, as I was going from Dolgelly to Machynlleth, and climbing up towards Cadair Idris, I considered it to be incumbent upon me to pray, however hard I felt my heart, and however worldly the frame of my spirit was. Having begun in the Name of Jesus, I soon felt as it were the fetters loosening, and the old hardness of heart softening, and, as I thought, mountains of frost and snow dissolving, and melting within me. This engendered confidence in my soul in the promise of the Holy Ghost. I felt my mind relieved from some great bondage: tears flowed copiously, and I was constrained to cry out for the gracious visits of God, by restoring to my soul the joy of His salvation.—CHRISTMAS EVANS.

I am sometimes downright staggered at the exceeding riches of His grace. How Christ can go on pardoning day after day, and hour after hour; sometimes I feel almost afraid to ask, for shame.—A. L. NEWTON.

> Man-like is it to fall in sin,
> Fiend-like is it to dwell therein,
> Christ-like is it for sin to grieve,
> God-like is it all sin to leave.
>                    —LONGFELLOW.

## CHAPTER 62

# DECIDED UNGODLINESS

*"They have refused to return"* (Jeremiah 5:3).

I. WHO HAVE REFUSED TO RETURN?

1. Those who have said as much. With unusual honesty or presumption, they have made public declaration that they will never quit their sinful ways.

2. Those who have made a promise to repent, but have not performed it.

3. Those who have offered other things instead of practical return to God: ceremonies, religiousness, morality, and the like.

4. Those who have only returned in appearance. Formalists, mere professors, and hypocrites.

## II. What This Refusal Unveils.

1. An intense love of sin.
2. A want of love to the great Father, Who bids them return.
3. A despising of God: they reject His counsel, His command, and even Himself.
4. A resolve to continue in evil. This is their proud ultimatum, "they have refused to return."
5. A trifling with serious concerns. They are too busy, too fond of gaiety, etc. There is time enough yet.

## III. What Is the Real Reason of This Refusal?

1. It may be self-conceit: perhaps they dream that they are already in the right road.
2. It is at times sheer recklessness. The man refuses to consider his own best interests. He resolves to be a trifler; death and hell and heaven are to him as toys to sport with.
3. It is a dislike of holiness. That lies at the bottom of it: men cannot endure humility, self-denial, and obedience to God.
4. It is a preference for the present above the eternal future.

From the cross the Lord Jesus calls on you to return. Hasten home! The door of heaven shuts from below, not from above. "Your iniquities have separated," saith the Lord.—WILLIAMS, *of Wern.*

Lord Byron, a short time before death, was heard to say, "Shall I sue for mercy?" After a long pause, he added, "Come, come, no weakness; let's be a man to the last!"

The reason why a wicked man doth not turn unto God is not because he cannot (though he cannot), but because he will not. He cannot say at the day of judgment, "Lord, Thou knowest I did my best to be holy, but I could not." The man that had not on a wedding-garment could not say, "Lord, I was not able to get one." But he was "speechless."—W. FENNER.

## Chapter 63

# REST AS A TEST

*"Ask for the old paths, where is the good way, and walk therein, and ye shall find rest for your souls"* (Jeremiah 6:16).

It is the distinguishing feature of the good old way that in it we find rest for our souls.

Rest is never found apart from the gospel, and faith in Jesus.

Rest comes not from wealth, health, honor, or any other earthly thing.

I. IN "THE GOOD WAY" WE FIND REST IF WE WALK THEREIN.

1. The way of pardon by an atonement gives rest to the conscience.
2. The way of believing the Word as a little child gives rest to the understanding.
3. The way of trusting our affairs with God gives rest to the mind.
4. The way of obedience to divine commands gives rest to the soul.
5. The way of communion with Christ gives rest to the heart.

II. REST FOUND BY WALKING IN "THE GOOD WAY" IS GOOD FOR THE SOUL.

1. It brings satisfaction, but not self-satisfaction.
2. It brings a sense of safety, but does not lead to presumptuous sin.
3. It creates content, but also excites desires for progress.

III. REST OF THIS KIND SHOULD BE ENJOYED NOW.

1. You should be in the way, know that you are there, and try to keep to the very middle of the road. Truly believe in Jesus, and perfect rest must come. "Therefore, being justified by faith, we have peace with God" (Rom. 5:1).
2. You should have no doubt that the way is good, and that it is the way of the Lord.
3. You should feel an intense satisfaction in Jesus. You will do so unless you live at a distance from Him, and so miss His presence and smile. A present Christ is a well of delight.

We challenge Romanists, sacramentarians, self-justiciaries, and the like, to say that they have any rest. Rome does not promise it even to her own votaries, either in this world or in the world to come; but goes on saying her masses for the repose of the souls of her own departed cardinals, who evidently are not at rest. If her most eminent divines go to purgatory, where do the common people go?

We invite all the laboring and laden to come and try the Lord Jesus, and see if He does not rest them at once, and forever.

We hear our own willing testimony to the sweetness, safety, perpetuity, and truthfulness of the rest of faith.

It is called "the good way." It is not the easy way; the idle and the foolish ask for that, but it is not worth seeking for, since it leads to poverty and perdition. Neither is it the popular way, for few there be that find it. But it is the good way, made by a good God, in infinite goodness to his creatures; paved by our good Lord Jesus, with pains and labors immeasurable; and revealed by the good Spirit to those whose eternal good He seeks.—C. H. S.

Here there is a well-beaten track under our feet. Let us keep it. It may be quite the shortest way; it may not take us through all the grandeur and sublimity which bolder pedestrians might see: we may miss a picturesque waterfall, a remarkable glacier, a charming view: but the track will bring us safe to our quarters for the night.—DR. DALE.

## CHAPTER 64

## THE ETHIOPIAN

*"Can the Ethiopian change his skin?"* (Jeremiah 13:23).

Jeremiah had spoken to these people, and they would not hear; He had wept over them, and they would not consider. Even God's judgments had failed to move them, and He came to the conclusion that they were incorrigible, and could no more improve than a black man could become white.

I. THE QUESTION AND ITS ANSWER. "CAN THE ETHIOPIAN CHANGE HIS SKIN?" The expected reply is, "HE CANNOT DO SO."

The outward impossibility is the Ethiopian's changing the color of his own skin: a physical experiment never yet accomplished.

The inward impossibility is a change of heart and character by one "accustomed to do evil."

Can he—will he—change himself? Never.

The difficulty in the sinner's case lies—

1. In the strength of habit. Use is second nature. Practice in transgression has forged chains, and bound the man to evil.
2. In the pleasure of sin, which fascinates and enslaves the mind.
3. In the appetite for sin, which gathers intensity from indulgence. Drunkenness, lechery, covetousness, etc., are a growing force.
4. In the blindness of the understanding, which prevents men from seeing the evil of their ways, or noting their danger.

For these reasons we answer the question in the negative: sinners can no more renew themselves than Ethiopians can change their skins.

*Why then preach to them?*

It is Christ's command, and we are bound to obey.

Their inability does not hinder our ministry, for power goes with the word.

*Why tell them it is their duty to repent?*

Because it is so: moral inability is no excuse: the law is not to be lowered because man has grown too evil to keep it.

*Why tell them of this moral inability?*

To drive them to self-despair, and make them look to Christ.

II. ANOTHER QUESTION AND ANSWER. CAN THE ETHIOPIAN'S SKIN BE CHANGED? OR, CAN THE SINNER BE MADE ANEW?

This is a very different affair, and in it lies the door of hope for men.

Assuredly the Lord can make a black man white.

The greatest sinner can be transformed into a saint.

The grounds for so believing are many.

Here are a few of them,—

1. All things are possible with God (Matt. 19:26).

2. The Holy Spirit has special power over the human heart.

3. The Lord Jesus has determined to work this wonder and for this purpose He came into this world and died, and rose again. "He shall save His people from their sins" (Matt. 1:21).

4. Many such jet-black sinners have been totally changed.

5. The gospel is prepared with that end.

Herein lies hope for the most inveterate sinner.

　　Not in the bath of baptism;

　　Nor in the scalding tears of remorse;

　　Nor in the medicine of vows and pledges;

　　But in His word of power, who doeth great wonders of grace.

If it were possible for those who have been for ages in hell to return to the earth (and not to be regenerated), I firmly believe that, notwithstanding all they have suffered for sin, they would still love it, and return to the practice of it.—JOHN RYLAND.

The Christian sects in Syria appear to consider a true case of Druze conversion to Christianity as out of the question. "The wolf's whelps," they say, "are not tamed." The conversion of many sinners appears equally impossible, and yet how many such triumphs of grace are recorded as that which John Newton described in himself: "I was a wild beast on the coast of Africa once, but the Lord Jesus caught me, and tamed me, and now people come to see me as they would go to look at the lions in the tower."

　　　　Can there no help be had?

　　Lord, Thou art holy, Thou art pure:

　　　　Mine heart is not so bad,

　　So foul, but Thou canst cleanse it sure.

　　Speak blessed Lord, wilt Thou afford

　　　　Me means to make it clean?

　　I know Thou wilt: Thy blood was spilt.

　　　　Should it run still in vain?

　　　　　　　CHRISTOPHER HARVEY, *in "Schola Cordis."*

## CHAPTER 65

# PRAYER ENCOURAGED

*"Call unto Me, and I will answer thee, and shew thee great and mighty things which thou knowest not"* (Jeremiah 33:3).

This is a prison-word: let those who are spiritually in prison prize it. This was the second time the Lord had spoken to the prophet while in the dungeon. God leaves not His people because of their being in ill odor with the world, nor even when they are put into prison. Nay, rather, He doubles his visits when they are in double trouble.

The text belongs to every afflicted servant of God.

It encourages him in a threefold manner,—

I. To CONTINUE IN PRAYER. "Call unto Me!"

1. Pray, though you have prayed. See previous chapter at 16th verse and onward.

2. Pray though you are still in prison after prayer. If deliverance tarries, make your prayers the more importunate.

3. Pray; for the Word of the Lord comes to you with this command.

4. Pray; for the Holy Spirit prompts you, and helps you.

II. To EXPECT ANSWERS TO PRAYER. "I will answer thee, and shew thee."

The Lord will answer us because—

1. He has appointed prayer, and made arrangements for its presentation and acceptance. He could not have meant it to be a mere farce: that were to treat us as fools.

2. He prompts, encourages, and quickens prayer; and surely He would never mock us by exciting desires which He never meant to gratify. Such a thought well-nigh blasphemes the Holy Ghost, Who indites prayer in the heart.

3. He has given His promise in the text; and it is often repeated elsewhere: He cannot lie or deny Himself.

III. To EXPECT GREAT THINGS AS ANSWERS TO PRAYER. "I will shew thee great and mighty things."

Read the previous chapter from verse 18, and learn from it that we are to look for things—

1. Great in counsel: full of wisdom and significance.

2. Divine things: "I will shew thee." These are enumerated in the verses which follow the text, even to the end of the chapter: such as these—
Health and cure (verse 6).
Liberation from captivity (verse 7).
Forgiveness of iniquity (verse 8).
See how sufferers may win unexpected deliverances.
See how workers may achieve surprising marvels.
See how seekers may find more than they dare expect.

A young engineer was being examined, and this question was put to him: "Suppose you have a steam-pump constructed for a ship, under your own supervision, and know that everything is in perfect order, yet, when you throw out the hose, it will not draw; what should you think?" "I should think, sir, there must be a defect somewhere." "But such a conclusion is not admissible; for the supposition is that everything is perfect, and yet that the pump will not work." "Then, sir," replied the student, "I should look over the side of the ship to see if the river had run dry." Even so it would appear that if true prayer is not answered the nature of God must have changed.

God's praying people get to know much more of His mind than others; like as John, by weeping, got the book opened; and Daniel, by prayer, had the king's secret revealed unto him in a night vision. —TRAPP.

Sir Walter Raleigh one day asking a favor from Queen Elizabeth, the latter said to him, "Raleigh, when will you leave off begging?" To which he answered, "When your Majesty leaves off giving." Ask great things of God. Expect great things from God. Let His past goodness make us "instant in prayer"—*New Cyclopaedia of Illustrative Anecdote.*

The dungeon of the Mamertine, where a probable tradition declares that Paul was for a while confined, is entered through a round hole in the floor of another dungeon above. The uppermost apartment is dark enough, but the lower one is darkness itself, so that the apostle's imprisonment was of the severest kind.

We noticed, however, a strange fact:—in the hard floor there is a beautiful fountain of clear crystal water, which doubtless was as fresh in Paul's day as it is now; of course the Papists believe the fountain to be miraculous; we who are not so credulous of traditions rather see in it a symbol full of instruction:—there never was a dungeon for God's servants which was without its well of consolation.—C. H. S.

## CHAPTER 66

# IS IT NOTHING TO YOU?

*"Is it nothing to you, all ye that pass by? Behold and
see if there be any sorrow like unto my sorrow, which is
done unto me wherewith the Lord hath afflicted me in the
day of His fierce anger"* (Lamentations 1:12).

When Christians think of Calvary and of their wounded, bleeding
Lord they cannot help imitating Jeremiah and picturing their Lord
as crying these words of our text from the Cross.  In all ages of the
church this has been a favorite text

I.  THE SUFFERINGS OF THE SON OF GOD UPON THE CROSS WERE AL-
TOGETHER UNPARALLELED.

1.  Because of the Divine Dignity of His Person.  Kings have
died, philosophers have died, but never such a One as this, for He
that bled on Calvary was Prophet, Priest and King, the Eternal Son
of God.

2.  Because of the Perfect Innocence of His Character.  Herein
is a sorrow never to be forgotten, that He must bleed and die and
moreover He must so suffer as to be connected with sin.

3.  Because in His case there was such a conjunction of griefs.
Sometimes you and I have grief on grief and things so hard.  But
with Christ it seemed as if every form of grief was let loose against
Him.

4.  Because all of His sorrow was voluntarily undertaken.  He was
under no compulsion from any force which He could not Himself
control.

II.  THE SUFFERINGS OF CHRIST HAVE A DEEP INTEREST IN THEM
FOR MANY.

1.  Multitudes have found in the sufferings of Christ the cure for
their despair.  And in curing their despair they have wrought a
complete transformation in their lives.

The apostle Paul on the way to Damascus breathing threatening
and slaughter, becomes the greatest of all preachers of Christ.

2.  The sufferings of Christ have girded them to heroic deeds.
The lifting up of the little finger of Christ was enough to move
hosts of men and women to court death and defy the flames.

3.  They teach men to hate sin.  When they see the agonies by
which redemption from sin was obtained.

III.  WHAT HAVE YOU TO DO WITH HIM?

1.  He means nothing to so many.  They rise like a balloon and
are filled and inflated with prosperity.  But when the wine is sour
and the gold corroded, what then?

2. He can mean everything to the heavy of heart. Are you guilty? Would you be forgiven? Turn aside and look at Him. Look till your eyes are full of tears.

3. If you won't take Him, what have you to offer in His place? You who say that we Christians are doing no good. Try your own hand at it. Go to the dying, the sick, take them bottles of your philosophy, comfort them with the elixir of scientific doubt. Go ahead!

I shall never forget when I shook the hand of Livingstone. I count it one of the great honors of my life to have known him. It was the love of Christ that made him tread pathless Africa and die among the heathen. . . . Over there at your Smithfield, why, there were men and women who were summoned to stand at fiery stakes and burn; and they were seen to clap their hands, when every finger was a candle and cry "None but Christ! None but Christ!"

There was a poor girl who had long been a Christian, but she was very sad at heart through sickness; and when her minister came to see her he said to her, "Well, Susan, how is your hope?" She said, "Sir, I am afraid I am not a Christian. I do not love the Lord Jesus Christ." He said, "Why, I always thought you did. You acted as if you did." "No," she said, "I am afraid I have deceived myself and that I do not love Him." The minister wisely walked to the window and wrote on a piece of paper, "I do not love the Lord Jesus Christ," and he said, "Susan, here is a pencil. Just put your name to that. "No sir," she said, "I could not sign *that*." "Why not?" "I would be torn to pieces before I would sign it, sir." But why not sign it if it is true?" "Ah, sir," said she, "I hope it is not true. I think I do love Him."

## Chapter 67

## BETTER THAN YOUR BEGINNINGS

*"I will settle you after your old estates, and will do better unto you than at your beginnings, and ye shall know that I am the Lord"* (Ezekiel 36:11).

To hypocrites and formalists an end cometh; but true children of God rise again after decays and declensions. As saith the prophet. (Micah 7:8).

A greater blessing than that which they have lost may yet be granted to restored wanderers.

## I. What Was There So Good In Our Beginnings?

As Israel's land in the beginning flowed with milk and honey, so our first estate had a singular richness about it.

1. We enjoyed a vivid sense of free and full forgiveness.
2. We gained repeated victories over sinful inclinations, and outward temptations; and this made us jubilant in Christ.
3. We felt great delight in prayer, the Word, communion, etc.
4. We abounded in zeal and service, and the joy of the Lord was our strength.

We read of "the first ways of David:" (II Chron. 17:3). We are bidden to do our "first works:" (Rev. 2:5).

## II. Can We Enjoy Something Better Than Our Beginnings?

Assuredly we shall, if the Lord will fulfil this promise; and that He is sure to do if we walk more closely with Him.

1. Our faith will be stronger, more steadfast, and intelligent.
2. Our knowledge will be fuller and deeper.
3. Our love will be more constant, practical, enduring.
4. Our prayer will be more prevalent.
5. Our usefulness will be more extended, more abiding.
6. Our whole being will be more mature.

We are to shine more and more unto the perfect day (Prov. 4:18).

## III. How Can We Enjoy This Betterness?

1. We must return to our first simple faith in Jesus.
2. We must quit the sins which alienated us from God.
3. We must be more thorough, and earnest.
4. We must seek after closer fellowship with Christ.
5. We must more resolutely strive to advance in divine things.

Admire the liberality of our God! He promises to do better unto us than at our beginnings. What more can He do?

God's dealings with His people are best at last; they may have much kindness and mercy in the morning, but they shall have more in the evening. "I will settle you after your old estates," etc. The Jews had the best wine at last; they had milk and honey before, but the feast of fat things full of marrow, and of wines on the lees well-refined, were at the latter end of their day given in; they had Christ and the Gospel at last.

Abraham had much of the world at first, and his Isaac afterward. "God blessed the latter end of Job more than his beginning." Simeon in his latter days saw Christ, and had Him in his arms.—William Greenhill.

Those that will not return to the duties they have neglected, cannot expect to return to the comforts they have lost.—G. S. Bowes.

He is a skillful physician indeed who, finding a man sorely afflicted, not only succeeds in restoring him to health, but actually causes him to be better than he was before, dealing with his medicine, not only with the disease which caused pain, but with some other which lay deeper, but had scarcely been perceived by the patient.

Such is the medicine of mercy. Thus graciously doth God deal with repenting sinners. He must be worse than a brute beast who would turn this into an argument for sinning. A true child of God feels the water standing in his eyes when he thinks of such super-abounding love.

CHAPTER 68

## MISTAKEN NOTIONS ABOUT REPENTANCE

> *"And I will multiply the fruit of the tree, and the increase of the field, that ye shall receive no more reproach of famine among the heathen.*
> *Then shall ye remember your own evil ways, and your doings that were not good, and shall loathe yourselves in your own sight for your iniquities, and for your abominations"* (Ezekiel 36:30, 31).

Repentance is wrought in the heart by a sense of love divine.

This sets repentance in its true light, and helps us to meet a great many mistakes which have darkened this subject. Many are kept from Christ and hope by misapprehensions of this matter. They have—

**I. MISTAKEN IDEAS OF WHAT REPENTANCE IS.**

They confound it with—

1. Morbid self-accusation, which is the fruit of dyspepsia, or melancholy, or insanity. This is an infirmity of mind, and not a grace of the Spirit. A physician may here do more than a divine.
2. Unbelief, despondency, despair: which are not even a help to repentance, but tend rather to harden the heart.
3. Dread of hell, and sense of wrath: which might occur even to devils, and yet would not cause them to repent. A measure of this may go with repentance, but it is no part of it.

Repentance is a hatred of evil

a sense of shame          Wrought by a sense
a longing to avoid sin          of divine love.

II. MISTAKEN IDEAS OF THE PLACE WHICH REPENTANCE OCCUPIES.

1. It is looked upon by some as a procuring cause of grace, as if repentance merited remission: a grave error.
2. It is wrongly viewed by others as a preparation for grace; a human goodness laying the foundation for mercy a meeting of God half way; this is a deadly error.
3. It is treated as a sort of qualification for believing, and even as the ground for believing: all which is legality, and contrary to pure gospel truth.
4. Others treat it as the argument for peace of mind. They have repented so much, and it must be all right. This is to build our confidence upon a false foundation.

III. MISTAKEN IDEAS OF THE WAY IN WHICH IT IS PRODUCED IN THE HEART.

It is not produced by a distinct and immediate attempt to repent.
Nor by strong excitement at revival meetings.
Nor by meditating upon sin, and death, and hell, etc.
But the God of all grace produces it—

1. By His free grace, which by its action renews the heart (verse 26).
2. By bringing His great mercy to our mind.
3. By making us receive new mercy (verses 28-30).
4. By revealing Himself and His methods of grace (verse 32).

There are no arguments like those that are drawn from the consideration of the great and glorious things Christ hath done for you; and if such will not take with you, and win upon you, I do not think the throwing of hell-fire in your faces will ever do it.—THOMAS BROOKS.

Repentance—the tear dropped from the eye of faith.

God's favor melts hard hearts sooner than the fire of His indignation; His kindness is very penetrative, it gets into the hearts of sinners sooner than His threats and frowns; it is like a small soaking rain, which goes to the roots of things, whereas a dashing rain runs away, and does little good. It was David's kindness that brake the heart of Saul (I Sam. 24) and it's God's kindness which breaks the hearts of sinners.

The milk and honey of the gospel affect the hearts of sinners more than the gall and wormwood of the law; Christ on Mount Zion brings more to repentance than Moses on Mount Sinai.—WILLIAM GREENHILL.

"Some people," says Philip Henry, "do not wish to hear much of repentance, but I think it so necessary that, if I should die in the pulpit, I wish to die preaching repentance; and if out of the pulpit practising it."

CHAPTER 69

# A MAN TROUBLED BY HIS THOUGHTS

*"His thoughts troubled him"* (Daniel 5:6).

To many men thinking is an unusual employment.

Yet it is a distinction of man that he can think.

No wonder that when thought is forced on some men they are troubled.

I. IT DID NOT APPEAR LIKELY THAT HIS THOUGHTS WOULD TROUBLE HIM.

1. He was an irresponsible and reckless monarch.
2. He had hardened his heart with pride (verses 22 and 23). Daniel said, "Thou hast lifted up thyself against the Lord of heaven."
3. He was drinking wine and it had worked upon him (verse 2)
4. He was rioting in gay company.
5. He was venturing far in profanity (verse 3); daring to abuse the sacred vessels, in his banquets, as an expression of his contempt for Israel's God, Whom he despised.

No man is rendered wise or thoughtful by the wine-cup.

No man is out of the reach of the arrows of God.

No conscience is so dead that God cannot arouse it.

II. YET WELL MIGHT HIS THOUGHTS TROUBLE HIM.

1. For what he saw was appalling: (verse 5).
2. For what he could not see was suggestive. Where was the hand? Where was the writer? What had he written? What did it mean?
3. For what he had done was alarming. His own past flashed before him. His cruel wars, oppressions, blasphemies and vices.

   What he had himself failed to do came before him (verse 23). What he was then in the act of doing startled him.

III. AND MIGHT NOT YOUR THOUGHTS TROUBLE SOME OF YOU?

1. You are prosperous. Are not beasts fattened for the slaughter?
2. You are trifling with holy things. You neglect, or ridicule, or use without seriousness the things of God.
3. You mix with the impure. Will you not perish with them?
4. Your father's history might instruct you, or at least trouble you.
5. The sacred writing "over against the candle-stick" is against you. Read the Holy Scripture, and see for yourself.

Conscience, from inaction is like a withered arm in the souls of many; but the Lord of conscience will one day say to it, "Be thou stretched forth, and do thine appointed work."

As the ant-hill, when stirred, sets in motion its living insects in every direction, so the conscience of the sinner, disturbed by the Spirit, or judgments of God, calls up before its vision thousands of deeds which fill the soul with agony and woe.—McCosh.

The Duke of Wellington once said that he could have saved the lives of a thousand men a year, had he had chaplains or any religious ministers. The uneasiness of their minds reacted on their bodies, and kept up continual fever, once it seized upon their frames. It is our blessed office to tell of One Who can "minister to a mind diseased," Whose grace can deliver from "an evil conscience," and through Whom all inward fear and trouble are removed.

Charles IX, of France, in his youth, had humane and tender sensibilities. The fiend who had tempted him was the mother who had nursed him. When she first proposed to him the massacre of the Huguenots, he shrunk from it with horror: "No, no, madam! They are my loving subjects." Then was the critical hour of his life. Had he cherished that natural sensitiveness to bloodshed, St. Bartholomew's Eve would never have disgraced the history of his kingdom, and he himself would have escaped the fearful remorse which crazed him on his death-bed.

To his physician he said in his last hours, "Asleep or awake, I see the mangled forms of the Huguenots passing before me. They drip with blood. They make hideous faces at me. They point to their open wounds and mock me. Oh, that I had spared at least the little infants at the breast!" Then he broke out in agonizing cries and screams. Bloody sweat oozed from the pores of his skin.

He was one of the very few cases in history which confirm the possibility of the phenomenon which attended our Lord's anguish in Gethsemane. That was the fruit of resisting, years before, the recoil of his youthful conscience from the extreme of guilt.—Austin Phelps.

## Chapter 70

## PRAYER FOR THE CHURCH

*"Now, therefore, O our God, hear the prayer of Thy servant, and his supplications, and cause Thy face to shine upon Thy sanctuary that is desolate, for the Lord's sake"* (Daniel 9:17).

This true-hearted man lived not for himself. Daniel was a fervent lover of his country.

His prayer is instructive to us.

It suggests our fervent entreaties for the church of God in these days.

### I.  THE HOLY PLACE.  "Thy sanctuary."

The temple was typical, and for our edification we shall read the text as if the spiritual house had been meant.  There are many points in the type worthy of notice, but these may suffice:—

1. The temple was unique; and as there could only be one temple for Jehovah, so there is but one church.
2. The temple was the result of great cost and vast labor; so was the church builded by the Lord Jesus at a cost which can never be estimated.
3. The temple was the shrine of God's indwelling.
4. The temple was the place of His worship.
5. The temple was the throne of His power: His word went forth from Jerusalem; there He ruled His people, and routed His foes.

### II.  THE EARNEST PRAYER.  "Cause Thy face to shine upon Thy sanctuary that is desolate."

1. It rose above all selfishness.  This was his one prayer, the center of all his prayers.
2. It cast itself upon God.  "O our God."
3. It was a confession that he could do nothing of himself. Honest men do not ask God to do what they can do themselves.
4. It asked a comprehensive boon.  "Cause Thy face to shine." This would mean many things which we also implore for the church of God.
   1) Ministers in their places, faithful in their service.
   2) Truth proclaimed in its clearness.  God's face cannot shine upon falsehood or equivocation.
   3) Delight in fellowship.
   4) Power in testimony.  When God is pleased His word is mighty.

### III.  THE CONSISTENT CONDUCT.  This is suggested by such a prayer.

1. Let us lay it earnestly to heart.  Whether for joy or sorrow, let the condition of the church concern us deeply.
2. Let us do all we can for her, or our prayer will be a mockery.
3. Let us do nothing to grieve the Lord; for all depends upon His smile.  "Cause Thy face to shine."
4. Let us pray much more than we have done.  Let each one of us be a Daniel.

During the troublous times of Scotland, when the Popish court and aristocracy were arming themselves to suppress the Reformation in that land, and the cause of Protestant Christianity was in imminent peril, late on a certain night John Knox was seen to leave his study, and to pass from the house down into an enclosure to the rear of it.

He was followed by a friend, when, after a few moments of silence, his voice was heard as if in prayer. In another moment the accents deepened into intelligible words, and the earnest petition went up from his struggling soul to heaven, "O Lord, give me Scotland, or I die!" Then a pause of hushed stillness, when again the petition broke forth, "O Lord, give me Scotland, or I die!"

Once more all was voiceless and noiseless, when, with a yet intenser pathos the thrice-repeated intercession struggled forth, "O Lord, give me Scotland, or I die!" And God gave him Scotland in spite of Mary and her Cardinal Beatoun; a land and a church of noble loyalty to Christ and His crown.

The church may be sick, yet not die. Die it cannot, for the blood of an eternal King bought it, the power of an eternal Spirit preserves it, and the mercy of an eternal God shall crown it.—THOMAS ADAMS.

## CHAPTER 71

## WAYS HEDGED UP

*"Therefore, behold, I will hedge up thy way with thorns, and make a wall, that she shall not find her paths. And she shall follow after her lovers, but she shall not overtake them; and she shall seek them, but shall not find them; then shall she say, I will go and return to my first husband; for then was it better with me than now"* (Hosea 2:6, 7).

This is a parenthesis of mercy in a passage of threatening.

I. THE STUBBORN CHARACTER OF MANY SINNERS.

1. Ordinary means have missed their aim. The details are given in previous verses; and then we read "therefore": showing that because of former failures the Lord is about to try further measures.

2. Extraordinary means are now to be used.

3. Even these means are to fail. Men will leap hedges, and scale walls, to get at their darling sins.

4. Only divine power can overcome the hardened one. God Himself must personally interpose, or none will turn to Him.

What sinners those must be whom neither hedge nor wall will stop unless God be there also in omnipotence of grace!

II. THE MEANS WHICH GOD USES TO RECLAIM THEM.

1. Sharp afflictions: "I will hedge up thy way with thorns." Many are checked and made to think by being made to smart.
2. Insurmountable difficulties: "and make a wall." The Lord of love places effectual stoppages in the road of those whom He means to save.
3. Blinding perplexities: "She shall not find her paths."
4. Utter failures: "she shall follow after, but not overtake."
5. Bitter disappointments: "she shall seek them but shall not find them."

These severe chastenings are frequently made useful in the early days of religious impression, they are the ploughing before the sowing.

III. THE BLESSED RESULT WHICH AT LAST IS ATTAINED.

1. Remembrance aroused: "It was better with me."
2. Confession of sad loss extorted: "then was it better with me than now."
3. Resolution formed: "I will go and return."
4. Affection stirred: "I will return to my first husband."

Let us turn to the Lord before He uses thorns to stop us.

If already hedged up, let us consider our ways.

"I will hedge up thy way."—There is a twofold hedge that God makes about His people. There is the hedge of protection, to keep evil from them; and the hedge of affliction, to keep from evil. The hedge of protection you have in Isa. 5:5, where God threatens that He "will take away the hedge" from His vineyard; and it is said of Job that God had "hedged him about." But the hedge here meant is the hedge of affliction. "I will hedge up thy way," that is I will bring sore and heavy afflictions upon you to keep you from evil.

A wounded conscience is a hedge of thorns; but this thorny fence keeps our wild spirits in the true way, which otherwise would be straggling; and it is better to be held in the right road with briars and brambles than to wander on beds of roses in a wrong path which leads to destruction.—THOMAS FULLER.

A popular and successful young minister in America became entangled in the meshes of infidelity, left the pulpit, joined an infidel club, and derided the name he had preached to others as the Savior of the world. But he sickened, and came to his death-bed. His friends gathered round him, and tried to comfort him with their cold and icy theories, but in vain. The old thought came back to him—the old experience came before him. He said, "Wife, bring me my Greek Testament."

88

8

Upon his bed he turned to the fifteenth chapter of the First Epistle to the Corinthians. When he had finished the chapter, great tears of joy rolled down his cheeks. He closed the book, and said, "Wife, back again at last upon the old rock to die."

## CHAPTER 72
## WHAT WILL THE HARVEST BE

*"For they have sown the wind, and they shall reap the whirlwind: it hath no stalk: the bud shall yield no meal: if so be it yield, the strangers shall swallow it up"* (Hosea 8:7).

Life is a seed-time. Of all men it may be said, "they have sown." Prudent men put the question, "What will the harvest be?"

I. THE RESULT OF CERTAIN SOWINGS WILL BE TERRIBLE. "They have sown the wind, and they shall reap the whirlwind."

1. Vicious men sow their wild oats, and we need not say what they reap. The debauched, drunken, and profligate are around us, bearing already in their own persons the first-fruits of the fearful harvest of transgression.
2. Immoral theories go far beyond their original intent. The speculation was an airy nothing, but the outcome is a whirlwind, breaking down all that is built up.
3. Heresies in the church also lead to unexpected evils. Apparently trifling errors grow to grievous evils. The use of a symbol develops into idolatry. A little laxity increases into absolute immorality. Small disputes lead on to heart-burnings and divisions.
4. Tolerance of sin in a family is a fruitful source of overwhelming evil. See the case of Eli.
5. Toleration of sin in yourself. Occasional indulgence becomes habit, and habit is as the Simoon of the desert, before which life expires, and hope is swept away. Even allowable acts may grow into dangerous excess.

II. THE RESULT OF SOME SOWINGS IS MANIFEST FAILURE. "It hath no stalk."
The seed feebly tries to grow, but it comes to nothing.
1. Self-conceit vainly endeavors to produce a reputation.
2. Self-righteousness strives unsuccessfully to obtain salvation.
3. Human wisdom idly struggles to make a new gospel.

4. Mere idlers and talkers affect to be useful, but it is a delusion. What appears to be accomplished soon vanishes away. Great talk, but "no stalk."

5. He who spends his life without faith in Christ, and obedience to His will, may dream of a happy future but he will be deceived: "it hath no stalk."

III. THE RESULT OF MANY SOWINGS IS UNSATISFACTORY. "The bud shall yield no meal."

1. The man lived for pleasure, and found satiety.
2. He lived for fame, and gathered vanity.
3. He lived for self and found misery.
4. He lived by his own works and religiousness, but reaped no peace of mind, and no real salvation.

Without God, nothing is wise, or strong, or worth the doing.

Only to live unto God is a wise sowing.

May the Lord destroy utterly all our sowings to the flesh, lest we reap corruption! (Gal. 6:8).

May the Lord Jesus supply us with good seed, and bless us in the sowing! Oh, for a consecrated life!

An Eastern apalogue tells us of Abdallah, to whom an evil spirit came at first as a fly, sipping an atom of syrup. He did not drive away the creature, and to his surprise it increased to the size of a locust. Being further indulged, the creature went on growing, and made such rapid increase that it became an enormous monster, devoured his substance, and in the end murdered him, leaving in the garden, where it slew its victim, a footprint six cubits long. Thus does sin grow upon men, till it becomes a giant habit, and slays them.

Augustine tells us of a young man who thought that the devil had made flies, and such like tiny things. By the influence of this apparently insignificant error, he was led on, step by step, till in the end he ascribed everything to Satan, and ceased to believe in God. Thus does error sow the wind, and reap the whirlwind. Scrupulous correctness of faith is as much a duty as careful practice in morals.

David Hume, the historian, philosopher and sceptic, spent his life in traducing the Word of God. In his last moments he joked with those around him; but the intervals were filled with sadness. He wrote, "I am affrighted and confounded with the forlorn solitude in which I am placed by my philosophy. When I turn my eye inward, I find nothing but doubt and ignorance. Where am I, and what? I begin to fancy myself in the most deplorable condition imaginable, environed in the deepest darkness."—*New Cyclopaedia of Anecdote.*

CHAPTER 73

# HEART DISEASE

*"Their heart is divided; now shall they be found faulty"*
(Hosea 10:2).

Israel, as a nation, divided its allegiance between Jehovah and Baal, and so became good for nothing, and was given up to captivity.

God has made one heart in man, and the attempt to have two, or to divide the one, is in every case injurious to man's life.

A Church divided into parties, or differing in doctrine, becomes heretical, or contentious, or weak and useless.

A Christian, aiming to another object besides his Lord's glory, is sure to spend a poor, unprofitable life. He is an idolater, and his entire character will be faulty.

A seeker after Christ will never find Him while his heart is hankering after sinful pleasures, or self-righteous confidences: his search is too faulty to be successful.

A minister, aiming at something else besides his one object, whether it be fame, learning, philosophy, rhetoric or gain, will prove to be a very faulty servant of God.

In any case this heart-disease is a dire malady. A broken heart is a blessing; but a divided heart is a mortal malady.

I. THE DISEASE. "Their heart is divided."
This evil is to be seen—
1. In their idea of their state: they say they are "miserable sinners," but they believe themselves to be exceedingly respectable.
2. In the ground of their trust: they profess faith in Christ, and yet they rely upon self; they try to mix grace and works.
3. In the aim of their life: God and mammon, Christ and Belial, heaven and the world.
4. In the object of their love. It is Jesus and some earthly love. They cannot say "Jesus only."

II. THE EVIL EFFECT OF IT. "Now shall they be found faulty."
1. God is not loved at all when not wholly loved.
2. Christ is insulted when a rival is admitted.
3. The life limps and halts when it has not a whole heart behind it.

III. ATTEMPTS AT A CURE.
1. That he condemns himself by yielding so much of his heart to God. Why any if not all? Why go this way at all, if not all the way?

2. That his salvation will require all his thought and heart; for it is no trifling matter. (Matt. 11:12; I Peter 4:18).

3. That Jesus gave His whole heart to our redemption, and therefore it is not consistent for us to be half-hearted.

4. That all potent beings in the universe are undivided in heart.
   Bad men are eager for their pleasure, gains, etc.
   The devil works evil with his whole power.
   Good men are zealous for Christ.

Read, hear, pray, repent, believe with your whole heart, and you shall soon rejoice with all your heart.

A minister in Brooklyn was recently called upon by a business man, who said to him, "I come, sir, to enquire if Jesus Christ will take me into the concern as a sleeping partner." "Why do you ask?" said the minister. "Because I wish to be a member of the firm, and do not wish anybody to know it." The reply was: "Christ takes no sleeping partners."

Some talk that the devil hath a cloven foot; but whatever the devil's foot be, to be sure his sons have a cloven heart; one half for God, the other half for sin; one half for Christ, the other half for this present world. God hath a corner in it, and the rest is for sin and the devil.—RICHARD ALLEINE.

As to the evil of being neither one thing nor the other, one finds an illustration in the water-ways of Southern China, which in wintertime are quite useless for purposes of commerce. The temperature is most tantalizing, for it is neither cold enough to freeze the canals, so that the ice would be able to bear traffic; nor warm enough to thaw them, so that they could be navigable by boats.

## CHAPTER 74

## THE STROKE OF THE CLOCK

*"Sow to yourselves in righteousness, reap in mercy, break up your fallow ground: for it is time to seek the Lord, till He come and rain righteousness upon you"* (Hosea 10:12).

What should we think of a farmer who allowed his finest field to lie fallow year after year? Yet men neglect their souls; and besides being unprofitable, these inward fields become full of weeds, and exceedingly foul.

I. WHEN IS IT TIME? "It is time."

1. In the very first hour of responsibility it is none too soon.
2. At the present it is late, but not too late. "It is time."
3. When chastening has come, seek the Lord instantly; for now it is high time, "lest a worse thing come unto thee:" (John 5:14).
4. Have you not sinned long enough? (I Peter 4:3).
5. When you assume great responsibilities, and enter on a new stage of life:—married, made a master, a father, etc. (I Chron. 22:19).
6. When God's Spirit is specially at work, and therefore others are saved. (Acts 3:19).

II. WHAT IS THE PECULIAR WORK? "to seek the Lord."

1. To draw nigh unto God; seeking Him in worship, prayer, etc. (Ps. 105:4).
2. To ask pardon at His hands through the atonement of Jesus. (Isa. 55:6).
3. To obtain the blessings connected with the new birth. (John 1:12, 13).
4. To live for His glory: seeking His honor in all things. (Matt. 6:33).

Suppose a pause between the seeking and the blessing, do not look in some other direction, but seek the Lord still.

What else can you do? (John 6:68).

It is sure to come. He will come, and will not tarry. (Heb. 10:37).

III. WHAT WILL COME OF IT?

1. He will come. God's coming in grace is all you need.
2. He will come in abundance of grace meeting your obedient sowing. Mark the precept, "Sow in righteousness."
   Then note the promise, "and rain righteousness upon you."
3. In consequence of the Lord's coming to you in righteousness, you shall "reap in mercy."

Come then, and seek the Lord at this very hour! If thou wouldst find Him, He is in Christ. Believe, and thou hast found Him, and righteousness in Him. (Rom. 3:22).

Sir Thomas More, whilst he was a prisoner in the Tower, would not so much as suffer himself to be trimmed, saying that there was a controversy betwixt the king and him for his head, and till that was at a happy end, he would be at no cost about it.

Let us but scum off the froth of his wit, and we may make a solemn use of it; for certainly all the cost we bestow upon ourselves, to make our lives pleasurable and joyous to us, is but mere folly, till it be decided what will become of the suit betwixt God and us, what will be the issue of the controversy that God hath against us, and that not for our heads, but for our souls, whether for heaven or hell. Were it not, then, the wisest course to begin with making our peace; and then we may the sooner lead a happy life?

It is said, "He who gets out of debt grows rich." Most sure it is that the pardoned soul cannot be poor; for as soon as peace is concluded, a free trade is opened between God and the soul. If once pardoned, we may then sail to any port that lies in God's dominions, and be welcome. All the promises stand open with their treasures, and say, "Here, poor soul, take in full lading of all precious things, even as much as thy faith can bear and carry away!"—JOHN SPENCER.

A little maiden stood trembling, weeping, timidly knocking at the door of a minister's library. "Come in," said a cheerful voice. The door handle slowly turned, and there she stood, sobbing with emotion. "What is the matter, my dear child?" said the sympathetic pastor. "Oh, sir," was the reply, "I have lived seven years without Jesus!" She had just been celebrating her seventh birthday.—*The British Messenger*.

THOMAS FULLER says, "God invites many with His golden sceptre whom He never bruises with His rod of iron." If the invitations of His grace were more freely accepted, we should often escape the chastisements of His hand.

Oh, that men did but know that a time of health, and happiness, and prosperity is as fit a season as can be for seeking the Lord! Indeed, any hour is a good time in which to seek the Lord, so long as it is present with us. He who would be wise will find no better day in the calendar for casting away folly than that which is now with him.

But let no man trifle with time, for in an instant the die may be cast, and then it is written concerning the ungodly, "I also will laugh at your calamity, and mock when your fear cometh" (Prov. 1:26).

## CHAPTER 75

## INWARD MORE THAN OUTWARD

*"Rend your heart and not your garments, and turn unto the Lord your God"* (Joel 2:13).

I. THE GENERAL DOCTRINE THAT TRUE RELIGION IS MORE INWARD THAN OUTWARD.

The expression "Rend your heart, and not your garments," casts somewhat of a slur upon the merely outward.

1. This respects forms and ceremonies of men's devising.
2. It bears also upon ordinances of God's own ordaining if practiced without grace, and relied upon as of themselves effectual.

Among good things which may become unprofitable we may mention—

The reading of Holy Scripture.

The holding of an orthodox creed.

The attendance upon sacraments.

All these things should have their place in our lives: but they do not prove saintship: since a sinner may practice them all, after a sort. The absence of a true heart will make them all vain.

## II. The Further Doctrine That Man Is More Inclined To the Outward Observance Than To Inward Matters.

Man is thus partial to externals—

1. Because he is not spiritual, but carnal by nature.
2. Because the inward is more difficult than the outward, and requires thought, diligence, care, humiliation, etc.
3. Because he loves his sin. He will rend his robes, for they are not himself; but to rend off his beloved sins is like tearing out his eyes.
4. Because he cares not to submit to God. Law and gospel are both distasteful to him; he loves nothing which necessitates the obedience of his heart to God.

Many throng the outer courts of religious observance who shun the holy place of repentance, faith and consecration.

## III. The Particular Doctrine That Heart-Rending Is Better Than Any External Act Of Piety.

1. Heart-rending should be understood. It is—
   To have the heart broken, contrite, tender, sensitive.
   To have the heart grieving over past evils.
   To have the heart rent away from sin, as by holy violence.
   The sight of sin should rend the heart, especially when it is seen by the light of the cross.
2. Heart-rending should be practised. "Rend your hearts."
   This would need a great tug. Can a man rend himself?
   This drives us to look to a higher power.
   This is met only by Jesus. Looking to Him Whom we have pierced, our hearts are rent.
   This, when fully done, leaves us at His feet. Who alone "healeth the broken in heart, and bindeth up their wounds."

An old Hebrew story tells how a poor creature came one day to the Temple, from a sick bed, on tottering limbs. He was ashamed to come, for he was very poor, and he had no sacrifice to offer; but as he drew near he heard the choir chanting, "Thou desirest not sacrifice; else would I give it: Thou delightest not in burnt offerings. The sacrifices of God are a broken spirit: a broken and contrite heart, O God, thou wilt not despise."

Other worshipers came, pressed before him, and offered their sacrifices; but he had none. At length he prostrated himself before the priest, who said, "What wilt thou, my son? Hast thou no offering?" And he replied, "No, my father, for last night a poor widow and her children came to me, and I had nothing to offer them but the two pigeons which were ready for the sacrifice." "Bring, then," said the priest, "an ephah of fine flour." "Nay, but, my father," said the old man, "this day my sickness and poverty have left only enough for my own starving children; I have not even an ephah of flour." "Why, then, art thou come to me?" said the priest. "Because I heard them singing, 'The sacrifices of God are a broken spirit.' Will not God accept my sacrifice if I say, 'Lord, be merciful to me, a sinner?' "

Then the priest lifted the old man from the ground, and he said, "Yes, thou art blessed, my son; it is the offering which is better than thousands of rivers of oil."—*"The World of Proverb and Parable," by* E. PAXTON HOOD.

If this hypocrisy, this resting in outward performances, was so odious to God under the law, a religion full of shadows and ceremonies, certainly it will be much more odious under the gospel, a religion of much more simplicity, and exacting so much the more sincerity of heart, even because it disburdens the outward man of the performances of legal rights and observances.

And therefore, if we now, under the gospel, shall think to delude God Almighty, as Michael did Saul, with an idol handsomely dressed instead of the true David, we shall one day find that we have not mocked God, but ourselves; and that our portion among hypocrites shall be greater than theirs.—WILLIAM CHILLINGWORTH.

As garments to a body, so are ceremonies to religion. Garments on a living body preserve the natural warmth; put them on a dead body and they will never fetch life. Ceremonies help to increase devotion; but in a dead heart they cannot breed it. These garments of religion upon a holy man are like Christ's garments on His own holy body; but joined with a profane heart, they are like Christ's garments on His crucifying murderers.—RALPH BROWNRIG.

CHAPTER 76

# THE PLUMBLINE

*"Thus He shewed me: and behold, the Lord stood upon a wall made by a plumbline, with a plumbline in His hand"* (Amos 7:7).

The metaphors of Amos are very forcible, though homely and simple.

The Lord continues to use the same infallible rule: wherever He is, He has a plumbline in His hand.

## I. A PLUMBLINE IS USED IN BUILDING.

In all that we build up, we must act by the sure rule of righteousness.

1. In God's building it is so.
   He removes the old walls when tested by the plumbline, and found faulty. Truth requires the removal of falsehood.
   He builds in truth and reality.
   He builds in holiness and purity.

2. In our own life-building it should be so.
   Not haste, but truth should be our object.
   Not according to the eye of man, but according to fact.
   We should build by the Word; in God's sight; after Christ's example; by the Spirit, unto holiness.

3. In our building of the church it should be so.
   Teaching the Scriptures only in all things.
   Preaching nothing but the gospel.
   Laying sinners low by the law, and exalting the grace of God.
   Leading men to holiness and peace by the doctrines of truth.
   Exercising discipline that the church may be pure.

## II. A PLUMBLINE IS USED FOR TESTING.

1. We may use it—
   On the wall of self-righteousness, conceit, boasting, etc.
   On the wall of careless living.
   On the wall of trust in ceremonials.

2. God uses it in this life.

3. He will use it at the last.

4. Let us use it on ourselves.

## III. A PLUMBLINE WILL BE USED FOR DESTROYING.

1. Even the saved will be saved justly through our Lord Jesus, and in their case every sin will be destroyed, and every trace of evil will be removed before they enter heaven.

2. Not a pain will be inflicted unjustly.
   Knowledge or ignorance will increase or abate the number of stripes (Luke 12:47, 48).

3. Rejectors of Christ will find their doom intolerable, because they, themselves, will be unable to deny its justice. (Luke 19:27). The lost know their misery to be deserved.

4. Since every sentence will be infallible, there will be no revision. So impartial and just will be each verdict that it shall stand for ever (Matt. 25:46).

The question, "What is truth?" was proposed at a Deaf and Dumb Institution, when one of the boys drew a straight line. "And what is falsehood?" The answer was a crooked line.—G. B. Bowes.

Whitefield often affirmed that he would rather have a church with ten men in it right with God, than one with five hundred at whom the world would laugh up its sleeve.—Joseph Cook.

Livingstone, as a missionary, was anxious to avoid a large church of nominal adherents. "Nothing," he wrote, "will induce me to form an impure church. 'Fifty added to the church' sounds well at home, but if only five of these are genuine, what will it profit in the Great Day?"—Blaikie.

Sinners on earth are always punished less, and in hell never more, than their iniquities deserve.—Benjamin Beddome.

## Chapter 77

## SELF-DECEIVED

> *"The pride of thine heart hath deceived thee"* (Obadiah 1:3).

This is true of all proud persons, for pride is self-deceit.
There may be proud persons in this congregation.
Those who are sure that they have no pride are probably the proudest of all. Those who are proud of their humility are proud indeed.

I. THEY WERE DECEIVED.
   1. As to the estimate formed of them by others. They thought themselves to be had in honor, but the prophet says,—"Thou art greatly despised." (See verse 2).

   2. As to their personal security. They felt safe, but were near their doom. (verses 3 and 4).

3. As to their personal wisdom. They talked of "The wise man out of Edom" (verse 8); but the Lord said, "There is none understanding in him" (verse 7).

4. As to the value of their confidences. Edom relied on alliances, but these utterly failed. "The men that were at peace with thee have deceived thee" (verse 7). Rich relatives, influential friends, tried allies—all will fail those who trust in them.

## II. THEIR OWN PRIDE DECEIVED THEM.

1. In each of the points mentioned above, pride lay at the bottom of their error.

2. In every way pride lays a man open to being deceived.
His judgment is perverted by it: he cannot hold the scales.
His standard is rendered inaccurate: his weights are false.
His desires invite flattery, and his folly accepts it.

## III. THIS PRIDE LED THEM INTO EVIL WAYS.

1. They were full of defiance. "Who shall bring me down to the ground?"

2. They were destitute of compassion. "Thou stoodest on the other side." (See verses 9-12). Pride is stony-hearted.

3. They even shared in oppression. (See verses 13 and 14).

4. They showed contempt of holy things. "Ye have drunk upon my holy mountain" (verse 16).

## IV. THESE EVIL WAYS SECURED THEIR RUIN.

1. Their defiance brought enemies upon them.

2. Their contempt of God made him say, "there shall not be any remaining of the house of Esau" (verse 18).

Hating all pride, let us humbly rest in Him.

If a man is a perfectionist, and thinks he is sinless, it is proof not that he is better, but only that he is blinder, than his neighbors.—RICHARD GLOVER.

Adam thought that the fair apple should make him like his Maker, but God resisted his pride, and that apple made him like the serpent that tempted him with it. Absalom thought that rebellion would make him a king, but God resisted his pride, and his rebellion hanged him on a tree.—HENRY SMITH.

The Venetian ambassador wrote of Cardinal Wolsey:—"I do perceive that every year he groweth more and more in power." When I first came to England, he used to say, "His Majesty will do so and so"; subsequently, he said, "We shall do so and so"; but now he says, "I shall do so and so." But history records how Wolsey's pride went before destruction, and his haughty spirit before a fall.

Napoleon Bonaparte, intoxicated with success, and at the height of his power, said, "I make circumstances." Let Moscow, Elba, Waterloo, and St. Helena, that rocky isle where he was caged until he fretted his life away, testify to his utter helplessness in his humiliating downfall.—J. B. GOUGH.

As God hath two dwelling-places, heaven and a contrite heart, so hath the devil—hell and a proud heart.—T. WATSON.

CHAPTER 78

# THE NINEVITES' REPENTANCE

*"And Jonah began to enter into the city a day's journey, and he cried, and said, Yet forty days, and Nineveh shall be overthrown"* (Jonah 3:4).

*"The men of Nineveh shall rise in judgment with this generation, and shall condemn it: because they repented at the preaching of Jonas; and, behold, a greater than Jonas is here"* (Matthew 12:41).

Our Lord never lost patience with an audience, and never brought railing accusation against any man: His rebuke was well deserved.

The men of Nineveh repented, and turned to God, and yet—

## I. THEIR CALLS TO REPENTANCE WERE NOT MANY.

Many unbelievers have been warned and entreated times without number, and yet they remain impenitent; but—

Nineveh enjoyed no privileges: it was in heathen darkness.

Nineveh heard but one prophet; and he was none of the greatest, or most affectionate.

Nineveh heard that prophet only once; and that was an open-air sermon, very short, and very monotonous.

Nineveh had heard no word of good tidings; she heard the thunder of the law, but nothing else.

Yet the obedience to the warning was immediate, universal, practical, and acceptable, so that the city was spared.

## II. THE MESSAGE OF THE PROPHET WAS NOT ENCOURAGING.

1. He proclaimed no promise of pardon.
2. He did not even mention repentance; and consequently he held out no hope to the penitent.
3. He foretold a crushing and final doom: "Nineveh shall be overthrown." His message began and ended with threatening.
4. He mentioned a speedy day: "yet forty days."

Yet out of this dreadful message the people made a gospel, and so acted as on it to find deliverance; while to many of us the rich, free, sure promise of the Lord has been of no force through our unbelief.

## III. THE PROPHET HIMSELF WAS NO HELPER TO THEIR HOPE.

Jonah was no loving, tender pastor, anxious to gather the lost sheep.

1. He disliked the ministry in which he was engaged, and no doubt discharged it in a hard, harsh manner.
2. He uttered no word of sympathetic love, for he had none in his heart. He was of the school of Elijah, and knew not the love which burned in the heart of Jesus.
3. He offered no prayer of loving pity.
4. He was even displeased that the city was spared.

Yet these people obeyed his voice, and obtained mercy through hearkening to his warnings. Does not this rebuke many who have been favored with tender and loving admonitions? Certainly it rebuked those who lived in our Lord's day, for no two persons could afford a more singular contrast than Jonah and our Lord.

Indeed, a "greater," better, tenderer than Jonah was there.

## IV. THE HOPE TO WHICH THE NINEVITES COULD REACH WAS BUT SLENDER.

It was no more than—"Who can tell?"

1. They had no revelation of the character of the God of Israel.
2. They knew nothing of an atoning sacrifice.
3. They had received no invitation to seek the Lord, not even a command to repent.
4. Their argument was mainly negative.
   Nothing was said against their repenting.
   They could not be the worse for repenting.
5. The positive argument was slender.
   The mission of the prophet was a warning: even a warning implies a degree of mercy; they ventured upon that bare hope, saying, "Who can tell!"

Have we not all at least this much hope?

Have we not far more in the gospel?

Will we not venture upon it?

God warns before He wounds, frights before He fights. "Yet forty days, and Nineveh shall be overthrown." Oh, let us fall down before the Lord our Maker! Then shall His anger be pleased to make in us a daily pass-over, and His bullets leveled at us must fly above us.—THOMAS FULLER.

"I have heard," says Mr. Daniel Wilson, in a sermon of his, "of a certain person whose name I could mention, who was tempted to conclude his day over, and himself lost; that, therefore, it was his best course to put an end to his life, which, if continued, would serve to increase his sin, and consequently his misery, from which there was no escape; and seeing he must be in hell, the sooner he was there the sooner he should know the worst; which was preferable to his being worn away with the tormenting expectation of what was to come.

"Under the influence of such suggestions as these, he went to a river, with a design to throw himself in; but as he was about to do it, he seemed to hear a voice saying to him, 'Who can tell?' as if the words had been audibly delivered. By this therefore, he was brought to a stand; his thoughts were arrested, and thus began to work on the passage mention: 'Who can tell? (Jonah 3:9) viz., What God can do when He will proclaim His grace glorious. Who can tell but such an one as I may find mercy? or what will be the issue of humble prayer to heaven for it? Who can tell what purposes God will serve in my recovery?'

"By such thoughts as these, being so far influenced as to resolve to try, it pleased God graciously to enable him, through all his doubts and fears, to throw himself by faith on Jesus Christ, as able to save to the uttermost all that come to God by Him, humbly desiring and expecting mercy for His sake, to his own soul. In this he was not disappointed, but afterwards became an eminent Christian and minister: and, from his own experience of the riches of grace, was greatly useful to the conversion and comfort of others."—*Religious and Moral Anecdotes.*

## CHAPTER 79

## THE WORST OF ENEMIES

*"Even of late my people is risen up as an enemy"* (Micah 2:8).

When men are in trouble they are apt to blame God.

The Lord here answers Israel's complaint of Him by a deeply truthful complaint of them.

I. LET US LISTEN TO THE GRIEVOUS CHARGE.

There is a deep pathos about this as coming from the God of love.

1. They were His own people. "My people." God has enemies enough without His own beloved ones becoming such. It is horrible ingratitude and treachery for the chosen to rebel.

2. They had risen up "as an enemy." Faithless **friends** wound keenly, and are often more bitter than other **antagonists**. For favored ones to rise up as foes is cruel indeed.

3. They had lately done this: "even of late,"—"yesterday," in the margin. The sin is fresh, the wound is bleeding, the offence is rank. A fit of wilfulness was on them.

4. They had done this wantonly. (See latter part of verse). They picked a quarrel with One Who is "averse from war." God would have our love, yet we turn against Him without cause.

## II. LET US HEAR THE MORE GRIEVOUS EVIDENCE BY WHICH THE CHARGE IS SUBSTANTIATED.

Taking the words "my people" as referring to all professing Christians, many of them "rise up as an enemy" from the fact of—

1. Their separation from their Lord. "He that is not with Me is against Me:" (Matt. 12:30).

2. Their worldliness. By this the Lord's jealousy is moved, for the world is set up as His rival in the heart. "The friendship of the world is enmity with God" (James 4:4).

3. Their unbelief, which stabs at His honor, His veracity, His immutability (I John 1:10).

4. Their heresies, fighting against His revealed truth. It is wretched work when the church and its ministers oppose the gospel.

5. Their unholiness. Unholy professors are, par excellence, "the enemies of the cross of Christ" (Phil. 3:18).

6. Their lukewarmness: by which they sicken their Savior (Rev. 3:16), grieve His Spirit (Eph. 4:30), encourage sinners in sin (Ezek. 16:54), and discourage seekers.

## III. LET US HEARKEN TO MOST GRIEVOUS WARNINGS.

No good can possibly come of opposition to the Lord; but the most painful evils will inevitably ensue.

1. In the case of true Christians, there will come to them heavy chastisements and humiliations. (Lev. 26:23, 24).

2. With these will come the keenest regrets, and agonies of heart.

3. In the case of mere professors, there will soon come abandonment of profession, immorality, sevenfold wickedness, etc.

The sins of the wicked pierce Christ's side, but the sins of the godly plunge the spear into His heart.

Carlyle, speaking of the changes made by time, says, "How tragic to me is the sight of old friends; a thing I always really shrink from!" Sin has made still more painful changes in some once numbered amongst the friends of God.

Pharnaces, the son of Mithridates, the king of Pontus, sending a crown to Cæsar at the time he was in rebellion against him, he refused the present, saying, "Let him first lay down his rebellion, and then I will receive his crown." There are many who set a crown of glory upon the head of Christ by a good profession, and yet plant a crown of thorns upon His head by an evil conversation.—SECKER.

After poor Sabat, an Arabian, who had professed faith in Christ by the means of the labors of the Rev. W. Martyn, had apostatized from Christianity, and written in favor of Mohammedanism, he was met at Malacca by the late Rev. Dr. Milne, who proposed to him some very pointed questions, in reply to which he said, "I am unhappy! I have a mountain of burning sand upon my head. When I go about, I know not what I am doing!" It is indeed an evil thing and bitter to forsake the Lord our God.—*Bate's Cyclopaedia.*

## CHAPTER 80

## THE LORD'S APPEAL TO HIS OWN PEOPLE

*"O my people, what have I done unto thee? And wherein have I wearied thee? Testify against Me"* (Micah 6:3).

Far be it from us to trifle when God has a controversy with us, for to Him it is a matter of deep solemnity. In condescending grace He makes much of the affection of His people, and He will not lose it without effort.

I. A PITEOUS EXCLAMATION. "O my people!"

Is it not remarkable that such language should be used by the Eternal God?

1. It is the voice of solemn earnestness.
2. It is the cry of sorrow. The interjection is wet with tears.
3. It is the appeal of love. Love injured, but living, pleading, striving, entreating.
4. It is the language of desire. Divine love yearns for the reconciliation of the rebel: it pines to have his loyal affection.

II. A PAINFUL FACT. "Wearied thee."

Israel acted as if they were tired of their God.

1. They were weary of His name. Baal and Ashtaroth had become the fashion, and the living God was despised.

2. They were weary of His worship. The sacrifice, the priest, the holy place, prayer, praise, etc., all these were despised.

3. They were weary of obedience to His laws, though they were right, and just, and meant for their good.

4. They were weary of His restraints: they desired liberty to ruin themselves by transgression.

III. A PATIENT ENQUIRY. "What have I done unto thee?" etc.

Amazing love! God Himself puts Himself upon trial.

1. What single act of God could induce us to forsake His way? "What have I done unto thee?"

2. What continuous way of the Lord could have caused us weariness? "Wherein have I wearied thee?"

3. What testimony of any kind can we bear against God? "Testify against me."

If wearied with our God, it is—
Because of our foolish waywardness.
Because of our fickle fancy
Because of our feeble love to Himself and holiness.

Now there is one thing to which we need to call the attention of backsliders; and that is,—that the Lord never forsook them; but that they forsook Him! The Lord never left them; but they left Him! And this, too, without a cause.

Love does not like to be forgotten. You mothers would break your hearts if your children left you, and never wrote you a word, or sent any memento of their affection for you; and God pleads over backsliders as a parent over loved ones who have gone astray and He tries to woo them back. He asks, "What have I done that you should have forsaken Me?" The most tender and loving words to be found in the whole of our Bible are from Jehovah to those who have left Him without a cause.—D. L. MOODY.

Let those tempted to depart from the Lord remember the answer of Christian to Appollyon, when the latter sought to persuade him to turn back, and forsake his Lord: "O thou destroying Appollyon, to speak truth, I like his service, his wages, his servants, his government, his company, and country, better than thine; and, therefore, leave off to persuade me further: I am His servant and I will follow Him."

Polycarp, being required by an infidel judge to blaspheme Christ, made him this witty and devout answer: "Eighty-six years have I lived, neither did He once harm me in any one thing; why, then, should I blaspheme my God, which hath neither hindered me nor injured me?"

CHAPTER 81

# THE STRONGHOLD

*"The Lord is good, a stronghold in the day of trouble;
and He knoweth them that trust in Him"* (Nahum 1:7).

Here we come upon an island in Nahum's stormy lake. All is calm
in this verse, though the whole contest is tossed with tempest.

The text is full of God, and brims over with His praise.

I. GOD HIMSELF. "Jehovah is good."

1. Good; in Himself essentially and independently.
2. Good; eternally and unchangeably.
3. Good in all His acts of grace.
4. Good in His present act, be it what it may.

Whoever else may or may not be good, we know that the Lord
is good (Matt. 19:17).

II. GOD TO US. "A stronghold in the day of trouble."

1. Under special circumstances our resort.
   The day of trouble, when trial is special and vehement.
   The day of trouble: temporary, but yet long enough to last
   through our life unless the Lord prevent.
   The day of trouble: when within, without, around, there seem
   to be only care, and fear, and want, and grief.
2. Maintaining our peace.
3. Defying our foes, who dare not attack such a fortress.
4. Abiding forever the same: always a sure refuge for the needy.

III. GOD WITH US. "He knoweth them that trust in Him."

1. His tender care to supply all their necessities.
2. His loving communion with them, which is the best proof
   that they are known to Him, and are His beloved friends.
3. His open acknowledgment: He owns them now, and will confess them before assembled worlds. (Rev. 3:5).

When we were in the Yosemite Valley, lately, our driver told us
of a series of terrific earthquakes, which visited the valley several
years ago. The few inhabitants who dwelt there were thrown out
of their beds in the night. Frail cottages were overturned. Loose
rocks were hurled down from the precipice into the valley. These
shocks were repeated for several days until the people were panic-
stricken and ready to despair.

"What did you do?" we inquired. The driver (pointing to the
mighty and immovable rock, El Capitan, which rises for three thousand feet on the south side of the valley, and has a base of three
solid miles) replied: "We determined to go and camp under old

Capitan; for if that ever moved we knew the world would be coming to an end."—DR. CUYLER.

Tamar may disguise herself, and walk in an unaccustomed path, so that Judah may not know her; Isaac, through the dimness of his sight, may bless Jacob, and pass over Esau; want of time may make Joseph forget, or be forgotten of, his brethren; Solomon may doubt to whom of right the child belongeth; and Christ may come to His own, and not be received: but the Lord knoweth them that are His, and His eye is always over them.

Time, place, speech, or apparel cannot obscure or darken His eye or ear. He can discern Daniel in the den; and Job, though never so much changed, on the dung-hill. Let Jonah be lodged in the whale's belly, Peter be put into a close prison, or Lazarus be wrapped in rags, or Abel rolled in blood, yet can He call them by name, and send His angels to comfort them. Ignorance and forgetfulness may cause love and knowledge to be estranged in the creature, but the Lord is not incident to either, for His eye, as His essence, is everywhere; He knoweth all things.—SPENCER'S *"Things New and Old."*

Many talk of trusting God when indeed they know nothing of real faith. How are we to know who is, and who is not, a believer? This question is hard to answer in times of prosperity, but not in the day of trouble: then the true truster is calm and quiet in his God, and the mere pretender is at his wit's end. Our text seems to hint as much. Everybody can find a bird's nest in winter when the trees are bare, but the green leaves hide them; so are believers discovered by adversity.

One thing, however, should never be forgotten: whether we know believers or not, God knows them. He does not include one hypocrite in the number, nor exclude one sincere truster, even though he be of little faith. He knows infallibly and universally. Does He know me, even me, as one of those who trust in Him? The Lord knoweth them that are His, and they know Him as their stronghold. Have I such knowledge?

## CHAPTER 82
## PRIDE THE DESTROYER

*"Behold, his soul which is lifted up is not upright in him: but the just shall live by his faith"* (Habakkuk 2:4).

Delay of deliverance is a weighing of men.

Suspense is very trying, and constitutes a searching test.

This divides men into two classes by bringing out their real character.

The proud and the just stand out in relief; the uplifted and the upright are far as the poles asunder; and the result of trial in the two cases is as different as death from life.

The tarrying of the promise—

## I. REVEALS A GREAT FAULT. "His soul which is lifted up."

The man is impatient, and will not endure to wait. This is pride full-blown, for it quarrels with the Lord, and dares to dictate to Him.

1. It is very natural to us to be proud. So fell our first father, and we inherit his fault.
2. Pride takes many shapes, and among the rest this vainglorious habit of thinking that we ought to be waited on at once.
3. In all cases pride is unreasonable. Who are we that God should make Himself our servant, and take His time from our watch.

## II. DISCOVERS A SERIOUS OPPOSITION.

He grows tired of the gospel, which is the sum of the promises, and he becomes averse to the exercise of the faith which it requires.

His pride makes him reject salvation by grace, through faith in Jesus.

1. He is too great to consider it.
2. He is too wise to believe it.
3. He is too good to need it.
4. He is too advanced in "culture" to endure it.

## III. DIRECTS US TO A PLEASING CONTRAST.

1. The man who is really just is truly humble.
2. Being humble, he does not dare to doubt his God, but yields to His Word an implicit faith.
3. His faith keeps him alive under trial, and conducts him into the joys and privileges of spiritual life.
4. His life conquers the trial, and develops into life eternal.

As the first step heavenward is humility, so the first step hellward is pride. Pride counts the gospel foolishness, but the gospel always shows pride to be so. Shall the sinner be proud who is going to hell? Shall the saint be proud who is newly saved from it? God had rather His people fared poorly than lived proudly.—MASON.

Poverty of spirit is the bag into which Christ puts the riches of His grace.—ROWLAND HILL.

We must be emptied of self before we can be filled with grace; we must be stripped of our rags before we can be clothed with righteousness; we must be unclothed that we may be clothed; wounded, that we may be healed; killed, that we may be made alive; buried in disgrace, that we may rise in holy glory. These words, "Sown in corruption, that we may be raised in incorruption; sown in dishonor, that we may be raised in glory; sown in weakness, that we may be raised in power," are as true of the soul as of the body.

To borrow an illustration from the surgeon's art: the bone that is set wrong must be broken again, in order that it may be set aright. I press this truth on your attention. It is certain that a soul filled with self has no room for God; and like the inn at Bethlehem, crowded with meaner guests, a heart preoccupied by pride and her godless train, has no chamber within which Christ may be born in us "the hope of glory."—GUTHRIE.

But for pride, the angels who are in hell should be in heaven (Jude 6); but for pride, Nebuchadnezzar, who is in the forest, should be in his palace (Daniel 4); but for pride, Pharaoh, who lies with the fishes, should be with his nobles (Exodus 14); no sin hath pulled so many down as this, which promised to set them up.

Of all the children of pride, the Pope is the father, which sitteth in the temple of God and is worshipped as God (II Thess. 2:4) ... But for pride, the Pharisees would have received Christ as gently as His disciples; but for pride, Herod would have worshipped Christ as humbly as the shepherds.

CHAPTER 83

# FAITH: LIFE

Habakkuk 2:4.  Romans 1:17.  Galatians 3:11.  Hebrews 10:38.

When the Spirit of God frequently repeats Himself, He thereby appeals for special attention.

A doctrine so often declared must be of first importance.

A doctrine so often declared should be constantly preached.

A doctrine so often declared should be unhesitatingly received by each one of our hearers.

I. WE WILL TREAT THE FOUR TEXTS AS ONE.

The teaching is clear. "The just shall live by his faith."

1. Life is received by the faith which makes a man just.

A man begins to live by a full acquittal from condemnation, and from penal death, so soon as he believes in Jesus. A man begins to live as one raised out of spiritual death so soon as he has faith in the Lord Jesus Christ.

2. Life is sustained by the faith which keeps a man just.

He who is forgiven and quickened lives ever afterwards as he began to live—namely, by faith.

He lives by faith in every condition,—

In joy and in sorrow; in wealth and in poverty;

In strength and in weakness; in laboring and in languishing; in life and in death.

He lives best when faith is at its best, even though in other respects he may be sorely put to it. He lives the life of Christ most blessedly when most intensely he believes in Christ.

## II. WE WILL TREAT THE FOUR TEXTS SEPARATELY.

If we read with precision, we shall see that Scripture contains no repetitions. The context gives freshness of meaning to each apparent repetition.

1. Our first text (Hab. 2:4) exhibits faith as enabling a man to live on in peace and humility, while as yet the promise has not come to its maturity. While waiting we live by faith, and not by sight.

   We are thus able to bear up under the temporary triumphs of the wicked.

   We are thus preserved from proud impatience at delay.

2. Our second text (Rom. 1:17) exhibits faith as working salvation from the evil which is in the world through lust. The chapter in which it stands presents an awful view of human nature, and implies that only faith in the gospel can bring us life in the form of—

   Mental enlightenment of life as to the true God: (Rom. 1:19-23).

   Moral purity of life: (Rom. 1 verse 24, and onward).

3. Our third text (Gal. 3:11) exhibits faith as bringing to us that justification which saves us from the sentence of death. Nothing can be plainer, more positive, more sweeping than this declaration that no man is justified before God except by faith. Both the negative and the positive are plain enough.

4. Our fourth text (Heb. 10:38) exhibits faith as the life of final perseverance.

   There is need of faith while waiting for heaven (verses 32-36). The absence of such faith would cause us to draw back (verse 38).

   That drawing back would be a fatal sign.

   That drawing back can never occur, for faith saves the soul from all hazards, keeping its face heavenwards even to the end.

What can you do who have no faith?

In what other way can you be accepted with God?

On what ground can you excuse your unbelief in your God?

Will you perish sooner than believe Him?

The Jews in the Talmud have the saying, "The whole law was given to Moses at Sinai, in six hundred and thirteen precepts." David, in the fifteenth Psalm, brings them all within the compass of eleven. Isaiah brings them to six (Isaiah 33:15); Micah to three (Micah 6:8); Isaiah, again, to two (Isaiah 56); Habakkuk to this one, "The just shall live by his faith."—LIGHTFOOT.

The soul is the life of the body. Faith is the life of the soul. Christ is the life of faith.—FLAVEL.

> Inscribed upon the portal from afar
> Conspicuous as the brightness of a star,
> Legible only by the light they give
> Stand the soul-quickening words
>        *—Believe and Live.*

To believe God is not a little thing; it is the index of a heart reconciled to God, and the token of true spirituality of mind; it is the essence of true worship, and the root of sincere obedience. He who believes his God in spite of his sins, does him more honor than cherubim and seraphim in their continual adoration.

A little thing faith! How is it then that unbelief is so great a crime that it is marked out for reprobation as the one damning evil which shuts men out of heaven? Whatever else you put in the second place, give faith the lead; it is not a vain thing, for it is your life.

## CHAPTER 84

## MAY BE

> *"Seek ye the Lord, all ye meek of the earth, which have wrought His judgment; seek righteousness, seek meekness: it may be ye shall be hid in the day of the Lord's anger"* (Zephaniah 2:3).

In spiritual things we may draw encouragement from the faintest sign of hope when it proceeds from God: "it may be ye shall be hid."

The seeking for refuge, here commanded, is directed only to the meek and righteous; but it is our joy to proclaim a hiding-place for the guilty, and to bid them seek the Lord even on the least encouragement.

I. IN MANY A RECORDED INSTANCE "MAY BE" HAS PROMPTED AND JUSTIFIED A RIGHT ACTION.

1. A "may be" led Jonathan to attack the garrison of the Philistines. (I Sam. 14:6). This should nerve saints for holy enterprises.
2. A "may be" cheered David when Absalom rebelled, and Shimei cursed. (II Sam. 16:12). Let us hope in God in our darkest hours.
3. A "may be" induced the lepers to visit the Syrian camp. (II Kings 7:4).
4. A "may be," in the form of "Who can tell?" brought all Nineveh to repentence. (Jonah 3:9).

If we fly to Jesus by childlike faith, there is more than a "may be" that the result will be happy.

II. IN THE INSTANCE OF A SINCERE SEEKER THE "MAY BE" IS OF UNUSUAL STRENGTH.

There is every probability of the penitent obtaining salvation if we—

1. Consider the gracious nature of our God. (Micah 7:18).
2. Consider the glorious work of Christ for sinners. (I Tim. 1:15).
3. Consider the number and character of those who have been saved. (Rev. 5:9; 7:9; I Cor. 6:11).
4. Consider the Omnipotence of the Holy Spirit. (John 3:8).

III. BUT IN THE SEEKER'S CASE HE HAS FAR MORE TO GO UPON THAN A MERE "MAY BE."

There are innumerable sure promises in the Word of God, and these are made to—

Repentance. (Prov. 28:13; Isa. 55:7).

Faith. (Mark 16:16; John 3:18; Acts 16:31).

Prayer. (Matt. 7:7; Acts 2:21).

Let these promises be studies, and their encouragement accepted by immediate compliance with their requirements.

Consider that God foresaw all events when He made these promises, and accordingly He has not made them in error.

Consider that He is the same as when He made the promise, and so in effect makes it again every day.

Dr. John Duncan was once heard thus addressing a beggar-woman in Edinburgh: "Now, you'll promise me that you'll seek: but mind, seeking will not save you, yet it is your duty; and if you seek you'll find, and finding will save you."

Our hope is not hung upon such untwisted thread as "I imagine so"; or, "it is likely"; but the cable, the strong rope of our fastened anchor, is the oath and promise of Him Who is eternal verity; our salvation is fastened with God's own hand, and Christ's own strength, to the strong stake of God's unchanging nature.—RUTHERFORD.

How long a beggar will wait, and how eagerly he will plead, although he has no promise of an alms, but only the bare chance of winning a penny from a passer-by! How laboriously will fishers cast their nets again and again, though nothing has been taken as yet, and their only encouragement is the possibility that fish may come that way! How desperately will men dive into the sea with the expectation of finding pearls in oyster-shells, encountering fierce monsters of the deep with the uncertain hope of being enriched.

And will not men draw near to God when their outlook is so much more bright, their expectation so much more justifiable? As for me, I will lay down my sick soul at Christ's feet, in sure and certain belief that He will heal me, and then I will follow Him whithersoever He goeth, in calm assurance that He will lead me to His eternal kingdom and glory.—C. H. S.

CHAPTER 85

## DEFILED AND DEFILING

*"Then said Haggai, If one that is unclean by a dead body touch any of these, shall it be unclean? And the priests answered and said, It shall be unclean.*
*"Then answered Haggai, and said, So is this people, and so is this nation before Me, saith the Lord; and so is every work of these hands; and that which they offer there is unclean"* (Haggai 2:13, 14).

The prophet makes the priests witness against themselves and the people. This was a powerful means of forcing home the truth.

What a picture! An unclean person making everything unclean wherever he laid his hand! He could not move without spreading defilement on all sides.

Such were the erring people of Haggai's day in the judgment of their God, and He never judges too severely.

Such are sinful men at this day.

I. THE TERRIBLE UNCLEANNESS. Here we keep to our text.

1. Common things are polluted by men of unclean nature.
   By making gods of them, saying, "What shall we eat?" etc.
   By excess in the use of them. By gluttony, drunkenness, etc.
   By excess in the keeping of them. A miser's goods are accursed.

2. **Holy** things are polluted by men of unclean nature.
   They use the gospel as an excuse for sin.
   They offer prayer in solemn mockery.
   They make praise into a musical performance.
   They turn the sacraments into hypocrisy or worse.
3. **Good works** are polluted when they come from evil men: "so is every work of their hands."
   They can be charitable for ostentation.
   They can be religious to be seen of men.
   They can be sternly righteous in order to be revenged.
   They can be humble to gain their ends.

Sin has cast a serpent's trail over the whole universe, making the creation itself subject to vanity. What does man touch which he does not degrade and pollute? Here is a wide field for thought, and abundant cause for humiliation.

II. THE ALL-SUFFICIENT REMEDY. Here we go beyond our text.
1. There was a sacrifice (Num. 19:2-4; Heb. 9:22).
2. There was a burning: (verses 5 and 6). Sin is hateful, and we must see it to be such; it must be burned without the camp.
3. There was a water of separation.
4. There was an application with hyssop. Faith must receive the cleansing. "Purge me with hyssop, and I shall be clean."

See, O sinner, your need of cleansing before you attempt anything. Before this, nothing you are, or have, or do, is clean before God. After this, all things shall be holy to you.

See to this cleansing at once, and all else will follow in due course.

"My friends say everywhere that I am not a Christian. I have just given them the lie direct by performing my Easter devotions (*mes paques*) publicly, thus proving to all my lively desire to terminate my long career in the religion in which I was born, and I have fulfilled this important act after a dozen attacks of consecutive fever, which made me fear I should die before I could assure you of my respect and my devotion."—VOLTAIRE, *to Madame du Barri.* (What a specimen of polluted holy things!)

Diogenes, standing beside a foul bath, was heard to exclaim, "Where shall those be washed who wash here?" When even the religious duties of men are defiled, what hope can they have making themselves clean? Those who turn prayer into a mockery, and sacraments into a show, have turned medicine into poison; and how shall they be healed?

A child has taken an infectious disease. He comes to fondle you, and you push him away. He moves the furniture, and you command him to take his hands off. He must be shut up, and kept from contact with the household.

Suppose he persists in leaving his room, and joining with the rest of the family. No matter how kind his motive, he is doing wrong and acting mischievously. The more industriously he works about the house, and runs to and fro, the more does he spread the disorder. The household work which he does would be well enough if he were but in health: as it is, his every movement is a danger, and his best endeavors are perilous.

The child must be healed before he can do real good in the family: while he is infected he pollutes all that he touches, and injures all whom he approaches.

Oh, that unconverted men were wise enough to see that what they need, at first, is not so much work to do, as cleansing from pollution, in order that they may be able to do good works.

At one of the Ragged-schools in Ireland, a clergyman asked the question, "What is holiness?" After some pause, a poor Irish convert, in dirty, tattered rags, jumped up, and said, "Plaise your Riverence, it's to be clane inside."—G. S. Bowes.

## Chapter 86
## SMALL THINGS NOT TO BE DESPISED

*"For who hath despised the day of small things!"* (Zechariah 4:10).

Great numbers of persons do despise "the day of small things."
It is usually God's way to begin His great works with a day of small things.

Thus it is seen that there is nothing in the means themselves.

Thus the divine power is more fully displayed.

Thus faith is exercised, and made to learn many lessons.

Why should men despise what God ordains?

They show their contempt in various ways.

They affect pity for such feebleness (Nehemiah 4:2).

They decry and find fault (I Sam. 17:28).

They sneer, and ridicule (Matt. 13:55; Acts 17:18).

I. Those Who Despise Others Who Are In the Day of Small Things.

1. Do you not know that there are babes in grace, and that these are true children of God? Do you doubt that evident fact?
2. Were you not once such little ones yourselves?
   If you never were, who are you to despise your betters?
3. Were not the greatest of the saints once very feeble?
   Would you have acted thus to them?
4. Does not our Lord care tenderly for the lambs? (Isa. 40:11).

## II. THOSE WHO DESPISE THE DAY OF SMALL THINGS IN THEMSELVES.

1. They will frequently fail to notice and nurture thoughts and feelings which would lead them to Christ.
2. They cannot believe that salvation can come by ordinary means, or through their present knowledge and emotions: these are too small in their esteem, they crave for signs and wonders.
3. If they would nurture their weak desires, and feeble resolves, and faint beliefs, and trembling hopes, good would come of them.
4. No doubt many think ill of their own condition when God thinks well of them. They judge that little faith, and little life and little strength are useless; but the Lord thinks not so.

## III. THOSE WHO DO NOT DESPISE THE DAY OF SMALL THINGS.

1. Hopeful pastors. We are looking out for gracious signs and are more apt to be misled by our sanguine hopes than to fall into the opposite fault of despising the day of small things.
2. Anxious parents. They long to see buds of grace in their children. The smallest signs of spiritual life would charm them.
3. Wise soul-winners. They rejoice to see "first the blade."
4. Jesus Himself. He loves the little ones (Mark 10:14).

Come ye to Him, all ye trembling souls!

When the boy began to draw portraits upon his slate, and to sketch with charcoal, the great artist was in him in embryo. It was not every eye that could perceive his budding genius, but he who did so, and encouraged the youth to pursue art as his vocation, found a life-long satisfaction in having helped him.

Had he sneered at the young draughts-man he would have lived to see his folly; but now he takes pleasure in every triumph of the renowned painter. Some such joy, only of a higher and more spiritual order, will be yours if you stimulate early piety, and teach the tender heart the way to peace and holiness.

To repress desires which are heavenward, because they are attended with something of childishness, is wicked cruelty: prune the vine of its wild shoots, but do not uproot it. Foster and nurture even the tiniest sign of grace. "Destroy it not; for a blessing is in it" (Isa. 65:8).

One afternoon, I noticed a young lady at the service, whom I knew to be a Sunday School teacher. After the service, I asked her where her class was. "Oh," said she, "I went to the school, and found only a little boy, and so I came away." "Only a little boy!" said I; "think of the value of one such soul! the fires of a Reformation may be slumbering in that tow-headed boy; there may be a young Knox, or a Wesley, or a Whitefield in your class."—D. L. MOODY.

The moss is but a very little plant, yet when its seeds fall on deep, swampy, treacherous morasses, they grow up, and bind the ground together with such bands that it becomes quite safe to pass over,—building, in fact, a broad and durable bridge. "Throughout creation the grandest and most complicated ends are obtained by the employment of the simplest means."—JAMES NEIL, *in "Rays from the Realms of Nature."*

CHAPTER 87

## PRISONERS OF HOPE

*"As for thee also, by the blood of thy covenant I have sent forth thy prisoners out of the pit wherein is no water. Turn you to the stronghold, ye prisoners of hope: even today do I declare that I will render double unto thee"* (Zechariah 9:11, 12).

This is a wonderful text for those who are in the lowest possible state of mind. May the Lord make it a blessing to them!

I. CONDITION OF THE SORROWING ONES. "Prisoners in the pit wherein is no water."

1. Prisoners: bound, freedom gone.
2. Prisoners in a pit: escape impossible, darkness intolerable, fate unavoidable, present discomfort terrible.
3. Prisoners in a pit wherein is no water: comfortless, and likely to perish of thirst. Comfort in sin is deadly: the absence of that comfort is hopeful.

II. CAUSE OF THEIR DELIVERANCE. "I have sent forth thy prisoners."

1. The Lord Omniscient spies them out in their dungeon, and He knows whose prisoners they are.
2. He has the power and the right to set free prisoners. Who can shut up those whom He delivers?
3. He sends them forth by "the blood."
   By the expiation made for sin before God.
   By the peace created in the conscience of the penitent.

Let a soul once know the blessedness of "the covenant," and the sealing power of "the blood," and it is a prisoner no longer.

III. COURSE COMMENDED TO THE DELIVERED ONES. "Turn you to the stronghold, ye prisoners of hope."
1. To make hope their characteristic. When they feel like prisoners, let them hope, and so become "prisoners of hope."
2. To make Christ their Stronghold.
3. To turn to Him every day, and all the day.
4. To turn to Him specially when they feel like prisoners.

IV. COMFORT GIVEN TO THOSE WHO TURN TO THE STRONGHOLD. "Even today do I declare that I will render double unto thee."
1. God is speedy in His comforts to those who turn to Jesus. "Even today do I declare."
2. God is abundant in His mercy: "I will render double unto thee."
The double of your trouble (Job 13:10).
The double of your expectation (Isa. 61:7).
The double of your attainments: "grace for grace" (John 1:16).
The double of your largest faith (Eph. 3:20).
3. God is consoling in His promise; for it is:
Plain: "I declare."
Present: "Even today do I declare."
Positive: "I will declare that I will."
Personal: "I will render unto thee."

With what gratitude and joy should these intimations of hope be received by those who are naturally in so miserable a condition! It is a celebrated story that, when Titus Flaminius, at the public games, proclaimed the liberty of Greece, after it had been conquered by the Romans the auditors were at first lost in a silent amazement, and then burst out into one continued shout for two hours together, "Liberty! Liberty!"

Methinks such joy, and greater than this, should appear amongst miserable sinners when these proclamations for liberty are made. And are they not now made? Have I not been telling you, from the Word of God, that though you were condemned under the righteous sentence of the law, through a Redeemer that sentence may be reversed, your souls may be restored to life and happiness? Have I not been proving that, though Satan held you in a dark captivity, yet by the law of the great Redeemer you may be rescued from his hands, and made more than conquerors through Him?

Have I not told you that, notwithstanding the painful and the fruitless struggle which you have hitherto had with the feebleness and corruptions of a depraved nature, you may still receive those communications of the Spirit which will purify and strengthen you, and enable you to perfect holiness in the fear of God? . . . Prisoners of hope, will you despair?—DR. DODDRIDGE, *Sermon on this text.*

CHAPTER 88

# SPIRITUAL CONVALESCENCE

*"And I will strengthen them in the Lord; and they shall walk up and down in His Name, saith the Lord"* **(Zechariah 10:12).**

They are so much forgotten, and so often persecuted, and so generally despised, that we do well to think upon the prophecies of a glorious future, which the Lord God has spoken concerning His chosen people.

But the heritage of the natural and typical Israel belongs, in its spiritual meaning, to the spiritual Israel; and this promise is ours.

I. DIVINE STRENGTHENING PROMISED. "I will strengthen them in the Lord."

1. It is painfully needed.
   We are naturally weak as water.
   In the presence of great labors we feel our weakness.
   We want strength for watching, walking, working, and warring.

2. It is freely promised. See also verse 6.
   Justice might have left us to ourselves.
   Tender love observes our need.
   Infinite power abundantly supplies it.

3. It is divinely bestowed: "I will strengthen them."
   Hence it is—Certain in accomplishment.

4. It is gradually received. We go from strength to strength.
   By use of the means of grace: prayer, communion with God, spiritual exercise, experience, etc.

5. It is delightfully perceived.
   An excellent illustration is that of a sick man recovering strength.
   As in his case, so in ours,—
   Appetite returns: we relish the Word.
   Difficulties vanish: burdens grow light, etc.
   Employment is desired: strength pines for exercise.

II. CHRISTIAN ACTIVITY PREDICTED. "They shall walk up and down in His Name."

1. They shall enjoy ease,—implied in walking up and down.
2. They shall possess freedom: it is the gait of liberty.

3. They shall persevere in such activity walking up and down; and evermore crying joyously, "Onward and Upward!"

4. They shall consecrate that activity with care: "They shall walk in His Name,"—doing all in the name of the Lord Jesus.

III. BOTH BLESSINGS GUARANTEED.

1. Here is the divine "I will" of Omnipotent grace.

2. Here is the divine "they shall" of consecrated free-agency.

3. Here is the divine "saith the Lord" of infallible faithfulness.

Sir Walter Scott relates in his autobiography that when he was a child, one of his legs was paralyzed and when medical skill failed, a kind uncle induced him to exert the muscles of the powerless limb by drawing a gold watch before him on the floor, tempting him to creep after it, and thus keeping up and gradually increasing vital and muscular force.

So God deals with us in our spiritual childhood, and the weakness of our faith. How weak our efforts; how slow our movements! But spiritual vitality is elicited, developed, strengthened by those efforts and movements slow and weak as they are.

Lack of strength is more serious than lack of any kind of outward possession. A weak rich man is in a far worse position than a strong poor man; and the strong poor man is really the wealthier. Weakness lessens work, reduces enjoyment, and greatly aggravates suffering of any kind.

In many instances, moreover, it is the cause of wickedness,— leading directly to transgression, and exposing the individual to fierce and exceedingly dangerous temptations. So that, as a means of preserving ourselves against sin, we should ask daily for strength.

Every man needs strength; but no man has within him strength to the demands that are made upon him. He requires strengthening.

The Christian is no exception to this rule. He needs strength. His conversion was not translation to inactivity, to ease and to unbroken quiet. His work is not the ceaseless singing of psalms while he reclines upon green pastures, and sits beside still waters. There are times when he lies down in green pastures; but he lies down wearied; and he lies down that he may rise again a stronger man, to enter upon fiercer battles, and to do harder work. We rest, not for resting's sake, but that we may work again.—SAMUEL MARTIN.

CHAPTER 89

# MOURNING AT THE CROSS

*"And I will pour upon the house of David, and upon the inhabitants of Jerusalem, the spirit of grace and of supplications: and they shall look upon Me Whom they have pierced, and they shall mourn for Him, as one mourneth for his only son, and shall be in bitterness for Him, as one that is in bitterness for his firstborn"* (Zechariah 12:10).

Note the remarkable change of persons: "look upon me," and "mourn for him." Such changes indicate unity and distinctiveness; and afford us a hint as to the Unity of the Godhead, and the Trinity of the Persons.

He Who speaks is Jehovah "which stretcheth forth the heavens," (see verse 1) and yet He says "Me, whom they have pierced."

It is Jehovah-Jesus Who is pierced, and pours out the Spirit of grace.

It is a marvel that Jesus should be crucified when the Jewish law required stoning; and that, when crucified, the Roman soldier, though ignorant of the prophecy, should pierce Him with his spear.

Evangelical sorrow for sin is to be our subject at this time.

I. IT IS CREATED BY THE HOLY SPIRIT, "the spirit of grace and supplications."

1. It is not produced by mere conscience, nor by terror, nor by the use of a form of penitence; much less by music, pictures, etc.

2. It comes as a gift of grace: "I will pour." The understanding is enlightened, the heart renewed, etc., by a distinct act of the Spirit of God, sent forth by the Father.

3. It is attended by prayer: "grace and of supplications." In this differing from remorse, which never prays.

II. IT IS CAUSED BY LOOKING TO JESUS. "They shall look upon Me, Whom they have pierced."

It cannot, therefore, prepare for that look: we look to Jesus as we are, and the look makes penitents of us.

1. We see the horrible hatred which sin bears toward purity, for it slew the Holy One, and that when He was arrayed in the most lovely and attractive form.

2. We see its ingratitude to love. Sin repays infinite compassion with inveterate hate, and therefore crucifies Jesus.

3. We see its abhorrence of God. It would slay Him if it could, and it did so in effect. Sin is Deicidal in intent and tendency.

4. We see that such is the terrible guilt of our sin that nothing but an infinite sacrifice could atone for it.

III. IT IS THE CHIEF OF SORROWS. "They shall mourn for Him, as one mourneth for his only son."

1. Comparable to a terrible parental agony, for an only son, or for a first-born child: both very special sources of grief.

2. It is personal and private. (See verses 12 to 14).

3. It is spreading and social. "The land shall mourn" (vs. 12).

IV. IT IS NOT IN ITSELF A CLEANSING FOR SIN.

By it we confess the crime, but cannot thereby remove it. Conviction is a glass to show our spots, not a bath to cleanse them.

1. It acknowledges our need of the fountain; but it is not itself a fountain of cleansing.

2. It goes with the saving look to Jesus, but it is no rival to it.

3. It leads away from self and even from its own self.

4. It leads to Jesus: we mourn for Him; and this linking us with Jesus is most operative upon our hearts.

Come, bleeding heart, and look to Jesus for healing!

Come, hard heart, and look to Jesus for brokenness!

Come, careless heart, for the sight of Jesus may arrest even thee!

## CHAPTER 90
## APART

*Zechariah 12:12-14.*

True repentance is attended with mourning. It may not in itself be sorrow, but a repentance which did not include sorrow for sin would be a mere pretence. It is a change of mind, and that change involves sorrow for the past.

We have need to stand in doubt of that repentance which hath no tear in its eye, no mourning in its heart.

I. THE INDIVIDUALIZING EFFECT OF SORROW FOR SIN. Observe the many times in which we here have the word "apart."

1. It is seen even when that mourning is universal. "The land shall mourn, every family apart." The widest spread of grace will not diminish its power over each separate person.

2. It is seen in the distinction between family and family even when both fear the Lord.
The royal family.
The prophet's family.
The priest's family.
The ordinary family.
The family of Shimei apart.

## II. How Does This Individuality Show Itself?

1. Each individual sees most his own sin: he is alone as to character.
2. Each individual desires to be alone as to place. No matter where whether at the bed-side, or in the field, or in the barn: but solitude is desired, and must be obtained.
3. Each individual has his own time. At once the penitent must mourn, whether it be morning, noon, or night: he cannot be timed by regulation.
4. Each individual has his own manner. Some are silent; others cry aloud. One weeps, another cannot literally do so, and it is all the more sad. One feels broken in heart, another laments his hardness, etc.
5. Each individual has his own secret. None can enter into it even if they would do so. Each mourner has a secret hidden away in his own soul, and he cannot reveal it to men.

## III. How Do You Account for This Individuality?

1. In part it is accounted for by a natural and justifiable shame, which prevents our confessing all our sins before another.
2. The heart desires to come to God Himself, and the presence of a third person would be an interruption.
3. The man is conscious that his guilt was all his own, and as he dissociates everyone else from it, he instinctively comes to God apart, and solely on his own account.
4. This is the sign of sincerity. Sham piety talks about religion as national, and delights to display itself as national, and delights to display itself in the assembly or in the street; true godliness is of the heart, and being "in spirit and in truth," it is deeply personal.

Realize the fact that you must die apart, and, in a sense, be judged, and sentenced apart. Never forget your own individuality. You must have Christ for yourself, and be born again yourself, or you are lost.

Let the question of eternity have a monopoly on you. It is an intensely personal question; but instead of making you selfish, it will expand your heart. He who has never felt for his own soul cannot feel for another's.—Brownlow North.

The question "Guilty?" or "Not Guilty?" must be put to each prisoner separately, and each one must answer to his name and put in his personal plea. Should a pardon be granted, it must bear the individual's name, and it must be issued distinctly to him, or it will be a document of no value to him. In every case, the guilt and the pardon must have a personal bearing: but how hard it is to make a man see this!

Oh, that we could preach in the "thousand-thee" style, and could make each hearer feel that we were as personal as Nathan when he said, "Thou art the man!" If our hearers will not cry, "Lord, is it I?" we must go to them with the word, "I have a message from God unto thee."

## CHAPTER 91

# LOVE QUESTIONED AND VINDICATED

*"I have loved you, saith the Lord. Yet ye say, Wherein hast Thou loved us?"* (Malachi 1:2).

I. GOD'S LOVE DECLARED. "I have loved you, saith the Lord."

To every believer this love has been shown in—
1. Election in Christ Jesus from of old.
2. Pardon of sin, justification by faith, adoption, sanctification, etc.
3. Preservation to this hour, and promise for all future time.

This is a scanty list of the ways by which the Lord has said to each regenerate soul, "I have loved you."

II. GOD'S LOVE QUESTIONED. "Yet ye say, Wherein hast Thou loved us?"

Such a question has been asked—
1. Under great afflictions in which there seemed no relief. Petulantly the sorrowing one has questioned divine love.
2. In sight of the prosperous wicked in their day of pride many a poor despised believer has rashly doubted the special love of God.
3. In times of grievous doubt as to one's personal salvation, and under heavy temptations of Satan, the same doubt has arisen.

III. GOD'S LOVE CONSIDERED.
1. Love lamenting. Is God to be thus treated?
   Shall He mournfully cry, "I have loved you? Yet ye say, Wherein hast Thou loved us?"

2. Love entreating. Does not each accent say, "Return to Me"?
3. Love abounding. Our question shames us. God loves us in ten thousand ways; loves us so as to be patient even when we wickedly question His love.

If it would be marvellous to see one river leap up from the earth full-grown, what would it be to gaze upon a vast spring from which all the rivers of the earth should at once come bubbling up, a thousand of them born at a birth? What a vision would it be! Who can conceive it? And yet the love of God is that fountain, from which all the rivers of mercy, which have ever gladdened our race—all the rivers of grace in time, and of glory hereafter—take their rise. My soul, stand thou at that sacred fountainhead, and adore and magnify for ever and ever God, even our Father, Who hath loved us.—C. H. S.

## CHAPTER 92

## SUNSHINE

*"But unto you that fear My Name shall the sun of righteousness arise with healing in his wings; and ye shall go forth, and grow up as calves of the stall"* (Malachi 4:2).

There is one grand distinction among men—"Him that serveth God, and him that serveth him not."

Fearing God is the mark which distinguishes man from man far more than wealth, rank or nationality.

The coming of Christ is a calamity or a blessing to men according to their character.

What a change of figures! To the wicked "an oven!" (see verse 1). To God-fearing men a "Sun"!

I. LET US THINK OF OUR LORD AS THE SUN.

1. He is the Center of the whole system of grace.
2. He is to us the Grand Attraction, and Holdfast, keeping us in our places, as the sun keeps the planets in their orbits.
3. He is without variableness or shadow of turning. (James 1:17). In Himself He is for ever the same, shining on without ceasing.
4. To us He has His risings, and His settings. If for a while we are in the shade, let us look for His arising.

What the world would be without the sun, that should we be without our Lord. Can we conceive the gloom, the death, etc.?

II. LET US ENJOY THE BLESSINGS WHICH HE SCATTERS.

1. What light of knowledge, what warmth of love, what radiance of joy we receive from Him! Let us walk in it.

2. What health He gives! Healing for the sick, health for the strong.
3. What liberty He brings! "Ye shall go forth."
   When the sun has reached a certain point in its annual course, the cattle which have been stalled are led forth to the mountain pastures; so the Lord Jesus sets His people free, and they go forth.
4. What growth He fosters!—"and grow up as calves of the stall." A heart which communes with Jesus possesses a freshness of youth, an ease of life, and other advantages, which admirably fulfil the comparison of "calves of the stall."

We have not to make a Sun, or move the Sun, or buy the Sun; but only to step into the free and blessed sunshine. Why do we hesitate?

Why do we not by faith pass from darkness into His marvelous light?

There is a beautiful fable of the ancient mythology, to the effect that Apollo, who represents the sun, killed a huge poisonous serpent by arrows surely aimed, and shot from afar. It intimates that sunbeams, darted straight from heaven, destroy many deadly things that crawl upon the ground, and so make the world a safer habitation.

The parable is, in this respect, a stroke of truth, and it coincides with a feature of the eternal covenant. Light from the face of Jesus, when it is permitted to stream right into a human heart, destroys the noisome things that haunt it, as Apollo's arrows slew the snake. —W. ARNOT.

A man scoffingly asked, "What advantage has a religious man over any one like myself? Does not the sun shine on me as on him?" "Yes," replied his companion, a pious laborer, "but the religious man has two suns shining on him at once,—one on his body, the other on his soul"—*The Biblical Treasury.*

CHAPTER 93

SONSHIP QUESTIONED

*"If Thou be the Son of God"* (Matt. 4:3).

There is no sin in being tempted (Heb. 4:15).
Temptation does not necessitate sinning.
It may be needful for us to be tempted—
    For test. Sincerity, faith, love, patience, are thus put to proof.
    For usefulness. We become able to comfort and warn others.
Solitude will not prevent temptation.

It may even aid it. Jesus was tempted in the wilderness.
Nor will fasting and prayer always keep off the tempter; for
these had been fully used by our Lord.

Satan knows how to write prefaces: our text is one.

He began the whole series of his temptations by a doubt cast
upon our Lord's Sonship, and a crafty quotation from Scripture.

I. THE TEMPTER ASSAILS WITH AN "IF."

1. Not with point-blank denial. That would be too startling.
   Doubt serves the Satanic purpose better than heresy.
2. He ifs a plain Scripture. "Thou art my Son" (Ps. 2:7).
3. He ifs a whole life. From the first Jesus had been about His
   Father's business; yet after thirty years His Sonship is
   questioned.

II. THE TEMPTER AIMS THE "IF" AT A VITAL PART.

1. At our sonship.
   In our Lord's case he attacks his human and divine Sonship.
   In our case he would make us doubt our regeneration.
2. At our Father's honor. He tempts us to doubt our Father's
   providence, and to blame Him for letting us hunger.

III. THE TEMPTER SUPPORTS THAT "IF" WITH CIRCUMSTANCES.

1. You are alone. Would a Father desert His child?
2. You are in a desert. Is this the place for God's Heir?
3. You are with the wild beasts. Wretched company for a Son
   of God!
4. You are an hungered. How can a loving Father let His perfect
   Son hunger?

Put all these together, and the tempter's question comes home
with awful force to one who is hungry, and alone.

When we see others thus tried, do we think them brethren? Do
we not question their sonship, as Job's friends questioned him?
What wonder if we question ourselves!

IV. WHEN OVERCOME, THE TEMPTER'S "IF" IS HELPFUL.

1. As coming from Satan, it is a certificate of our true descent.
   He only questions *truth:* therefore we are true sons.
   He only leads *sons* to doubt their sonship; therefore we are sons.
2. It takes the sting out of man's questionings and suspicions; for
   if we have answered the devil we do not fear men.
3. As past, it is usually the prelude to angels coming and minis-
   tering to us, as in our Lord's case. No calm is so deep as
   that which follows a great storm. (Mark 4:39).

How different is the use which Jesus makes of this word "if" in those lessons of Divine instruction and heavenly consolation, which He so frequently delivered to His disciples when He was on earth! He always employed it to inspire confidence; never to excite distrust. Take a single instance of this:—"If God so clothe the grass of the field, which today is, and tomorrow is cast into the oven, shall He not much more clothe you, O ye of little faith?" What a contrast between this divine remonstrance and the malicious insinuation of the great enemy of God and man!—DANIEL BAGOT.

God had but one Son without corruption, but He had none without temptation. Such is Satan's enmity to the Father, that the nearer and dearer any child is to Him, the more will Satan trouble him, and vex him with temptations. None so well-beloved as Christ; none so much tempted as He.—THOMAS BROOKS.

Oh, this word "if"! Oh, that I could tear it out of my heart! O thou poison of all my pleasures! Thou cold icy hand, that touchest me so often, and freezest me with the touch! "If!" "If!"—ROBERT ROBINSON.

CHAPTER 94

## THE MAKING OF MEN-CATCHERS

*"And He said unto them, Follow Me, and I will make you fishers of men"* (Matthew 4:19).

Conversion is most fully displayed when it leads converts to seek the conversion of others: we most truly follow Christ when we become fishers of men.

I. SOMETHING TO BE DONE BY US. "FOLLOW ME."
  1. We must be separated to Him that we may pursue His object. We cannot follow Him unless we leave others (Matthew 6:24).
  2. We must abide with Him, that we may catch His spirit.
  3. We must obey Him that we may learn His method.
     Teach what He taught (Matthew 28:20).
     Teach as He taught (Matthew 11:29; I Thess. 2:7).
     Teach such as He taught, namely, the poor, the base, children, etc.

II. SOMETHING TO BE DONE BY HIM. "I WILL MAKE YOU."
  1. By our following Jesus He works conviction and conversion in men; He uses our example as a means to this end.
  2. By His Spirit He qualifies us to reach men.
  3. By His secret working on men's hearts He speeds us in our work.

III. A FIGURE INSTRUCTING US. "FISHERS OF MEN."

The man who saves souls is like a fisher upon the sea.

1. A fisher is dependent and trustful.
2. He is diligent and persevering.
3. He is intelligent and watchful.
4. He is laborious and self-denying.
5. He is daring, and is not afraid to venture upon a dangerous sea.
6. He is successful. He is no fisher who never catches anything.

I love your meetings for prayer, you cannot have too many of them: but we must work while we pray, and pray while we work. I would rather see a man, who has been saved from the gulf below, casting life lines to others struggling in the maelstrom of death, than on his knees on that rock thanking God for his own deliverance; because I believe God will accept action for others as the highest possible expression of gratitude that a saved soul can offer.—THOMAS GUTHRIE.

The minister is a fisherman. As such he must fit himself for his employment. If some fish will bite only by day, he must fish by day; if others will bite only by moonlight, he must fish for them by moonlight.—RICHARD CECIL.

I watched an old man trout-fishing the other day, pulling them out one after another briskly. "You manage it cleverly, old friend," I said: "I have passed a good many below who don't seem to be doing anything." The old man lifted himself up and stuck his rod in the ground. "Well, you see, Sir, there be three rules for trout-fishing, and 'tis no good trying if you don't mind them. The first is, Keep yourself out of sight; and the second is, Keep yourself farther out of sight; and the third is, Keep yourself farther still out of sight. Then you'll do it." "Good for catching men, too," thought I.—MARK GUY PEARSE.

## CHAPTER 95
## THE DISOWNED

*"Not every one that saith unto Me"* (Matthew 7:21-23).

One of the best tests of everything is how it will appear in the moment of death, in the morning of resurrection, and at the day of judgment. Our Lord gives us a picture of persons as they will appear "in that day."

## I. THEY WENT A LONG WAY IN RELIGION.

1. They made an open profession. They said, "Lord, Lord."
2. They undertook Christian service, and that of a high class.
3. They had obtained remarkable success.
4. They were noted for their practical energy.
5. They were diligently orthodox.
   They did everything in the name of Christ. The words "Thy name" are mentioned three times.

## II. THEY KEPT IT UP A LONG TIME.

1. They were not silenced by men.
2. They were not openly disowned by the Lord Himself during life.
3. They expected to enter the Kingdom, and they clung to that false hope to the last. They dared to say, "Lord, Lord," to Christ Himself, at the last.

## III. THEY WERE FATALLY MISTAKEN.

1. They prophesied, but did not pray.
2. They cast out devils, but the devil was not cast out of them.
3. They attended to marvels, but not to essentials.
4. They wrought wonders, but were also workers of iniquity.

## IV. THEY FOUND IT OUT IN A TERRIBLE WAY.

1. The solemnity of what He said. "I never knew you." He had been omitted from their religion. What an oversight!
2. The terror of what it implied: they must depart from all hope, and continue forever to depart.
3. The awful truth of what He said. They were utter strangers to His heart. He had not chosen them, nor communed with them nor approved them, nor cared for them.
4. The solemn fixedness of what He said. His sentence would never be recalled, altered, or ended. It stood, "depart from Me."

In many simple works God is more seen than in wonderful works. The Pharisee at heaven's gate says, "Lord, I have done many wonderful works in Thy Name"; but, alas! has he ever made the Lord's Name wonderful?—T. T. LYNCH.

I knew you well enough for "black sheep," or, rather, for reprobate goats: I knew you for hirelings and hypocrites, but I never knew you with a special knowledge of love, delight, and complacency. I never acknowledged, approved, and accepted of your persons and performances. (See Psalm 1:6; Romans 11:2).—JOHN TRAPP.

Not "I once knew you, but cannot own you now"; but "I *never* knew you;—as real penitents, suppliants for pardon, humble believers, true followers."—E. R. CONDER.

Note our Lord's open confession before men and angels, and specially to the men themselves—"I never knew you." I knew about you; I knew that you professed great things; but you had no acquaintance with Me; and whatever you knew about Me, you did not know *Me*. I was not of your company and did not know you. Had He once known them, He would not have forgotten them.

Those who accept His invitation, "Come unto Me," shall never hear Him say, "Depart from Me."—C. H. S.

"Depart *from me*,"—a fearful sentence, a terrible separation. "From me," saith Christ, that made Myself man for your sakes, that offered My Blood for your redemption. "From Me," that invited you to mercy, and ye would not accept it. "From Me," that purchased a kingdom of glory for such as believed on Me, and have resolved to honor their heads with crowns of eternal joy. "Depart from Me:" from My friendship, My fellowship, My paradise, My presence, My heaven.—THOMAS ADAMS.

## CHAPTER 96

## "A MAN NAMED MATTHEW"

*"And as Jesus passed forth from thence, He saw a man, named Matthew sitting at the receipt of custom: and He saith unto him, Follow Me. And he arose, and followed Him"* (Matthew 9:9).

Matthew is here writing about himself. Note his modesty in the expression—"a man, named Matthew," and his omission of the fact that the feast mentioned in verse 10 was held in his own house.

The story is placed immediately after a miracle, as if to hint that Matthew's conversion was a miracle.

There are points of similarity between the miracle and the conversion.

Matthew was spiritually palsied by his sin, and his money-making; hence he needed the divine command, "Arise, and walk."

I. HIS CALL SEEMED ACCIDENTAL AND UNLIKELY.

1. Jesus had often been at Capernaum, which He had selected to be "His own city"; and yet Matthew remained unsaved. Was it likely that he would now be called? Had not his day of grace closed? Jesus was about other business; for we read, "as Jesus passed forth from thence." Would He now be likely to call Matthew? "He saw a man, named Matthew," for He foresaw him. He knew him, for He foreknew him.

In all of which there is a parallel between Matthew and ourselves.

## II. HIS CALL WAS ALTOGETHER UNTHOUGHT OF AND UNSOUGHT.

1. He was in a degrading business. None but the lowest of the Jews would care to gather taxes for the Roman conqueror. His discipleship would bring no honor to the Lord Jesus.
2. He would not have dared to follow Jesus even if he had wished to do so. He felt himself to be too unworthy.
3. He would have been repulsed by the other disciples had he proposed to come without the Lord's open invitation.
4. The call was of pure grace, as it is written, "I am found of them that sought Me not."

## III. HIS CALL WAS GIVEN BY THE LORD, WITH FULL KNOWLEDGE OF HIM.

1. He saw all the evil that had been in him, and was yet there.
2. He saw in him His chosen, His redeemed, His convert, His disciple, His apostle, His biographer.

The Lord calls as He pleases, but He sees what He is doing. Sovereignty is not blind: but acts with boundless wisdom.

## IV. HIS CALL WAS SUBLIMELY SIMPLE.

1. Few were the words: "Follow Me."
   It is very tersely recorded, "He saw ... He saith ... he arose."
2. Clear was the direction: "Follow Me."
3. Personal was the address: "He saith *unto him.*"
4. Royal was the command: "He saith."

## V. HIS CALL WAS IMMEDIATELY EFFECTUAL.

1. Matthew followed at once. "He arose and followed Him."
2. He followed wholly: bringing his voice and his pen with him.
3. He followed ever after, never deserting his Leader.

## VI. HIS CALL WAS A DOOR OF HOPE FOR OTHERS.

1. His salvation encouraged other publicans to come to Jesus.
2. His open house gave opportunity to his friends to hear Jesus.
3. His personal ministry brought others to the Savior.
4. His written gospel has convinced many, and will always do so.

Are *you* up to your neck in business? Are you "sitting at the receipt of custom"? Yet may a call come to you at once. It does come. Hear it attentively, rise earnestly, and respond immediately.

An old writer says: "Our calling is uncertain in respect of place, for God calls some from their ships, and some from their shops; some from under the hedges, and others from the market; so that, if a man can but make out unto his own soul that he is certainly called, the time when and the place where, matter little."

How I now loved those words that spake of a Christian's calling!
As when the Lord said to one, "Follow Me"; and to another, "Come
after Me." Oh! I thought, that He would say so to me: how gladly
would I run after Him! I could seldom read of any that Christ did
call, but I presently wished, "Would I had been in their clothes!
Would I had been born Peter, or John!" I often thought, "Would I
had heard Him when He called *them,* how would I have cried, 'O Lord,
call me also!'" But I feared He would not call me.—JOHN BUNYAN.

We read in classic story how the lyre of Orpheus enchanted with
its music, not only the wild beasts, but the very trees and rocks upon
Olympus, so that they moved from their places to follow him; so
Christ, our heavenly Orpheus, with the music of His gracious speech,
draws after Him those less susceptible to benign influences than
beasts and trees and stones even poor, hardened, senseless, sinful
souls. Let Him but strike His golden harp and whisper in thy heart,
"Come, follow Me," and thou, like another Matthew, shalt be won.

## CHAPTER 97

## LEARNING IN PRIVATE WHAT TO TEACH IN PUBLIC

> *"What I tell you in darkness, that speak ye in light: and
> what ye hear in the ear, that preach ye upon the house-
> tops"* (Matthew 10:27).

Usefulness is the great desire of our souls if we are disciples of
Jesus.

We must not run till we are prepared. This verse describes, and
by implication promises, the needful preparation of heart.

I. AN INVALUABLE PRIVILEGE.

1. We are permitted to realize our Lord's presence with us personally.

2. We are enabled to feel His word as spoken *to* us.
   Immediately: "*I* tell *you.*" Personal contact.
   Forcefully: "in the ear."

3. We are privileged to receive such communications again and
   again.
   We need for a thousand reasons this private tuition, this personal communication with our Commander-in-chief.

## II. A PREPARATORY PROCESS.

We see by reason of personal contact with our Lord—

1. Truth in its personality; living, acting, feeling; for He is "the way, the truth, and the life."
   Truth is no theory or phantom in Christ. Substantial truth is spoken by Him.
2. Truth in its purity is found in Him, in His written teaching, and in that which He speaks to the heart. Truth from man is mixed and adulterated; from Jesus it is unalloyed.
3. Truth in its power. It comes strikingly, persuasively, convincingly, omnipotently from Him. It quickens, and sustains.
4. Truth in its certainty. "Verily, verily," is His motto.

## III. THE CONSEQUENT PROCLAMATION.

Courting publicity, we are to preach "upon the house-tops."
What is this message which we have heard in the ear? We bear our willing witness that—

1. There is peace in the Blood of Jesus.
2. There is sanctifying power in His Holy Spirit.
3. There is rest in faith in our Lord and God.
4. There is safety in conformity to our great Exemplar.

Of a certain preacher it was said: "He preaches as if Jesus Christ were at his side. Don't you see how every now and then he turns around as if he were saying: 'Lord Jesus, what shall I say next?'"

> Take my lips, and let them be
> Filled with messages from Thee.
> —F. R. HAVERGAL.

Possessors of divine truth are eager to spread it. "For," as Carlyle says, "if new-got gold is said to burn the pockets till it be cast forth into circulation; much more may new-found truth."

Often in the South of France have I needed to have a fire lighted; but I have found little or no comfort from it when my wish had been granted. The dwellers in that mild region build their fireplaces so badly that all the heat goes up the chimney. No matter how big the blaze, the hearth only seems to warm itself.

Thus many professors of our holy faith would seem to get grace, and light, and pious feeling for themselves only: their heat goes up their own chimney. What is told them in the dark they keep in the dark, and that which is spoken in their ear never blesses any other ear.—C. H. S.

## CHAPTER 98

# CROSS-BEARING

*"He that taketh not his cross and followeth after Me, is not worthy of Me"* (Matthew 10:38).

Picture to the mind's eye a procession led by a cross-bearing Jesus, and made up of His cross-bearing train. This is not a pageant, but a real march of suffering. It reaches through all time.

Let us obediently inquire—

## I. WHAT IS MY PECULIAR CROSS?

"He that taketh not *his* cross."

1. It may be the endurance of reproach and unkindness, or remaining in poverty and obscurity for the good of others.
2. It may be the suffering of losses and persecutions, for Christ's sake.
3. It certainly means the consecrating of all to Jesus, the bowing of my whole self beneath the blessed burden of service with which He honors me.

## II. WHAT AM I TO DO WITH IT?

"Taketh . . . followeth after Me."

1. I am deliberately to take it up.
   Not to choose a cross, or pine after another form of trial.
   Not to make a cross by petulance and obstinacy.
   Not to murmur at the cross appointed me.
   Not to despise it, by callous stoicism, or wilful neglect of duty.
   Not to faint under it, fall beneath it, or run from it.
2. I am boldly to face it. It is only a wooden cross after all.
3. I am patiently to endure it, for I have only to carry it a little way.
4. I am cheerfully to resign myself to it, for my Lord appoints it.

It is a royal burden, a sanctified burden, a sanctifying burden, a burden which gives communion with Christ.

## III. WHAT SHOULD ENCOURAGE ME?

1. Necessity: I cannot be a disciple without cross-bearing.
2. Society: better men than I have carried it.
3. Love: Jesus bore a far heavier cross than mine.
4. Faith: grace will be given equal to the weight of the cross.
5. Expectation: glory will be the reward of it. No cross, no crown.

When Alexander the Great marched through Persia, his way was stopped with ice and snow, insomuch that his soldiers, being tired out with hard marches, were discouraged, and would have gone no further, which he perceiving, dismounted his horse, and went on foot through the midst of them all, making himself a way with a pickaxe, whereat they all being ashamed, first his friends, then the captains of his army, and, last of all, the common soldiers followed him.

So should all men follow Christ their Saviour, by that rough and unpleasant way of the cross that He hath traversed before them. He having drunk unto them in the cup of His passion, they are to pledge Him when occasion is offered; He having left them an example of His suffering, they are to follow Him in the self-same steps of sorrow.—JOHN SPENCER.

The cross is easier to him who takes it up than to him who drags it along.—J. E. VAUX.

We are bid to *take*, not to make our cross. God in His providence will provide one for us. And we are bid to *take it up;* we hear nothing of laying it down. Our troubles and our lives live and die together.—W. GURNALL.

Christ's cross is the sweetest burden that ever I bore; it is such a burden as wings are to a bird, or sails to a ship, to carry me forward to my harbor.—SAMUEL RUTHERFORD.

Whatever the path is, Christ is there, and to be with Him is joy enough for any creature, whether man or angel. He does not send us to walk in a dreary, desolate road. He does not say, "Go ye," pointing to a lonely way in which He is not to be found; He says, "Come after Me," so that we need not take a single step where His footprints cannot be seen, and where His presence may not still be found.

If the sharp flints cut our feet, they have wounded His before. If the darkness gathers thickly here and there, it was a denser gloom that surrounded Him. If ofttimes we must stand and fight, it was through fiercer conflicts that He passed. If the cross is heavy to our shoulder, it is light when compared with the one He bore. "Christ leads me," said Baxter, "through no darker room than He went through before." If the road were a thousand times rougher than it is, it would be well worth while to walk in it for the sake of walking with Christ there. Following Jesus means fellowship with Jesus and the joy of that fellowship cannot be told.

When Christ gives us the cross to carry He crys, "Halves, My love!" —ANON.

CHAPTER 99

# REST FOR THE RESTLESS

*"Come unto Me, all ye that labor and are heavy laden, and I will give you rest."*
*"Take My yoke upon you, and learn of Me; for I am meek and lowly in heart; and ye shall find rest unto your souls. For My yoke is easy, and My burden is light"* (Matthew 11:28-30).

Jesus had first taught the solemn truth of *human responsibility* (verses 20-24), and afterwards He had joyfully proclaimed in prayer the doctrine of *election:* now He turns to give a free and full invitation to those who are needing rest. These three things are quite consistent, and should be found in all Christian preaching.

I. A CHARACTER WHICH DESCRIBES YOU.

1. Laboring, "all ye that labor," in whatever form.
   In the service of formal religion, in attempt to keep the law, or in any other way of self-justification.
   In the service of self to get gain, honor, ease, etc.
   In the service of Satan, lust, drink, infidelity.
2. Laden. All who are "heavy laden," are called.
   Laden with sin, guilt, dread, remorse, fear of death.
   Laden with care, anxiety, greed, ambition, etc.
   Laden with sorrow poverty, oppression, slander, etc.

II. A BLESSING WHICH INVITES YOU.

1. Rest to be given. "I will give you rest."
   To the conscience, by atonement and pardon.
   To the mind, by infallible instruction and establishment.
   To the heart a rest for love.
   To the energies, by giving an object worth attaining.
   To the apprehensions, assuring that all things work for good.

III. A DIRECTION TO GUIDE YOU.

1. *"Come* unto Me."
   Come to a Person, to Jesus, the living Savior and Example.
   Come at once, Jesus is ready now. Are you?
2. *"Take* My yoke upon you."
   Be obedient to My command.
   Be willing to be conformed to Me in service and burden-bearing.
3. *"Learn* of Me."
   You do not know; but must be content to learn.
   You must not cavil; but have a mind to learn.
   You must learn by heart, and copy My meekness and lowliness.

"*I will give you rest.*" Rest for the burdened conscience, in pardon; for the unquiet intellect, in truth; for the aching, thirsty heart, in divine love; for the care-fretted spirit, in God's providence and promises; for the weary with sorrow and suffering, in the present foretaste, and shortly in the actual enjoyment of "His rest."—E. R. CONDER.

"Come," saith Christ, "and I will give you rest." I will not *show* you rest, nor barely *tell* you of rest, but I will *give* you rest. I am faithfulness itself, and cannot lie, I *will* give you rest. I that have the greatest power to give it, the greatest will to give it, the greatest right to give it, come, laden sinners, and *I* will give you rest.

Rest is the most desirable good, the most suitable good, and to you the greatest good. Come, saith Christ; that is, believe in Me, and I will give you rest; I will give you peace with God, and peace with conscience: I will turn your storm into an everlasting calm; I will give you such rest, that the world can neither give to you nor take from you.—THOMAS BROOKS.

Lord, Thou madest us for Thyself, and we can find no rest till we find rest in Thee!—AUGUSTINE.

There are many heads resting on Christ's bosom, but there's room for yours there.—SAMUEL RUTHERFORD.

## CHAPTER 100

## THE WHY AND THE WHEREFORE OF DOUBT

> "*And immediately Jesus stretched forth His hand, and caught him, and said unto him, O thou of little faith, wherefore didst thou doubt?*" (Matthew 14:31).

Our Lord did not question the doubter till He had saved the sinker. His rebukes are always timely.

When the grace of faith is really present doubt has to answer for itself, and to die if it cannot defend itself.

I. WHEREFORE DOST THOU DOUBT, O CHRISTIAN?

1. *Let us mention some supposable valid reasons.*

Can you quote past experience of broken promises?

Is the present evil beyond the power of Omnipotence?

Are the promises abolished? Are the purposes of grace annulled?

Has God Himself changed? Is His mercy clean gone forever?

None of these supposable reasons have any existence.

2. *Let us hear your actual reasons; if you dare state them.*
   My sense of guilt is peculiarly deep and clear.
   My failures justify despair when viewed by the side of other
   men's attainments, and my own obligations.
   My trials are so peculiar, so fierce, so long, so varied.
   My heart fails me. I can bear up no longer.
3. *Shall we hint at the true reasons of your doubting?*
   You were self-confident, and that confidence has failed you.
   You looked too much to things seen by the light of sense; and
   now that it is dark, you are in consequence troubled.
   You took your eye off from your Lord.

## II. Wherefore Dost Thou Doubt, O Sinner?

1. *Let us suppose good reasons for your doubtings.*
   Have others believed and perished?
   Have you yourself tried faith in Jesus, and found it vain?
   Has the Blood of Jesus lost its power?
   Has the Holy Spirit ceased to comfort, enlighten, renew?
   Is the Gospel abrogated? Is God's mercy clean gone forever?
   None of these can be answered in the affirmative.
2. *Let us hear your apparent reasons.*
   Your sins are great, numerous, aggravated and singular.
   You cannot think that salvation is for you.
   You have refused the Gospel call so long.
   Your heart is so dreadfully hard and unfeeling.
   None of these are sufficient reasons for doubting Almighty
   love.
3. *Let us learn the way to deal with such unreasonable doubting.*
   Repent of it, for it dishonors the power and promise of the
   Father, the Blood of Jesus, and the grace of the Holy Spirit.
   End it by simply believing what is so surely true.
   Run as far as possible the other way. Believe up to the hilt.
   In every case, let us be sure that to believe God is sanctified
   common-sense, and to doubt Him is an extravagance of folly.

I have great sympathy with Billy Bray, whose wife said to him,
when he came home, having given all his money away, "I never saw
such a man in my life. Thee'lt go and look after other people's
wives and children, and help them, and thee own wife and children
starve." Billy, with great force said, "Well, woman, thee'st never
starved yet"; and that was the fact, for there she stood, a living
witness to his word.—Henry Varley.

Good old Mr. Crisp, who had been President of the Baptist College
at Bristol for fifty years, was towards the end of his life fearful
that his faith would fail. Being reminded of the passage, "He that
spared not His own Son, but delivered Him up for us all, how shall

He not with Him also freely give us all things?" he said, after repeating and dwelling on the last words, "No, it would be wrong to doubt; I cannot, I dare not, I will not doubt!"—S. A. SWAINE, in *"Faithful Men."*

Certain persons think that doubting is a needful part of Christian experience, but it is by no means the case. A child may have a deep experience of its father's love, and yet it may never have known a doubt of him. All the experience of a Christian is not Christian experience. If many Christians are despondent, it is no reason why I must be; it is rather a reason why I should watch against it. What if many sheep suffer from the fly; am I to be anxious to have my fleece fly-blown in order to be like them? Never doubt the Lord till you have cause for it; and then you will never doubt Him as long as you live.

## CHAPTER 101

## GUESTS FOR THE WEDDING FEAST

*(Matthew 22:8-10).*

The grand design of God is to make a marriage for His Son.
Our Lord Jesus has espoused His Church, and there must be a feast at the wedding.

### I. THE FIRST INVITATION WAS A FAILURE.

This is seen in Jewish history.
The invitation was refused—
1. Not because it involved suffering, for it was a wedding-feast to which they were bidden.
2. Nor because there were no adequate preparations,—"The wedding is ready."
3. Nor because the invitations were not delivered, or were misunderstood,—they "were bidden."
4. But because they were not fit for the high joy.
   They were not loyal to their King.
   They were wrapt up in self-interest.

Love must reign: mercy must be glorious; Christ must reveal His grace; otherwise He has no joy of His union with mankind.

### II. THE COMMISSION WAS ENLARGED.

1. Disappointment must arouse activity and enterprise,—"Go ye."
2. Disappointment suggests change of sphere,—"into the highways."

3. A keen outlook is to be kept,—"as many as ye shall find."
4. Publicity is to be courted,—"went out into the highways."

III. THE NEW MISSION WAS FULFILLED.
1. The former servants, who had escaped death, went out again.
2. They went out at once. Not an hour could be left unused.
3. They pointed all they met to one center.
4. They welcomed all sorts of characters,—"as many as they found."
5. They found them willing to come.

The wicked, for the slight breakfast of this world, lose the Lamb's supper of glory (Rev. 19:9); where these four things concur, they make a perfect feast:—A good time, eternity; a good place, heaven; a good company, the saints; good cheer, glory.—THOMAS ADAMS.

The devil does not like field-preaching; neither do I. I love a commodious room, a soft cushion, a handsome pulpit; but where is my zeal if I do not trample all these under foot in order to save one more soul?—JOHN WESLEY.

We are fools to waste time in the shallows of our churches and chapels when the deep outside teems with waiting fishers. We need *fresh* hearers: the newer the news to any man, the more likely is he to regard it as good news.

## CHAPTER 102

# ENTRANCE AND EXCLUSION

*"They that were ready went in with Him to the marriage: and the door was shut"* (Matthew 25:10).

During the waiting period, the virgins seemed much alike, even as at this day one can hardly discern the false professor from the true.

When the midnight cry was heard the difference began to appear, as it will do when the Second Advent approaches.

I. THE READY, AND THEIR ENTRANCE.
1. What is this readiness? "They that were ready."
   It is not a fruit of nature.
   It must be a work of grace.
   It mainly consists in a secret work wrought in us.
   In being reconciled to God by the death of His Son.
   In being regenerated, and so made meet for glory.
   In being anointed with the Spirit, and fitted for holy service

2. What is this entrance?

Immediate. "They that were ready *went in.*"
No sooner was the Bridegroom come, than they went in. Love brooks no delays.
Intimate. They "went in *with Him.*"
Joyous. They went in with Him "*to the marriage.*"

## II. The Unready, and Their Exclusion.

1. What is this unreadiness?

It was the absence of a secret essential; but that absence was consistent with much apparent preparation.
These persons had the name and character of virgins.
They had the lamps or torches of true bridesmaids.
They were companions of the true virgins.
They acted like the true; in their virtues and in their faults.
They awakened as the true did, startled by the same cry.
They prayed also, after a fashion,—"give us of your oil."
Yet were they never ready to enter in with the King.
They had no heart-care to be found ready, hence flaming external lamps, but no hidden internal oil.

2. What is this exclusion?

It was universal to all who were not ready.
It was complete; "the door was shut,"—shut for those without quite assuredly as for those within.
It was just; for they were not ready, and so slighted the King.
It was final. Since the fatal news that the door was shut, no news has come that it has been opened, or that it ever will be.

A lady, who heard Whitefield, in Scotland, preach upon the words, "And the door was shut," being placed near two dashing young men, but at a considerable distance from the pulpit, witnessed their mirth; and overheard one to say, in a low tone, to the other, "Well, what if the door *be* shut? Another will open." Thus they turned off the solemnity of the text.

Mr. Whitefield had not proceeded far when he said, "It is possible there may be some careless, trifling person here today, who may ward off the force of this impressive subject by lightly thinking, 'What matter if the door be shut? Another will open.'" The two young men were paralyzed, and looked at each other. Mr. Whitefield proceeded: "Yes; another *will* open. And I will tell you what door it will be: it will be the door of the bottomless pit!—the door of hell! —the door which conceals from the eyes of angels the horrors of damnation!"

## CHAPTER 103

# MOCKED OF THE SOLDIERS

*"And when they had platted a crown of thorns, they put it upon His head, and a reed in His right hand: and they bowed the knee before Him, and mocked Him, saying, Hail, king of the Jews!"* (Matthew 27:29).

I. HERE LEARN A LESSON FOR YOUR HEART.

In the Lord of glory thus made the center of cruel scorn—

1. See what sin deserved. It is all laid on Him. Ridicule for its folly. It should be despised for its mad rebellion against the omnipotent will of the great King.
Scorn for its pretensions. How dared it propose to usurp dominion over hearts and lives which belonged alone to God? Shame for its audacity. It dared defy the Eternal to battle. Oh, wretched, braggart sin!

2. See how low your Savior stooped for your sake. He is made the Substitute for foolish, sinful man; and is treated as such.
He is scoffed at by soldiers of the meanest grade.
He is made a puppet for men who play the fool.

3. See how your Redeemer loved you.
He bears immeasurable contempt, bears in silence, bears to the bitter end; and all for love of His people.

4. Bernard used to say, "The more vile Christ hath made Himself *for* us, the more dear He ought to be *to* us."

II. HERE LEARN A LESSON FOR YOUR CONSCIENCE.

1. Jesus may still be mocked.
By condemning His doctrine. Many do this who affect to admire His character. This is the peculiar sin of the present age. By resolves never fulfilled. Sinners vow but never pay; confess faults, and cling to them. This is to insult the Lord. By beliefs never obeyed. It is common to pretend to a belief which never affects the life, mocking great truths by acting contrary to them.

2. If guilty of mocking Him, what shall you do?
Do not despair, but confess and lament your sin.
Do not give all up for lost. Believe and live.
Do not repeat the sad offence. Repent, and quit the crime.

3. What shall you do in any case?
Crown Him with love.
Sceptre Him with obedience.

Ye sinners, destroy the sins which grieved your Savior!

Ye saints, defy all the contempt of the world for His sake!

Whither, O whither, dost Thou stoop, O Thou co-eternal Son of thine eternal Father? Whither dost Thou abase Thyself for me? I have sinned, and Thou art punished; I have exalted myself, and Thou art dejected; I have clad myself with shame, and Thou art stripped; I have made myself naked, and Thou art clothed with robes of dishonor; my head hath devised evil, and Thine is pierced with thorns; I have smitten Thee, and Thou art smitten for me; I have dishonored Thee, and Thou, for my sake, art scorned; Thou art made the sport of men, for me that have deserved to be insulted by devils!—BISHOP HALL.

Christ's head hath sanctified all thorns; His back, all furrows; His hands, all nails; His side, all spears; His heart, all sorrows that can ever come to any of His children.—SAMUEL CLARK, *in "The Saint's Nosegay."*

To be ridiculed may give us communion with the Lord Jesus, but to ridicule others will place us in fellowship with His persecutors. —C. H. S.

During the last moments of a gracious lady, speech had left her; but she managed to articulate the word "Bring." Her friends in ignorance of her meaning, offered her food, but she shook her head, and again repeated the word "Bring." They then offered her grapes, which she also declined, and, for the third time uttered the word "Bring." Thinking she desired to see some absent friends, they brought them to her: but again she shook her head; and then, by a great effort, she succeeded in completing the sentence—

> "Bring forth the royal diadem,
> And crown Him Lord of all;"

and then passed away to be with Jesus.—NEWMAN HALL.

## CHAPTER 104

## HEARING WITH HEED

*"And He said unto them, Take heed what ye hear: with what measure ye mete, it shall be measured to you: and unto you that hear shall more be given"* (Mark 4:24).

In these days we have many instructions as to preaching; but our Lord principally gave directions as to hearing. The art of attention is as difficult as that of homiletics.

I. HERE IS A PRECEPT. "Take heed what ye hear."
   1. Hear with discrimination, shunning false doctrine (John 10:5).
   2. Hear with attention; really and earnestly hearing (Matt. 13:23).
   3. Hear retentively endeavoring to remember the truth.
   4. Hear desiringly, praying that the' Word may be blessed to you.

II. HERE IS A PROVERB. "With what measure ye mete, it shall be measured to you."
   1. Those who desire to find fault find faults enough.
   2. Those who seek solid truth learn it from any faithful ministry
   3. Those who hunger find food.
   4. Those who bring faith receive assurance.
   5. Those who come joyfully are made glad.
      But no man finds blessing by hearing error.

III. HERE IS A PROMISE. "Unto you that hear shall more be given."
   You that hear shall have—
   1. More desire to hear.
   2. More understanding of what you hear.
   3. More convincement of the truth of what you hear.

*Hear well.* God's teaching deserves the deepest attention. It will repay the best consideration.

*Hear often.* Waste no Sabbath, nor any one of its services.

What care I to see a man run after a sermon if he cozens and cheats as soon as he comes home.—JOHN SELDEN.

Ebenezer Blackwell was a rich banker, a zealous Methodist, and a great friend of the Wesleys. "Are you going to hear Mr. Wesley preach?" said one to Mr. Blackwell. "No," he answered, "I am going to hear God; I listen to Him, whoever preaches; otherwise I lose all my labor."—JOHN BUNYAN.

Some can be content to hear all pleasant things, as the promises and mercies of God; but judgments and reproofs, threats and checks, these they cannot brook; like unto those who, in medicine, care only for a pleasant smell or appearance in the remedy, as pills rolled in gold, but have no regard for the efficacy of the physic.

Some can willingly hear that which concerns other men and their sins, their lives and their manners, but nothing touching themselves or their own sins; as men can willingly abide to hear of other men's deaths, but cannot abide to hear their own.—RICHARD STOCK.

The meaning of this passage is brought out in the words of the old Rabbi: "Much have I learnt from my tutors; more from my companions; but most of all from my pupils." The more light you give another, the more you get yourself. You get a better grip of truth by pondering it with the wish to impart it. The love, which imparts what you have, opens your heart to receive something still higher.—RICHARD GLOVER.

## CHAPTER 105

## HE RAN, AND HE RAN

*"But when he saw Jesus afar off, he ran and worshipped Him"* (Mark 5:6).

*"But when he was yet a great way off, his father saw him, and had compassion, and ran, and fell on his neck, and kissed him"* (Luke 15:20).

These two texts have a measure of apparent likeness: the man runs to Jesus from afar, and the Father runs to the prodigal from afar.

I. THE SINNER'S PLACE. "Afar off."

Jesus is afar off in the sinner's apprehension.

1. As to character. What a difference between the demoniac and the Lord Jesus: between the prodigal son and the great Father!

2. As to knowledge. The demoniac knew Jesus but knew little of His love. The prodigal knew little of his Father's great heart.

3. As to possession. The demoniac had no hold upon the Savior; on the contrary he cried, "What have I to do with Thee?" The prodigal thought he had lost all claim to his Father, and therefore said, "I am no more worthy to be called Thy son."

Immeasurable is the distance between God and a sinner: it is wide as the gulf between sin and holiness, death and life, hell and heaven.

II. THE SINNER'S PRIVILEGE. "He saw Jesus."

This much you, who are most under Satan's influence, are able to see concerning Jesus: you know that—

1. There is such a Person. He is God and Man, the Savior.

2. He has done great things.

3. He is able to cast out the powers of evil.

4. He may cast them out from you, and deliver you.

III. THE SECRET OF HOPE FOR SINNERS. "His father saw him."

1. The returning sinner was seen from afar by Omniscience.

2. He was recognized as a son is known by his Father.

3. He was understood, beloved, and accepted by his Father.

God will pardon a repentant sinner more quickly than a mother would snatch her child out of the fire.—VIANNEY.

When either God or man is strongly moved, the pace is running. A soul in distress runs to Jesus: God in compassion runs to meet returning wanderers. A slow pace evidences an unwilling heart;

hence delay to repent is a deadly sign. With sin within thee, Christ before thee, time pressing thee, eternity awaiting thee, hell beneath thee, heaven above thee; O sinner, thou mayest well run! It is the pace of one hunting after the game he desires, one anxious to win a prize, one escaping the avenger of blood. He that would have heaven must run for it.—C. H. S.

CHAPTER 106

## THE FREE-AGENCY OF CHRIST

*Mark 8:22-25.*

Men arrive at Christ by different processes: one is found by Christ Himself, another comes to Him, another is borne of four, and this blind man is led. This matters little, so long as we do come to Him.

I. IT IS A COMMON WEAKNESS OF FAITH TO EXPECT THE BLESSING IN A CERTAIN FIXED WAY.

"They besought Him to touch Him."

1. We dream that deliverance from trouble must come in one way.
2. We look for sanctification either by afflictions or by ecstasies.
3. We expect a revival to take the stereotyped shape.

II. WHILE OUR LORD HONORS FAITH, HE DOES NOT DEFER TO ITS WEAKNESS.

He did nothing to the blind man before their eyes; but led him out of the town. He would not indulge their observation or curiosity.

He did not heal him instantly, as they expected.

He used a means never suggested by them—"spit on his eyes," etc.

1. Thus He refused to foster the superstition which limited His power.
2. Thus He used a method more suited to the case.

III. WHILE OUR LORD REBUKES THE WEAKNESS, HE HONORS FAITH ITSELF.

1. The blind man had consented to be led to Jesus, and Jesus leads him further.
2. His friends had asked for sight, and the Lord gave sight. If we have praying faith, He will keep pace with it.

Is the sick man the doctor, that he would choose the remedy?— MADAM SWETCHINE.

So apt are people, as in the case of Naaman, to settle in their own minds the method of the work of grace, that it is hard to overcome their preconceptions. I met with one young woman, before whom I set the way of salvation by faith alone. She was long in accepting, or even understanding it; and when she did grasp it, and the joy of it filled her heart, she exclaimed with surprise, "I never thought that people could find peace in this way." "Why not?" I asked her, and she replied very energetically, "I always believed that one must almost go to hell to get to heaven. My father was so full of despair that they locked him up in the asylum for six months, and then at last he got religion."—C. H. S.

## CHAPTER 107

## THE BLIND BEGGAR OF JERICHO

### *Mark 10:49, 50.*

This man is a picture of what we would fain have every seeker of Christ to become.

In his lonely darkness, and deep poverty, he thought and became persuaded that Jesus was the Son of David.

Though he had no sight, he made good use of his hearing. If we have not all gifts, let us use those which we have.

I. HE SOUGHT THE LORD UNDER DISCOURAGEMENTS.

1. No one prompted his seeking.
2. Many opposed his attempts. "Many charged him that he should hold his peace" (verse 48).
3. For a while he was unheeded by the Lord Himself.
4. He was but a blind beggar, and this alone might have checked some pleaders.

II. HE RECEIVED ENCOURAGEMENT.

This came from our Lord's commanding him to be called.

There are several kinds of calls which come to men at the bidding of our Lord Jesus. There is the—

1. Universal call. Jesus is lifted up that all who look to Him may live. (John 3:14, 15). The Gospel is preached to every creature.
2. Character call. To those who labor, and are heavy laden. Many are the Gospel promises which call the sinful, the mourning, the weary to Jesus (Is. 55:7; Matt. 11:28; Acts 2:38, 39).
3. Ministerial call. Given by the Lord's sent servants, and so backed by His authority (Acts 13:26, 38, 39; 16:31).

III. BUT ENCOURAGEMENT DID NOT CONTENT HIM; HE STILL SOUGHT JESUS.

To stop short of Jesus and healing would have been folly indeed.

1. He arose. Hopefully, resolutely, he quitted his begging posture. In order to receive salvation we must be on the alert, and in earnest.
2. He cast away his garment, and every hindrance. Our righteousness, our comfortable sin, our habit—anything, everything we must quit for Christ.
3. He came to Jesus. In the darkness occasioned by his blindness, he followed the Savior's voice.
4. He stated his case. "Lord that I might receive my sight!"
5. He received salvation. Jesus said unto him, "Thy faith hath made thee whole." He obtained perfect eyesight; and in all respects he was in complete health.

IV. HAVING FOUND JESUS, HE KEPT HIM.

1. He used his sight to see his Lord.
2. He became his avowed disciple. (See verse 52).
3. He went with Jesus on his way to the cross, and to the crown.
4. He remained a well-known disciple, whose father's name is given.

*"And commanded him to be called."* By this circumstance he administered reproof and instruction: reproof, by ordering those to help the poor man who had endeavored to check him: instruction, by teaching us that, though he does not stand in need of our help, he will not dispense with our services; that we are to aid each other; that though we cannot recover our fellow-creatures, we may frequently bring them to the place and means of cure.—WILLIAM JAY.

Success in this world comes only to those who exhibit determination. Can we hope for salvation unless our mind is truly set upon it? Grace makes a man to be as resolved to be saved as this beggar was to get to Jesus, and gain his sight. "I must see him," said an applicant at the door of a public person. "You cannot see him," said the servant; but the man waited at the door. A friend went out to him, and said, "You cannot see the master, but I can give you an answer." "No," said the unfortunate pleader, "I will stay all night on the doorstep, but I will see the man himself. He alone will serve my turn."

You do not wonder that, after many rebuffs, he ultimately gained his point: it would be an infinitely greater wonder if an importunate sinner did not obtain an audience from the Lord Jesus. If you must have grace, you shall have it. If you will not be put off, you shall not be put off. Whether things look favorable, or unfavorable, press you on till you find Jesus, and you shall find Him.—C. H. S.

CHAPTER 108

# GETHSEMANE

*"And they came to a place which was named Gethsemane"*
(Mark 14:32).

It was a killing change from the cheerful communion of the Supper to the lone agony of the garden.

I. THE CHOICE OF THE SPOT.

1. Showed His serenity of mind, and His courage.
   He goes to His usual place of secret prayer.
   He goes there though Judas knew the place.

2. Manifested His wisdom.
   Holy memories there aided His faith.
   Deep solitude was suitable for His prayers and cries.

3. Bequeathed us lessons.
   In a garden, Paradise was lost and won.
   In Gethsemane, the olive-press, our Lord Himself was crushed.

II. THE EXERCISE UPON THE SPOT.

1. He took all due precautions for others.
   He would not have His disciples surprised, and therefore bade them watch.

2. He solicited the sympathy of friends.
   We may not despise this; though, like our Lord, we shall prove the feebleness of it, and cry, "Could ye not watch with Me?"

3. He prayed and wrestled with God.
   In lowliest posture and manner. (See verse 35).
   In piteous repetition of His cry. (See verses 36 and 39).
   In awful agony of spirit even to a bloody sweat (Luke 22:44).

4. He again and again sought human sympathy, but made excuse for his friends when they failed Him. (See verse 38). We ought not to be soured in spirit even when we are bitterly disappointed.

III. THE TRIUMPH UPON THE SPOT.

1. Behold His perfect resignation. He struggles with "If it be possible," but conquers with "not what I will, but what Thou wilt." He is our example of patience.

2. Mark the angelic service rendered. The Blood-bestained Sufferer has still all heaven at His call. (Matt. 26:53).

3. Remember His majestic bearing towards His enemies.
   He meets them bravely (Matt. 26:55).
   He makes them fall (John 18:6).
   He yields Himself, but not to force (John 18:8).
   He goes to the cross but transforms it to a throne.

The late Rev. W. H. Krause, of Dublin, was visiting a lady in a depressed state, "weak, oh, so weak!" She told him that she had been very much troubled in mind that day, because in meditation and prayer she had found it impossible to govern her thoughts, and kept merely going over the same things again and again.

"Well, my dear friend," was his prompt reply, "there is provision in the Gospel for that too. Our Lord Jesus Christ, when *His* soul was exceeding sorrowful, even unto death, three times prayed, and spoke *the same words*." This seasonable application of Scripture was a source of great comfort to her.

"My will, not thine, be done," turned paradise into a desert. "Thy will, not mine, be done," turned the desert into Paradise, and made Gethsemane the gate of heaven.—E. DE PRESSENSE.

*"And there appeared an angel unto Him, from heaven, strengthening Him."*—What! The Son of God receives help from an angel, who is but His creature? Yes. And we learn thereby to expect help and comfort from simple persons and common things. When God pleases. All strength and comfort come from God, but He makes creatures His ministers to bring it. We should thank both them and Him.— *Practical Reflections on every verse of the Holy Gospels, by a Clergyman.*

CHAPTER 109

# FOUNTAINS OF REPENTANT TEARS

*"And when he thought thereon, he wept"* (Mark 14:72).

Repentance is wrought by the Spirit of God. But He works it in us by leading us to think upon the evil of sin.

I. STUDY PETER'S CASE, AND USE IT FOR OUR OWN INSTRUCTION.
   1. He considered that he had denied his Lord.
      Have we never done the like?
      This may be done in many ways.
   2. He reflected upon the excellence of the Lord Whom he had denied.

3. He remembered the position in which his Lord had placed him,
   —making him an apostle, and one of the first of them.
   Have we not been placed in positions of trust?

4. He bethought him of the special intercourse which he had
   enjoyed. He and James and John had been most favored.
   (Matt. 17:1-13; 26:36-46; Mark 5:37-43.)
   Have not we known joyous fellowship with our Lord?

5. He recollected that he had been solemnly forewarned by his
   Lord.
   Have we not sinned against light and knowledge?

6. He recalled his own vows, pledges and boasts. "Although all
   shall be offended, yet will not I" (verse 29).
   Have we not broken very earnest declarations?

II. STUDY OUR OWN LIVES, AND USE THE STUDY FOR OUR FURTHER
HUMILIATION.

1. Think upon our small progress in the divine life.
2. Think upon our backslidings and heart-wanderings.
3. Think upon our neglect of the souls of others.
4. Think upon our little communion with our Lord.
5. Think upon the little glory we are bringing to His great Name.
6. Think upon our matchless obligations to His infinite love.

III. STUDY THE EFFECT OF THESE THOUGHTS UPON OUR OWN MINDS.

1. Can we think of these things without emotion? This is possible, for many excuse their sin on the ground of their circumstances, their constitution, their company, their trade,
   their fate; they even lay the blame on Satan or some other
   tempter. Certain hard hearts treat the matter with supreme
   indifference.
   This is perilous. It is to be feared that such a man is not
   Peter but Judas; not a fallen saint, but a son of perdition.

2. Are we moved by thoughts of these things?
   There are other reflections which may move us far more.
   Our Lord forgives us, and numbers us with His brethren.
   He asks us if we love Him, and He bids us feed His sheep.
   Surely, when we dwell on these themes, it must be true of
   each of us—"When he thought thereon, he wept."

Peter's recollection of what he had formerly heard was another
occasion of his repentance. We do not sufficiently consider how much
more we need recollection than information. We know a thousand
things, but it is necessary that they should be kept alive in our
hearts by a constant and vivid recollection. It is, therefore, extremely absurd and childish for people to say, "You tell me nothing but
what I know." I answer, you forget many things; and therefore, it
is necessary that line should be upon line, and precept upon precept.

Peter, himself, afterwards said, in his Epistles, "I will not be negligent to put you always in remembrance of these things, though ye know them." We are prone to forget what we know; whereas we should consider that, whatever good thing we know is only so far good to us as it is remembered to purpose.—RICHARD CECIL.

Peter falls dreadfully, but by repentance rises sweetly; a look of love from Christ melts him into tears. He knew that repentance was the key to the kingdom of grace. At once his faith was so great that he leaped, as it were, into a sea of waters to come to Christ; so now his repentance was so great that he leaped, as it were, into a sea of tears, for that he had gone from Christ.

Some say that, after his sad fall, he was ever and anon weeping, and that his face was even furrowed with continual tears. He had no sooner taken in poison but he vomited it up again, ere it got to the vitals; he had no sooner handled this serpent but he turned it into a rod, to scourge his soul with remorse for sinning against such clear light, and strong love, and sweet discoveries of the heart of Christ to him.

Clement notes that Peter so repented that, all his life after, every night when he heard the cock crow, he would fall upon his knees, and, weeping bitterly, would beg pardon for his sin. Ah! souls, you can easily sin as the saints, but can you repent with the saints? Many can sin with David and Peter, who cannot repent with David and Peter, and so must perish for ever.—THOMAS BROOKS.

Nothing will make the faces of God's children more fair than for them to wash themselves every morning in their tears.—SAMUEL CLARK.

The old Greeks thought that memory must be a source of torture in the next world, so they interposed between the two worlds the waters of Lethe, the river of forgetfulness; but believers in Christ want no river of oblivion on the borders of Elysium. Calvary is on this side, and that is enough.—ALEXANDER MACLAREN.

# CHAPTER 110

## A SAD INTERIOR AND A CHEERY MESSENGER

*"And she went and told them that had been with Him, as they mourned and wept"* (Mark 16:10).

I. A SORROWFUL ASSEMBLY. "As they mourned and wept."

What a scene! We behold a common mourning, abundantly expressed by tears and lamentations. They mourned—

1. Because they had believed in Jesus, and loved Him; and therefore they were concerned at what had happened.

2. Because they felt their great loss in losing Him.
3. Because they remembered their ill-conduct **towards Him.**

## II.  A CONSOLING MESSENGER.
Mary Magdalene came and told them that **Jesus had risen, and had** appeared unto her.

1. She was one of themselves.  The witnesses to our Lord's resurrection were such as His disciples, and, indeed all the world, might safely trust.

2. She came with the best of news.
She declared that Jesus was indeed risen.  The resurrection of our divine Lord—
Removes the cause of our sorrow.
Assures us of the help of a living Redeemer (John 14:19).
Secures our own personal resurrection (I Cor. 15:23).
Brings us personal justification (Rom. 4:25).

3. She was not believed.
Unbelief is apt to become chronic: they had not believed the Lord when He foretold His own resurrection, and so they do not believe an eye-witness who reported it.
Unbelief is cruelly unjust; they made **Mary Magdalene a liar,** and yet all of them esteemed her.

## III.  A REASSURING REFLECTION.
1. We are not the only persons who have mourned an absent Lord.
2. We are not the only messengers who have been rejected.
3. We are sure beyond all doubt of the resurrection of Christ.
The evidence is more abundant than that which testifies to any other great historical event.
The apostles so believed it as to die as witnesses of it.

In the famous picture-gallery of Bologna, there is a striking picture by Domenichino, representing an angel standing beside the empty cross, from which the body of Christ has just been removed. He holds in his hands the crown of thorns, that had just fallen from the august Sufferer's brow; and the expression that passes over his face, as he feels with his finger the sharpness of one of the protruding thorns, is full of meaning.  It is a look of wonder and surprise.

To the pure, unstained, immortal nature of the angel, all that suffering is a profound mystery.  The death of Christ was equally a mystery to His disciples.—HUGH MACMILLAN.

A sorrow is none the less sharp because it is founded upon a mistake. Jacob mourned very bitterly for Joseph, though his darling was not torn in pieces, but on the way to be lord over all Egypt.

Yet while there is of necessity so much well-founded sorrow in the world, it is a pity that one unnecessary pang should be endured, and endured by those who have the best possible grounds for joy. The case in the text before us is a typical one. Thousands are at this day mourning and weeping who ought to be rejoicing.

Oh, the mass of needless grief! Unbelief works for the father of lies in this matter, and works misery out of falsehood among those who are not in truth children of sadness, but heirs of light and joy. Rise, faith, and with thy light chase away this darkness! And if even thou must have thy lamp trimmed by a humble Mary, do not despise her kindly aid.

## CHAPTER 111

## STRANGE THINGS

*"We have seen strange things to-day"* (Luke 5:26).

The world is aweary, and longs for something novel.

The greatest stranger in the world is Jesus; and, alas, He is the least seen, and the least spoken of by most of men!

If men would come and watch Him, they would see strange things.

His person, His life, His death, His teaching, are full of strange things.

What He is now doing has as much as ever the element of strangeness and wonder about it.

I. MARK THE STRANGE THINGS OF THAT PARTICULAR DAY.

1. Power present to heal doctors! (Verse 17).
2. Jesus pardoning sin with a word. (Verse 20).
3. Jesus practising thought-reading. (Verse 22).
4. Jesus making a man carry the bed which had carried him. Verse 25).

II. MARK THE STRANGE THINGS OF CHRIST'S DAY.

1. The Maker of men born among men. The Infinite an infant.
2. The Lord of all serving all.
3. The Just One accused, condemned, and sacrificed for sin.
4. The Crucified rising from the dead.
5. Death slain by the dying of the Lord.

These are but incidents in a life which is all strange and marvelous.

III.   MARK THE STRANGE THINGS SEEN BY BELIEVERS IN THEIR DAY
WITHIN THEMSELVES AND OTHERS.

1. A self-condemned sinner justified by faith.
2. A natural heart renewed by grace.
3. A soul preserved in spiritual life amid killing evils, like the
   bush which burned with fire and was not consumed.
4. Strength made perfect in weakness.

Life never grows stale to a companion of Jesus.

Do you find it becoming so, and are you a believer?

Seek the conversion of your family, and your neighborhood.

Seek to know more of Jesus at work among men.

This will cause you to see stranger and stranger things, till you
see the strangest of all with Christ in glory.

A holy grateful wonder should be indulged to the full; but a cold,
skeptical wonder should be resisted as a suggestion from Satan.
Faith accounts all things possible with God; it is unbelief that in-
credulously marvels at the work of His hand.

Guthrie, of Fenwick, a Scotch minister, once visited a dying
woman.  He found her anxious about her state, but very ignorant.
His explanation of the Gospel was joyfully received by her, and soon
after she died.  On his return home, Guthrie said, "I have seen a
strange thing today—a woman whom I found in a state of nature,
I saw in a state of grace, and left in a state of glory."

In a manuscript by an old Scotch minister, in the early part of
the last century, there is a remarkable account of the conversion of
Lord Jeddart who had been famous for his recklessness in sin, and
of the astonishment it caused among Christian people.

A little after his conversion, and before the thing was known, he
came to the Lord's table.  He sat next a lady who had her hands
over her face, and did not see him till he delivered the cup out of
his hand.  When she saw that it was Lord Jeddart, who had been
so renowned for sin, she fell a-trembling terribly for very amazement that such a man should be there.  He noticed it, and said,
"Madam, be not troubled: the grace of God is free!"  This calmed
the lady: but when we consider what sort of man Lord Jeddart had
been, we can account for her surprise.

When I get to heaven, I shall see three wonders there—the first
wonder will be to see many people there whom I did not expect to
see; the second wonder will be to miss many people whom I did
expect to see; and the third and greatest wonder of all will be to find
myself there.—JOHN NEWTON.

# CHAPTER 112

## "AT HIS FEET"

*Luke 7:38.*

### I. IT IS A BECOMING POSTURE.

The posture is admirable for many reasons.

1. As He is divine, let us pay Him lowliest reverence.
2. As we are sinful, let us make humble confession.
3. As He is Lord, let us make full submission.

The best are at His feet joyfully, bowing before Him.

The worst *must* come there, whether they will or no.

### II. IT IS A HELPFUL POSTURE.

1. For a weeping penitent. (Luke 7:38).
   Our humility will help penitence.
   Our lowly submission will bring assurance.
   Our full obeisance will prepare for service.
2. For a resting convert. (Luke 8:35).
   In such a position devils are driven out, and no longer rule us.
3. For a pleading intercessor (Luke 8:41).
   We plead best when we are lowliest.
   We may be rulers of the synagogue, but when our heart is breaking we find most hope "at His feet."
4. For a grateful worshipper. (Luke 17:16).
   So the healed leper expressed his thanks.
   So angels adore, giving Him thanks while bending low.
5. For a saint beholding his Lord's glory. (Rev. 1:17).
   Overwhelmed, humbled, overjoyed, exhausted with excess of ecstasy.
   He is so worthy: pay Him all reverence.
   He has received from you so much despite: kiss His feet.

### III. IT IS A SAFE POSTURE.

1. Jesus will not refuse us that position, for it is one which we ought to occupy.
2. Jesus will not spurn the humbly submissive, who in self-despair cast themselves before Him.
3. Jesus will not suffer any to harm those who seek refuge at His feet.
4. Jesus will not deny us the eternal privilege of abiding there.

When the Danish missionaries, stationed at Malabar, set some of their converts to translate a catechism, in which it was asserted that believers become the sons of God, one of the translators was so startled that he suddenly laid down his pen, and exclaimed, "It is too much. Let me rather render it, 'They shall be permitted to kiss His feet.' "—G. S. BOWES.

The Rev. Mr. Young was, one stormy day, visiting one of his people, an old man, who lived in great poverty, in a lonely cottage, a few miles from Edinburgh. He found him sitting with the Bible open on his knees, but in outward circumstances of great discomfort, the snow drifting through the roof and under the door, and scarcely any fire on the hearth. "What are you about to-day, John?" was Mr. Young's question on entering. "Ah! sir," said the happy saint, "I am sitting under His shadow wi' great delight."—*The Christian Treasury*.

The end of all Christian preaching is to cast the sinner trembling at the feet of mercy.—VINET.

## CHAPTER 113

## LOVE'S FOREMOST

*"Tell me, therefore, which of them will love him most?"* (Luke 7:42).

I. WE MUST FIRST BE SAVED IN THE SAME MANNER AS OTHERS.

The road to eminence in love is just the plain way of salvation, which all who are in Christ must travel.

1. All are in debt; we must heartily own this to be our own case.

2. The loving Lord forgives in each case: personally we have exceeding great need of such remission. We must feel this.

3. In each case He forgives frankly, or without any consideration or compensation; it must be so with us. We must accept free grace and undeserved favor.

II. WE MUST AIM AT A DEEP SENSE OF SIN.

1. It was the *consciousness* of great indebtedness which created the great love in the penitent woman. Not her sin, but the consciousness of it was the basis of her loving character.

2. It is to be cultivated. The more we bewail sin the better, and we must aim at great tenderness of heart in reference to it. In order to cultivate it we must seek to get—
A clearer view of the law's requirements. (Luke 10:26, 27).

A deeper consciousness of the love of God to us. (I John 3:1, 2).

A keener valuation of the cost of redemption. (I Peter 1:18, 19).

A surer persuasion of the perfection of our pardon will also help to show the baseness of our sin. (Ezek. 16:62, 63).

III. THIS WILL LEAD TO A HIGHLY LOVING CONDUCT TOWARDS OUR LORD.

1. We shall desire to be near Him, even at His feet.
2. We shall show deep humility, delighting even to wash His feet.
3. We shall exhibit thorough contrition, beholding Him with tears.
4. We shall render earnest service; doing all that lies in our power for Jesus, even as this woman did.

A spiritual experience which is thoroughly flavored with a deep and bitter sense of sin is of great value to him that hath had it. It is terrible in the drinking, but it is wholesome in the bowels, and in the whole of the after-life. Possibly much of the flimsy piety of the day arises from the ease with which men reach to peace and joy in these evangelistic days.

We would not judge modern converts, but we certainly prefer that form of spiritual exercise which leads the soul by the way of the Weeping-cross, and makes it see its blackness before it assures it that it is "clean every whit." Too many think lightly of sin, and therefore lightly of a Savior.

He who has stood before His God, convicted, and condemned, with the rope about his neck, is the man to weep for joy when he is pardoned, to hate the evil which has been forgiven him, and to live to the honor of the Redeemer by Whose Blood he has been cleansed.

Bold blasphemers ought to be enthusiasts for the honor of their Lord when they are washed from their iniquities. As they say reclaimed poachers make the best game-keepers, so should the greatest sinners be the raw material out of which the Lord's transforming grace shall create great saints.

I have heard say the depth of a Scotch loch corresponds with the height of the surrounding mountains. So deep thy sense of obligation for pardoned sin, so high thy love to Him Who has forgiven thee.—C. H. S.

Love to the Saviour rises in the heart of a saved man in proportion to the sense which he entertains of his own sinfulness on the one hand, and of the mercy of God on the other. Thus the height of a saint's love to the Lord is as the depths of his own humility: as this root strikes down unseen into the ground, the blossoming branch rises higher in the sky.—WILLIAM ARNOT.

CHAPTER 114

## A WELCOME FOR JESUS

*"And it came to pass, that, when Jesus was returned, the people gladly received Him: for they were all waiting for Him"* (Luke 8:40).

Jesus went to those who refused Him in the land of Gadara; and there He saved one, to show the freeness and sovereignty of His grace.

He then quitted the inhospitable country, to show that He forces Himself on none. Wisdom abandons those who refuse her counsels. (Prov. 1:24.) Those whom the Lord has chosen shall be willing in the day of His power. (Ps. 110:3.)

I. A BEAUTIFUL SIGHT. "They were all waiting for Him."

This waiting may be seen in several different forms.

1. A praying company, an earnest church, looking for revival, and prepared to cooperate in labor for it.
2. A seeking sinner, sighing for mercy, searching the Scriptures, hearing the Word, inquiring of Christians, constantly praying, and thus "waiting for Him."
3. A departing saint, longing for home: saying like Jacob, "I have waited for Thy salvation, O Lord" (Gen. 49:18).

II. A SURE ARRIVAL. "Jesus was returned."

1. His spirit is there already, making them wait. (Romans 8:23).
2. His promise is there, "Lo, I am with you always" (Matt. 28:20).
3. His custom is to be there. His delights are still with the sons of men. (Proverbs 8:31).

III. A HEARTY WELCOME. "The people gladly received Him."

1. Their fears made Him welcome.
   They feared lest He might have gone forever from them. (Ps. 77:7).
2. Their hopes made Him welcome.
   They trusted that now their sick would be cured, and their dead would be raised.
3. Their prayers made Him welcome.
   Those who pray that Jesus may come are glad when He comes.
4. Their faith made Him welcome.
   Jairus now looked to have his child healed. (See verse 41).
5. Their love made Him welcome.
   When our heart is with Him, we rejoice in His appearing.
6. Their care for others made Him welcome.

Jesus never disappoints those who wait for Him.
Jesus never refuses those who welcome Him.

A congregation cannot be said to welcome the Lord Jesus unless they are all there, which requires *punctuality;* unless they have come with design to meet Him, which implies prayerful *expectancy;* unless they are ready to hear Him, which involves *attention;* and unless they are resolved to accept His teaching, which demands *obedience.*

When the inhabitants of Mentone desired a visit from the Prince of Savoy, they made a way for him over the mountains. Hills were tunnelled, and valleys bridged, that the beloved sovereign might receive the welcome of his subjects.

If we would really welcome the Lord Jesus, we must make a road for Him by abasing our pride, elevating our thoughts, removing our evil habits, and preparing our hearts. Never did a soul cast up a highway for the Lord, and then fail to enjoy His company.—C. H. S.

## CHAPTER 115

## LOVE AT HOME

*"And she had a sister called Mary, which also sat at Jesus' feet, and heard His word"* (Luke 10:39).

Martha sought to serve the Lord with her very best.

Mary was full of love to Jesus, as we know by her anointing Him, and therefore she also would serve Him with her very best.

She did so by attending to His words.

I. LOVE AT LEISURE. "Which also sat as Jesus' feet."

Like Mary—

We would feel ourselves quite at home with Jesus our Lord. We would be free from worldly care—leaving all with Jesus. All our future, for time and for eternity, safe in His dear hands.

Let us, without fear, enjoy leisure with Jesus—leisure, but not laziness—leisure to love, to learn, to commune, to copy.

II. LOVE IN LOWLINESS. "At Jesus' feet."

1. A penitent, which is an acknowledgment of my unworthiness.
2. A disciple, which is a confession of my ignorance.
3. A receiver, which is an admission of my emptiness.

III. LOVE LISTENING. "And heard His word."

Listening to Himself. Studying *Him,* reading His very heart.

Listening, and not obtruding our own self-formed thoughts, notions, reasonings, questionings, desires, and prejudices.

Listening, and forgetting the observations and unbeliefs of others.

God delighteth to deal with us when we are most in private: He appeared to Abraham sitting in the door of his tent. (Gen. 18). The Holy Ghost came down upon the Apostles, and filled all the house where they were sitting. (Acts 2). The eunuch, sitting in his chariot, was called and converted by Philip's preaching. (Acts 8).—HENRY SMITH.

Which shall we praise more, Mary's humility or her docility? I do not see her take a stool and sit by Him, or a chair and sit above Him; but, as desiring to show her heart was as low as her knees, she sits at His feet. She was lowly set and richly warmed with His heavenly beams. The greater submission, the more grace. If there be one hollow in the valley lower than other, thither the waters go.—BISHOP HALL.

Dr. Chalmers complained: "I am hustled out of my spirituality."

CHAPTER 116

# THE GOOD SHEPHERD IN THREE POSITIONS

*Luke 15:4-6.*

The love of Jesus is not mere sentiment; it is active and energetic.

It is prevenient love, going after sheep that have no notion of returning to the fold from which they have wandered.

It is engrossing, making Him leave all else.

I. IN THE SEARCH. "Until he find it."

Mark him well, as, with his eyes, and heart, and all his faculties, he goes "after that which is lost."

1. No rejoicing is on His countenance. He is anxious for the lost.

2. No hesitation is in His mind. Despite the roughness of the way, or the length of the time or the darkness of the night, He still pursues His lost one.

3. No anger is in His heart. The many wanderings of the sheep cost Him dear, but He counts them as nothing, so that He may but find it.

II. AT THE CAPTURE. "When he hath found it."

1. Wanderer held. How firm the grip!

2. Weight borne. No chiding, driving; but a lift, a self-loading an easing of the wanderer.

**3.** Distance travelled. Every step is for the Shepherd.
He must tread painfully all that length of road over which
the sheep had wandered so wantonly.
The sheep is carried back with no suffering on its own part.

III. IN THE HOME-BRINGING. "When he cometh home."

1. Heaven is home to Christ.
2. Jesus must carry us all the way there.
3. Jesus loves others to rejoice with Him over the accomplishment of His design.
4. One sinner can make all heaven glad. See verses 7 and 10.

Let us learn a lesson from each of the three pictures which we
have looked upon—

Of perseverance till souls are saved.

Of patience with souls who are newly found.

Of encouragement in expectation of the gathering into glory of
those for whom we labor on behalf of Jesus.

One evening, in 1861, as General Garibaldi was going home, he met
a Sardinian shepherd lamenting the loss of a lamb out of his flock.
Garibaldi at once turned to his staff, and announced his intention of
scouring the mountain in search of the lamb. A grand expedition
was organized. Lanterns were brought, and old officers of many a
campaign started off, full of zeal, to hunt the fugitive. But no lamb
was found, and the soldiers were ordered to their beds.

The next morning, Garibaldi's attendant found him in bed, fast
asleep. He was surprised at this, for the General was always up
before anybody else. The attendant went off softly, and returned in
half-an-hour. Garibaldi still slept. After another delay, the attendant awoke him. The General rubbed his eyes, and so did the attendant, when he saw the old warrior take from under the covering the
lost lamb, and bid him convey it to the shepherd. The General had
kept up the search through the night, until he found it. Even so
doth the Good Shepherd go in search of His lost sheep until He
find them.—*The Preachers' Monthly.*

Christ a Shepherd.—He is the Good Shepherd that laid down His
life for the sheep (John 10:11); the Great Shepherd that was brought
again from the dead (Heb. 13:20); the Chief Shepherd Who shall
appear again (I Peter 5:4); the Shepherd and Bishop of souls
(I Peter 2:25); He is the Shepherd of the sheep, who gathers the
lambs with His arm, and carries them in His bosom (John 10; Isaiah
40:11); the Shepherd of Israel (Ezekiel 34:23); Jehovah's Shepherd
(Zechariah 13:7).—JOHN BATE.

Why doth He not drive the sheep before Him, especially seeing it
was lively enough to lose itself? First, because, though it had wildness more than enough to go astray, it had not wisdom enough to

go right. Secondly, because probably the silly sheep had tired itself with wandering. "The people shall weary themselves for very vanity" (Hab. 2:13). Therefore the kind Shepherd brings it home on His own shoulders.—THOMAS FULLER.

Yam Sing, on his examination for membership on experience before the Baptist Church, San Francisco, in response to the question, "How did you find Jesus? answered, "I no find Jesus at all; He find me." He passed.

## CHAPTER 117

## THE ORDAINED MEMORIAL

*Luke 22:19, 20.*

Here we have full directions for observing the Lord's Supper.
You see what it was, and how it was done.
The directions are plain, clear, definite.

I. THE MAIN OBJECT OF THE SUPPER IS A PERSONAL MEMORIAL.

"In remembrance of *Me*." We are to remember not so much His doctrines, or precepts, as His Person.

Remember the Lord Jesus at this Supper—

1. As the trust of your hearts.
2. As the object of your gratitude.
3. As the Lord of your conduct.
4. As the joy of your lives.

II. THE MEMORIAL ITSELF IS STRIKING.

1. Simple, and therefore like Himself, Who is transparent and unpretentious truth. Only bread broken and wine poured out.
2. Frequent,—"as oft as ye drink it," and so pointing to our constant need. He intended the Supper to be often enjoyed.
3. Universal, and so showing the need of all. "Drink ye all of it." In every land, all His people are to eat and drink at this table.
4. His death is the best memory of Himself, and it is by showing forth *His death* that we remember *Him.*

III. THE OBJECT AIMED AT IS ITSELF INVITING.

1. We may come to it, though we have forgotten Him often and sadly. In fact, this will be a reason for coming.
2. We may come, though others may be forgetful of Him. We come not to judge *them*, but to remember Him ourselves.

Let us at the sacred table quit all other themes.
Let us not burden ourselves with regrets, resolves, etc.

Let us muse wholly and alone on Him Whose flesh is meat indeed, Whose Blood is drink indeed (John 6:55).

Our Lord Jesus has His own memorials of us, even as He has given us a memorial of Himself. The prints of the nails constitute forget-me-nots of a peculiarly personal and abiding kind: "Behold, I have graven thee upon the palms of My hands" (Isaiah 49:16). By these marks He sees what He has already suffered, and He pledges Himself to do nothing apart from those sufferings, for His hands, with which He works, are pierced. Since He thus bears in His hands the marks of His passion, let us bear them on our hearts.—C. H. S.

*"This do in remembrance of Me."* 1. This command implies a knowledge of Himself. To remember, we must first know. It is no use saying to a man born blind, "Remember the sunshine." 2. It reveals the love of Christ. Why should He care about our remembering Him? Dying voices have said to some of us, "Think of me sometimes; don't forget me." It is the very nature of love to want to be remembered. 3. It implies a tendency to forget. God never founds a needless institution. It is a sin that we do not remember Christ more. We should thankfully use every help to memory.—*Outline of an Address by* DR. STANFORD.

# CHAPTER 118

## SERVUS SERVORUM

*"I am among you as He that serveth"* (Luke 22:27).

Singular fact with regard to the apostles. They were at the same time troubled with two questions: "Which of them should be accounted the greatest?" and "Which of them should betray His Master?"

Where humility should have abounded ambition intruded.

The remedy which He used was His own conduct (John 13:12-17).

I. OUR LORD'S POSITION.

  1. In the whole course of His life, Jesus on earth ever took the place of the servant, or slave.

    His ear was bored by His entering into covenant. "Mine ears hast thou digged, or pierced" (Ps. 40:6 Margin; Ex. 21:6).

    His office was announced at His coming, "Lo, I come to do Thy will!" (Ps. 40:7; Heb. 10:5-9).

    His nature was fitted for service: He "took upon Him the form of a servant" (Phil. 2:7).

    He assumed the lowest place among men. (Ps. 22:6; Is. 53:3).

He cared for others, and not for Himself. "The Son of man came not to be served but to serve" (Mark 10:45).
He laid aside His own will. (John 4:34; 6:38).
He bore patiently all manner of hardness. (I Peter 2:23).

II. THE WONDER OF IT. THAT HE SHOULD BE A SERVANT AMONG HIS OWN SERVANTS.

The marvel of it was rendered the greater—

1. As He was Lord of all by nature and essence. (Col. 1:15-19).
2. As He was superior in wisdom holiness, power, and in every other way, to the very best of them. (Matt. 8:26, 27; John 14:9).
3. As He was so greatly their Benefactor. (John 15:16).

III. THE EXPLANATION OF IT.

We must look for this to His own nature.

1. He is so infinitely great. (Heb. 1:2-4).
2. He is so immeasurably full of love. (John 15:9; I John 3:16).

IV. THE IMITATION OF IT.

Let us copy our Lord—

1. In cheerfully choosing to fulfil the most lowly offices.
2. In manifesting great lowliness of spirit, and humility of bearing. (Eph. 4:1-3; Phil. 2:3; I Peter 5:5).
3. In gladly bearing injustice rather than break the peace, avenge ourselves, or grieve others. (I Peter 2:19, 20; 3:14).
   Does not the text rebuke our pride?
   Does it not arouse our adoring love?

Why is it that so many professed Christians "feel above" undertaking humble work for God and humanity? We have heard of a minister of Christ complaining that his station was "beneath his talents!" As if the soul of a beggar were beneath the genius of a Paul!

Some are unwilling to enter a mission-school or to distribute tracts through a poor district, strangely forgetting that their divine Master was Himself a missionary. Have such never learned that the towel wherewith Jesus wiped His disciples' feet outshone the purple that wrapped Cæsar's limbs? Do they not know that the post of honor is the post of service? "My seat in the Sunday-school is higher than my seat in the Senate," said an eminent Christian statesman.—DR. CUYLER.

CHAPTER 119

"FATHER, FORGIVE THEM"

*"Then said Jesus, Father, forgive them; for they know not what they do"* (Luke 23:34).

Let us go to Calvary to learn how we may be forgiven;
And then let us linger there to learn how we may forgive
There shall we see what sin is, as it murders the Lord of love.

I. WE SEE THE LOVE OF JESUS ENDURING.

To the closing act of human malice.
To the utmost endurance of shame. (Phil. 2:8; Heb. 12:2).
To the extreme limit of personal suffering. (Psalm 22:1-18).

II. WE SEE THAT LOVE REVEALING ITSELF.

Love, when in a death-agony, still prays.
Love thus brings heaven to the succor of those for whom it cares.

III. WE SEE HOW THE LOVING JESUS PRAYS.

For His wanton murderers in the very act.
For their full and immediate forgiveness.
For no other reason except their ignorance; and this plea grace alone could suggest or accept.

IV. WE SEE HOW HIS PRAYER BOTH WARNS AND WOOS.

It warns, for it suggests that there is a limit to the possibility of pardon.
Men may so sin that there shall remain no plea of ignorance; nay, no plea whatever. It woos, for it proves that if there be a plea, Jesus will find it.

V. WE SEE HOW HE INSTRUCTS FROM THE CROSS.

He teaches us to forgive the utmost wrong. (Mark 11:25).
He teaches us to pray for others to our last breath. (Acts 7:59, 60).

There is something in this plea that at first confounds me, and that makes me ask with reverence in what sense Christ used it. Surely ignorance is not the gospel plea. Ignorance gives no man a claim on God . . . We are not to say, "Being justified by ignorance, we have peace with God." . . . Ignorance is not innocence, it is often a sin; and one sin is no salvation from another.

The ignorance of Christ's enemies of what is involved in their capital crime brings them within the pale of mercy, and allows their pardon to be a possibility—a possibility on the ground which his cross supplies. Perhaps no mere men really know what they do in repudiating Christ. Satan knew what he did, and nothing has been said in our hearing of any gospel for him; but human sinners cannot fully know; and their ignorance, though it does not make sin sinless, leaves it pardonable.—CHARLES STANFORD.

O Saviour, Thou couldst not but be heard! Those who out of ignorance and simplicity thus persecuted Thee, find the happy issue of Thine intercession. Now I see whence it was that three thousand souls were converted soon after, at one sermon. It was not Peter's speech, it was Thy prayer, that was thus effectual. Now they have grace to know and confess whence they have both forgiveness and salvation, and can recompense their blasphemies with thanksgiving.

What sin is there, Lord, whereof I can despair of the remission? Or what offence can I be unwilling to remit,. when Thou prayest for the forgiveness of Thy murderers and blasphemers?—BISHOP HALL.

It was a mark of true moral grandeur in the character of Phocion, that, as he was about to be put to death, when one asked him whethei he had any commands to leave for his son, he exclaimed, "Yes, by all means, tell him from me to forget the ill-treatment I have received from the Athenians."

Such a spirit of forgiveness, if it became a heathen, will much more become a disciple of the gentle and loving Christ, Who, in His dying hour, prayed, "Father, forgive them; for they know not what they do." No one has a right to claim the Christian spirit who refuses to forgive a foe, and even cement his forgiveness by some act of self-denying love.

A great boy in a school was so abusive to the younger ones, that the teacher took the vote of the school whether he should be expelled. All the small boys voted to expel him except one, who was scarcely five years old. Yet he knew very well that the bad boy would continue to abuse him.

"Why, then, did you vote for him to stay?" said the teacher. "Because if he is expelled, perhaps he will not learn any more about God, and so he will become still more wicked." "Do you forgive him, then?" said the teacher. "Yes," said he, "father and mother forgive me when I do wrong; God forgives me too; and I must do the same."
—*The Biblical Treasury.*

## CHAPTER 120
## A DIVINE VISITATION

*"And as they thus spake, Jesus Himself stood in the midst of them, and saith unto them, Peace be unto you"* (Luke 24:36).

I. WHEN HE APPEARED.

1. When they had been acting unworthily by fleeing from Him at His betrayal, and deserting Him at His trial.

2. When they were unprepared, and unbelieving, doubting His express promise, and refusing the testimony of His messengers.
3. When they greatly needed His presence, for they were like sheep without a shepherd.

II. WHAT HE SAID. "Peace be unto you."
 1. It was a benediction: He wishes them peace.
 2. It was a declaration: they were at peace with God.
 3. It was a fiat: He inspired them with peace.
 4. It was an absolution: He blotted out all offences which might have spoiled their peace.

III. WHAT CAME OF HIS APPEARING.
 1. He banished their doubts. Even Thomas had to shake off his obstinate unbelief.
 2. He revealed and sealed His love upon their hearts by showing them His hands and His feet.
 3. He refreshed their memories. "These are the words which I spake unto you" (verse 44).
 4. He opened their understandings. (verse 45).
 5. He showed them their position. "Ye are witnesses of these things." (verse 48).
 6. He filled them with joy. (John 20:20).

There are depths in the ocean, I am told, which no tempest ever stirs; they are beyond the reach of all storms, which sweep and agitate the surface of the sea. And there are heights in the blue sky above to which no cloud ever ascends, where no tempest ever rages, where all is perpetual sunshine, and naught exists to disturb the deep serene. Each of these is an emblem of the soul which Jesus visits; to whom He speaks peace, whose fear He dispels, and whose lamp of hope He trims.—TWEEDIE.

In the life of Dr. John Duncan there is a touching passage which relates how much he suffered from religious melancholy. His mental struggles were often very distressing, casting a shadow over his whole life and work.

On one occasion, he went to his college-class in a state of extreme dejection. During the opening prayer, however, the cloud passed away. His eye brightened, his features relaxed, and before beginning his lecture he said, with pathetic sympathy, "Dear young gentlemen, I have just got a glimpse of Jesus."

We are soldiers of Jesus Christ. Now, that which nerves the soldier's arm, and strengthens his heart, as he goes forth to battle, is not so much the multitude of the army of which he forms a part, as the character of the chief whom he is following.

It is related that, in one of the Duke of Wellington's battles, a portion of the army was giving way, under the charge of the enemy, when he rode into the midst of them. A soldier called out in ecstasy, *"There's the Duke—God bless him! I'd rather see his face than a whole brigade";* and these words, turning all eyes to their chief, so reassured his comrades that they repulsed the foe; they felt, he is beside us who was never defeated yet, and who will not be defeated now.

A military friend, with whom I conversed on this subject, said that, though he had never heard the anecdote, he could well conceive it to be true: the presence of the distinguished General, he added, was at any time worth five thousand men.—TAIT *on the Hebrews.*

## CHAPTER 121

## OUR LORD'S ATTITUDE IN ASCENSION

*"And He led them out as far as Bethany, and He lifted up His hands, and blessed them"* (Luke 24:50).

The scene itself was very remarkable.
So unlike what superstition would have devised.
So quiet—no chariot of fire and horses of fire.
So majestic—no angels, nor other agents to lend imaginary splendor; but the Lord's own power and Godhead in sublime simplicity working all.

I.  HIS HANDS WERE UPLIFTED TO BLESS.

1. This blessing was with authority. He blessed them while His Father acknowledged Him by receiving Him to heaven.
2. This blessing was so full that, as it were, He emptied His hands. They saw those dear hands thus unladen of their benedictions.
3. The blessing was for those beneath Him, and beyond the sound of His voice: He scattered benedictions upon them all.

II.  THOSE HANDS WERE PIERCED.

This could be seen by them all as they gazed upward.
1. Thus they knew that they were Christ's hands.
2. Thus they saw the price of the blessing. His crucifixion has purchased continual blessing for all His redeemed.
3. Thus they saw the way of blessing: it comes from those human hands, through those sacrificial wounds.

III.  THOSE HANDS SWAY THE SCEPTRE.

His Hands are omnipotent. Those very hands, which blessed His disciples, now hold, on their behalf, the sceptre—
1. Of providence: both in small affairs and greater matters.
2. Of the future judgment, and the eternal reign.

What spot did Jesus select as the place of His ascension? He selected, not *Bethlehem,* where angelic hosts had chanted His praises; nor *Tabor,* where celestial beings had hovered around Him in homage; nor *Calvary,* where riven rocks and bursting graves had proclaimed His Deity; nor the *Temple-court,* in all its sumptuous glory, where, for ages, His own Shekinah had blazed in mystic splendor: but He hallows afresh the name of a lowly village, *Bethany;* He consecrates a Home of Love.—DR. MACDUFF'S *"Memories of Bethany."*

The manner of Christ's ascension into heaven may be said to have been an instance of divine simplicity and sublimity combined, which scarcely has a parallel. While in the act of blessing His disciples, He was parted from them, and was carried up, and disappeared behind a cloud. There was no pomp; nothing could have been more simple.

How can the followers of this Lord and Master rely on pomp and ceremony to spread His religion, when He, its Founder, gave no countenance to such appeals to the senses of men? Had some good men been consulted about the manner of the ascension, we can imagine the result.—N. ADAMS.

This is no death-bed scene. "Nothing is here for tears." We are not at the close, but at the beginning of a life. There is no sign of mourning that a great career is over, that the lips of a great Teacher are forever dumb; no ground for that melancholy question that twice rang in the ears of Elisha, "Knowest thou that the Lord will take away thy master from thy head today? And he said, Yea, I know it; hold ye your peace." No, the scene before us is one of calm victory.

The earthly work of the Redeemer is over; the work which that short sojourn on earth was designed to inaugurate is now to begin. We are in the presence of One Who said, "All power is given unto Me in heaven and in earth"; and again, "Be of good cheer, I have overcome the world."—DR. BUTLER, *Head Master of Harrow.*

That wonderful hand of Christ! It was that same hand which had been so quickly stretched out to rescue Peter when sinking in Galilee's waves. It was that same hand which had been held in the sight of the questioning disciples on the third evening after they had seen it laid lifeless in the tomb. It was that same hand which incredulous Thomas must see before he would believe its risen power; it was that same hand which was extended to him not only to see, but to touch the nail-prints in its palm. It was that same hand which the disciples last saw uplifted in a parting blessing when the cloud parted Him from them.

It was only after ten days that they realized the fulness of blessing which came from that extended, pierced hand of Christ. Peter at Pentecost must have preached with that last sight of it fresh in his memory, when he said, "God hath made that same Jesus, *whom ye have crucified*, both Lord and Christ." That hand, with its nail-prints, knocks at the heart's door for entrance. That hand, with its deep marks of love, beckons on the weary runner in the heavenly way.—F. B. PULLAN.

CHAPTER 122

## THE BAPTIST'S MESSAGE

*"The next day John seeth Jesus coming unto him, and saith, Behold the Lamb of God, which taketh away the sin of the world"* (John 1:29).

In the case before us the preacher was a notable man, and his theme more notable still. John the Baptist preaches Jesus.

We have here a model for every minister of Christ.

I. THE TRUE MESSENGER.

1. He is one who sees Jesus for himself. (Verse 33).
   He rejoices to preach Jesus as One Whom he has himself seen and known, and still hopes to see.
   He preaches Him as come, and as coming.
2. He calls upon men to see Jesus. "Behold the Lamb of God."
   This he does plainly and confidently.
   This he does continually: it is his one message. John preached the same sermon "again the next day after." (verse 35).
3. He leads His own followers to Jesus. John's disciples heard John speak, and followed Jesus. (Verse 37).
   He had enough force to induce men to be His followers.
   He had enough humility to induce his followers to leave him for Jesus. This is the glory of John the Baptist.
   He had enough grace to make him rejoice that it was so.
   Our speech should make men go beyond ourselves to Christ. "We preach not ourselves but Christ Jesus the Lord" (II Cor. 4:5).
4. He loses himself in Jesus.
   He sees the necessity of this. "He *must* increase, but I *must* decrease" (John 3:30).

II. THE TRUE MESSAGE.

John's word was brief, but emphatic.

1. He declared Jesus to be sent and ordained "of God."
2. He declared Him to be the one real, divinely appointed sacrifice for sin,—"the Lamb of God."
   He declared Him to be the only remover of human guilt,—"which taketh away the sin of the world."

III. THE TRUE RECEPTION OF THAT MESSAGE.
1. To believe it, and so to acknowledge Jesus as our sin-removing sacrifice.
2. To follow Jesus. (See verse 37).
3. To follow Jesus, even if we be alone.
4. To abide with Jesus. (See verse 39).
5. To go forth and tell others of Jesus. (See verses 40 and 41).

In 1857, a day or two before preaching at the Crystal Palace, I went to decide where the platform should be fixed; and, in order to test the acoustic properties of the building, cried in a loud voice, "Behold the Lamb of God, which taketh away the sin of the world."

In one of the galleries, a workman, who knew nothing of what was being done, heard the words, and they came like a message from heaven to his soul. He was smitten with conviction on account of sin, put down his tools, went home, and there, after a season of spiritual struggling, found peace and life by beholding the Lamb of God. Years after, he told this story to one who visited him on his death-bed.—C. H. S.

Notice, how simple the means, how grand the result! John simply declared, "Behold the Lamb of God!" Here is no vehement appeal, no angry rebuke, no feverish, would-be impressive urging; it is a simple, earnest declaration of God's truth. What else have Christ's servants to do but to set forth the truth, the Gospel, the will of God, as revealed in the Person and work of Christ?

How much more important to give all our energy and strength to this, than to the attempt of enforcing and applying, threatening and inviting, urging and pressing, in perorations thundering or melting! The truth itself thunders and melts, rouses and whispers, bruises and comforts; entering into the soul, it brings with it light and power. How calm and objective do Christ's sermons, and those of the apostles, appear! How powerful by the consciousness which pervades them: this is the truth of God, light from heaven, power from above! "Behold the Lamb of God."—ADOLPH SAPHIR.

It is related of John Wesley that, preaching to an audience of courtiers and noblemen, he used the "generation of vipers" text, and flung denunciation right and left. "That sermon should have been preached at Newgate," said a displeased courtier to Wesley, on passing out. "No," said the fearless apostle, "my text *there* would have been, 'Behold the Lamb of God, which taketh away the sin of the world.'"

No *herald* could live long in the wilderness on locusts and wild honey, if he had not to tell of a man or an era nobler than himself, and brighter than his own twilight-hour. John lived more truly on the prophecy he proclaimed than on the honey and locusts—DR. PARKER.

CHAPTER 123

## JESUS SITTING ON THE WELL

*"Now Jacob's well was there. Jesus therefore, being
wearied with His journey, sat thus on the well: and it
was about the sixth hour"* (John 4:6).

How worn was His humanity!  He was more weary than the
disciples.

His self-denials were even then remarkable.

He would not exempt Himself from fatigue.

He would not work a miracle for His own refreshment.

I. LET YOUR CONSCIENCE DRAW A SPIRITUAL PICTURE OF YOUR
WEARIED SAVIOR.

1. He is wearied with our sins. (Is. 43:24).
2. He is wearied with our formal worship. (Is. 1:14)
3. He is wearied with our erring through unbelief. (Ps. 95:10).
4. He is wearied with our resistance of His Spirit. (Is. 63:10).
5. He is wearied with our cavillings and rebellions. (Mal. 2:17).

Perhaps we have specially wearied the Lord, as we read in Amos
2:13, where singular provocations are mentioned.

That is a grave question asked by the prophet Isaiah, "Will ye
weary my God also?" (Is. 7:13).

II. LET YOUR CONSCIENCE DRAW A SPIRITUAL PICTURE OF YOUR
WAITING SAVIOR.

1. He waits for comers to the well: He seizes on all occasions to
   bless, such as affliction, the hearing of the Word, the recur-
   rence of a birthday, or even the simplest event of life.
2. He waits for the most sinful; she that had five husbands.
3. He waits to accept and to commission.
4. He waits to begin by one convert the ingathering of a great
   harvest of souls, as in the case of the Samaritans.

How long He has waited for some of you!

III. LET YOUR PENITENCE DRAW ANOTHER PICTURE.

Alter the position of the character.

1. Be yourself weary of your sinful way.
2. Wait and watch till your Savior comes.
3. Ask Him to give you to drink, and, in so doing, give Him to
   drink, for this is His best refreshment.
4. Drink yourselves of the living water, and then run to tell
   others.

While we sympathize with the bodily weariness of our Lord, it
will be well to remember the soul weariness which sin must have

occasioned Him. He hungered to bless men, and they refused the bread of life. He would have gathered them, but they would not be gathered. He must have been specially wearied with the ostentatious hypocrisy of the Pharisees, and the silly legalisms of the Scribes with their tithing of mint and anise. He was often wearied with the dogged unbelief of the Jews, and the provoking want of faith among His own disciples.

The sin, the cavilling, the slander, the selfishness, the hardness of heart of those about Him, must have worn down His holy soul, and made Him every day a Man of sorrows. Yet He never left the well, never refused to give the living water to a thirsting soul, never ceased to entreat men to come to Him and drink.—C. H. S.

When wearied, let us still be on the watch to do good. Wearied, and sitting on the well, our Lord is still in the attitude of observation. "I am never too tired to pray," said a minister, who, after a hard day's toil, found his host ready to excuse him from conducting family prayer.

When God is blessing the Word, true ministers forget their fatigue, and hold on long into the night with inquiries. Alas! when the Holy Spirit has nothing to do with a man's heart, the man excuses himself from "making overtime," as I once heard a professor call it, when he quitted the room the instant the service was over. Another, in describing a minister, said, "Oh, he is cold! He is one who thinks it is wrong to be too religious. He cannot endure zeal." Be it ours to show a more excellent way.

Holy Brainerd, when he could not preach, because he was on his dying bed, called to him a little Indian boy, and tried to teach him his letters. Let us live soul-saving, and so let us die.—C. H. S.

## CHAPTER 124
## SABBATH-WORK

*"On the same day was the Sabbath"* (John 5:9).

Six special cases of cures wrought on the Sabbath are recorded.
1. The evil spirit cast out. (Luke 4:31-35).
2. The withered hand restored. (Luke 6:6-10).
3. The crooked woman made straight. (Luke 13:10-17).
4. The man with the dropsy cured. (Luke 14:1-6).
5. The impotent man made whole. (John 5:1-9).
6. The blind man's eyes opened. (John 9:1-14).

As God rested on the Sabbath, and hallowed it; so as God it was rest to Jesus to heal, and thus He hallowed the day.

## I. THESE CURES MEET MANY CASES.

1. Those conscious of spiritual inability. (Luke 6:6-10).
2. Those bowed down with great distress. (Luke 13:10-17).
3. Those blind from birth. (John 9:1-14). Many are in this condition. They see no spiritual truth, but abide in total darkness as to all the Gospel truth.

## II. THESE CURES REPRESENT USUAL PROCESSES.

1. A word personal to the sufferer. "Stretch forth thy hand" (Luke 6:10). He was unable, and yet he was commanded; and he obeyed. This is the Gospel method.
2. A word accepted as done. "Thou art loosed from thine infirmity" (Luke 13:12). Faith turns promise into fact, Gospel-teaching into actual salvation.
3. Power without a word. (Luke 14:4).

## III. THESE CURES WERE ALL UNSOUGHT.

This is one special feature about them all.

1. The possessed man entreated Christ to leave him alone. (Luke 4:34).
2. The man with the withered hand did not think of cure. (Luke 6:6).
3. The infirm woman did not hope for healing. (Luke 13:11).
4. The man with the dropsy did not ask for the blessing. (Luke 14:2).
5. The infirm man was too paralyzed to seek Christ. (John 5:5).
6. It was an unheard-of thing that the eyes of a man born blind should be opened, and therefore he did not expect it. (John 9:32).

On his death-bed, Brainerd said: "I was born on a Sabbath-day; I have reason to hope I was new-born on a Sabbath-day; and I hope I shall die on this Sabbath-day."

The first day of the week was signalized by the giving of the light of nature, and it is most delightful that now it should be a chosen day for bestowing the light of grace.—C. H. S.

CHAPTER 125

## "WHERE IS HE?"

*"Then the Jews sought Him at the feast, and said, Where is He?"* (John 7:11).

No man, having once heard of Jesus, can any longer remain indifferent to Him; he *must* take some sort of interest in the Lord Jesus.

I. CONSIDER THE WAYS IN WHICH THE QUESTION HAS BEEN ASKED.
1. Hate, ferociously desiring to slay Him, and overthrow His cause. Herod was the type of this school.
2. Infidelity, sneeringly denying His existence, taunting His followers because His cause does not make progress. (II Peter 3:4).
3. Timorous fear, sadly doubting His presence, power, and prevalence. "Where is he that trod the sea?" (Job 23:8, 9).
4. Penitence, humbly seeking Him that she may confess her sin, trust her Lord, and show her gratitude to Him. (Job 23:3).

II. GIVE THE SAINTS' EXPERIMENTAL ANSWER.
1. He is at the mercy-seat when we cry in secret.
2. He is in the Word as we search the sacred page.
3. He is in the furnace of trial, revealing Himself, sanctifying the trial, bearing us through.
4. He is near us, yea, with us, and in us.

III. RETURN THE QUESTION TO YOU.
1. Is He at the bottom of your trust?
2. Is He at the root of your joys?
3. Is He on the throne of your heart?
4. Is His presence manifested in your spirit, your words, your actions?
5. Is He before you, the end of your journey, the terminus towards which you are daily hastening?

IV. ASK IT OF THE ANGELS.
They with one voice reply that the Lord Jesus Christ is—
1. In the bosom of the Father.
2. In the center of glory.
3. On the throne of government.

# CHAPTER 126

# CHRIST THE CAUSE OF DIVISION

*"So there was a division among the people because of Him"* (John 7:43).

To this day the greatest division in the world is *"because of Him."*

I. THERE WAS A DIVISION AMONG NON-DISCIPLES.
1. Some admitted none of His claims.
2. Others admitted a portion, but denied the rest.
3. Certain admitted His claims, but neglected to follow out the legitimate consequences of them.

    **4.** A few became His sincere hearers, going as far with Him as they had yet learned of Him.

**II. THERE WAS A DIVISION OF BELIEVERS FROM NON-BELIEVERS.**
There is a great division at this present hour—
1. In opinion: especially as to the Lord Jesus.
2. In trust: many rely on self; only the godly on Jesus.
3. In love. Differing pleasures and aims prove that hearts go after differing objects.
4. In obedience, character, and language.
5. In development, growth, tendency.
6. In destiny. The directions of the lines of life point at different places as the end of the journey.

This cleavage divides the dearest friends and relatives.
This is the most real and deep difference in the world.

**III. YET WHEN FAITH COMES, UNITY IS PRODUCED.**
1. Nationalities are blended. Calvary heals Babel.
   Jews and Gentiles are one in Christ.
2. Personal peculiarities cease to divide.
   Workers for Christ are sure to be blended in one body by their common difficulties.
3. Mental specialties feel the touch of unity.
   Saints of all styles of education are one in Jesus.
   Saints in heaven will be many as the waves, but one as the sea.
   Ambitions, which else would disintegrate, are overcome, and laid at Jesus' feet.

Let us divide, if there be a division.
Let us closely unite, if there be real union in Christ.

Christ, Who is properly the Author of peace, is, on account of the wickedness of men, the occasion of discord.—JOHN CALVIN.

There never lived any one who has so deeply moved the hearts of men as Jesus Christ has done. The greatest monarchs that ever reigned, the greatest warriors that ever fought, the greatest masters in art, or science, or literature, have never affected so many, and that to so great an extent, as Jesus of Nazareth has done.

He has changed the course of the world's history, and made its condition almost inconceivably different from what it would have been but for His coming. His teachings are received by the foremost nations of the earth. Millions of men call themselves by His name. He occupies the highest place in the esteem and affection of multitudes. For His sake men have lived as none others were able or willing to live: for His sake they have died as none others could or would have died.

But in proportion to the faith, the veneration, the love with which Christ is regarded by a portion of mankind, are the unbelief, the contempt and the hatred, which others display towards Him. The poles are not more widely sundered than are the sentiments of men respecting Christ. There is nothing about which they are more completely at variance.

Do you sing, "How sweet the name of Jesus sounds"? To this day the Jew curses that name, and the infidel brands it as the name of an imposter. Do you regard Christ as worthy of your warmest love? There are those who regard Him with a passionate hate. Satan himself cannot be more bitterly hostile to Christ than some men are.

Originating among the Jews, the Christian religion was regarded at first by great Rome as a mere Jewish sect, and shared alike in the impunity and the contempt with which that people were ever treated by their imperial masters. What did a Claudius or a Vespasian know, or care to know, of this new sect of Christians or Nazarenes, any more than of those other party names of Pharisee, Sadducee, Essene, Libertine, and the like? . . . Christ was then only "one Christus," and the controversies between His followers and the Jewish priests only one of those paltry squabbles to which that restless people were chronically subject.

By-and-by, as the young church became strong, it began to make its existence and its presence felt in the world, and then it stood in its genuine character and distinctive spirit, face to face with Rome. Once met, they instinctively recognized each other as its natural and irreconcilable enemy, and straightway a war of deadliest hate began between them, which was from the first one of extermination, and could terminate only by the fall of the one or the other. There was no room in the world for Christ and Cæsar, so one or the other must die.—ISLAY BURNS.

## CHAPTER 127
## PLACE FOR THE WORD

*"My word hath no place in you"* (John 8:37).

I. WHAT PLACE THE WORD SHOULD HAVE IN MEN'S HEARTS.

1. An inside place: in the thoughts, the memory, the conscience, the affections. "Thy Word have I hid in mine heart" (Ps. 119:11). See also Jer. 15:16; Col. 3:16.

2. A place of honor; it should receive attention, reverence, faith, obedience. (John 8:47; Luke 6:46; Matt. 7:24, 25.)

3. A place of trust. We ought in all things to rely upon the sure Word of promise, since God will neither lie, nor err, nor change. (Is. 7:9; I Sam. 15:29; Titus 1:2.)

4. A place of love. It should be prized above our daily food, and defended with our lives. (Job 23:12; Jude 3).

II. WHY IT HAS NO PLACE IN MANY MEN.

1. You are too busy and so you cannot admit it.
2. It does not come as a novelty and therefore you refuse it. You are weary of the old, old story.
    Are you wearied of bread? of air? of water? of life?
3. You are too wise, too cultured, too genteel, to yield yourself to the government of Jesus. (John 5:44; Rom. 1:22).
4. Is the reason of your rejection of the Word one of these?
    That you are not in earnest?
    That you are fond of sin?
    That you are greedy of evil gain?
    That you need a change of heart?

III. WHAT WILL COME OF THE WORD HAVING NO PLACE IN YOU?

1. Every past rejection of that Word has involved you in sin.
2. The Word may cease to ask for place in you.
3. You may become the violent opponent of that Word, like these Jews.
4. The Word will condemn you at the last great day. (John 12:48).

The only reason why so many are against the Bible, is because they know the Bible is against them.—G. S. BOWES.

# CHAPTER 128

## TRUE AND NOT TRUE

*"Now we know that God heareth not sinners: but if any man be a worshipper of God, and doeth His will, him He heareth"* (John 9:31).

It is ill to wrench passages of the Bible out of their context, and treat them as infallible Scripture, when they are only the sayings of men.

By acting thus foolishly we could prove that there is no God (Psalm 14:1), that God hath forgotten His people (Isaiah 49:14), that Christ was a winebibber (Matt. 11:19), and that we ought to worship the devil (Matt. 4:9).

This will never do. We must inquire who uttered the sentence before we begin to preach from it.

Our text is the saying of a shrewd blind man, who was far from being well instructed. It is to be taken for what it is worth; but by no means to be regarded as Christ's teaching.

## I. IT IS NOT TRUE IN SOME SENSES.

1. God does hear men who sin, or else He would hear no one; for there is not a man upon earth that sinneth not. (I Kings 8:46). Not a saint would be heard; for even saints are sinners.

2. God does sometimes hear and answer unregenerate men.
   To lead them to repentance. (I Kings 21:27).
   To leave them without excuse. (Exodus 10:16, 17).

3. God does graciously hear sinners when they cry for mercy.
   Not to believe this were to render the gospel no gospel.
   Not to believe this were to deny facts. David, Manasseh, the dying thief, the publican, the prodigal, confirm this testimony. (Isaiah 55:7).

## II. IT IS TRUE IN OTHER SENSES.

1. He hears no sinner's prayer apart from the mediation of our Lord Jesus. (I Tim. 2:5; Ephesians 2:18).

2. He will not hear a wicked, formal, heartless prayer. (Prov. 15:29).

3. He will not hear the man who wilfully continues in sin, and abides in unbelief. (Jer. 14:12; Is. 1:15).

4. He will not hear the unforgiving. (Mark 11:25, 26).

5. He will not hear even His people when sin is wilfully indulged, and entertained in their hearts. (Ps. 66: 18).

6. He will not hear sinners who die impenitent.
   At the last He will close His ear to them as to the foolish virgins, who cried, "Lord, Lord, open to us!" (Matt. 25:11).

It is our sins that block up the passage of our prayers. It is not the vast distance between heaven and earth, not the thick clouds, not the threefold regions, not the sevenfold orbs, not the firmament of heaven, but only our sins, that hinder the ascent of our prayers. "When ye make many prayers, I will not hear you." Why? "Because your hands are full of blood." God will have none of those petitions that are presented to Him with bloody hands.

Our prayers are our bills of exchange, and they are allowed in heaven when they come from pious and humble hearts; but if we be broken in our religion, and bankrupt of grace, God will protest our bills; He will not be won with our prayers.—THOMAS ADAMS.

God is "neither hard of hearing, nor hard of giving."

The blood of sheep and the blood of swine are both alike; yet the blood of swine was not to be offered, because it was the blood of swine; so the prayer of an unregenerate man may be as well framed, both for the petitions and for everything that is required immediately to a prayer, and yet not be accepted, because of the heart and person from whom it comes.—SAMUEL CLARK.

It is difficult to illustrate this truth, because, in human life, nothing ever takes place corresponding to what occurs when an impenitent sinner presumes to pray to God.

To every government many petitions are presented, but never one by any who are in rebellion against its authority. It is universally recognized, that rebellion against any government of itself cuts off all right of petition to it. So that, for an impenitent sinner to pray to God is one of the most unnatural and monstrous things that can be conceived of.

What rebellious city, besieged by the forces of the lawful government, would venture to ask aid from the government, on the ground that great distress prevailed in it, while all the time its inhabitants had not the slightest intention of surrendering to the government?— *The Preachers' Monthly.*

## CHAPTER 129

## THE DOOR

*"I am the door: by Me if any man enter in, he shall be saved, and shall go in and out, and find pasture"* (John 10:9).

Our Lord sets Himself forth very condescendingly.

The most sublime and poetical figures are none too glorious to describe Him; but He chooses homely ones, which the most prosaic minds can apprehend.

A door is a common object. Jesus would have us often think of Him.

A door to a sheepfold is the poorest form of door. Jesus condescends to be anything, so that He may serve and save His people.

I. THE DOOR. IN THIS HOMELY ILLUSTRATION WE SEE—

1. Necessity. Suppose there had been none, we could never have entered in to God, peace, truth, salvation, purity, or heaven.
2. Singularity. There is only one door; let us not weary ourselves to find another. Salvation is by entrance at that door, and at none other. (Acts 4:12).
3. Personality. The Lord Jesus is Himself the door. "I am the door," saith He; not ceremonies, doctrines, professions, achievements, but the Lord Himself, our Sacrifice.

II. THE USERS OF IT.

1. They are not mere observers, or knockers at the door, or sitters down before it, or guards marching to and fro in front of it. But they *enter in* by faith, love, experience, communion.

2. They are persons who have the one qualification: they do *"enter in."* The person is "any man," but the essential distinction is entrance.

A door which is conspicuously marked as THE DOOR is evidently meant to be used. The remarkable advertisement of "I am the door," and the special promises appended to it, are the most liberal invitation imaginable.

III. THE PRIVILEGES OF THESE USERS.

1. Salvation. "He shall be saved." At once, forever, altogether.
2. Liberty. He "shall go in and out." This is no prison-door, but a door for a flock whose Shepherd gives freedom.
3. Access. "Shall go in," for pleading, hiding, fellowship, instruction, enjoyment.
4. Egress. "He shall go out," for service, progress, etc.
5. Nourishment. "And find pasture." Our spiritual food is found through Christ, in Christ, and around Christ.

The work of the Reformation was thus described by Stern, a German statesman: "Thank heaven, Dr. Luther has made the entrance into heaven somewhat shorter, by dismissing a crowd of door-keepers, chamberlains, and masters of ceremony."—JOHN BATE.

We cannot go abroad or return home without passing through an emblem of our Lord. So near as He is in the type, so near let Him be in reality.—C. H. S.

There are not half-a-dozen ways out of our sin and misery—not a choice of ways over the steep hills and desolate waste-places of this mortal life, so that by any of them we may reach heaven at last, but only one way.

But, if this is the only way, it is likewise a perfectly secure way. *Via unica, via certa,* is a Latin proverb in which the truth is stated very forcibly.—DEAN HOWSON.

## CHAPTER 130

## LOVE'S IMPORTANCE

*"Ye have heard how I said unto you, I go away, and come again unto you. If ye loved Me, ye would rejoice, because I said, I go unto the Father: for My Father is greater than I"* (John 14:28).

I. WE SHOULD TRY TO SEE THINGS IN CHRIST'S LIGHT.

1. He sees the whole of things. He says not only, "I go away," but also, "I come again unto you."

2. He sees through things. He does not say, "I die," but He looks beyond, and says, "I go unto the Father."

3. He sees the true bearing of things. The events which were about to happen were in themselves sad, but they would lead to happy results. "If ye loved Me, ye would rejoice."

## II. OUR LOVE SHOULD GO FORTH TOWARDS HIS PERSON.

1. He is the source of all the benefits He bestows.
2. Loving Him, we have Him, and so His benefits.
3. Loving Him, we prize His benefits the more.
4. Loving Him, we sympathize in all that He does.
5. Loving Him, we love His people for His sake.
6. Loving Him, our love endures all sorts of rebuffs for His sake.
7. Loving Him, the Father loves us. (John 14:23).

## III. OUR SORROW OUGHT NOT TO PUT OUR LOVE IN QUESTION.

Yet, in the case of the disciples, our Lord justly said, "*If* ye loved Me."

He might sorrowfully say the same to us—

1. When we repine at His will, because of our severe afflictions.
2. When we fear to die, and thus display an unwillingness to be with our Lord. Surely, if we loved Him, we should rejoice to be with Him.

## IV. OUR LOVE SHOULD MAKE US REJOICE AT OUR LORD'S EXALTATION THOUGH IT BE OUR PERSONAL LOSS.

1. It was apparently the disciples' loss for their Lord to go to the Father; and we may think certain dispensations to be our loss—
   When we are afflicted, and He is glorified, by our sorrows.
   When we are eclipsed, and in the result the Gospel is spread.
   When we are deprived of privileges for the good of others.

2. It was greatly to our Lord's gain to go to His Father.
   Thus He left the field of suffering forever.
   Thus He reassumed the glory which He had laid aside.
   Thus He received the glory awarded by the Father.

A saint cares not how ill it goes with him so it goes well with Jesus Christ; he saith, as Mephibosheth to David, "Yea, let him take all, forasmuch as my lord the king is come again in peace unto his own house" (II Sam. 19:30). So it may go well with God's name, Moses cares not though his be blotted out of the book of life; and, said John the Baptist, "He must increase, but I must decrease; this my joy, therefore, is fulfilled."—RALPH VENNING.

CHAPTER 131

# A WATCHWORD

*"Arise, let us go hence"* (John 14:31).

Our Lord was under marching-orders, and He knew it: for Him there was no stay upon this earth.

Hear how He calls Himself, and all His own, to move on, though bloody sweat, and bloody death be in the way.

I. OUR MASTER'S WATCHWORD.

By this stirring word—

1. He expressed His desire to obey the Father.
   He was not hindered by expected suffering.
2. He indicated His readiness to meet the arch-enemy. "The prince of this world cometh. Arise, let us go hence."
   He was prepared for the test. He "hath nothing in Me."
3. He revealed His practical activity. All through the chapter observe our Lord's energy. He is ever on the move. "I go. I will come again. I will do it. I will pray. Arise, let us go hence."
   He prefers action to the most sacred rites, and so leaves the Supper-table with this word on His lips.
   He prefers action to the sweetest converse. "I will not talk much with you. Arise, let us go hence."

II. OUR OWN MOTTO. "Arise, let us go hence."

Ever onward, ever forward, we must go. (Exodus 14:15).

1. Out of the world when first called by grace. (II Cor. 6:17).
2. Out of forbidden associations, if, as believers, we find ourselves like Lot in Sodom. "Escape for thy life" (Gen. 19:17).
3. Out of present attainments when growing in grace. (Phil. 3:13, 14).
4. Out of all rejoicing in self. There we must never stop for a single instant. Self-satisfaction should startle us.
5. To suffer when the Lord lays affliction upon us. (II Cor. 12:9).
6. To die when the voice from above calls us Home. (II Tim. 4:6).

It was well said once by a remarkable man, and the words are worth remembering,—"Bear in mind that you are just then beginning to go wrong when you are a little pleased with yourself because you are going right." Let us watch against this as a snare of Satan, and endeavor ever to maintain the apostolic attitude: "In lowliness of mind let each esteem other better than himself."

And let me caution you not to make the mistake of supposing that this self-complacency can be effectually guarded against by a mere use of the recognized theological expressions duly ascribing all the merit and all the praise to God. These are too often merely the garments of spiritual pride, and by no means must they be mistaken for true humility.—W. H. M. H. AITKEN.

Pressed on all sides by the enemy, the Austrian General Melas sent a messenger to Suwarrow, asking whither he should "retire." Suwarrow wrote with a pencil, *"Forward."*

The zealous are impatient of any hindrances. As Edmund Burke said to the electors of Bristol, "Applaud us when we run; console us when we fall; cheer us when we recover; but let us pass on—for God's sake, let us pass on!"

Brethren, let this be our motto, and our cry, "Onward." Until the last wandering sheep, far out upon the bleak mountain-side hears Christ's voice, and is gathered into His fold.—A. H. BAYNES.

## CHAPTER 132

## "BEHOLD YOUR KING!"

*"He saith unto the Jews, Behold your king"* (John 19:14).

I. BEHOLD HIM PREPARING HIS THRONE.
  1. He lays the foundation of it in His suffering nature.
  2. He makes it a throne of grace by His atoning griefs.

II. BEHOLD HIM CLAIMING OUR HOMAGE.
  He claims and wins our adoration—
  1. By the right of supreme love.
  2. By the right of complete purchase.
  3. By the right of grateful consecration, which we heartily accord to Him under a sense of loving gratitude.

III. BEHOLD HIM PROVING THE CERTAINTY OF HIS KINGDOM.
  1. Is He King there in His shame? Then, assuredly He is King now that He has risen from the dead, and gone into the glory.
  2. Is He King amid shame and pain? Then He is able to help us if we are in like case.
  3. Is He King while paying the price of our redemption? Then, certainly, He is King now that it is paid, and He has become the author of eternal salvation.
  4. Is He King at Pilate's bar? Then, truly, He will be so when Pilate stands at His bar to be judged.

It is far worse to despise a Saviour in His robes than to crucify Him in His rags. An affront is more criminal to a prince upon his throne than when he is disguised as a subject, and masked in the clothes of his servant. Christ is entered into glory after His sufferings; all who are His enemies must enter into misery after their prosperity: and whosoever will not be ruled by His golden sceptre shall be crushed by His rod.—STEPHEN CHARNOCK.

Did Pilate hope to melt the Jewish heart to a sort of scornful pity? Did he think that they would turn away from so wretched an object, and be ashamed of having accused *Him* of treason? Perhaps so. But he failed. The sorrows of Jesus do not of themselves overcome the hate of man; but this fact proves how desperately hardened his heart has become.

Given the Holy Spirit, there is nothing more likely to win men to Jesus than beholding Him in His sorrows. Behold, O man, and see what thy sin has done, what thy Redeemer has borne, and what He claims of thee! Behold Him not as another's, but as thine! Behold Him not only as thy Friend, thy Saviour, but thy King! Behold Him, and at once fall at His feet, and own thyself His loving subject! —C. H. S.

CHAPTER 133

## A HANDKERCHIEF

*"Jesus saith unto her, Woman, why weepest thou? Whom seekest thou?"* (John 20:15).

Woman has had many reasons for weeping since the fall.

Jesus went to His death amid weeping women, and on His rising He met a little company of them.

The first words of a risen Savior are to a weeping woman.

He Who was born of woman has come to dry up woman's tears.

I. IS IT NATURAL SORROW?

1. Art thou bereaved? The risen Savior comforts thee; for—
   He assures thee of the resurrection of the departed.
   He is with thee, thy living Helper.
   He sympathizes with thee, for He once lost His friend Lazarus; yea, He Himself has died.

2. Are thy beloved ones sick?
   He lives to hear prayer for healing.

3. Art thou thyself sick?
   Jesus lives to moderate thy pains.
   Jesus lives to sustain thy heart under suffering.
   Jesus lives to give life to thy body, as He has done to thy soul.

## II. Is It Spiritual Sorrow?

1. *Distinguish.* See whether it be good or ill. "Why weepest thou?"

   Is it selfish sorrow? Be ashamed of it.

   Is it rebellious? Repent of it.

   Is it ignorant? Learn of Jesus, and so escape it.

   Is it hopeless? Believe in God and hope ever.

2. *Declare.* Tell Jesus all about it. "Why weepest thou?"

   Is it sorrow for others? He weeps with thee.

   Are loved ones abiding in sin?

   Is the church cold and dead?

   Is it the sorrow of a seeking saint? He meets thee.

   Do thy prayers appear to fail?

   Does thine old nature rebel?

   Is it the sorrow of one in doubt? He will strengthen thee.

   Come to Jesus as a sinner.

   Is it the sorrow of a seeking sinner? He will receive thee.

   Dost thou weep because of past sin?

   He accepts thee: in Him thou hast all thou art seeking for.

A Hindoo woman said to a missionary, "Surely your Bible was written by a woman." "Why?" "Because it says so many kind things for women. Our pundits never refer to us but in reproach."—BISHOP HALL.

The first words that ever Christ spake after His resurrection to them He appeared to, were, "Woman, why weepest thou?" It is a good question after Christ's resurrection. What cause of weeping remains now that Christ is risen? Our sins are forgiven, because He, our Head and Surety, hath suffered death for us; and if Christ be risen again, why weep we? If we be broken-hearted, humbled sinners, that have interest in His death and resurrection, we have no cause to grieve.—RICHARD SIBBES.

"Good men weep easily," says the Greek poet; and the better any are, the more inclined to weeping, specially under affliction. As you may see in David, whose tears, instead of gems, were the ornaments of his bed; in Jonathan, Job, Ezra, Daniel, etc. "How," says one, "shall God wipe away my tears in heaven if I shed none on earth? And how shall I reap in joy if I sow not in tears? I was born with tears, and I shall die with tears; and why then should I live without them in this valley of tears?"—THOMAS BROOKS.

## CHAPTER 134

# NOLI ME TANGERE

*"Jesus saith unto her, Touch Me not; for I am not yet as-
cended to My Father: but go to My brethren, and say
unto them, I ascend unto My Father, and your Father;
and to My God, and your God"* (John 20:17).

I. THE CAUTION. "Touch me not."

    1. We may carnalize the spiritual.
This has ever been a tendency with even the best of the saints;
and it has misled many in whom affection has been stronger
than intellect.

    2. We may seek most passionately what is by no means essential.
The assurance of sense, by touch or otherwise: when the
assurance of faith is far better, and quite sufficient.

    3. We may crave what were better further on.
When we are raised to eternal glory we shall be able to enjoy
what now we must not ask.

II. THE MISSION. "Go to My brethren."

    1. This was better for her. Contemplation alone may degenerate
into the sentimental, the sensuous, the impracticable.

    2. This was unquestioningly done by this holy woman. What she
had seen she declared.
What she had heard she told.
Women are said to be communicative; and so there was wisdom in the choice.

III. THE TITLE. "My brethren."

    1. His brethren, though He was about to ascend to His throne.

    2. His brethren though they had forsaken Him in His shame.
Relationship owned more than ever; since their sense of guilt
made them afraid. He was a true Joseph to them. (Gen.
45:4).

IV. THE TIDINGS. "I ascend unto My Father, and your Father."

    1. By the news of His departure they are to be aroused.

    2. By His ascension to the common Father they are to be com-
forted with the prospect of coming there themselves. He is
not going into an unknown country, but to His home and
theirs. (John 14:2).

It is this that men will labor after, and have labored for, even from
the beginning of the world,—to be too much addicted to the things of
sight and sense. They will worship Christ, but they must have a
picture before them. They will adore Christ, but they must bring

His body down to a piece of bread. They must have a presence, and so, instead of raising their hearts to God and Christ in a heavenly manner, they pull down God and Christ to them.

This the pride and base earthliness of man will do. And therefore saith Christ, "Touch Me not" in that manner; it is not with Me now as it was before. We must take heed of mean and base conceits of Christ. What saith Paul in II Cor. 5:16? "Henceforth know we no man after the flesh, yea, though we have known Christ after the flesh, yet now henceforth know we Him no more."—RICHARD SIBBES.

To whom doest Thou send her? "Go to *My brethren*." Blessed Jesus! who are these? Were they not Thy followers? Yea, were they not Thy forsakers? Yet still Thou stylest them Thy brethren. O admirable humanity! O infinite mercy! How doest thou raise their titles with Thyself? At first they were Thy servants, and then Thy disciples; a little before Thy death they were Thy friends; now, after Thy resurrection, they were Thy brethren. Thou that wert exalted infinitely higher from mortal to immortal, descendest so much lower to call them brethren who were before friends, disciples, servants.—BISHOP HALL.

While the going up of Elias may be compared to the flight of a bird which none can follow, the ascension of Christ is, as it were, a bridge between heaven and earth, laid down for all who are drawn to Him by His earthly existence.—BAUMGARTEN.

## CHAPTER 135

## SIGNS AND EVIDENCES

*"Then saith He to Thomas, Reach hither thy finger, and behold My hands; and reach hither thy hand, and thrust it into my side: and be not faithless, but believing"* (John 20:27).

Thomas set His Lord a test, and thus tried His patience.
The Lord accepted the test, and so proved His condescension.
Peradventure, certain among us would desire tests of some such sort.

I. CRAVE NO SIGN.

  1. It is dishonoring to your Lord.
  2. It is damaging to ourselves. Faith must be weak while we demand for it such proofs; and in this weakness lies incalculable mischief.

3. It is dangerous. We may readily be driven either into infidelity or superstition, if we give way to this craving for signs.

Picture what Thomas could and would have become under the influence of his unbelief, had not His Lord interposed.

## II. YET TURN TO CHRIST'S WOUNDS.

1. The seals of His death. He did actually and truly die. How could He outlive that wound in His side?

2. The identification of His person as actually risen.

3. The tokens of His love. He has graven us upon the palms of His hands.

4. The ensigns of His conflict, of which He is not ashamed, for He displays them.

5. The memorials of His passion, by which He is manifested in glory as the Lamb that was slain. (Rev. 5:6).

Tell the inhabitant of the sultry climes, that, at a certain season of the year, water, which he has only seen in a fluid state, becomes solid and hard enough to walk upon—and it will seem to him an idle tale: he has witnessed no such thing, and reasoning from what he knows, deems it incredible. If Thomas had constantly judged according to the rule he professed, how little could he have believed at all! . . .

To believe no more than we can comprehend, or reduce to some of our modes of knowledge, is not to honor the authority of God at all; yea, it is a reflection upon His wisdom, and upon His veracity: upon His wisdom—as if He could tell us no more than we know; and upon His veracity—as if He were not to be trusted if He could.—WILLIAM JAY.

## CHAPTER 136

## BONDS WHICH COULD NOT HOLD

*"Whom God hath raised up, having loosed the pains of death: because it was not possible that He should be holden of it"* (Acts 2:24).

## I. IT WAS NOT POSSIBLE THAT THE BANDS OF DEATH SHOULD HOLD OUR LORD.

He derived His superiority to the bondage of death—

1. From the command of the Father that He should have power to take His life again. (John 10:18).

2. From the dignity of His human person.
   As in union with Godhead.
   As being in itself absolutely perfect.

3. From the nature of things, since without it we should have—
   No assurance of our resurrection. (I Cor. 15:17).
   No certainty of justification. (Rom. 4:25).
   No representative possession of heaven. (Heb. 9:24).

II. IT IS NOT POSSIBLE THAT ANY OTHER BANDS SHOULD HOLD HIS KINGDOM.

1. The firm establishment of error shall not prevent the victory of truth. The colossal systems of Greek philosophy and Roman priestcraft have passed away; and so shall other evil powers.

2. The scholarship of His foes shall not resist His wisdom. He baffled the wise in His life on earth; much more will He do it by His Holy Spirit. (I Cor. 1:20).

3. The ignorance of mankind shall not darken His light. "The poor have the Gospel preached to them" (Matt. 11:5). Degraded races receive the truth. (Matt. 4:16).

4. The power, wealth, fashion, and prestige of falsehood shall not crush His kingdom. (Acts 4:26).

III. IT IS NOT POSSIBLE TO HOLD IN BONDAGE ANYTHING THAT IS HIS.

1. The poor struggling sinner shall escape the bonds of his guilt, his depravity, his doubts, Satan, and the world. (Ps. 124:7).

2. The bondaged child of God shall not be held captive by tribulation, temptation, or depression. (Ps. 34:19; Ps. 116:7).

3. The bodies of His saints shall not be held in the grave. (I Cor. 15:23; I Peter 1:3-5).

4. The groaning creation shall yet burst into the glorious liberty of the children of God. (Rom. 8:21).

The Emperor Theodosius, having on a great occasion opened all the prisons, and released his prisoners, is reported to have said, "And now, would to God I could open all the tombs, and give life to the dead!"

But there is no limit to the mighty power and royal grace of Jesus. He opens the prisons of justice, and the prisons of death with equal and infinite ease: He redeems not the soul only, but the body.—DR. STANFORD.

## CHAPTER 137

# LIFE-WOUNDS

*"Now when they heard this, they were pricked in their heart"* (Acts 2:37).

Peter's sermon was not a fine display of eloquence;
Neither was it a very pathetic plea;
Nor a loud but empty cry of "Believe, believe!"
It was a simple, a plain statement, and a soberly earnest argument.

I. SAVING IMPRESSION IS A PRICK IN THE HEART.

To be cut to the heart is deadly (Acts 5:33): to be pricked in the heart is saving.

1. All true religion must be of the heart.
   Without this—
   Ceremonies are useless. (Is. 1:13).
   Orthodoxy of head is in vain. (Jer. 7:4).
   Profession and a constrained morality fail. (II Tim. 3:5).
2. Impressions which do not prick the heart may even be evil.
   They may excite to wrath and opposition.
   They may lead to sheer hypocrisy.
   They may create and foster a spurious hope.

II. WHAT TRUTHS PRODUCE SUCH A PRICK?

1. The truth of the Gospel has often, by the power of the Holy Ghost, produced an indelible wound in minds sceptical and opposed.
2. A sense of some one specially startling sin has frequently aroused the conscience. (II Sam. 12:7).
3. Instruction in the nature of the law, and the consequent heinousness of sin, has been blessed to that end. (Rom. 7:13).
4. The exactness, severity, and terror of the judgment, and the consequent punishment of sin, are stirring thoughts. (Acts 16:25-30).
5. The great goodness of God has led many to see the cruel wantonness of sin against Him. (Rom. 2:4).

III. WHAT HAND MAKES THESE PAINFUL PRICKS?

1. The same hand which wrote the piercing truths also applies them.
2. He is well acquainted with our hearts, and so can reach them.
3. He is the Quickener, the Comforter, the Spirit helping our infirmities, showing to us the things of Jesus: His fruit is love, joy, peace, etc. We need not utterly despair when wounded by such a tender Friend.

IV. How Can These Pricks Be Healed?

1. Only One Who is Divine can heal a wounded heart.
2. The only medicine is the Blood of His heart.
3. The only hand to apply it is that which was pierced.
4. The only fee required is gladly to receive Him.

Conversion is a work of *argument*, for the judgment is gained by the truth. It is a work of *conviction*, for the awakened are pricked in their hearts. It is a work of *enquiry*, for they ask, "What must we do to be saved?" And, lastly, it is a work of *comfort*, for its subjects have received remission of sins, and the gift of the Holy Ghost.—Joseph Sutcliffe.

"Therefore let Jerusalem know assuredly that God hath made Him Lord." I call that Peter's colossal "therefore." It is the strongest word in the first oration delivered in the defence of Christianity. The Holy Spirit was promised; He has been poured out; therefore let those who receive Him know that the power behind natural law—our Lord, Who was, and is, and is to come—is now breathing upon the centuries as He breathed upon us symbolically. He hath shed forth this; therefore, let all men know assuredly that God hath made Him Lord. When they who were assembled at Jerusalem at that time heard this *"therefore,"* they were pricked in the heart.—Joseph Cook.

Heart-work must be God's work. Only the great heart-Maker can be the great heart-Breaker.—Richard Baxter.

The Comforter came to convince the world. The Comforter! Does it seem a strange name to any of you, my brethren, for Him Who came on such an errand? Does it seem to you that, in convincing you of your sins, instead of comforting you, He must needs cover you with shame and confusion, and make you sink to the ground in unutterable anguish and dismay?

No, dear brethren, it is not so. Those among you whom the Spirit has indeed convinced of sin, will avouch that it is not. They will avouch that, in convincing them of sin, He has proved that He is indeed the Comforter. If the conviction and consciousness of sin arise from any other source, then indeed it is enough to crush us with shame, and to harrow us with unimaginable fears. But when it comes from the Spirit of God, it comes with healing and comfort on its wings.

Remember what the sin is, of which He convinces us—that we believe not in Christ. All other conviction of sin would be without hope; here the hope accompanies the conviction, and is one with it. If we have a deep and lively feeling of the sin of not believing in Christ, we must feel at the same time that Christ came to take away this along with all other sins.—J. C. Hare.

When a man is wounded with a barbed arrow, the agonies he suffers will cause him to toss about in pain; but the harder he strives to release the weapon from his flesh, the more does it become entangled in his sinews, the wound becomes enlarged, and the torture is increased.

When, by the power of the Holy Spirit, a man is wounded on account of sin, and the arrows of the Most High tear his soul, he frequently tries to pluck them out with his own hand, but finds that the misery becomes worse, and the inflaming wounds at last cause faintness and despair. Only the Good Physician knows how to relieve the pain without tearing and festering the spirit.—*Handbook of Illustration.*

## CHAPTER 138

## THE GOLDEN MUZZLE

*"And beholding the man which was healed standing with them, they could say nothing against it"* (Acts 4:14).

The opposition of ungodly men is—
Natural, seeing that the heart of man is depraved.
Endurable, since our Lord and His apostles suffered it.
Harmless, if we commit the case to God.
Overruled for good by Divine grace and wise Providence.

Those who would say *anything* if they could, can say *nothing* of what they would, when they see before their eyes the cures wrought by the Word of the Lord Jesus.

I. THE GOSPEL IS VINDICATED BY ITS RESULTS.

1. On a broad scale in nations. England, the islands of the Pacific, Jamaica, Madagascar, etc.
2. In individual conversions from open sin. Some of the worst of men have become clear instances of the purifying power of the Gospel.
3. In holy and happy death-beds. These are plentiful throughout history, among all ranks; and they never fail to convince the candid.

II. GOSPEL-WORKS AND WORKERS MUST LOOK FOR LIKE VINDICATION.

Nowadays men ask for results: the tree must bear fruit, or the cry is, "Cut it down." We do not shrink from this test.

1. The minister must find in his converts a proof of his call, and a defence of his doctrines, methods, peculiarities, etc.
2. Even our Lord Himself loses or gains honor among men according as His followers behave themselves.

### III. The Gospel and Its Workers Deserve Vindication At Our Hands.

Those who are healed should boldly stand with Peter and John, as witnesses and fellow-workers.

This suggests a series of practical questions:

1. Has it produced blessed results in us?
2. Have we come forward to stand with the preachers of it in evidence that it has wrought our cure? Are we continually witnessing to the truth and value of the Gospel of Christ?
3. Does the influence of the Gospel upon us so continue and increase unto holiness of life as to be a credit to its influence?

In the course of one of his journeys, preaching the word, Mr. Wesley went to Epworth. Having offered to assist the curate on the following day (Sunday), and his offer being refused, he took his stand upon his father's tombstone in the evening, and preached to the largest congregation Epworth had ever witnessed.

This he did night after night. He preached also during his stay of eight days at several of the surrounding villages, where societies had been formed and a great work wrought among the people, and some of them had suffered for it. "Their angry neighbors," says Wesley, "had carried a whole wagon-load of these new heretics before a magistrate. But when he asked what they had done, there was a deep silence; for it was a point their conductors had forgotten. At length one said, 'They pretended to be better than other people, and prayed from morning to night!' and another said, 'They have *converted* my wife. Till she went among them she had such a tongue! and now she is as quiet as a lamb!' 'Take them back, take them back,' replied the justice, 'and let them convert all the scolds in the town.'" *Tyerman's Life of Wesley.*

Lord Peterborough, more famed for his wit than for his religion, when he had lodged with Fenelon, the Archbishop of Canterbury, was so charmed with his piety and beautiful character, that he said to him at parting, "If I stay here any longer I shall become a Christian in spite of myself."—G. S. Bowes.

Certain gentlemen waited upon Rev. Matthew Wilks to complain of the eccentricities of his discourses. Wilks heard them through, and then produced a long list of names. "There," said the quaint divine, "all those precious souls profess to have found salvation through what you are pleased to call my whims and oddities. Can you produce a similar list from all the sober brethren you have been so much extolling?" This was conclusive: they withdrew in silence.

The behavior of some professors has often given the wicked an opportunity to reproach religion. Lactantius reports, that the heathen were wont to say, "The Master could not be good, when His disciples were so bad."

The malice of sinners is such that they will reproach the rectitude of the law, for the obliquity of their lives who swerve from it. Oh that your pure life did but hang a padlock upon their impure lips! —WILLIAM SECKER.

## CHAPTER 139

## STEPHEN AND SAUL

*"The witnesses laid down their clothes at a young man's feet, whose name was Saul"* (Acts 7:58).

The Holy Spirit records Stephen's martyrdom, but does not enter into details of his sufferings and death, as uninspired recorders would have been so apt to do.

The object of the Holy Ghost is not to indulge curiosity nor to harrow the feelings, but to instruct and move to imitation.

He tells us of the martyr's posture,—"He kneeled down"; his prayer,—"Lord, lay not this sin to their charge", and his composure, —"he fell asleep." Upon each of these points volumes might be written.

I. A SUGGESTED CONTRAST. STEPHEN AND SAUL.

1. Stephen spiritual; giving in his address great prominence to the spiritual nature of religion, and the comparative insignificance of its externals. (See verses 48-50).
Saul superstitious, worshipping form and ritual, full of reverence for the temple and the priests, and so forth.

2. Stephen, a humble believer in the Lord Jesus, saved by faith alone.
Saul, a self-righteous Pharisee as proud as he could live.

II. A SINGULAR INTRODUCTION TO TRUE RELIGION.

Many have been brought to God by means somewhat similar.

The young man whose name was Saul, met with the religion of Jesus in the person of Stephen, and thus he saw it with the following surroundings:

1. The vision of a shining face.
2. The hearing of a noble discourse.
3. The sight of a triumphant death.

These did not convert Saul, but they made it harder for him to be unconverted, and were, no doubt, in after days thought of by him.

Let us so introduce religion to men, that the memory of its introduction may be worth their retaining.

## III. A Remarkable Instance of the Lord's Care For His Church.

1. Stephen's death was a terrible blow to the cause; but at that moment his successor was close at hand.
2. That successor was in the ranks of the enemy.
3. That successor was far greater than the martyr, Stephen, himself.

## IV. A Gracious Memorial of Repented Sin.

Did not Paul give Luke this information concerning himself? and cause it to be recorded in the Acts of the Apostles?

It was well for Paul to remember his sin before conversion.

It will be well for us to remember ours.

1. To create and renew feelings of humility.
2. To inflame love and zeal.
3. To deepen our love to the doctrines of sovereign grace.

A Spanish painter, in a picture of Stephen conducted to the place of execution, has represented Saul as walking by the martyr's side with melancholy calmness. He consents to his death from a sincere, though mistaken, conviction of duty: and the expression of his countenance is strongly contrasted with the rage of the baffled Jewish doctors and the ferocity of the crowd who flock to the scene of bloodshed.

Literally considered, such a representation is scarcely consistent either with Saul's conduct immediately afterwards, or with his own expressions concerning himself at the later periods of his life. But the picture, though historically incorrect, is poetically true. The painter has worked according to the true idea of his art in throwing upon the persecutor's countenance the shadow of his coming repentance.

We cannot dissociate the martyrdom of Stephen from the conversion of Paul. The spectacle of so much constancy, so much faith, so much love, could not be lost. It is hardly too much to say with Augustine, that "the church owes Paul to the prayer of Stephen." —Conybeare and Howson.

As soon as Satan heard of the conversion of Saul, he ordered the devils into deep mourning.—John Ryland, Senior.

Among the leaders of the great revival of the eighteenth century were Captain Scott and Captain Toriel Joss, the former a captain of dragoons, the latter a sea-captain. Both became famous preachers. Whitefield said of them, "God, Who sitteth upon the flood, can bring a shark from the ocean, and a lion from the forest, to show forth His praise."

The following lines by William Hone, author of the "Every-Day Book," were written to describe his own experience—

> The proudest heart that ever beat
> Hath been subdued in me;
> The wildest will that ever rose
> To scorn Thy cause, and aid Thy foes,
> Is quell'd, my God, by Thee.
>
> Thy will, and not my will, be done;
> My heart be ever Thine;
> Confessing Thee, the mighty Word,
> My Saviour Christ, my God, my Lord,
> Thy cross shall be my sign.

## CHAPTER 140

## "TO YOU"

*"To you is the word of this salvation sent"* (Acts 13:26).

I. WHAT IS THE WORD OF THIS SALVATION?

1. It is the testimony that Jesus is the promised Savior. (Verse 23).
2. The word which promises forgiveness to all who exhibit repentance of sin, and faith in the Lord Jesus. (Verses 38, 39).
3. In a word, it is the proclamation of perfect salvation, through the risen Savior. (Verses 32, 33).

It is a word *of salvation;* for it declares, describes, presents, and presses home salvation.

It is a word *sent,* for the Gospel dispensation is a mission of mercy from God, the Gospel is a message, Jesus is the Messiah, and the Holy Ghost Himself is *sent* to work salvation among men.

II. IN WHAT MANNER IS THE GOSPEL SENT TO YOU?

1. In the general commission, which ordains that it be preached to every creature.
2. In the providence which has brought you this day to hear the word.
3. In the peculiar adaptation of it to your case, character, and necessity. A medicine which suits your disease is evidently meant for you.

It would be a sad thing if we had to single out even one, and say,— "This word is *not* sent to you."

III. IN WHAT POSITION DOES IT PLACE YOU?

 1. Of singular favor. Prophets and kings died without hearing
    what you hear. (Matt. 13:16).
 2. Of notable indebtedness to martyrs and men of God, in past
    **ages**, and in these days; for these have lived and died to bring
    you the Gospel.
 8. Of great hopefulness; for we trust you will accept it and live.
 4. Of serious responsibility; for if you neglect it, how will you
    escape? (Heb. 2:3).

IV. IN WHAT MANNER WILL YOU TREAT THIS WORD?

 1. Will you basely and foolishly delay your reply?
    This is a very dangerous course, and many perish in it.
 2. Will you play the hypocrite, and pretend to receive it, while
    in your heart you reject it?
 3. Will you act the part of the temporary convert?
 4. Will you not rather accept the word of salvation with delight?

Jesus said, "Preach the Gospel to every creature." I can imagine
Peter was asking Him: "What, Lord! shall we offer salvation to the
men who crucified You?" And I imagine Jesus answering him:
"Yes, Peter, I want you to preach My Gospel to everybody, beginning at Jerusalem. Proclaim salvation to the men who crucified Me.

"Peter, I'd like you to find that man who put the crown of thorns
on My head. Tell him, if he'll take salvation as a gift, he shall have
a crown of glory from Me, and there sha'n't be a thorn in it. Look
up that Roman soldier who thrust that spear into My side, to My
very heart, and tell him that there's a nearer way to My heart than
that. My heart is full of love for his soul. Proclaim salvation to
him."—D. L. MOODY.

*To whom* is it that the God of salvation sent "the word of salvation"? He sent it to all sinners that hear it. It is a word that
suits the case of sinners; and therefore it is sent to them. If it be
inquired, for what *purpose* is it sent to sinners? . . . It is sent as
a word of *pardon* to the condemned sinner. Hence may every condemned sinner take hold of it, saying, This word is sent to me. It
is sent as a word of *peace* to the rebellious sinner.

It is sent as a word of *life* to the dead. It is a word of *liberty*
to the captives, of *healing* for the diseased, of *cleansing* to the polluted. It is a word of *direction* to the bewildered, and of *refreshment* to the weary. It is sent as a *comforting* word to the discon-
solate; and as a *drawing* word and a *strengthening* word to the soul
destitute of strength. It is sent, in short, as a *word of salvation*,
and *all sorts* of salvation and redemption to the lost soul, saying,
"Christ came to seek and to save that which was lost."—*Condensed
from* RALPH ERSKINE.

CHAPTER 141

# GROWING AND PREVAILING

*Acts 19:18-20.*

The Gospel is the same as ever.
The human race is unchanged at heart.
The sins to be overcome are the same.
The Holy Spirit is just as mighty to convince and renew.

## I. THE WORD OF GOD PLANTED.

Planted it was, or it could not have grown.
The work proceeded in the following fashion—

1. Certain disciples were further enlightened, aroused, and led to seek a higher degree of grace.
2. A bold ministry proclaimed and defended the truth.
3. Opposition was aroused. This is always a needful sign. God is not at work long without the devil working also.
4. Deceitful counterfeiting commenced.

## II. THE WORD OF GOD GROWING.

1. In a church formed with many suitable elders.
2. In a people converted, and openly confessing their conversion.

Is the Word of God growing among us? If not, why not?
It is a living seed, and should grow.
It is a living seed, and will grow unless we hinder it.

## III. THE WORD OF GOD PREVAILING.

Growth arouses opposition; but where the Word grows with inward vitality it prevails over outward opposition.

1. Paul does not appear to have dwelt continually upon the evil habit of using magical arts; but Gospel light showed the guilt of witchcraft, and providence cast contempt on it.
2. The sin being exposed, it was confessed by those who had been guilty of it, and by those who had commenced its study.
3. Their destruction involved expense, which was willingly incurred, and that expense gave weight to the testimony.

It's a blessed time in a soul, it's a blessed time in a family, it's a blessed time in a congregation, it's a blessed time in a country—when the Word of God grows mightily and prevails. . . . .

It's a blessed time when open sinners are seen leaving their sins and seeking the Saviour; when men are seen giving up their unholy gains; when tavern-keepers take down their signs and burn them—when they give up their licenses; and it's a blessed time when card-players throw away their cards and take the Bible instead. It's a blessed time when the lovers of gaudy dress take their gaudy dresses and destroy them.—ROBERT MURRAY M'CHEYNE.

The Gospel, like a plant of great vigor, will grow almost among stones. Thus have I seen it grow among hypocrites, formalists, and worldlings; and I have seen it laying hold of one, and another, and indeed, of many, however untoward the surrounding soil. "So mightily grew the Word of God and prevailed."—RICHARD CECIL.

The Earl of Rochester, of whom it has been said that he was "a great wit, a great scholar, a great poet, a great sinner, and a great penitent," left a strict charge to the person in whose custody his papers were, to burn all his profane and lewd writings, as being only fit to promote vice and immorality; by which he had so highly offended God, and shamed and blasphemed the holy religion into which he had been baptized.

## CHAPTER 142

## THE OX AND THE GOAD

*"Saul, Saul, why persecutest thou Me? It is hard for thee to kick against the pricks"* (Acts 26:14).

Jesus even out of heaven speaks in parables, according to His wont.

I. THE OX. A FALLEN MAN DESERVES NO HIGHER TYPE.

1. You are acting like a brute beast, in ignorance and passion. You are unspiritual, thoughtless, unreasonable.
2. Yet God values you more than a man does an ox.
3. Therefore He feeds you, and does not slay you.

II. THE OX-GOAD. YOU HAVE DRIVEN THE LORD TO TREAT YOU AS THE HUSBANDMAN TREATS A STUBBORN OX.

1. The Lord has tried you with gentle means, a word, a pull of the rein, etc.: by parental love, by tender admonitions of friends and teachers, and by the gentle promptings of His Spirit.
2. Now He uses the more severe means—
Of solemn threatening by His law.
Of terrors of conscience, and dread of judgment.
Of loss of relatives, children, friends.
Of sickness, and varied afflictions.
Of approaching death, with a dark future beyond it.

III. THE KICKS AGAINST THE GOAD.

1. There are early childish rebellions against restraint.
2. There are sneers at the Gospel, at ministers, at holy things.
3. There are wilful sins against conscience and light.

4. There are revilings and persecutions against God's people.
5. There are questionings, infidelities, and blasphemies.

IV. THE HARDNESS OF ALL THIS TO THE OX.

It hurts itself against the goad, and suffers far more than the driver designs.

1. In the present. You are unhappy: you are full of unrest and alarm, you are increasing your chastisement, and fretting your heart.
2. In the best possible future. You will feel bitter regrets, have desperate habits to overcome, and much evil to undo. All this if you do at last repent and obey.

Dr. John Hall, in one of his sermons, compared the attacks of infidelity upon Christianity to a serpent gnawing at a file. As he kept on gnawing, he was greatly encouraged by the sight of the growing pile of chips; till, feeling pain, and seeing blood, he found that he had been wearing his own teeth away against the file, but the file was unharmed.—POLLOK.

The Spirit of God can make use of any agency to bring sinners to repentance and faith in the Redeemer. Commenting once upon the words, "The ox knoweth his owner, and the ass his master's crib; but Israel doth not know, My people doth not consider," the speaker sought to impress upon his people how strangely guilty the human heart is, despising the goodness of God, and forgetting His very existence.

Three or four days after, a farmer, who had been present, was giving provender to his cattle, when one of his oxen, evidently grateful for his care, fell to licking his bare arm. Instantly, with this simple incident, the Holy Spirit flashed conviction on the farmer's mind. He burst into tears, and exclaimed, "Yes, it is all true. How wonderful is God's word! This poor dumb brute is really more grateful to me than I am to God, and yet I am in debt to Him for everything. What a sinner I am!" The lesson had found its way to his heart, and wrought there effectually to lead him to Christ.

## CHAPTER 143
## KINDLING A FIRE

*"And the barbarous people showed us no little kindness:
for they kindled a fire, and received us every one, because of the present rain, and because of the cold"* (Acts
28:2).

I. THAT WE ARE APT TO BE COLD.

1. The world is a cold country for gracious men.
2. By reason of our inbred sin, we are cold subjects, and far too apt to be lukewarm, or frozen.

**3.** Cold seasons also come, when all around lies bound in frost. Ministers, churches, saints, are too often cold as ice.

**4.** Chilling influences are now abroad. Modern thought, worldliness, depression in trade, depreciation of prayer, etc.

If we yield to the power of cold, we become first uncomfortable, next inactive, and then ready to die.

## II. That There Are Means of Warmth.

**1.** The Word of God is as a fire. Heard or read, it tends to warm the heart.

**2.** Private, social, and family prayer. This is as coals of juniper.

**3.** Meditation and communion with Jesus. "While I was musing the fire burned" (Ps. 39:3). "Did not our heart burn within us, while He talked with us by the way?" (Luke 24:32).

**4.** Fellowship with other Christians. (Malachi 3:16).

## III. That We Should Kindle Fires For Others.

Concerning a true revival, let it be remembered that it both resembles the fire in the text, and differs from it.

**1.** It must be lighted under difficulties,—"because of the present rain." The sticks are wet, the hearth is flooded, the atmosphere is damp. It is not easy to make a fire in such circumstances; and yet it must be done.

**2.** The fire we need cannot, however, be kindled by barbarians: the flame must come from above.

**3.** Once get the flame, the fire begins with littles. Small sticks are good for kindling.

**4.** It is well to nourish the flame by going down on your knees, and breathing upon it by warm and hearty supplications.

**5.** It must be fed with fuel. Think of the great Paul picking up a bundle of sticks. Let each one bring his share.

**6.** The fire will be of great service, and yet it may warm into life more than one viper. Thank God, the fire which revived the creature into venomous life will also destroy it.

How to maintain spiritual warmth. Philip Henry's advice to his daughter was: "If you would keep warm in this cold season (January, 1692), take these four directions: 1. Get into the sun. Under his blessed beams there are warmth and comfort. 2. Go near the fire. 'Is not My Word like a fire?' How many cheering passages are there! 3. Keep in motion and action—stirring up the grace and gift of God that is in you. 4. Seek Christian communion. 'How can one be warm alone?' "—*Feathers for Arrows*.

## CHAPTER 144

# CONCERNING THE FORBEARANCE OF GOD

*"Or despisest thou the riches of His goodness and for-*
*bearance and longsuffering; not knowing that the good-*
*ness of God leadeth thee to repentance?"* (Romans 2:4).

It is an instance of divine condescension that the Lord reasons
with men, and asks this question, and others like it. (Is. 1:5, 55:2;
Jer. 3:4; Ezek. 33:11).

It is a sad thing that any who have seen God's judgments on others,
and have escaped themselves, should draw from this special mercy a
reason for adding sin to sin. (Jer. 3:8).

I. LET US HONOR THE LORD'S GOODNESS AND FORBEARANCE.

1. It is manifested to us in a threefold form—
   Goodness which has borne with past sin. (Ps. 78:38).
   Forbearance which bears with us in the present. (Ps. 103:10).
   Longsuffering which, in the future as in the past and the
   present, is prepared to bear with the guilty. (Luke 13:7-9).

2. It is manifested in its excellence by three considerations.—
   The person who shows it. It is "the goodness *of God*" Who is
   Omniscient to see sin, just to hate it, powerful to punish it,
   yet patient towards the sinner. (Ps. 145:8).
   The being who receives it. It is dealt out to man, a guilty,
   insignificant, base, provoking, ungrateful being. (Gen. 6:6).
   The conduct to which it is a reply. It is love's response to
   sin. Often God forbears, though sins are many, wanton,
   aggravated, daring, repeated, etc. (Mal. 3:6).

II. LET US CONSIDER HOW IT MAY BE DESPISED.

1. By claiming it as our due, and talking as if God were bound
   to bear with us.

2. By perverting it into a reason for hardness of heart, presumption, infidelity, and further sin. (Zeph. 1:12; Eccl. 8:11).

3. By urging it as an apology for procrastination. (II Pet. 3:3-4)

III. LET US FEEL THE FORCE OF ITS LEADING.

1. He is not hard and unloving, or He would not have spared us.

2. To go on to offend would be cruel to Him, and disgraceful to
   ourselves. Nothing can be baser than to make forbearance a
   reason for provocation.

3. It is evident from His forbearance that He will rejoice to
   accept us if we will turn to Him. He spares that He may save.

The forbearance and longsuffering of God toward sinners is truly astonishing. He was longer in destroying Jericho than in creating the world.—BENJAMIN BEDDOME.

According to the proverb of the Jews, "Michael flies but with one wing, and Gabriel with two"; God is quick in sending angels of peace, and they fly apace; but the messengers of wrath come slowly: God is more hasty to glorify His servants than to condemn the wicked—JEREMY TAYLOR.

It is observable that the Roman magistrates, when they gave sentence upon any one to be scourged, a bundle of rods tied hard with many knots was laid before them. The reason was this: that whilst the beadle, or flagellifer, was untying the knots, which he was to do in a certain order, and not in any other hasty or sudden way, the magistrate might see the deportment and carriage of the delinquent, whether he were sorry for his fault, and showed any hope of amendment, that then he might recall his sentence, or mitigate the punishment; otherwise he was to be corrected the more severely.

Thus God, in the punishment of sinners, how patient is He! how loath to strike! how slow to anger if there be but any hopes of recovery! How many knots doth He untie! How many rubs doth He make in His way to justice! He doth not try us by martial law, but pleads the case with us, "Why will ye die, O house of Israel?"

To sin against law is daring, but to sin against love is dastardly. To rebel against justice is inexcusable, but to fight against mercy is abominable. He who can sting the hand which nourishes him is nothing less than a viper. When a dog bites his own master, and bites him when he is feeding him, and fondling him, no one will wonder if his owner becomes his executioner.

## CHAPTER 145

## "JESUS OUR LORD"

*"Jesus our Lord"* (Romans 4:24).

This Name, Lord, is a great contrast to incarnation, and humiliation.

In the manger, in poverty, shame, and death, Jesus was still Lord.

I. HIS TENDER CONDESCENSIONS ENDEAR THE TITLE.

1. We acknowledge Him as Lord the more fully and unreservedly, because He loved us, and gave Himself for us.

2. In all the privileges accorded to us in Him He is Lord:—
In our salvation, we have "received Christ Jesus the Lord" (Col. 2:6).

In entering the church we find Him the head of the body, to Whom all are subject. (Eph. 5:23).

In our life-work He is Lord. "We live unto the Lord" (Rom. 14:8). We glorify God in His name. (Eph. 5:20).

In resurrection He is the firstborn from the dead. (Col. 1:18).

At the Advent His appearing will be the chief glory. (Titus 2:13).

In eternal glory He is worshipped forever. (Rev. 5:12, 13).

II. OUR LOVING HEARTS READ THE TITLE WITH PECULIAR EMPHASIS.

1. We yield it to Him only. Moses is a servant, but Jesus alone is Lord. "One is your Master" (Matt. 23:8, 10).

2. To Him unreservedly. We wish our obedience to be perfect.

3. To Him in all matters of administration in the church, and in providence. "It is the Lord, let Him do what seemeth Him good" (I Sam. 3:18).

III. WE FIND SWEETNESS IN THE WORD "OUR."

1. It makes us remember our personal interest in the Lord.
Each believer uses this title in the singular, and calls Him from his heart, "My Lord."
David wrote, "Jehovah said unto my Lord."
Elizabeth spoke of "The mother of my Lord."
Magdalene said, "They have taken away my Lord."
Thomas said, "My Lord and my God."
Paul wrote, "The knowledge of Christ Jesus my Lord," etc.

2. Our zeal to make Him Lord forbids all self-exaltation. "Be not ye called Rabbi: for one is your Master, even Christ. Neither be ye called masters," etc. (Matt. 23:8, 10).

3. Our common joy in Jesus as our Lord becomes an evidence of grace, and thus of union with each other. (I Cor. 12:3).

It ought to be the great care of every one of us to follow the Lord fully. We must in a course of obedience to God's will, and service to His honor, follow Him universally, without dividing; uprightly, without dissembling; cheerfully, without disputing; and constantly, without declining; and this is following Him fully.—MATTHEW HENRY.

A disciple of Christ is one that gives up himself to be wholly at Christ's disposing; to learn what He teaches, to believe what He reveals, to do what He commands, to avoid what He forbids, to suffer what is inflicted by Him or for Him, in expectation of that reward which He hath promised. Such a one is a disciple of Christ, and he, and none else, is a Christian.—DAVID CLARKSON.

It was thought a wondrous act of condescension when King George III visited the tent of the dying gipsy woman in Windsor forest, and entered into religious conversation with her. What shall we think of Him, who, though He was the King of glory, came down to us, and took our sins and sorrows upon Himself, that He might bring us into fellowship with Himself for ever?

## CHAPTER 146

## HEIRS OF GOD

*"And if children, then heirs; heirs of God, and joint heirs with Christ; if so be that we suffer with Him, that we may be also glorified together"* (Romans 8:17).

This chapter is like the garden of Eden, which had in it all manner of delights. If one were shut up to preach only from the eighth of Romans he would have a subject which might last a lifetime. Every line of the chapter serves for a text. It is an inexhaustible mine. Paul sets before us a golden ladder, and from every step he climbs to something yet higher: from sonship he rises to heirship, and from heirship to joint-heirship with the Lord Jesus.

I. THE GROUND OF HEIRSHIP. "If children, then heirs."

1. It does not follow from ordinary creation. It is not written—if creatures, then heirs.

2. Neither is it found in natural descent. It is not written—if children of Abraham, then heirs. (Rom. 9:7, 13).

3. Nor can it come by meritorious service. It is not written—if servants, then heirs. (Gal. 4:30).

4. Nor by ceremonial observances. It is not written—if circumcised or baptized, then heirs (Rom. 4:9, 12).
   Our being regenerated or born again unto God by His Holy Spirit is our one ground of heirship.

II. THE UNIVERSALITY OF THE HEIRSHIP. "Children, then heirs."

1. The love of God is the same to them all.

2. They are all blessed under the same promise. (Heb. 6:17).

3. The inheritance is large enough for them all.

III. THE INHERITANCE WHICH IS THE SUBJECT OF HEIRSHIP. "Heirs of God."

Our inheritance is divinely great. We are—
Heirs of all things. "He that overcometh shall inherit all things" (Rev. 21:7). "All things are yours" (II Cor. 3:21).
Heirs of salvation. (Heb. 1:14).
Heirs of eternal life. (Tit. 3:7).

**Heirs of** Promise. (Heb. 6:17).

**Heirs of** the grace of life. (I Pet. 3:7).

**Heirs of** righteousness. (Heb. 11:7).

Heirs of the kingdom. (James 2:5).

IV.   THE PARTNERSHIP OF THE CLAIMANTS TO HEIRSHIP.   "And joint-heirs with Christ."

1. This ·is the test of our heirship.  We are not heirs except with Christ, through Christ and in Christ.
2. This ensures it to us; for Jesus will not lose it, and His title-deed and ours are one and indivisible.
3. This joint heirship binds us faster to Jesus, since we are nothing, and have nothing apart from Him.

How God treats men.  "He pardons them and receives them into His house, He makes them all children, and all His children are His heirs, and all His heirs are princes, and all His princes are *crowned*." —JOHN PULSFORD.

As a dead man cannot inherit an estate, no more can a dead soul inherit the kingdom of God.—SALTER.

As justification is union and communion with Christ in His righteousness; and sanctification is union and communion with Christ in His holiness, or His holy character and nature; so, by parity of reasoning, adoption must be held to be union and communion with Christ in His Sonship; surely the highest and best union and communion of the three.—DR. CANDLISH.

*Inheritance.*—What is it?  The pay of a soldier is not inheritance; neither are the fees of a lawyer, nor of a physician; nor the gains of trade; nor the wages of labor.  The rewards of toil and skill, these are earned by the hands that receive them.  What is inherited, on the other hand, may be the property of a new-born babe; and so the coronet, won long ago by the stout arm of valor, and first blazoned on a battered shield, now stands above the cradle of a wailing infant. —DR. GUTHRIE.

# CHAPTER 147

# DISOBEDIENCE TO THE GOSPEL

*"But they have not all obeyed the gospel.  For Esaias saith, Lord, who hath believed our report?"* (Romans 10:16).

Man is the same disobedient creature under all dispensations.  We bemoan his rejection of the gospel, and so did Isaiah, who spoke in the name of the whole company of the prophets.

It is one of the greatest proofs of the depravity of man's heart that he will no more obey the gospel than the law, but disobeys his God, whether He speaks to him in love or in law.

## I. THE GOSPEL COMES TO MEN WITH THE FORCE OF A COMMAND.

It is not optional to men to accept or refuse it at pleasure. (Acts 17:30).

It is so put—

1. To secure the honor of God. It is not the offer of an equal to an equal, but of the great God to a condemned sinner.
2. To embolden the proclaimer of it. The minister now speaks boldly with his Master's authority.
3. To encourage the humble seeker. He must be at full liberty to believe in Jesus, since he is commanded to do so, and threatened if he does not do so.

## II. WHAT, THEN, ARE THE CLAIMS OF THE GOSPEL TO OBEDIENCE?

1. The authority of the sender. Whatever God commands, man is under bonds to do.
2. The motive of the sender. Love shines in the gospel command, and no man should slight infinite love.
3. The great gift of the sender: He has given us His only begotten Son.
4. The earnestness of the sender. His whole heart is in the gospel. Note the high position which the scheme of salvation occupies in the esteem of God.

## III. WHAT IS THE OBEDIENCE REQUIRED BY THE GOSPEL?

Not mere hearing, crediting, liking, professing, or proclaiming; but a hearty obedience to its command.

It claims,

1. Faith in the Lord Jesus Christ.
2. Renunciation of self-righteousness, and confession of guilt.
3. Repentance and practical quittance of sin.
4. Public confession of His name, in His own way, namely, by baptism.

A powerful argument to prove the enmity of man's heart against God is the unsuccessfulness of the gospel; which can be resolvable into nothing else but such an enmity. The design of the gospel is to bring us into a union with the Son of God, and to believe on Him Whom the Father hath sent. Christ seeks to gather in souls to God, but they will not be gathered.

This is a matter of fearful consideration, that when God is calling after men by His own Son, there be so few that will come to Him. How few there are that say, "Give me Christ, or I am lost! None can reconcile me to God, but Christ!" You are daily besought in

Christ's stead, to be reconciled, but in vain! What does this signify, but obstinate, invincible enmity?—JOHN HOWE.

To disobey the gospel is far worse than to break the law. For disobedience to the law there is remedy in the gospel, but for disobedience to the gospel no remedy can be found. "There remaineth no more sacrifice for sins."

## CHAPTER 148

## PATIENCE, COMFORT AND HOPE

*"For whatsoever things were written aforetime were written for our learning, that we through patience and comfort of the Scriptures might have hope"* (Romans 15:4).

This is the text from which old Hugh Latimer was wont to preach continually in his latter days. Certainly it gave him plenty of searoom.

The apostle declares that the Old Testament Scriptures are meant to teach New Testament believers.

Things written aforetime were written for our time.

The Old Testament is not outworn; apostles learned from it.

Nor has its authority ceased; it still teaches with certainty.

I. THE PATIENCE OF THE SCRIPTURES.

    1. Such as they inculcate.

    Patience under every appointment of the divine will.

    Patience under human persecution and satanic opposition.

    Patience under brotherly burdens. (Gal. 6:2).

    Patience in waiting for divine promises to be fulfilled.

    2. Such as they exhibit in examples.

    Job under divers afflictions triumphantly patient.

    Joseph patiently forgiving the unkindness of his brethren, and bearing the false accusation of his master.

    David in many trials and under many reproaches, patiently waiting for the crown, and refusing to injure his persecutor.

    Our Savior patient under all the many forms of trial.

II. THE COMFORT OF THE SCRIPTURES.

    1. Such as they inculcate.

    They bid us to rise above fear. (Ps. 46:1-3).

    They urge us to think little of all transient things.

    They command us to find our joy in God.

    2. Such as they exhibit.

    Enoch walking with God.

Abraham finding God his shield and exceeding great reward.
David strengthening himself in God.
Hezekiah spreading his letter before the Lord.

III. THE HOPE OF THE SCRIPTURES.

Scripture is intended to work in us a good hope.
The hope of salvation. (I Thess. 5:8).
"The blessed hope, and the appearing of our Lord." (Titus 2:13).
The hope of the resurrection of the dead. (Acts 23:6).
The hope of glory. (Col. 1:27).

How much important matter do we find condensed in this single
verse! What a light and glory does it throw on the Word of God!
It has been well noted, that we have here *its authority*, as it is a
written word; *its antiquity*, as it was written aforetime; *its utility*,
as it is written for our learning.—JAMES FORD.

Oliver Cromwell once read aloud Phil. 4:11-13, and then remarked,
"There, in the day when my poor child died, this Scripture did go
nigh to save my life."

When George Peabody was staying at Sir Charles Reed's house, he
saw the youngest child bringing to his father a large Bible for family prayers. Mr. Peabody said, "Ah! my boy, you carry your Bible
now; but the time is coming when you will find that *the Bible must
carry you.*"

"Speak to me now in Scripture language alone," said a dying
Christian. "I can trust the words of God; but when they are the
words of man, it costs me an effort to think whether I may trust
them."—G. S. BOWES.

As an instance of the patience, comfort, and hope, which come from
the gospel, note the following from *Dr. Payson:*—Christians might
avoid much trouble if they would believe that God is able to make
them happy without anything else. God has been depriving me of
one blessing after another; but as every one was removed, he has
come in and filled up its place; and now, when I am a cripple, and
not able to move, I am happier than ever I was in my life before, or
ever expected to be. If I had believed this twenty years ago, I might
have been spared much anxiety.

CHAPTER 149

## BOUGHT WITH A PRICE

*"And ye are not your own, for ye are bought with a
price: therefore glorify God in your body, and in your
spirit, which are God's"* (I Cor. 6:19, 20).

With what ardor does the apostle pursue sin to destroy it!
He is not so prudish as to let sin alone, but cries out, in plainest

language, "Flee fornication." The shame is not in the rebuke, but in the sin which calls for it.

He chases this foul wickedness with arguments. (See verse 18).

He drags it into the light of the Spirit of God. "What? Know ye not that your body is the temple of the Holy Ghost?" (Verse 19).

He slays it at the cross. "Ye are bought with a price."

Let us consider this last argument, that we may find therein **death** for our sins.

## I. A BLESSED FACT. "Ye are bought with a price."

"Ye are bought." This is that idea of Redemption which modern heretics dare to style *mercantile*. The mercantile redemption is the Scriptural one; for the expression, "bought with a price," is a double declaration of that idea.

1. This is either a fact or not. "Ye are bought, or ye are un-redeemed." Terrible alternative.
2. If a fact, it is *the* fact of your life. A wonder of wonders.
3. It will remain to you eternally the greatest of all facts. If true at all, it will never cease to be true, and it will never be outdone in importance by any other event.
4. It should therefore operate powerfully upon us both now and ever.

## II. A PLAIN CONSEQUENCE. "Ye are not your own."

*Negative.* It is clear that if bought, ye are *not* your own.

1. This involves privilege.

   You are not your own provider: sheep are fed by their shepherd.

   You are not your own guide: ships are steered by their pilot.
2. This also involves responsibility.

   We are not our own to injure. Neither body nor soul.

   Not our own to waste, in idleness, amusement, or speculation.

   Not our own to exercise caprice, and follow our own prejudices, depraved affections, wayward wills, or irregular appetites.

*Positive.* "Your body and your spirit, which are God's."

   We are altogether God's. Body and spirit include the whole man.

   We are always God's. The price once paid, we are forever His.

## III. A PRACTICAL CONCLUSION. "Glorify God in your body, and in your spirit, which are God's."

Glorify God *in your body*.

By cleanliness, chastity, temperance, industry, cheerfulness, self-denial, patience, etc.

Glorify God—

In a suffering body by patience unto death.
In a working body by holy diligence.
In a worshipping body by bowing in prayer.
In a well-governed body by self-denial.
In an obedient body by doing the Lord's will with delight.
Glorify God *in your spirit*.

By holiness, faith, zeal, love, heavenliness, cheerfulness, fervor, humility, expectancy, etc.

But why should so vast a price be required? Is man worth the cost? A man may be bought in parts of the world for the value of an ox. It was not man simply, but man in a certain relation, that had to be redeemed. See one who has been all his days a drunken, idle, worthless fellow. All appropriate to him the epiphet "worthless"—worth nothing.

But that man commits a crime for which he is sentenced to be hanged, or to be imprisoned for life. Go and try to buy him now. Redeem him and make him your servant. Let the richest man in Cambridge offer every shilling he possesses for that worthless man, and his offer would be wholly vain, why? Because now there is not only the man to be considered, but the law. It needs a very great price to redeem one man from the curse of the law of England; but Christ came to redeem all men from the curse of the Divine law.—WILLIAM ROBINSON.

# CHAPTER 150
## EXAMINATION BEFORE COMMUNION

*"But let a man examine himself, and so let him eat of that bread, and drink of that cup"* (I Cor. 11:28).

The Lord's Supper is not for all men, but only for those who are able spiritually to discern the Lord's body.

It is not meant for the conversion of sinners, but for the edification of disciples.

Hence the need of examination, lest we intrude ourselves where we have no right to be.

I. THE OBJECT OF THE EXAMINATION.

1. That he may know that the responsibility rests with himself. The examination is not by priest or minister: he examines *himself*.

2. That he may communicate solemnly, and not come to the table carelessly, and as a matter of course. He is to make heart-searching enquiry, and so approach the table with self-humiliation.

   3. That he may come to the table intelligently, knowing to what he comes and why, and wherefore.

## II. THE MATTER OF THE EXAMINATION.

   1. It is a feast.

      Have I life? The dead sit not at banquets.

      Have I appetite? Else how can I eat?

      Have I a friendship toward the Lord Who is the Host?

      Have I put on the wedding garment?

   2. Jesus bids us show forth His death.

      Have I faith in His death?

      Do I live by His death?

   3. Jesus bids us do this by eating bread.

  Is this eating a symbol of a fact, or is it a mere mockery?

  Is Jesus really and truly the food of my soul?

   4. Jesus bids each believer do this in union with others.

      Am I truly one of His people, and one with them?

   5. Jesus calls His people to remember Him in this Supper.

      Are my past dealings with Him such as I wish to remember?

      Is He so loved by me that I wish to bear Him in my memory?

Ye who have come to this table heedlessly, repent of your wicked intrusion, and keep away till ye can come aright.

Ye who have never come at all, remember, if you are not fit for the communion below, you are not fit for heaven above.

All of you, bethink yourselves of Jesus, and having examined yourselves to your humbling, behold Him to your consolation.

The three questions which Philip Henry advised people to put to themselves in self-examination before the sacrament were, What am I? What have I done? and, What do I want?—JOHN WHITECROSS.

The duty required for preventing the sin and danger of unworthy communicating is the great and necessary duty of self-examination. It is a metaphor taken from goldsmiths, who try the truth of their gold by the touchstone, the purity of their gold by the fire, and the weight of it by the scale. We have here, 1. The person examining: "Let a man examine." 2. The person examined; it is "himself"; he is to call himself to the bar of conscience, and to put questions to himself. (1) Concerning his state, whether he has a right to come or not. (2) His sins and shortcomings. (3) His wants and necessities. (4) His ends and designs; whether it be to obey the charge of his dying Saviour, to show forth His death, renew and seal his covenant with God, get nearness and communion with Him, nourishment to his soul, and supply to his wants. And (5) concerning his graces and qualifications, particularly as to knowledge, faith, repentance, fear, love, thankfulness, holy desires, and new obedience.—JOHN WILLISON.

CHAPTER 151

## FALLEN ASLEEP

*"Some are fallen asleep"* (I Cor. 15:6).

Yes, the companions of Jesus died one by one.

Yet no work of lamentation is used. It is not said that they have perished, or passed into the land of shades, but that "they are fallen asleep."

The spirit is with Jesus in glory; the body rests till His appearing.

I. THE FIGURE HERE USED.

    1. An act of the most natural kind: "fallen asleep."
      It is the fit ending of a weary day.
      It is not painful, but the end of pain.
    2. A position of safety from a thousand dangers.
    3. A condition by no means destructive.
      Neither sleep nor death destroys existence, nor even injures it.
    4. A posture full of hope.
      We shall awake from this sleep.
      We shall awake without difficulty.
      We shall arise greatly refreshed.

II. THE THOUGHTS AROUSED BY THAT FIGURE.

    1. How did we treat those who are now asleep?
      Did we value their living presence, work, and testimony?
      Ought we not to be more kind to those who are yet alive?
    2. How fit that we also should be prepared to fall asleep!
      Is our house in order?
      Is our heart in order?
      Is our Christian work in order?
    3. How patiently should we bear up under the labors and sufferings of the day, since there remaineth a rest for the people of God!

III. THE HOPES CONFIRMED BY THAT FIGURE.

    1. The sleepers will yet awake.
      Their Father's voice will arouse them.
      They shall be awake indeed: full of health and energy.
      They shall have new clothes to dress in.
      They shall not again fall asleep.
    2. The sleepers and ourselves will enjoy sweet fellowship.
      Sleep does not destroy the love of brothers and sisters now.
      We shall arise as one unbroken family, saved in the Lord.

Let us not hopelessly sorrow over those asleep.

Let us not fear to sleep in such good company.

A pious Scotch minister being asked by a friend during his last illness, whether he thought himself dying, answered: "Really, friend, I care not whether I am or not; for if I die, I shall be with God; if I live, He will be with me."—ARVINE.

God's finger touched him, and he slept.—TENNYSON.

S. T. COLERIDGE, speaking of a dear friend's death, said, "It is recovery, and *not death.* Blessed are they that sleep in the Lord; his life is hidden in Christ. In His Redeemer's life it is hidden, and in His glory will it be disclosed. Physiologists hold that it is during sleep chiefly that we grow; what may we not hope of such a sleep in such a bosom?"

There must be life in Christ before death can become sleep in Him. "Louis, the beloved, sleeps in the Lord," said the priest who announced the death of Louis the Fifteenth. "If," was THOMAS CARLYLE'S stern comment, "if such a mass of laziness and lust sleeps in the Lord, who, think you, sleeps elsewhere?"

## CHAPTER 152

## COMFORTED AND COMFORTING

*II Cor. 1:3, 4.*

I. THE COMFORTABLE OCCUPATION. Blessing God. "Blessed be God."

If a man under affliction blesses the Lord—

1. It argues that his heart is not vanquished,
   So as to gratify Satan by murmuring, or
   So as to kill his own soul with despair.
2. It prophesies that God will send to him speedy deliverances to call forth new praises. It is natural to lend more to a man when the interest on what he has is duly paid.
   Never did man bless God but sooner or later God blessed him.
3. It profits the believer above measure.
   It takes the mind off from present trouble.
   It lifts the heart to heavenly thoughts and considerations.
4. It is the Lord's due in whatsoever state we may be.

II. THE COMFORTABLE FACT. "The God of all comfort comforteth us in all our tribulation."

1. God personally condescends to comfort the saints.
2. God habitually does this. He has always been near to comfort us in all past time, never once leaving us alone.
3. God effectually does this. He has always been able to comfort us in all tribulation. No trial has baffled His skill.

4. God everlastingly does this, He will comfort us to the end, for He is "the God of all comfort," and He cannot change.

III. THE COMFORTABLE DESIGN. "That we may be able to comfort."

1. To make us comforters of others. The Lord aims at this: the Holy Ghost, the Comforter, trains us up to be comforters. There is great need for this holy service in this sin-smitten world.

2. To make us comforters on a large scale. "To comfort them which are in any trouble." We are to be conversant with all kinds of grief, and ready to sympathize with all sufferers.

> Many an alleluia
> That rings through the Father's home,
> Sobbed out its first rehearsal
> In the shades of a darkened room.

We have no more religion than what we have in times of trial.— ANDREW FULLER.

He would put off a meditated journey, rather than leave a poor parishioner who required his services; and from his knowledge of human nature, he was able, and in a remarkable manner, to throw himself into the circumstances of those who needed his help. No sympathy was like his.—CHAMBERS, *on George Crabbe.*

# CHAPTER 153

## THE TENSES

*"Who delivered us from so great a death, and doth deliver: in whom we trust that He will yet deliver us"* (II Cor. 1:10).

Grammarians have here a lesson in the tenses; and Christians may profitably join in the exercise.

We may consider the past, present, and future, each one by itself.

We may also view them in their relation to each other.

I. THE TEXT SUGGESTS THREE TRAINS OF THOUGHT.

1. Memory tells of deliverances in the past—
From violent death. In Paul's case, "so great a death" may mean death by fierce mobs, or by the emperor.
From our death in sin: "So great a death" indeed.
From fierce despair when under conviction.
From destruction by slander and the like.

2. Observation calls attention to present deliverance.
   By the good hand of the Lord, we are at this time preserved—
   From unseen dangers to life.
   From the subtle assaults of Satan.
   From the rampant errors of the times.
   From inbred sin and natural corruption.

3. Expectation looks out of the window upon the future.
   Faith rests alone in God, "in Whom we trust," and through
   Him she looks for future deliverance—
   From all future common trials.
   From coming losses and afflictions, and from sicknesses, which
   may be coming upon us.
   From the infirmities and wants of age.
   From the peculiar glooms of death.
   This expectation makes us march on with cheerfulness.

II. THE TEXT SUPPLIES THREE LINES OF ARGUMENT.

1. From the Lord's beginning to deliver we argue that He will
   yet deliver, for
   There was no reason in us for His beginning to love us. If
   His love arises out of His own nature it will continue.
   He has obtained no fresh knowledge. He foreknew all our
   misbehaviors: hence, there is no reason for casting us off.

2. From the Lord's continuing to deliver we argue that He will
   yet deliver; for
   His deliverances have been so many;
   They have displayed such wisdom and power;
   They have come to us when we have been so unworthy;
   They have continued in such an unbroken line.

III. THE TEXT IS OPEN TO THREE INFERENCES.

1. We infer that we shall always be so in danger as to need to
   be delivered: wherefore we are not high-minded, but fear.

2. We infer our constant need of God's own interposition. He
   alone has met our case in the past, and He only can meet it in
   the future: wherefore, we would ever abide near our Lord.

3. We infer that our whole life should be filled with the praise
   of God, who, for past, present and future, is our Deliverer.

First, God hath a time, as for all things, so for our deliverance.
Secondly, God's time is the best time. He is the best discerner of
opportunities. Thirdly, this shall be when He hath wrought His
work upon our souls, especially when He hath made us to trust in
Him. As here, when Paul had learned to trust in God, then He
delivered him.—RICHARD SIBBES.

The Roman noblemen could give no greater proof of their confidence in their city and army, than when they bought the land on which their Carthaginian enemies were encamped around the city.

And we can give no greater proof of our confidence in God, than by trusting Him in the land which our enemies, darkness, and sickness, and trouble, seem to possess, and acting as if God were their master, and mightier than they all. This is but to act upon the truth. —*Sword and Trowel, 1887.*

## CHAPTER 154

## ALL THE PROMISES

*"For all the promises of God in Him are yea, and in Him amen, unto the glory of God by us"* (II Cor. 1:20).

I. THE DIGNITY OF THE PROMISES. "They are "the promises of God."

1. They were each one made by Him according to the purpose of His own will.

2. They are links between His decrees and His acts; being the voice of the decree, and the herald of the act.

3. They display the qualities of Him who uttered them. They are true, immutable, powerful, eternal, etc.

4. They remain in union with God. After the lapse of ages, they are still His promises as much as when He first uttered them.

II. THE RANGE OF THE PROMISES. *"All* the promises."

1. They are found both in the Old and New Testaments; from Genesis to Revelation, running through centuries of time.

2. They are of both sorts—conditional and unconditional: promises to certain works, and promises of an absolute order.

3. They are of all kinds of things—bodily and spiritual, personal and general, eternal and temporal.

4. They contain blessings to varied characters, such as—
The Penitent: Lev. 26:40-42; Isa. 55:7, 57:15; Jer. 3:12-13.
The Believing: John 3:16, 18, 6:47; Acts 16:31; I Pet. 2:6.
The Serving: Ps. 37:3, 9:40; Prov. 3:9, 10; Acts 10:35.
The Praying: Isa. 45:11; Lam. 3:25; Matt. 6:6; Ps. 145:18.
The Obeying: Ex. 19:5; Ps. 119:1-3; Isa. 1:19.
The Suffering: Matt. 5:10-12; Rom. 8:17; I Pet. 4:12-14.

III. THE STABILITY OF THE PROMISES. "All the promises *in Him are yea, and in Him Amen.*"

A Greek word "Yea," and a Hebrew word "Amen," are used to mark certainty, both to Gentile and Jew.

1. Their stability is in Christ Jesus beyond all hazard: for He is—
   The witness of the promise of God,
   The surety of the covenant,
   The sum and substance of all the promises,
   The fulfilment of the promises, by His actual incarnation,
   His atoning death, His living plea, His ascension power, etc.

IV. THE RESULT OF THE PROMISES. "The glory of God by us."

1. We glorify His condescending love in making the promise.

2. We glorify His power as we see Him keeping the promise.

3. We glorify Him by our faith, which honors His veracity, by expecting the boons which He has promised.

4. We glorify Him in our experience which proves the promise true.

A speaker at the Fulton Street prayer-meeting said, "I count all cheques as cash when I am making up my money and striking a balance"; and so, when we feel that we have not much of this world's goods, we can at least take hold of God's promises, for they are just so many drafts at sight upon divine mercy, and we may count them among our possessions. Then we shall feel rich, and the soul is rich who trusts God's word and takes His promises as something for present use.

Promises are like the clothes we wear; if there is life in the body they warm us, but not otherwise. When there is living faith the promise will afford warm comfort, but on a dead, unbelieving heart it lies cold and ineffectual. It has no more effect than pouring a cordial down the throat of a corpse.—WILLIAM GURNELL.

If thou lean upon the promises of God themselves, and not upon Jesus Christ in them, all will come to nothing. . . . Whence is it that so many souls bring a promise to the throne of grace, and carry so little away from it? They lean upon the promises without leaning on Christ in the promise.—FAITHFUL TEATE.

It is when these promises are reduced to experience—when they are seen cleansing us from all filthiness of flesh and spirit, making us partakers of the divine nature, leading us to walk worthy of the vocation wherewith we are called, filling us with kindness and benevolence, supporting us cheerfully under all our trials—it is then they glorify God "by us."—WILLIAM JAY.

## CHAPTER 155

# SORROW AND SORROW

*"For godly sorrow worketh repentance to salvation not to be repented of: but the sorrow of the world worketh death"* (II Cor. 7:10).

Time was when inner experience was considered to be everything, and experimental preaching was the order of the day.

Sinners were unwisely influenced by certain ministries to look to their own feelings, many began to seek comfort from their own misery.

Now it is "only believe." And rightly so: but we must discriminate. *There must be sorrow for sin working repentance.*

I. REMOVE CERTAIN ERRONEOUS IDEAS WITH REGARD TO REPENTANCE AND SORROW FOR SIN.

Among popular delusions we must mention the suppositions—
1. That mere sorrow of mind in reference to sin is repentance.
2. That there can be repentance without sorrow for sin.
3. That we must reach a certain point of wretchedness and horror, or else we are not truly penitent.
4. That repentance happens to us once, and is then over.

II. DISTINGUISH BETWEEN THE TWO SORROWS MENTIONED IN THE TEXT.

1. The godly sorrow which worketh repentance to salvation is—
   Sorrow for sin as committed against God.
   Sorrow for sin arising out of an entire change of mind.
   Sorrow for sin which joyfully accepts salvation by grace.
   Sorrow for sin leading to future obedience.
2. The sorrow of the world is
   Caused by shame at being found out;
   Is attended by hard thoughts of God;
   Leads to vexation and sullenness;
   Incites to hardening of heart;
   Lands the soul in despair;
   Works death of the worst kind.

This needs to be repented of, for it is in itself sinful and terribly prolific of more sin.

III. INDULGE OURSELVES IN GODLY SORROW FOR SIN.

Come, let us be filled with a wholesome grief that we:
1. Have broken a law, pure and perfect.
2. Have disobeyed a gospel, divine and gracious.
3. Have grieved a God, good and glorious.
4. Have slighted Jesus, whose love is tender and boundless.

5. Have been ungrateful, though loved, elected, redeemed, forgiven, justified and soon to be glorified.

A cognate text in Rom. 2:2, 4, will help us here. These two allied but distinct intimations may be placed in parallel lines, and treated like an equation; thus—

"The goodness of God leadeth thee to repentance."

"Godly sorrow worketh repentance."

We learn, as the result of the comparison, that the goodness of God leads to repentance by the way of godly sorrow. The series of cause and effect runs thus: goodness of God; godly sorrow; repentance.

Do not mistake; a fear of hell is not sorrow for sin; it may be nothing more than a regret that God is holy.

So hard is a heart long accustomed to evil, that nothing can melt it but goodness; and no goodness but God's; and no goodness of His but the greatest. Thanks be to God for His unspeakable gift. "Looking unto Jesus" is the grand specific for producing godly sorrow in a human heart.

It was a hard heart that quivered under the beams of His loving eye on the threshold of Pilate's judgment hall. When Jesus looked on Peter, Peter went out and wept. Emmanuel's love has lost none of its melting power; the hardest hearts laid fairly open to it must ere long flow down. God's goodness, embodied in Christ crucified, becomes, under the ministry of the Spirit, the cause of godly sorrow in believing men.—WILLIAM ARNOT.

Sin, repentance, and pardon are like to the three vernal months of the year, March, April and May. Sin comes in like March, blustering, stormy, and full of bold violence. Repentance succeeds like April, showering, weeping, and full of tears. Pardon follows like May, springing, singing, full of joy and flowers. Our eyes must be full of *April*, with the sorrow of repentance; and then our hearts shall be full of *May*, with the true joy of forgiveness.—THOMAS ADAMS.

## CHAPTER 156

## A CONFERENCE TO BE AVOIDED

*"Immediately I conferred not with flesh and blood"* (Gal. 1:16).

Paul, being converted, took an independent course.

Being taught of God,

He did not consult those who were already believers, lest he should seem to have received his religion at second-hand.

He did not consult his relatives, who would have advised caution.

He did not consult his own interests, which all lay in the opposite direction. These he counted loss for Christ.

He did not consult his own safety, but risked life itself for Jesus.

## I. FAITH NEEDS NO WARRANT BUT THE WILL OF GOD.

1. Good men in all ages have acted upon this conviction.
Noah, Abraham, Jacob, Moses, Samson, David, Elijah, Daniel, the three who were cast into the furnace, etc.

2. To ask more is virtually to renounce the Lord as our Commander and Guide, and to lift man into his place.

3. To hesitate from self-interest is openly to defy the Lord.

## II. THE PRINCIPLE HAS A WIDE RANGE OF APPLICATION.

1. To known duties.
In forsaking sin we are not to consult society.
In upright dealing we are not to consult the custom of trade.
In consecration to Christ we are not to follow the lower standard so common among our fellow Christians.
In service we are not to consult personal liking, ease, honor, prospect of advancement, or remuneration.

2. To special service. We are not to be held back from this by—
Considerations of personal weakness.
Considerations of want of visible means.
Considerations of how others will interpret our actions.
Consult not even your brethren here; for—
Good men may not have your faith.
They cannot judge your call.
They cannot remove your responsibility.

## III. THE PRINCIPLE COMMENDS ITSELF TO OUR BEST JUDGMENT.

It is justified by—

1. The judgment which we exercise upon others.
We blame them if they have no mind of their own.
We applaud them if they are bravely faithful.

2. The judgment of an enlightened conscience.

3. The judgment of a dying bed.

4. The judgment of an eternal world.

"Sir," said the Duke of Wellington to an officer of engineers, who urged the impossibility of executing the directions he had received, "I did not ask your opinion, I gave you my orders, and I expect them to be obeyed."

Such should be the obedience of every follower of Jesus. The words which he has spoken are our law. We are not permitted to oppose thereto our judgments or fancies. Even if death were in the way, it is—

> "Not ours to reason why—
> Ours but to dare and die";

and, at our Master's bidding, advance through flood or flame.— *"Feathers for Arrows."*

But this is a hard lesson to learn. I read some time ago of a German captain who found this out. He was drilling a company of volunteers. The parade ground was a field by the seaside. The men were going through their exercises very nicely, but the captain thought he would give them a lesson about obeying orders. They were marching up and down in the line of the water at some distance from it. He concluded to give them an order to march directly towards the water, and see how far they would go.

The men are marching along. "Halt, company," says the captain. In a moment they halt. "Right face," is the next word, and instantly they wheel around. *"Forward march,"* is then the order. At once they begin to march directly towards the water; on they go, nearer and nearer to it. Soon they reach the edge of the water. Then there is a sudden halt. "Vat for you stop? I no say halt," cried the captain. "Why, captain, here is the water," said one of the men. "Vell, vot of it," cried he, greatly excited, "Vater is nothing; fire is nothing; everything is nothing. Ven I say, Forwart martch, then you must forwart martch." The captain was right; the first duty of a soldier is to learn to obey.—Dr. RICHARD NEWTON.

What God calls a man to do He will carry him through. I would undertake to govern half-a-dozen worlds if God called me to do it; but if He did not call me to it, I would not undertake to govern half-a-dozen sheep.—Dr. PAYSON.

# CHAPTER 157
## UNDER ARREST

> *"But before faith came, we were kept under the law, shut up unto the faith which should afterwards be revealed"* (Gal. 3:23).

Here we have a condensed history of the world before the gospel was fully revealed by the coming of our Lord Jesus.

This history of each saved soul is a miniature likeness of the story of the ages. God acts upon the same principles both with the race and with individuals.

I. THE UNHAPPY PERIOD: "Before faith came."

   1. We had no idea of faith by nature. It would never occur to the human mind that we could be saved by believing in Jesus.

   2. When we heard of faith as the way of salvation we did not understand it. We could not persuade ourselves that the words used by the preacher had· their common and usual meaning.

   3. We saw faith in others, and wondered at its results; but we could not exercise it for ourselves.

   4. The reason of this inability was moral, not mental:
We were proud, and did not care to renounce self-righteousness. We could not grasp the notion of salvation by faith, because it was contrary to the usual run of our opinions.

II. THE CUSTODY WE WERE IN: "Kept under the law, shut up."

   1. We were always within the sphere of law. In fact, there is no getting out of it. As all the world was only one prison for a man who offended Caesar, so is the whole universe no better than a prison for a sinner.

   2. We were always kicking against the bounds of the law, sinning, and pining because we could not sin more.

   3. We dared not overleap it altogether, and defy its power. Thus, in the case of many of us, it checked us, and held us captive with its irksome forbiddings and commandings.

   4. We could not find rest. The law awakened conscience, and fear and shame attend such an awakening.

   5. We could not even fall into the stupor of despair; for the law excited life, though it forbade hope.

III. THE REVELATION WHICH SET US FREE: "The faith which should afterwards be revealed." The only thing which could bring us out of prison was faith. Faith came, and then we understood—

   1. What was to be believed.
Salvation by Another.
Salvation of a most blessed sort, gloriously sure, and complete.
Salvation by a most Glorious Person.

   2. What it was to believe.
We saw that it was "trust," implicit and sincere.
We saw that it was ceasing from self, and obeying Christ.

   3. Why we believed.
We were shut up to this one way of salvation.
We were shut out of every other.
We were compelled to accept free grace, or perish.

The Law and the Gospel are two keys. The law is the key that shutteth up all men under condemnation, and the gospel is the key which opens the door and lets them out.—WILLIAM TYNDALE.

The law is made to act the part of a sentry, guarding every avenue but one, and that one leads those who are compelled to take it to the faith of the gospel. They are shut up to this faith as their only alternative—like an enemy driven by the superior tactics of an opposing general, to take up the only position in which they can maintain themselves, or fly to the only town in which they can find a refuge or a security. This seems to have been a favorite style of argument with Paul, and the way in which he often carried on an intellectual warfare with the enemies of his Master's cause. It forms the basis of that masterly and decisive train of reasoning which we have in his epistle to the Romans.

The law was meant to prepare men for Christ, by showing them that there is no other way of salvation except through Him. It had two especial ends: the first was to bring the people who lived under it into a consciousness of the deadly dominion of sin, to shut them up, as it were, into a prison-house out of which only one door of escape should be visible, namely, the door of faith in Jesus.

The second intention was to fence about and guard the chosen race to whom the law was given—to keep as a peculiar people separate from all the world, so that at the proper time the gospel of Christ might spring forth, and go out from them as the joy and comfort of the whole human race.—T. G. ROOKE.

# CHAPTER 158

## VARIOUS HINDRANCES

*"Ye did run well; who did hinder you that ye should not obey the truth?"* (Gal. 5:7).

Never censure indiscriminately; admit and praise that which is good, that you may the more effectually rebuke the evil. Paul did not hesitate to praise the Galatians, and say, "Ye did run well."

I. WE SHALL USE THE TEXT IN REFERENCE TO HINDERED BELIEVERS.
1. You are evidently hindered.
   You are not so loving and zealous as you were.
   You are quitting the old faith for new notions.
   You are losing your first joy and peace.
2. Who has hindered you?
   Did I do it? Pray, then, for your minister.
   Did your fellow-members do it? You ought to have been proof against them; they could not have intended it. Pray for them.
   Did the world do it? Why so much in it?
   Did the devil do it? Resist him.

Did you not do it yourself? This is highly probable.
Did you not by pride become self-satisfied?
Did you not neglect prayer, Bible reading, the public means of grace, the Lord's Table, etc.?

3. You must look to it, and mend your pace.
Your loss has been already great. You might by this time have been far on upon the road.
Your natural tendency will be to slacken still more.
Your danger is great of being overtaken by error and sin.

## II. WE SHALL USE THE TEXT IN REFERENCE TO DELAYING SINNERS.

1. You have sometimes been set a-running.
God has blessed His Word to your arousing.
God has not yet given you up; this is evident.
God's way of salvation still lies open before you.

2. What has hindered you?
Self-righteousness and trust in yourself?
Carelessness, procrastination, and neglect?
Love of self-indulgence, or the secret practice of pleasurable sins?
Frivolous, skeptical, or wicked companions?
Unbelief and mistrust of God's mercy?

3. The worst evils will come of being hindered.
Those who will not obey truth will become the dupes of lies.
Truth not obeyed is disobeyed, and so sin is multiplied.
Truth disregarded becomes an accuser, and its witness secures our condemnation.

God have mercy on *hinderers*. We must rebuke them.
God have mercy on the *hindered*. We would arouse them.

CECIL says that some adopt the Indian maxim, that it is better to walk than to run, and better to stand than to walk, and better to sit than to stand, and better to lie than to sit.

Such is not the teaching of the gospel. It is a good thing to be walking in the ways of God, but it is better to be running—making real and visible progress, day by day advancing in experience and attainments. David likens the sun to a strong man rejoicing to run a race; not dreading it and shrinking back from it, but delighting in the opportunity of putting forth all his powers. Who so runs, runs well.—*The Christian.*

Some are too busy, they run about too much to run well; some run too fast at the outset; they run themselves out of breath.—T. T. LYNCH.

It is possible that *fellow professors* may hinder. We are often obliged to accommodate our pace to that of our fellow-travellers. If they are laggards we are very likely to be so too. We are apt to sleep as do others. We are stimulated or depressed, urged on or held back, by those with whom we are associated in Christian fellowship.

There is still greater reason to fear that in many cases *worldly friends and companions* are the hinderers. Indeed, they can be nothing else. None can help us in the race but those who are themselves running it: all others must hinder. Let a Christian form an intimate friendship with an ungodly person, and from that moment all progress is stayed; he must go back; for when his companion is going in the opposite direction, how can he walk with him except by turning his back upon the path which he has formerly trodden?—P.

A sailor remarks—"Sailing from Cuba, we thought we had gained sixty miles one day in our course; but at the next observation we found we had lost more than thirty. It was an under-current. The ship had been going forward by the wind, but going back by the current."

So a man's course in religion may often seem to be right and progressive, but the under-current of his besetting sins is driving him the very contrary way to what he thinks.—CHEEVER.

## CHAPTER 159

## THE OFFENCE OF THE CROSS

*"Then is the offence of the cross ceased"* (Gal. 5:11).

Paul intends here to declare the offence of the cross never has ceased, and never can cease. To suppose it to have ceased is folly.

The religion of Jesus is most peaceful, mild and benevolent.

Yet its history shows it to have been assailed with bitterest hate all along. It is clearly offensive to the unregenerate mind.

There is no reason to believe that it is one jot more palatable to the world than it used to be. The world and the gospel are both unchanged.

### I. WHEREIN LIES THE OFFENCE OF THE CROSS?

1. Its doctrine of atonement offends man's pride.
2. Its simple teaching offends man's wisdom, and artificial taste.
3. Its being a remedy for man's ruin offends his fancied power to save himself.
4. Its addressing all as sinners offends the dignity of Pharisees.
5. Its coming as a revelation offends "modern thought."
6. Its lofty holiness offends man's love of sin.

## II. How Is This Offence Shown?

1. Frequently by the actual persecution of believers.
2. More often by slandering believers, and sneering at them as old-fashioned, foolish, weak-minded, morose, self-conceited, etc.
3. Often by omitting to preach the cross. Many nowadays preach a Christless, bloodless gospel.
4. Or by importing new meanings into orthodox terms.

## III. What Then?

1. Herein is folly, that men are offended:
   With that which God ordains;
   With that which must win the day;
   With the only thing which can save them;
   With that which is full of wisdom and beauty.
2. Herein is grace,
   That we who once were offended by the cross, now find it to be:
   The one hope of our hearts,
   The great delight of our souls,
   The joyful boast of our tongues.
3. Herein is heart-searching.
   Perhaps we are secretly offended at the cross.
   Perhaps we give no offence to haters of the cross. Many professed Christians never cause offence to the most godless.

   Is this because they bear no testimony to the cross?

Preachers who have caught the spirit of the age are of the world, and the world loves its own; but we must disown them.

Let us not be distressed by the offence of the cross, even when it comes upon us with bitterest scorn.

Let us look for it and accept it as a token that we are in the right.

There is a want in the human mind which nothing but the Atonement can satisfy, though it may be a stumbling-block to the Jew, and foolishness to the Greek. In the words of Henry Rogers: "It is adapted to human nature, as a bitter medicine may be to a patient. Those who have taken it, tried its efficacy, and recovered spiritual health, gladly proclaim its value. But to those who have not, and will not try it, it is an unpalatable potion still."

I open an ancient book, written in opposition to Christianity by Arnobius, and I read: "Our gods are not displeased with you Christians for worshipping the Almighty God: but you maintain the deity of one who was put to death on the cross, you believe Him to be yet alive, and you adore Him with daily supplications."

"Men showed me at Rome, in the Kircherian Museum, a square foot of the plaster of a wall of a palace not many years ago uncovered on the Palatine Hill. On the poor clay was traced a cross bearing a human figure with a brute's head. The figure was nailed to the cross, and before it a soldier was represented kneeling, and extending his hands in the Greek posture of devotion. Underneath all was scratched in rude lettering in Greek, *"Alexanmenos adores his god."*

That representation of the central thought of Christianity was made in a jeering moment by some rude soldier in the days of Caracalla; but it blazes there now in Rome, the most majestic monument of its age in the world.—JOSEPH COOK.

The cross is the strength of a minister. I, for one, would not be without it for the world. I should feel like a soldier without weapons, like an artist without his pencil, like a pilot without his compass, like a laborer without his tools.

Let others, if they will, preach the Law and morality.

Let others hold forth the terrors of hell and the joys of heaven. Let others drench their congregations with teachings about the sacraments and the church. Give me the cross of Christ. This is the only lever which has ever turned the world upside down hitherto, and made men forsake their sins.

And if this will not do it, nothing will. A man may begin preaching with a perfect knowledge of Latin, Greek and Hebrew; but he will do little or no good among his hearers unless he knows something of the cross. Never was there a minister who did much for the conversion of souls who did not dwell much on Christ crucified. Luther, Rutherford, Whitefield, M'Cheyne, were all most eminent preachers of the cross. This is the preaching that the Holy Ghost delights to bless. He loves to honor those who honor the cross.— J. C. RYLE.

> My thoughts once prompt round hurtful things to twine,
> What are they now, when two dread deaths are near?
> The one impends, the other shakes his spear.
> Painting and sculpture's aid in vain I crave:
> My one sole refuge is that love Divine,
> Which from the cross stretched forth its arms to save.
>
> *Last lines written by Michael Angelo, when over eighty.*

## CHAPTER 160

## SOWING AND REAPING

*"Be not deceived; God is not mocked: for whatsoever a man soweth, that shall he also reap"* (Gal. 6:7).

I. GOD IS NOT TO BE TRIFLED WITH.

    1. Either by the notions that there will be no rewards and punishments.

2. Or by the idea that a bare profession will suffice to save us.
3. Or by the fancy that we shall escape in the crowd.
4. Or by the superstitious supposition that certain rites will set all straight at last, whatever our lives may be.

## II. THE LAWS OF HIS GOVERNMENT CANNOT BE SET ASIDE.

1. It is so in nature. Law is inexorable. Gravitation crushes the man who opposes it.
2. It is so in providence. Evil results surely follow social wrong.
3. Conscience tells us it must be so. Sin must be punished.

## III. EVIL SOWING WILL BRING EVIL REAPING.

1. This is seen in the present result of certain sins.
   Sins of lust bring disease into the bodily frame.
   Sins of idolatry have led men to cruel and degrading practices.
   Sins of temper have caused murders, wars, strifes and misery.
   Sins of appetite, especially drunkenness, cause want, misery, delirium, etc.
2. This is seen when the sinner becomes himself disappointed in the result of his conduct.
   His malice eats his heart; his greed devours his soul; his infidelity destroys his comfort; his raging passions agitate his spirit.

## IV. GOOD SOWING WILL BRING GOOD REAPING.

1. What are its seeds?
   Towards God, we sow in the Spirit, faith and obedience.
   Towards men, love, truth, justice, kindness, forbearance.
   Towards self, control of appetite, purity, etc.
2. What is the reaping of the Spirit?
   Life everlasting dwelling within us and abiding there forever.

It is not an open question at all whether I shall sow or not today; the only question to be decided is: Shall I sow good seed or bad? Every man always is sowing for his own harvest in eternity either tares or wheat. According as a man soweth, so shall he also reap; he that sows the wind of vanity shall reap the whirlwind of wrath.

Suppose a man should collect a quantity of small gravel and dye it carefully, so that it should resemble wheat, and sow it in his fields in spring, expecting that he would reap a crop of wheat like his neighbor's in the harvest. The man is mad; he is a fool to think that by his silly trick he can evade the laws of nature, and mock nature's God.

Yet equally foolish is the conduct, and far heavier the punishment, of the man who sows wickedness now, and expects to reap safety at last. Sin is not only profitless and disastrous; it is eminently a deceitful work. Men do not of set purpose cast themselves away: sin cheats a sinner out of his soul.

But sowing righteousness is never, and nowhere, lost labor. Every act is done by God's grace, and at His bidding, is living and fruitful. It may appear to go out of sight, like seed beneath the furrow; but it will rise again. Sow on Christians! Sight will not follow the seed far; but when sight fails, sow in faith, and you will reap in joy soon.—WILLIAM ARNOT.

Doth any think he shall lose by his charity? No worldling, when he sows his seed, thinks he shall lose his seed; he hopes for increase at harvest. Darest thou trust the ground, and not God? Sure God is a better paymaster than the earth; grace doth give a larger recompense than nature. Below, thou mayest receive forty grains for one; but in heaven (by the promise of Christ) a hundred-fold: a measure heapen, and shaken, and thrust together, and yet running over.

"Blessed is he that considereth the poor"; there is the seeding: "The Lord shall deliver him in the time of trouble" (Ps. 41:1); there is the harvest. Is that all? No. Matt. 25:35: "Ye fed Me when I was hungry, and gave Me drink when thirsty"—comforted Me in misery; there is the sowing. *Venite, beati.* "Come, ye blessed of my Father, inherit the kingdom prepared for you"; there is the harvest.—THOMAS ADAMS.

## CHAPTER 161

## MEASURING THE IMMEASURABLE

*Ephesians 3:16-19.*

He would have us measure the immeasurable, but He would first have us made fit to do so.

We shall make our chief point the fourfold measurement, but we shall note that which comes before, and that which follows after.

I. THE PREVIOUS TRAINING REQUIRED FOR THIS MEASUREMENT.

   1. He would have their spiritual faculties vigorous.

      "Your inner man": understanding, faith, hope, love, all need power from a divine source.

      "By His Spirit." The power required is spiritual, holy, heavenly, divine, actually imparted by the Holy Ghost.

   2. He would have the subject always before them.

      "That Christ may dwell in your heart by faith."

      "In your heart." Love must learn to measure Christ's love. It is revealed to the heart rather than to the head.

      "By faith." A carnal man measures by sight, a saint by faith.

   3. He would have them exercised in the art of measurement.

      "That ye, being rooted and grounded in love," etc.

We must love Him ourselves, if we would measure Christ's love.

## II. THE MENSURATION ITSELF.

1. *The breadth.* Immense.

   Comprehending all nations. "Preach the gospel to every creature."

   Covering hosts of iniquities. "All manner of sin."

   Compassing all needs, cares, etc.

   Conferring boundless boons for this life and worlds to come.

2. *The length.* Eternal.

   Eternal love in the fountain. Election and the covenant.

   Ceaseless love in the flow. Redemption, calling, perseverance.

   Endless love in endurance. Long suffering, forgiveness, faithfulness, patience, immutability.

   Boundless love, in length exceeding our length of sin, suffering, backsliding, age, or temptation.

3. *The depth.* Incomprehensible.

   Stoop of divine love, condescending to consider us, to commune with us, to receive us in love, to bear with our faults, and to take us up from our low estate.

   Stoop of love personified in Christ.

   He stoops, and becomes incarnate; endures our sorrows; bears our sins; and suffers our shame and death.

   Where is the measure for all this?

   Our weakness, meanness, sinfulness, despair, make one factor of the measurement.

   His glory, holiness, greatness, Deity, make up the other.

4. *The height.* Infinite.

   As developed in present privilege, as one with Jesus.

   As to be revealed in future glory.

   As never to be fully comprehended throughout the ages.

## III. THE PRACTICAL RESULT OF THIS MENSURATION. "That ye might be filled with all the fulness of God."

Here are words full of mystery, worthy to be pondered.

Be *filled.* What great things man can hold!

Filled *with* God. What exaltation!

Filled *with the fulness* of God. What must this be?

Filled *with all the fulness* of God. What more can be imagined?

In the gospel history we find that Christ had a fourfold entertainment amongst the sons of men; some received Him into house, not into heart, as Simon the Pharisee, who gave Him no kiss, nor water to His feet; some received Him into heart, but not into house, as Nicodemus, and others; some neither into heart nor house, as the graceless, swinish Gergesenes; some both into house and heart, as Lazarus, Mary, Martha.

And thus let all good Christians do; endeavor that Christ may dwell in their hearts by faith, that their bodies may be fit temples of His Holy Spirit, that now in this life, whilst Christ stands at the door of their hearts, knocking for admission, they will lift up the latch of their souls, and let Him in; for if ever they expect to enter into the gates of the city of God hereafter, they must open their hearts, the gates of their own city, to Him here in this world.—JOHN SPENCER.

"The wider the diameter of light, the greater is the circumference of darkness." The more a man knows, he comes at more points into contact with the unknown.

## CHAPTER 162

## TRUE LEARNING

*"But ye have not so learned Christ.*
*"If so be that ye have heard Him, and have been taught by Him, as the truth is in Jesus"* (Eph. 4:20, 21).

I. OUR LESSON. "Learned Christ."

This learning Christ is—
Much more than learning doctrine, precept or ceremony.
Much more than knowing about Christ, or learning from Christ.
It includes several forms of knowledge.

1. To know Him as a personal Christ.
2. To know His nature, and to treat Him accordingly.
3. To know His offices, and how to use them.
4. To know His finished work for God and for us.
5. To know His influence over men, and to test it.
6. To know by learning Christ, the way to live like Him.

II. HOW WE HAVE NOT LEARNED IT.

1. So as to remain as we were before. Unchanged, and yet at peace.
2. So as to excuse sin, because of His atonement.
3. So as to feel a freedom to sin because of pardon.
4. So as even to commit sin in Christ's name.
5. So as to reckon that we cannot conquer sin, and so sit down under the dominion of some constitutional temptation.
6. So as to profess reverence for His name and character, and then think little of the truth which He reveals.

### III. How We Have Learned It.

We know the truth, and know it in its best light—

1. As directly taught by His own self, and by His own Spirit.
2. As distinctly embodied in His life and character.
3. As it relates to Him and honors Him.

"If so be," saith he, "ye have learned the truth as it is in Jesus." Which doeth not, as other doctrines of philosophers, etc. teach you to put off the evils of your outward converse only, and to put on a new conversation over an old nature, as a sheep-skin over a wolfish nature; he that doth no more falls short of that truth of grace which Christ requires; but it teacheth principally to put off the old man, as the cause of all the evils in the outward converse; and that is His meaning, when He saith, "As concerning the outward converse, put off the old man," without which it is impossible to reform the converse.—THOMAS GOODWIN.

An illustration of the foregoing remarks is found in Lord Chesterfield, who trained his only son, not to abandon vice, but to be a gentleman in the practice of it.

Some persons, instead of "putting off the old man," dress him up in a new shape.—ST. BERNARD.

Unsanctified wisdom is the devil's greatest tool.

A handful of good life is worth a bushel of learning.

## CHAPTER 163

## HEAVENLY SHOES

*"And your feet shod with the preparation of the gospel of peace"* (Eph. 6:15).

### I. Let Us Examine the Shoes.

1. They come from the blessed Maker. One Who is skilful in all arts, and knows by experience what is wanted, since He has Himself journeyed through life's roughest ways.
2. They are made of excellent material: "the preparation of the gospel of peace." Well seasoned, soft in wear, lasting long.
   Peace with God as to the past, the future, the present.
   Peace with the Word and all its teachings.
   Peace with one's inner self, conscience, fears, desires, etc.
3. They are such shoes as Jesus wore, and all the saints.
4. They are such as will never wear out: they are old, yet ever new; we may wear them at all ages and in all places.

II. LET US TRY THEM ON.

Observe with delight—

1. Their perfect fitness. They are made to suit each one of us.
2. Their excellent foothold: we can tread with holy boldness upon our high places with these shoes.
3. Their marching powers for daily duty. No one grows weary or footsore when he is thus shod.
4. Their wonderful protection against trials by the way. "Thou shalt tread on the lion and adder" (Ps. 91:13).

III. LET US LOOK AT THE BAREFOOTED AROUND US.

The sinner is unshod. Yet he kicks against the pricks. How can he hope to fulfill the heavenly pilgrimage?

The professor is slipshod, or else he wears tight shoes. His fine slippers will soon be worn out. He loves not the gospel, knows not its peace, seeks not its preparation.

The gospel alone supplies a fit shoe for all feet. To the gospel let us fly at once. Come, poor shoeless beggar!

"*Put shoes on his feet!*" were among the first words of welcome to the returning prodigal. To be shoeless was in Israel a mark of great disgrace, indicating a lost inheritance, a state of misery and penury. (See Deut. 25:10).

"Your feet shod with the preparation of the gospel of peace" (Eph. 6:15). The passage has been paraphrased, "Shod with the firm footing of the solid knowledge of the gospel." The word "preparation" signifies *preparedness or readiness.* Compare II Tim. 4:2: "Instant in season, out of season"; also Rom. 1:15: "I am ready to preach the gospel." This preparedness is well-pleasing to God. "How *beautiful* are thy feet with shoes, O prince's daughter!" (Song of Solomon 7:1; Isa. 52:7).—MRS. GORDON.

The gospel shoe will not come on thy foot so long as thy foot is swelled with any sinful humor (I mean any unrighteousness or unholy practice). This evil must be purged out by repentance, or thou canst not wear the shoe of peace.

Is not thy shoe, Christian, yet on? art thou not yet ready to march? If thou hast it, what hast thou to dread? Canst fear that any stone can hurt thy foot through so thick a sole?—WILLIAM GURNALL.

Paul was thus shod: Rom. 8:38, "I am persuaded, nothing shall separate me from the love of God." "All things, I know, work together for the good of them that are beloved of God" (Rom. 8:28). And this furniture made him go such hard ways cheerfully, in which showers of afflictions did fall as thick as hailstones. This doth make God's children, though not in the letter, yet in some sort, tread upon the adder and the basilisk; yea, to defy vipers, and receive no hurt; whereas, if the feet be bared a little with the absence of this peace, anything causeth us to sore smart.—PAUL BAYNE.

CHAPTER 164

## JOY A DUTY

*"Rejoice in the Lord alway: and again I say, rejoice"*
(Phil. 4:4).

I. THE GRACE COMMANDED. "Rejoice."

1. It is delightful: our soul's jubilee has come when joy enters.
2. It is demonstrative: it is more than peace; it sparkles, shines, sings. Why should it not? Joy is a bird; let it fly in the open heavens, and let its music be heard of all men.
3. It is stimulating, and urges its possessor to brave deeds.
4. It is influential for good. Sinners are attracted to Jesus by the joy of saints. More flies are caught with a spoonful of honey than a barrel of vinegar.
5. It is contagious. Others are gladdened by our rejoicing.
6. It is commanded:
   Because joy makes us like God.
   Because it is for our profit.
   Because it is good for others.

II. THE JOY DISCRIMINATED. "In the Lord."

1. As to sphere. "In the Lord." This is that sacred circle wherein a Christian's life should be always spent.
2. As to object. "In the Lord."
   We should rejoice in the Lord God, Father, Son, and Spirit.
   We should rejoice in the Lord Jesus, dead, risen, etc.
   Not in temporals, personal, political, or pecuniary.
   Nor in self and its doings. (Phil. 3:3).

III. THE TIME APPOINTED. "Always."

1. When you cannot rejoice in any other, rejoice in God.
2. When you can rejoice in other things, sanctify all with joy in God.
3. When you have not before rejoiced, begin at once.
4. When you have long rejoiced, do not cease for a moment.
5. When others are with you, lead them in this direction.
6. When you are alone, enjoy to the full this rejoicing.

IV. THE EMPHASIS LAID ON THE COMMAND. "Again I say, Rejoice."
Paul rejoiced. He was habitually a happy man.
This epistle to the Philippians is peculiarly joyous. Let us look it through. The apostle is joyful throughout:
   He sweetens prayer with joy: 1:4.
   He rejoices that Christ is preached: 1:18.
   He wishes to live to gladden the church: 1:25.

To see the members like-minded with his joy: 2:2.
It was his joy that he should not run in vain: 2:16.
His farewell to them was, "Rejoice in the Lord": 3:1.
He speaks of those who rejoice in Christ Jesus: 3:3.
He calls his converts his joy and his crown: 4:1.
He expresses his joy in their kindness: 4:4, 10, 18.

Upon working days rejoice in the Lord, who giveth thee strength to labor, and feedeth thee with the labor of thy hands. On holidays rejoice in the Lord, who feasteth thee with the marrow and fatness of His house. In plenty, rejoice again and again, because the Lord giveth; in want rejoice, because the Lord taketh away, and as it pleaseth the Lord, so come things to pass.—EDWARD MARBURY.

The calendar of the sinner has only a few days in the year marked as festival days; but *every day* of the Christian's calendar is marked by the hand of God as a day of rejoicing.—ANON.

*'Tis impious in a good man to be sad.*—EDWARD YOUNG.

Napoleon, when sent to Elba, adopted, in proud defiance of his fate, the motto, *"Ubicunque felix."* It was not true in his case; but the Christian may be truly "happy everywhere" and always.


CHAPTER 165

## CHRIST THE CREATOR

*"For by Him were all things created, that are in heaven, and that are in earth, visible and invisible, whether they be thrones, or dominions, or principalities, or powers: all things were created by Him, and for Him"* (Col. 1:16).

Any theme which exalts the Savior is precious to the saints.

This is one in which the preacher cannot hope to do more than to show how vastly his Theme is above him.

I. CONSIDER THE STATEMENT ITSELF.

1. Heaven itself was created by and for Christ Jesus.
   There is such a place, as well as such a state, and of that place Jesus is the center. Enoch and Elijah in their bodies are there, Jesus as man is there, and there all His people will be. God, as a pure Spirit, needed no such place; nor angels, for everywhere they would see God.
   It was created for Jesus, and for the people whom He will bring there to be one forever with Himself.
   It exists by Jesus and for Jesus.
   Everything in heaven is prepared by Jesus. He is the designer of it.

Everything in heaven reflects Jesus.  He is the soul of it.
Everything in heaven praises Jesus.  He is the King of it.

2.  The angels.  All their ranks were made by Him for Him.
    To worship Him, and glorify Him with their adoration.
    To rejoice with Him and in Him, as they do when sinners repent.
    To guard Christ's people in life, and bring them to Him in death.
    To carry out His purposes of judgment, as with Pharaoh, etc.
    To achieve His purposes of deliverance, as Peter from prison.

3.  This world was made by Him to be—
    A place for Him to live and die upon.
    A stage for His people to live and act upon.

## II.  REVIEW THE REFLECTIONS HENCE ARISING.

1.  Jesus then is God.  "By Him were all things created."
2.  Jesus is the clue of the universe; its center and explanation. All things are to be seen in the light of the cross, and all things exist.
3.  To live to Jesus, then, is to find out the true object of our being, and to be in accord with all creation.
4.  Not living to Jesus, we can have no blessing.
5.  We can only live *for* Him as we live *by* Him, for so all things do.
6.  It is clear that He must triumph.  All is going well.  If we look at history from His throne, all things are "for Him." "He must reign."  Let us comfort one another with these words.

What an honor to be the smallest page in the retinue of such a prince!

When the Christian martyr Pionius was asked by his judges, "What God dost thou worship?" he replied: "I worship Him Who made the heavens, and Who beautified them with stars, and Who has enriched the earth with flowers and trees."  "Dost thou mean," asked the magistrates, "Him Who was crucified (*illum dicis qui crucifixus est*)?" "Certainly," replied Pionius, "Him Whom the Father sent for the salvation of the world."

As Pionius died, so died Blandina and the whole host of those who, in the first three centuries, without knowing anything of the Nicene Creed, held it implicitly, if not explicitly, and proclaimed it in flames and in dungeons, in famine and in nakedness, under the rack and under the sword.—JOSEPH COOK.

In creation God shows us His hand, but in redemption God gives us His heart.—ADOLPHE MONOD.

It was well said of a heathen, *Si essem luscinia*—if I were a nightingale I would sing as a nightingale; *si alauda*—if I were a lark I would soar as a lark. Since I am a man, what should I do but know, love, and praise God without ceasing, and glorify my Creator?

Things are unprofitable or misplaced when they do not seek or serve their end; therefore, for what use are we meet, if we are unmeet for our proper end? We are like the wood of the vine, good for nothing, not so much as to make a pin whereon to hang anything (Ezek. 15:2); good for nothing but to be cast into the fire, unless it be fruitful. What are we good for if we be not serviceable to the ends for which we were created?—THOMAS MANTON.

## CHAPTER 166

## CHRIST IS ALL

*"Where there is neither Greek nor Jew, circumcision nor uncircumcision, barbarian, Scythian, bond nor free: but Christ is all, and in all"* (Col. 3:11).

There are two worlds, the old and the new. These are peopled by two sorts of manhood, the old man, and the new man, concerning whom, see verses 9, 10.

In the first are many things which are not in the second.

In the second are many things which are not in the first.

I. WHAT THERE IS NOT IN THE NEW.

1. National distinctions: "Where there is neither Greek nor Jew." Jesus is a man. In the broadest sense He is neither Jew nor Gentile. We see in Him no restrictive nationality: and our own peculiar nationality sinks before union with Him.

2. Ceremonial distinctions: "There is neither circumcision nor uncircumcision." The typical separation is removed.
Both Jew and Gentile are united in one body by the cross.

3. Social distinctions: "There is neither bond nor free."
We are enabled through divine grace to see that:
These distinctions are transient.
These distinctions are superficial.
These distinctions are of small value.
These distinctions are non-existent in the spiritual realm.

II. WHAT THERE IS IN THE NEW.

"Christ is all and in all"; and that in many senses.

1. Christ is all our culture. In Him we emulate and excel the "Greek."

2. Christ is all our revelation. We glory in Him even as the "Jew" gloried in receiving the oracles of God.

3. Christ is all our natural traditions. He is more to us than the freshest ideas which cross the mind of the "Barbarian."

4. Christ is all our unconquerableness and liberty. The "Chythian" had not such boundless independence as we find in Him.

Christ is not valued at all unless He be valued above all.— AUGUSTINE.

> He is a path, if any be misled;
>   He is a robe, if any naked be;
> If any chance to hunger, He is bread;
>   If any be a bondman, He is free;
>   If any be but weak, how strong is He!
> To dead men life He is, to sick men health,
> To blind men sight, and to the needy wealth;
> A pleasure without loss, a treasure without stealth.
>                                   —GILES FLETCHER.

I cannot but reverence the memory of that reverend divine (Mr. Welsh) who, being in a deep muse after some discourse that had passed of Christ, and tears trickling abundantly from his eyes before he was aware, being urged for the cause thereof, he honestly confessed that he wept because he could not draw his dull heart to prize Christ aright. I fear this is a rare mind in Christians, for many think a very little to be quite enough for Jesus, and even too much for him!—SAMUEL WARD.

"At length, one evening, while engaged in a prayer-meeting, the great deliverance came. I received the full witness of the Spirit that the blood of Jesus had cleansed me from all sin. I felt I was nothing, and Christ was all in all. Him I now cheerfully received in all His offices: my Prophet, to teach me; my Priest, to atone for me; my King, to reign over me. Oh what boundless, boundless happiness there is in Christ, and all for such a poor sinner as I am! This happy change took place in my soul March 13th, 1772."—WILLIAM CARVOSSO.

*Dannecker*, the German Sculptor, spent eight years in producing a face of Christ; and at last wrought out one in which the emotions of love and sorrow were so perfectly blended that beholders wept as they looked upon it.

Subsequently, being solicited to employ his great talent on a statue of Venus, he replied, "After gazing so long into the face of Christ, think you that I can now turn my attention to a heathen goddess?" Here is the true secret of weanedness from worldly idols, "the expulsive power of a new affection."

### CHAPTER 167

## A HAPPY MINISTER'S MEETING

*I Thess. 2:13, 14.*

Paul unbosoms his heart to the loving church at Thessalonica.

He knew what it was to be worried by the Corinthians and the Galatians, but he found rest when thinking of the Thessalonians.

The most tried ministers have some bright spots.

In setting forth his joyful memories of Thessalonica, Paul gives us a sight of three things.

I. MINISTERS GIVING THANKS. "We also thank God."

Ministers are not always groaning and weeping, though they often do so. They have their time of thanksgiving, as in Paul's case.

1. This followed upon sore travail. (See verse 9). Only as we sow in tears do we reap in joy.

2. This was backed by holy living. Dwell upon each point in verses 10 and 11. Unholy ministers will have scant cause for joy.

3. It prevented all self-laudation. They thanked God, and this is the opposite of glorifying self.

4. It was of a social character. "We thank God"; Paul, and Silas, and Timothy. We hold a fraternal meeting of joy when God blesses us among our beloved people.

5. It was of an abiding character,—"without ceasing." We can never cease praising the Lord for His goodness in saving souls.

II. HEARERS RECEIVING THE WORD. "Ye received the word of God."

1. They received the Word of God: they heard it calmly, attended to it candidly, considered it carefully.

2. They received the word of God with a hearty welcome. They accepted it by faith, with personal confidence and joy.

3. They did not receive the word of man. It is well to keep the doors locked in that direction.

4. They received it as God's revealed word, and therefore received it.
With reverence of its divine character.
With assurance of its infallibility.
With obedience to its authority.
With experience of its sacred power.

III. CONVERTS EXHIBITING THE FAMILY LIKENESS.

1. They were like Judean Christians, the best of them, in faith; in experience; in afflictions.

2. They had never seen the church of God in Judea, and were no copyists, yet they came to be fac-similes of them.

3. This is a singular confirmation of the divine character of the work.

   The same Lord works in all believers, and in the main the same experience occurs in all the saints, even though they may never have seen each other.

   This similarity of all regenerated men furnishes a valuable set of experimental evidences of the divine origin of conversion.

Let us not be daunted by opposition, for at Thessalonica Paul was persecuted and yet triumphant.

"Whoever made this book," said a Chinese convert, "made me; it tells me the thoughts of my heart."

LOSKIEL'S "Account of the Moravian Missions among the North American Indians," has taught me two things. I have found in it a striking illustration of the uniformity with which the grace of God operates on men. CRANTZ, in his "Account of the Missions in Greenland," has shown the grace of God working on a man-fish—on a stupid, sottish, senseless creature, scarcely a remove from the fish on which he lived.

LOSKIEL shows the same grace working on a man-devil—a fierce, bloody, revengeful warrior, dancing his infernal war-dance with the mind of a fury. Divine grace brings these men to the same point: it quickens, stimulates, and elevates the Greenlander—it raises him to a sort of new life—it seems almost to bestow on him new senses— it opens his eye, and bends his ear, and rouses his heart; and what it adds, it sanctifies. The same grace tames the high spirit of the Indian—it reduces him to the meekness, and the docility, and simplicity of a child.

The evidence arising to Christianity from these facts is perhaps seldom sufficient, by itself, to convince the gainsayer; but, to a man who already believes, it greatly strengthens the reason of his belief. I have seen, also, in these books, that the fish boat, and the oil, and the tomahawk, and the cap of feathers excepted, a Christian minister has to deal with just the same sort of creatures as the Greenlander and the Indian among civilized nations.—RICHARD CECIL.

The Edition of those living Epistles is the same the world over; the binding only may differ.

## CHAPTER 168

# WEARINESS IN WELL-DOING

*"But ye, brethren, be not weary in well-doing"* (II Thess. 3:13).

Read the two previous verses, and mark the apostle's censure of those who are busy-bodies, "working not at all."

I. A SUMMARY OF CHRISTIAN LIFE. He calls it "well-doing."

1. Religious work is well-doing. Preaching, teaching, writing books and letters, temperance meetings, Bible-classes, tract-distributing, personal conversation, private prayer, praise, etc.
2. Charitable work is "well-doing." The poor, the widow and the fatherless, the ignorant, the sick, the fallen, and the despondent, are to be looked after with tender care.

Everything is "well-doing" which is done from a sense of duty, with dependence upon God, and faith in His word; out of love to Christ, in good-will to other workers, with prayer for direction, acceptance, and blessing.

Common actions become holy, and drudgery grows divine when the motive is pure and high.

II. A WARNING AS TO CAUSES OF WEARINESS IN WELL-DOING.

1. Idle examples tempt the industrious to idleness: verse 11.
2. Busy-bodies, and disorderly persons in the church, hinder many from their diligent service: verses 11, 12.
3. Troublers, such as "unreasonable and wicked men," dispirit those who would serve the Lord: verse 2.

III. AN ARGUMENT AGAINST WEARINESS IN WELL-DOING.

"But ye, brethren, be not weary in well-doing."

1. Lose not what you have already wrought.
2. Consider what self-denials others practise for inferior things: soldiers, wrestlers, rowers in boat-race, etc.
3. Remember that the eye of God is upon you, His hand with you, His smile on you, His command over you.
4. Reflect upon the grandeur of the service in itself as done unto the Lord, and to His glorious cause.

But more than this. I must be "well-doing." The Greek word expresses beauty, and this enters into the apostolic thought. True piety is lovely. Just so far as it comes short in the beautiful, it becomes monstrous. But, as used by Paul, it goes far beyond this, and signifies all moral excellence.

Activity is not enough; for activity the intensest may be evil. Lucifer is as active, as constant, and earnest as Gabriel. But the one is a fiend, and the other a seraph. Any activity that is not good is a curse always and only. Better be dead, inert matter—a stone, a clod—than a stinging reptile, or a destroying demon; and herein lies the great practical change in regeneration. It transforms the mere doer into a well-doer. It is not so much a change in the energy as in the direction.—CHARLES WADSWORTH, D.D.

The Hebrews have a saying, that God is more delighted in adverbs than in nouns: 'tis not so much the matter that's done, but the matter how 'tis done, that God minds. *Not how much, but how well!* 'Tis the well-doing that meets with a well-done. Let us therefore serve God, not nominally or verbially, but adverbially.—RALPH VENNING.

## CHAPTER 169

## THE FAITHFUL SAYING

*"This is a faithful saying, and worthy of all acceptation, that Christ Jesus came into the world to save sinners: of whom I am chief"* (I Tim. 1:15).

Paul had described his ordination in verse 12. He then went on to speak of the grace manifested in the call of such a person to the ministry (verse 13), and of the further grace by which he was sustained in that ministry.

I. HOW WE PREACH THE GOSPEL.

1. As a certainty. It is a "faithful saying." *We* do not doubt the truth of our message, or how could we expect *you* to believe it. We believe, and are sure, because
   It is a revelation of God.
   It is attested by miracles.
   It bears its witness within itself.
   It has proved its power upon our hearts.
2. As an everyday truth. It is to us a "saying" or proverb.
3. As claiming your attention. "Worthy of all acceptation."
   You must believe it to be true.
   You must appropriate it to yourself.
   You ought to do so, for it is worthy of your acceptance.

II. WHAT GOSPEL DO WE PREACH?

1. The gospel of a person: "Christ Jesus."
   He is the anointed of God: "Christ."
   He is the Saviour of men: "Jesus."
   He is God and Man in One Person.
   He died, and yet He lives forever.

2. The gospel for sinners.
   For such Jesus lived and labored.
   For such He died and made atonement.
   For such He has sent the gospel of pardon.
   For such He pleads in heaven.
3. The gospel of effectual deliverance. "To save sinners."
   Not to half save them.
   Nor to make them savable.
   Nor to help them to save themselves.
   Nor to save them as righteous.
   But to save them wholly and effectually from their sins.

## III. WHY DO WE PREACH IT?

1. Because we have been saved by it.
2. Because we cannot help it, for an inward impulse compels us to tell of the miracle of mercy wrought upon us.
   Will you not believe a saying so sure?
   Will you not accept a truth so gladsome?
   Will you not come to a Saviour so suitable?

A visitor to Rome says, "I was struck with the frequency with which the priests and other exhibitors of church curiosities use the phrase, "It is said"—*on dit*—when describing relics and rarities. They do not vouch for their being what they are reputed to be. "It is said." Are they ashamed of their curiosities? Do they thus try to satisfy their consciences? They do not express their personal belief; but— *it is said*. Not thus do gospel preachers speak. "That which we have seen and heard declare we unto you."

There's a nice word in the text—it is the word "acceptation." It's all provided for you. It's very much like a supper. You'll find the table laid, and everything all ready. You're not expected to bring anything at all.

I was once invited out to tea by a poor widow, and I took something in my pocket. But I'll never do it again. It was two cakes; and when I brought them out and laid them on the table, she picked them up and flung them out into the street, and said, "I asked you to tea; I didn't ask you to provide tea for me." And so with Christ; He asks, He provides, and He wants nothing but ourselves; and if we take aught else, he'll reject it. We can only sup with Him when we come as we are.

Luther says, "Once upon a time the devil said to me, 'Martin Luther, you are a great sinner, and you will be damned!' 'Stop! Stop!' said I; 'one thing at a time; I am a great sinner, it is true, though you have no right to tell me of it. I confess it. What next?' 'Therefore you will be damned.' 'That is not good reasoning. It is true that I am a great sinner, but it is written, "Jesus Christ came to save sinners;" therefore I *shall be saved!* Now go your way.' So I cut the devil off with his own sword, and he went away mourning because he could not cast me down by calling me a sinner."

## CHAPTER 170

## OUR GOSPEL

> *"For the which cause I also suffer these things; neverthe-*
> *less I am not ashamed: for I know Whom I have believed,*
> *and am persuaded that He is able to keep that which I*
> *have committed unto Him against that day"* (II Tim. 1:12).

I. WHAT HE HAD DONE.

1. His soul's case was there for Jesus to heal him as a *Physician.*
2. His soul's calls were there to be supplied by Jesus as a *Shepherd.*
3. His soul's course was there to be directed by Jesus as a *Pilot.*
4. His soul's cause was there to be pleaded by Jesus as an *Advocate.*
5. His soul's care was there to be guarded by Jesus as a *Protector.*

II. WHAT HE KNEW. "I know Whom I have believed."

1. He knew the Lord Jesus by his personal meeting with Him on the road to Damascus, and at other times.
2. By communion with Him. This way is open to all the saints.
3. By experience, through which he had tried and proved his love and faithfulness.
   Have we this personal acquaintance with the Lord?
   If so, we shall gladly commit our all to Him.

III. WHAT HE WAS SURE OF. "That He is able to keep," etc.

1. The ability of Jesus to keep all souls committed to Him.
   He is divine, and therefore omnipotent to save.
   His work is finished, so that He meets all the demands of the law.
   His wisdom is perfect, so that He will ward off all dangers.
   His plea is constant, and ever prevails to preserve His own.
2. The ability of Jesus to keep Paul's own soul.
3. The ability of Jesus to keep his soul under the heavy trials which were then pressing upon him. "I suffer . . . I am not ashamed, for I am persuaded that He is able to keep."

4. The ability of Jesus to keep his soul even to the close of all things: "against that day."

IV. WHAT, THEREFORE, HE WAS.

1. Very cheerful. He had all the tone and air of a thoroughly happy man.
2. Very confident. Though a prisoner, he says, "I am not ashamed." Neither of his condition, nor of the cause of Christ, nor of the cross, was he ashamed.
3. Very thankful. He gladly praised the Lord in whom he trusted. The text is a confession of faith, or a form of adoration.

When DR. JAMES W. ALEXANDER was dying, his wife sought to comfort him with precious words, as she quoted them to him: "I know in whom I have believed." Dr. Alexander at once corrected her by saying, "Not *in* whom I have believed; but 'I know *whom* I have believed.'" He would not even suffer a little preposition to be between his soul and his Saviour.

"I have lost that weary bondage of doubt, and almost despair, which chained me for so many years. I have the same sins and temptations as before, and I do not strive against them more than before, and it is often just as hard work. But whereas I could not before see why I *should* be saved, I cannot now see why I should *not* be saved if Christ died for sinners. On that word I take my stand, and *rest there*."—F. R. HAVERGAL.

JUSTYN MARTYR was asked ironically by the Roman prefect if he believed that after his decapitation he would ascend to heaven. He replied: "I am so sure of the grace which Jesus Christ hath obtained for me, that not a shadow of doubt can enter my mind."

DONALD CARGILL, on the scaffold, July 27th, 1681, as he handed his well-used Bible to one of his friends that stood near, gave his testimony: "I bless the Lord that these thirty years and more I have been at peace with God, and was never shaken loose of it. And now I am as sure of my interest in Christ, and peace with God, as all within this Bible, and the Spirit of God can make me. And I am no more terrified at death, or afraid of hell because of sin, than if I had never had sin: for all my sins were freely pardoned and washed thoroughly away through the precious blood and intercession of Jesus Christ."

## CHAPTER 171
## MERCY IN THE DAY OF JUDGMENT

*"The Lord grant unto him that he may find mercy of the Lord in that day"* (II Tim. 1:18).

The best method of showing our gratitude to some men for their kindness would be to pray for them.

Even the best of men will be the better for our prayers.

## I.  "THAT DAY."

"That day": it is not specifically described, because well known and much thought of among Christians.  Do we sufficiently think of that day?  If so, we shall feel our great need to find of the Lord mercy when it comes.

Its date is not given.  It would but gratify curiosity.

Its length is not specified.  Will it be a common day?  It will be long enough for the deliberate judgment of all men.

Its glory, the revelation of Jesus from heaven upon the throne of judgment.  This will make it most memorable.

Its decisions will be strictly just, indisputable, unchangeable, etc. It will be the last day, and henceforth the state of men will be fixed for joy or woe.

## II.  THE MERCY.

All will need it.  Assuredly we shall need it ourselves.

To arouse us, let us think of those who will find no mercy of the Lord in that day:

Those who had no mercy on others.

Those who lived and died impenitent.

Those who neglected salvation.  How shall they escape?

Those who said they needed no mercy: the self-righteous.

Those who sought no mercy: procrastinators, and the indifferent.

Those who scoffed at Christ, and refused the gospel.

## III.  TO-DAY.

We would not have you despair as to the future, but hope to find mercy in the present, that you may find it in "that day."

Remember that now is the accepted time, for—

You are not yet standing at the judgment bar.

You are yet where prayer is heard.

You are where faith will save all who exercise it towards Christ.

You are where the Spirit strives.

You are where sin may be forgiven, at once, and forever.

You are where grace reigns, even though sin abounds.

An infidel was introduced by a gentleman to a minister with a remark, "He never attends public worship."  "Ah!" said the minister, "I hope you are mistaken."  "By no means," said the stranger; "I always spend Sunday in settling my accounts."  "Then, alas!" was the calm, but solemn reply, "you will find, sir, that the day of judgment will be spent in the same manner."—G. S. BOWES.

When THOMAS HOOKER was dying, one said to him, "Brother, you are going to receive the reward of your labors." He humbly replied, "Brother, I am going to receive *mercy.*"

By that tremendous phrase, *"eternal* judgment," consider your ways and be wise! If its true meaning could lighten upon you at this moment, what consternation would strike upon each spirit! Every man, though serene as death before, would spring to his feet, and cry, Tell me, tell me this moment, what must I do!—CHARLES STANFORD, D.D.

## CHAPTER 172

## THE WORD OF GOD UNBOUND

*"Wherein I suffer trouble, as an evil-doer, even unto bonds; but the word of God is not bound"* (II Tim. 2:9).

The resurrection of Christ was Paul's sheet-anchor. Enlarge upon verse 8, wherein he mentions it as the essence of the gospel.

He himself is suffering and bound, but he is not without comfort.

His great joy is that the Word of God is not bound.

I.  IN WHAT SENSES THIS IS TRUE.

The Word of God is not bound—

1.  So that it cannot be made known.

The ministers who preach it may be imprisoned, but not the Word.

The Book which contains it may be burned, but the truth abides.

2.  So that it cannot comfort the soul.

Conviction of sin will not hinder consolation when faith is given.

Confirmed despair shall be overcome, even as Samson snapped the cords wherewith he had been bound.

3.  So that it cannot prevail over error.

Infidelity, Ritualism, Popery, fanaticism, etc., shall not bind the gospel so as to retain their mischievous power over men.

The gospel must and will accomplish the purposes of God.

II.  FOR WHAT REASONS THIS IS TRUE.

The Word of God cannot be bound, since—

1.  It is the voice of the Almighty.

2.  It is attended by the energetic working of the Holy Ghost.

3. It creates such enthusiasm in the hearts wherein it dwells, that men must declare it abroad: it must be free.

## III.  WHAT OTHER FACTS ARE PARALLEL WITH THIS?

As the binding of Paul was not the binding of the Word of God, so:
The death of ministers is not the death of the gospel.
The feebleness of workers is not its feebleness.
The bondage of the preacher's mind is not its bondage.
The coldness of men is not its coldness.
The falsehood of hypocrites does not falsify it.
The spiritual ruin of sinners is not the defeat of the gospel.
The rejection of it by unbelievers is not its overthrow.

In a portrait of Tyndale, still preserved in this country, beside the heroic man is a device: a burning book is tied to a stake, while a number of similar books are seen flying out of the fire. The meaning is an historic fact. Tonstal, the Bishop of London, had bought up some scores of Tyndale's Testaments, and burned them. The money paid for them enabled Tyndale to bring out a new and more correct edition.

Towards the close of the last century, before the days of the great Bible Societies, there was, for a season, a woeful want of Bibles in America, caused partly by the prevalence of French infidelity, and partly by the general religious apathy which followed the Revolutionary War. In that period a man went into a book-store in Philadelphia and asked to buy a Bible. "I have none," said the bookseller. "There is not a copy for sale in the city: and I can tell you further," said he (for he was of the French way of thinking), "in fifty years there will not be a Bible in the world." The rough answer of the customer was, "There will be plenty of Bibles in the world a thousand years after you are dead and gone to hell."— *The Christian Age.*

As a bird of the air, truth flies abroad on swift wings; as a ray of light it enters palaces and cottages; as the unfettered wind it laughs at laws and prohibitions. Walls cannot confine it, nor iron bars imprison it; it is free, and maketh free. Let every freeman be upon its side, and being so, let him never allow a doubt of its ultimate success to darken his soul.—C. H. S.

The truth is more incomprehensible than water. If compressed in one way, it will exude through the compressing mass, the more visible through the attempts to compress it.—DR. PUSEY.

## CHAPTER 173

# GOSPEL JEWELRY

*"That they may adorn the doctrine of God our Saviour in all things"* (Titus 2:10).

I. A NAME OF ADORNMENT FOR THE GOSPEL. "The doctrine of God our Saviour."

   1. It sets forth its greatness: "doctrine of God."
     Our fall, ruin, sin, and punishment were great.
     Our salvation and redemption are great.
     Our safety, happiness, and hopes are great.

   2. It sets forth its certainty. It is "of God."
     It comes by revelation of God.
     It is guaranteed by the fidelity of God.
     It is as immutable as God Himself.

   3. It sets forth its relation to Christ Jesus: "of God our Saviour."
     He is the Author, Substance and Proclaimer of it.
     He is the object of it. The gospel glorifies Jesus.

II. A METHOD OF ADORNMENT FOR THE GOSPEL.

   1. The persons who are to adorn the gospel.
     In Paul's day, bond-servants or slaves.
     In our day, poor servants of the humblest order.

   2. The way in which these persons could specially adorn the gospel.
     By restraining their tongues: "not answering again."
     By scrupulous honesty: "not purloining," verse 10.
     By trustworthy character: "showing all good fidelity."
  All this would make their masters admire the Gospel of Christ.

   3. The way of adornment of the doctrine in general
     Negatively: it is found.
     Nor in the finery of philosophical thought.
     Nor in the tawdriness of rhetorical speech.
     Positively: it lies in another direction.
     Adornment, if really so, is *suitable to beauty*.
     Holiness, mercifulness, cheerfulness, etc., are congruous with the gospel.
     Adornment is often a *tribute to beauty*. Such is a godly conversation: it honors the gospel.
     Adornment is an *advertisement of beauty*. Holiness calls attention to the natural beauty of the gospel.
     Adornment is an *enhancement of beauty*. Godliness gives emphasis to the excellence of doctrine.

Let us all endeavor to adorn the gospel, by:
> Strict integrity in business.
> Constant courtesy of behavior.
> Unselfish love to all around us.
> Quick forgiveness of injuries.
> Abundant patience under trials.
> Holy calm and self-possession at all times.

Yes, and mark you, this is to be done not as the prerogative of a few grandly gifted spirits, and on some occasion which may lift them proudly up to the gaze of the universe.

As found in the text, it was of the power of the poor Cretan slaves the apostle was writing; of their power, too, not in some tremendous trial, as of torture or martyrdom, to which the cruelty of their mas· ters sometimes subjected their faith, but of their power to do it "in all things"—in the daily, lowly, degrading service of a menial—in the small things as well as the great, in the squalid stall and fold as well as in the splendor of the palace; absolutely, in "all things" to adorn the glorious gospel of God.

O blessed bondsmen of Crete! going forth under the lash and the chain, yet with hearts of faith under their burdens, and smiles of love amid their tears, doing work for God impossible to an angel!— CHARLES WADSWORTH, D.D.

We have all heard the story of the girl who said she had been converted, for she now "swept under the mats." Koba, an Indian warrior, recently gave evidence of his conversion by saying, "I pray every day, and hoe onions." An Indian could not give a much better evidence of his sincerity than that. Manual labor is not the chief joy or pride of an Indian warrior.

A Brahmin wrote to a missionary: "We are finding you out. You are not as good as your Book. If your people were only as good as your Book, you would conquer India for Christ in five years."

## CHAPTER 174

## THE STORY OF A RUNAWAY SLAVE

*"Perhaps he therefore departed for a season, that thou shouldest receive him forever"* (Philemon 15).

Nature is selfish, but grace is loving. He who boasts that he cares for nobody, and nobody cares for him, is the reverse of a Christian. The apostle Paul was eminently large hearted and sympathetic.

I. Look At Onesimus As An Instance Of Divine Grace.

1. We see the grace of God in his *election*.

Were there no free men, that God must elect a slave? Onesimus was part and parcel of the dregs of a sink of sin. Yet eternal love which passed by kings and princes fixed its eye upon this slave.

2. In his *conversion*. How unlikely he appears to become a convert. An Asiatic slave of about the same grade as any heathen of our day. He was dishonest, and daring enough to make the long trip to Rome. But everlasting love means to convert the man and converted he shall be.

3. We see the grace of God in the *character* wrought in Onesimus.

We meet odd people who doubtless will go to heaven but they are cross grained; sort of spiritual hedgehogs. They illustrate the wisdom and patience of God but not good companions. Onesimus was of a kind, tender and loving spirit, and this was brought out by God's grace.

II. Note An Interesting Instance Of Sin Overruled.

Onesimus had no right to rob his master and run away; but God was pleased to make use of that crime for his conversion.

1. See how God overruled all. Nobody shall be able to touch the heart of this slave but Paul, but he is in prison at Rome and Onesimus at Colosse. The devil shall bring him to Rome by tempting him to steal and then run away. The devil didn't know that he would lose a willing servant thereby. The devil so often plays the fool.

III. Witness An Example Of Relations Improved.

It takes a long time often to learn great truths. Perhaps Philemon had not quite found out that it was wrong for him to have a slave. The text speaks of Onesimus as a "brother beloved," no longer a slave.

When Onesimus comes back he will be a better servant and Philemon a better master. Philemon could have refused to take him back, suspected him, treated him unkindly, but not if he was a true Christian.

Much better that you should overlook a fault which you might have noticed than notice a fault which you ought to have overlooked.

———

Rowland Hill used to say that he would not give a halfpenny for a man's piety if his dog and his cat were not better off after he was converted. There is much weight in that remark. Everything in the house goes better when grace oils the wheels . . . I do not believe in your Christianity, my friend, if it belongs to the church, and the prayer meeting and not to your home.

———

Some three years ago I was talking with an aged minister, and he began fumbling about in his coat pocket, but he was a long while before he found what he wanted. At last he brought out a letter that was well nigh worn to pieces, and he said, "God Almighty bless you! God Almighty bless you!" And I said, "Friend, what is it?" He said, "I had a son. I thought he would be the stay of my old age, but he disgraced himself, and he went away from me, and I could not tell where he went, only he said he was going to America. He took a ticket to sail for America from the London docks, but he didn't go on the particular day that he expected." The aged minister bade me read the letter and I read it, and it was like this: "Father, I am here in America. I have found a situation and God has prospered me. I write to ask your forgiveness for the thousand wrongs that I have done you, and the grief I have caused you, for, blessed be God, I have found the Saviour, I have joined the church of God here, and hope to spend my life in God's service.

"It happened thus: I did not sail for America the day I expected. I went down to the tabernacle to see what it was like and God met with me. Mr. Spurgeon said, 'Perhaps there is a runaway son here. The Lord call him by His grace.' And He did." "Now," said the minister, putting the letter away, "that son of mine is dead, and he is in heaven, and I love you and I shall do so as long as I live because you were the means of bringing him to Christ."

## CHAPTER 175

## THE SWORD OF THE LORD

*"For the word of God is quick, and powerful, and sharper than any two-edged sword, piercing even to the dividing asunder of soul and spirit, and of the joints and marrow, and is a discerner of the thoughts and intents of the heart"* (Heb. 4:12).

I. THE QUALITIES OF THE WORD.
   1. It is divine. It is the word of God.
   2. It is living. "The word of God is quick."
      In contrast to our words, which pass away, God's Word lives on.
      It has life in itself. It is "the living and incorruptible seed."
      It creates life where it comes.
      It can never be destroyed and exterminated.
   3. It is effectual: "Quick, and powerful."
      It carries conviction and conversion.
      It works comfort and confirmation.

It has power to raise us to great heights of holiness and happiness.

4. It is cutting, "Sharper than any two-edged sword."
   It wounds more or less all who touch it.
   It kills self-righteousness, sin, unbelief, etc.
5. It is piercing. "Even to the dividing asunder."
   It forces its way into the hard heart.
   It penetrates the smallest opening.
6. It is discriminating. "To the dividing asunder of soul and spirit."
   It separates things much alike: natural and spiritual religion.
   It divides the outer from the inner: external and internal religion, "joints and marrow."
7. It is revealing. "A discerner of the thoughts and intents of the heart."
   It cleaves the man as the butcher cleaves the carcass, and opens up the secret faculties and tendencies of the soul.

## II. THE LESSONS WE SHOULD LEARN THEREFROM.

That we do greatly reverence the Word, as truly spoken of God.

That we come to it for quickening for our own souls.

That we come to it for power when fighting the battles of truth.

That we come to it for cutting force to kill our own sins and to help us in destroying the evils of the day.

That we let it criticize us, and our opinions, and projects, and acts, and all about us.

Bless God for the efficacy of the Word upon thy soul. Did ever its point prick thy heart, its edge fetch blood of thy lusts? Bless God for it; you would do as much to a surgeon for lancing a sore and severing a putrified part from thy body, though he put thee to exquisite torture in doing it.

And I hope thou thinkest God hath done thee a great kindness. . . . There is not another sword like this in all the world, that can cure with cutting; not another arm could use this sword, to have done thus with it, besides the Spirit of God.

The Word of God is too sacred a thing, and preaching too solemn a work, to be toyed and played with, as is the usage of some, who make a sermon but matter of wit and fine oratory. If we mean to do good, we must come unto men's hearts, not in word only, but with power. Satan moves not for a thousand squibs and wit-cracks of rhetoric. Draw, therefore, this sword out of your scabbard, and strike with its naked edge; this, you will find, the only way to pierce your people's consciences, and fetch blood of their sins.—WILLIAM GURNALL.

MISS WHATELEY says, "To rouse the torpid and unexercised mind of a Moslem woman is wonderful, for they are sunk in ignorance and degradation; but while I was reading to one of them a few weeks ago, she exclaimed, 'Why it is just as if I were out in the dark and you held a lamp to me, that I might see my way.'"

The Rev. James Wall, of Rome, relates the following instances of conversion through the reading of the Scriptures: One of the converts, when first presented with a New Testament, said, "Very well; it is the very size for me to make my cigarettes," and so he began to smoke it away. He smoked away all the Evangelists, till he was at the tenth Chapter of John, when it struck him that he must read a bit of it, for if he didn't there would soon be no more left to read. The first word struck home, and the man read himself into Christ.

## Chapter 176

## BOLDNESS AT THE THRONE

*"Let us therefore come boldly unto the throne of grace, that we may obtain mercy, and find grace to help in time of need"* (Heb. 4:16).

Prayer occupies a most important place in the life of the Christian. This verse is one of the sweetest of invitations to prayer.

I. Here Is Our Great Resort Described: "The throne of grace." Once it was called "the mercy-*seat*," but now the "throne."
In drawing near to God in prayer, we come—
1. To God as a King, with reverence, confidence and submission.
2. To One who gives as a King: therefore we ask largely and expectantly. He has riches of grace and power.
3. To One who sits upon a throne "of grace," on purpose to dispense grace. It is His design, His object in displaying Himself as King.

II. Here Is A Loving Exhortation: "Let us come."
1. From Paul, a man like ourselves, but an experienced believer, who had much tried the power of prayer.
2. From the whole church speaking in him.
3. From the Holy Spirit; for the apostle spoke by inspiration. The Spirit, making intercession in us, says, "Let us come."

III. Here Is A Qualifying Adverb: "Let us come boldly."
Not proudly, presumptuously, nor with the tone of demand, for it is the throne; yet "boldly," for it is the throne *of grace*.
1. We may come unreservedly, with all sorts of petitions.
2. We may come freely, with simple words.
3. We may come hopefully, with full confidence of being heard.
4. We may come fervently, with importunity of pleading.

IV. **HERE IS A REASON GIVEN FOR BOLDNESS:** "Let us *therefore* come."

   1. We may come when we need great mercy, because of our sin. We may come when we have little grace.
   2. There are many other reasons for coming at once, and boldly. The character of God encourages us to be bold. Our relation to Him as children gives us great freedom. Christ is already given to us, and therefore God will deny us nothing. Our former successes at the throne give us solid confidence.
   3. The great reason of all for bold approach is in Jesus. He once was slain, and the mercy-seat is sprinkled with His blood.

He is risen and has justified us by His righteousness.

Let us come to the throne, when we are sinful, to find mercy.

Let us come to the throne, when we are weak, to find help.

Let us come to the throne, when we are tempted, to find grace.

When God enacts laws, He is on a throne of legislation: when He administers these laws, He is on a throne of government: when He tries His creatures by these laws, He is on a throne of judgment: but when He receives petitions, and dispenses favors, He is on a *throne of grace.*

A holy boldness, a chastened familiarity, is the true spirit of right prayer. It was said of Luther that, when he prayed, it was with as much reverence as if he prayed to an infinite God, and with as much familiarity as if he were speaking to his nearest friend.—G. S. BOWES.

This word *boldly* signifies liberty without restraint. You may be free, for you are welcome. You may use freedom of speech. The word is so used in Acts 2:29 and 4:13. You have liberty to speak your minds freely, to speak all your heart, your ails, and wants, and fears, and grievances. As others may not fetter you in speaking to God by prescribing what words you should use; so you need not restrain yourselves, but freely speak all that your condition requires. —DAVID CLARKSON.

When men pray with a slavish bondage upon them, with cold, set phrases, and a crouching solemnity, the free Spirit of the Lord may well rebuke them. Art thou coming to a tyrant? Holy boldness, or at least a childlike hope, is most becoming in a Christian.

Obtaining mercy comes first; then finding grace to help in time of need. You cannot reverse God's order. You will not find grace to help in time of need till you have sought and found mercy to save.

You have no right to reckon on God's help and protection and guidance, and all other splendid privileges which He promises to "the children of God by faith in Jesus Christ," until you have this first blessing, the mercy of God in Christ Jesus; for it is *"in"* Jesus Christ that all the promises of God are yea and Amen.—F. R. HAVERGAL.

CHAPTER 177

# THE EDUCATION OF SONS OF GOD

*"Though He were a Son, yet learned He obedience by the things which He suffered"* (Heb. 5:8).

I. SONSHIP DOES NOT EXEMPT FROM SUFFERING.

1. Not even Jesus, as a Son, escaped suffering.
   He was *the* Son, peculiarly, and above all others.
   He was the honored and beloved first-born.
   He was the faithful and sinless Son.
2. No honor put upon the sons of God will exempt them from suffering.
3. No holiness of character, nor completeness of obedience can exempt the children of God from the school of suffering.
4. No prayer of God's sons, however earnest, will remove every thorn in the flesh from them.
5. No love in God's child, however fervent, will prevent his being tried.

II. SUFFERING DOES NOT MAR SONSHIP.

The case of our Lord is set forth as a model for all the sons of God.
1. His poverty did not disprove His Sonship. (Luke 2:12).
2. His temptations did not shake His Sonship. (Matt. 4:3).
3. His endurance of slander did not jeopardize it. (John 10:36).
4. His fear and sorrow did not put it in dispute. (Matt. 26:39).
5. His desertion by men did not invalidate it. (John 16:32).
6. His being forsaken of God did not alter it. (Luke 23:46).
7. His death cast no doubt thereon. (Mark 15:39).
   He arose again, and thus proved His Father's pleasure in Him. (John 20:17).

There never was a truer, or lovelier, or more beloved Son, than the chief of all sufferers. "A Man of sorrows, and acquainted with grief."

III. SUFFERING HAS A PECULIAR POWER TO TEACH TRUE SONS.

1. It touches the man's self; his bone, his flesh, his heart.
2. It tests his graces, and sweeps away those shams which are not proofs of obedience, but pretences of self-will.

3. It goes to the root, and tests the truth of our new nature. It shows whether repentance, faith, prayer, etc., are mere importations, or home-grown fruits.

4. It tests our endurance, and makes us see how far we are established in the obedience which we think we possess. Can we say, "Though he slay me, yet will I trust in Him"?

The anxious question—Am I a son?

The aspiring desire—Let me learn obedience.

The accepted discipline—I submit to suffer.

Corrections are pledges of our adoption, and badges of our sonship. One Son God hath without sin, but none without sorrow. As God corrects none but His own, so all that are His shall be sure to have it; and they shall take it for a favor too. (I Cor. 11:32).—JOHN TRAPP.

I bear my willing witness that I owe more to the fire, and the hammer, and the file, than to anything else in my Lord's workshop. I sometimes question whether I have ever learned anything except through the rod. When my school-room is darkened, I see most.—C. H. S.

"I never," said Luther, "knew the meaning of God's Word, until I came into affliction. I have always found it one of my best school-masters."

A minister was recovering from a dangerous illness, when one of his friends addressed him thus: "Sir, though God seems to be bringing you up from the gates of death, yet it will be a long time before you will sufficiently retrieve your strength, and regain vigor enough of mind to preach as usual." The good man answered: "You are mistaken, my friend, for this six weeks' illness has taught me more divinity than all my past studies and all my ten years' ministry put together."—*New Cyclopaedia of Anecdote.*

## CHAPTER 178

## LAME SHEEP

*"And make straight paths for your feet, lest that which is lame be turned out of the way; but let it rather be healed"* (Heb. 12:13).

We sometimes meet with those who are fleet of foot and joyous of spirit. Would to God that all were so! But as they are not, the lame must be considered.

I. IN ALL FLOCKS THERE ARE LAME SHEEP.

1. Some are so from their very nature and birth.
   Ready to despond and doubt.
   Ready to disbelieve and fall into error.

2. Some have been ill-fed. This brings on a foot-rot and lameness. Many are taught false doctrine.
3. Some have been worried, and so driven to lameness.
   By persecutors, with their slander, taunting, ridicule, etc.
   By proud professors, unkindly pious, severely critical, etc.
4. Some have grown weary through the roughness of the road.
   Exceeding much worldly trouble has depressed them.
   Exceeding much inward conflict has grieved them.
   Exceeding much controversy has worried them.
5. Some have had a terrible fall.
   This has broken their bones so as to prevent progress.
   This has snapped the sinew of their usefulness.
   This has crippled them as to holy joy.

II. THE REST OF THE FLOCK MUST SEEK THEIR HEALING.

1. By seeking their company, and not leaving them to perish by the way through neglect, contempt and despair.
2. By endeavoring to comfort them and to restore them.
3. By making straight paths for our own feet.
   By unquestionable holiness of life.
   By plain gospel teaching in our own simple way.
   By manifest joy in the Lord.

III. THE SHEPHERD OF THE FLOCK CARES FOR SUCH.

1. Their comfort: He has provided all the means of healing the lame.
2. Their hope: He is very gentle and tender and wills not that any one of them should wander and perish.
3. Their confidence: healing will win him much honor and grateful affection: wherefore we conclude that he will keep them.

Sheep are liable to many diseases, many of them are weak and feeble; these a good shepherd taketh pity on and endeavors to heal and strengthen.

So the saints of God are subject to manifold weaknesses, temptations, and afflictions, which moved the Almighty to great compassion, and sorely to rebuke the shepherds of Israel for their cruelty and great remissness toward his flock: "The diseased have ye not strengthened, neither have ye healed that which was sick," etc. And therefore he saith he would himself take the work into his own hands; "I will bind up that which was broken, and will strengthen that which was sick," etc.—BENJAMIN KEACH.

Studied expressions and high notions in a sermon, are like Asahel's carcase in the way, that did only stop men and make them gaze, but did no ways profit them or better them. It is better to present Truth in her native plainness than to hang her ears with counterfeit pearls.
—THOMAS BROOKS.

It should be between a strong saint and a weak as it is between two lute strings that are tuned one to another: no sooner one is struck but the other trembles; no sooner should a weak saint be struck, but the strong should tremble. "Remember them that are in bonds, as bound with them" (Heb. 13:3).—THOMAS BROOKS.

CHAPTER 179

## HEAR! HEAR!

*"See that ye refuse not Him that speaketh. For if they escape not who refused Him that spake on earth, much more shall we not escape, if we turn away from Him that speaketh from heaven"* (Heb. 12:25).

Jesus still speaks to us in the gospel.

What a privilege to hear such a voice, with such a message!

What cruel sin to refuse Jesus a hearing!

I. THERE IS NEED OF THIS EXHORTATION FROM MANY CONSIDERATIONS.

1. The excellence of the Word. It claims obedient attention.

2. The readiness of Satan to prevent our receiving the divine word.

3. Our own indisposition to receive the holy, heavenly message.

4. We have rejected too long already.

II. THERE ARE MANY WAYS OF REFUSING HIM THAT SPEAKETH.

1. Not hearing. Absence from public worship, neglect of Bible reading. "Turn away from Him."

2. Refusing to believe. Intellectually believing, but not with the heart.

3. Being offended. Angry with the gospel, indignant at plain speech, opposing honest personal rebuke.

III. THERE ARE MANY CAUSES FOR THIS REFUSING.

1. Self-reliant wisdom, which is too proud to hear the voice of God.

2. Hatred of holiness, which prefers the wilful to the obedient, the lustful to the pure, the selfish to the divine.

3. Fear of the world, which listens to threats, or bribes, or flatteries, and dares not act aright.

4. Procrastination, which cries "tomorrow," but means "never."

### IV. THE DOOM TO BE FEARED IF WE REFUSE CHRIST.

Those to whom Moses spake on earth, who refused Him, escaped not.

1. Let us think of their doom, and learn that equally sure destruction will happen to all who refuse Christ.
   Pharaoh and the Egyptians.
   The murmurers dying in the wilderness.
   Korah, Dathan and Abiram.

2. Let us see how some have perished in the church.
   Judas, Ananias, and Sapphira, etc.

3. Let us see how others perish who remain in the world, and refuse to quit it for the fold of Christ.
   They shall not escape by Annihilation, nor by Purgatory, nor by Universal Restitutions.

We seem to have done with the Word as it has passed through our ears; but the Word, be it remembered, will never have done with us, till it has judged us at the last day.—JUDGE HALE.

A nobleman, skilled in music, who had often observed the Hon. and Rev. Mr. Cadogan's inattention to his performance, said to him one day, "Come, I am determined to make you feel the force of music; pay particular attention to this piece." It was accordingly played. "Well, what do you say now?" "Why, just what I said before." "What! can you hear this and not be charmed? Well, I am quite surprised at your insensibility. Where are your ears?"

"Bear with me, my Lord," replied Mr. Cadogan, "since I, too, have had my surprise. I have often, from the pulpit, set before you the most striking and affecting truths; I have sounded notes that might have raised the dead; I have said, 'Surely he will feel now,' but you never seem to be charmed with my music, though infinitely more interesting than yours. I, too, have been ready to say, with astonishment, 'Where are his ears?'"

One of the modern thinkers had been upholding the doctrine of universal salvation at a certain house with much zeal. A child who had listened to his pestilent talk, was heard to say to his companion, "We can now steal and lie, and do wicked things, for there is no hell when we die." If such preachers gain much power in this country, we shall not need to raise the question of a hell hereafter, for we shall have one here.—C. H. S.

## CHAPTER 180

# THE TRIED MAN THE BLESSED MAN

*"Blessed is the man that endureth temptation: for when he is tried, he shall receive the crown of life, which the Lord hath promised to them that love Him"* (James 1:12).

To be *blessed* is to be happy, favored, prosperous, etc.

But it has a secret, sacred emphasis all its own; for the favor and prosperity are such as only God Himself can bestow.

Who would not desire to be blessed of God?

I. THE BLESSED IN THIS LIFE.

1. Blessedness is not in our text connected with ease, freedom from trial, or absence of temptation.

    Untested treasures may be worthless; not so those which have endured the fire. No man may reckon himself blessed if he has to fear that a trial would wither all his excellence.

2. Blessedness belongs to those who endure tests.

    These have faith, or it would not be tried; and faith is blessed. These possess uprightness, purity, truth, patience; and all these are blessed things.

3. Blessedness comes out of patient experience.

    Blessedness of thankfulness for being sustained.

    Blessedness of holy dependence under conscious weakness.

    Blessedness of familiarity with God enjoyed in the affliction.

II. THE BLESSED IN THE LIFE TO COME.

1. Of being crowned. How crowned if never in the wars?

    Crowned because victorious over enemies.

    Crowned because they have kept the conditions of the award

2. Of attaining the glory and "crown of life" by enduring trial, thus only can life be developed till its flower and crown appear.

3. Of possessing a living crown of endless joy.

    If such fierce trials do not kill them, nothing will.

4. Of receiving this life-crown from God.

    His own promise reveals and displays it.

    His peculiar regard to those who love Him doubly ensures it.

    His own hand shall give it.

Afflictions do not make the people of God miserable. There is a great deal of difference between a Christian and a man of the world: his best estate is vanity (Psalm 39:5); and a Christian's worst is happiness. He that loveth God is like a die; cast him high or low, he is still upon the square: he may be sometimes afflicted, but he is always happy.—THOMAS MANTON.

Many were the sorts of crowns which were in use amongst the Roman victors; at first, *corona civica*, a crown made of oaken boughs, which was given by the Romans to him that saved the life of any citizen in battle against his enemies.

*Muralis*, which was of gold, given to him that first scaled the wall of any town or castle.

*Triumphalis*, which was of laurel, given to the chief general or consul who after some signal victory, came home triumphing.

These, with many others, as imperial, regal, and princely crowns (rather garlands or coronets than crowns), are not to be compared to the crown of glory which God hath prepared for those that love Him. Who is able to express the glory of it; or to what glorious thing shall it be likened? If I had the tongue of men and angels, I should be unable to decipher it as it worthily deserveth. It is not only a crown of glory, but hath divers other titles of preëminency given unto it, of which all shall be true partakers that are godly; a crown of righteousness by the imputation of Christ's righteousness; a crown of life, because those that have it shall be made capable of life eternal; a crown of stars, because they that receive it shall shine as stars for ever and ever.—JOHN SPENCER.

## CHAPTER 181

## MORE AND MORE

*"But He giveth more grace"* (James 4:6).

Practical as is the Epistle of James, the apostle does not neglect to extol the grace of God, as unevangelical preachers do in these times.

We err if we commend the fruits regardless of the root from which they spring. Every virtue should be traced to grace.

I. OBSERVE THE TEXT IN ITS CONNECTION.

1. It presents a contrast. "But He giveth more grace."
   Two potent motives are confronted. "The spirit that dwelleth in us lusteth to envy"; on God's part this is met by, "but He giveth more grace."

2. It suggests a note of admiration.
   When we discover more of our weakness, God gives more grace.

3. We learn where to obtain the weapons of our warfare: we must look to Him who gives grace.

4. It encourages us in continuing the conflict.
   As long as there is one passion in the believing soul that dares to rise God will give grace to struggle with it.

5. It plainly indicates a victory.
   "He giveth more grace" is a plain promise that—
   God will not give us up; but that He will more and more augment the force of grace, so that sin must and shall ultimately yield to its sanctifying dominion.

## II. OBSERVE THE GENERAL TRUTH OF THE TEXT.

God is ever on the giving hand. The text speaks of it as the Lord's way and habit: "He giveth more grace."

This should be—

1. A truth of daily use for ourselves.
2. A promise daily pleaded for others.
3. An assurance in prospect of the severe tests of sickness and death.

## III. BRING IT HOME BY SPECIAL APPROPRIATION.

1. My spiritual poverty, then, is my own fault, for the Lord giveth more grace to all who believe for it.
2. My spiritual growth will be to His glory, for I can only grow because He gives more grace. Oh, to grow constantly!

When Matthew Henry was a child he received much impression from a sermon on the parable of the "mustard-seed." On returning home, he said to his child sister, "I think I have received a grain of grace." It was the seed of the Commentary "cast upon the waters."
—CHARLES STANFORD.

I have grace every day! every hour! When the rebel is brought, nine times a-day, twenty times a-day, for the space of forty years, by his prince's grace, from under the axe, how fair and sweet are the multiplied pardons and reprievals of grace to Him! In my case here are multitudes of multiplied redemptions! Here is plenteous redemption! I defile every hour, Christ washeth; I fall, grace raiseth me; I come this day, this morning, under the rebuke of justice, but grace pardoneth me; and so it is all along, till grace puts me into heaven.
—SAMUEL RUTHERFORD.

A little grace will bring us to heaven hereafter, but great grace will bring heaven to us now.—ARNOLD DIVINE.

Oh, what a sad thing it is when Christians are what they always were! You should have more grace; your word should be, *ego non sum ego*—I am not the same I, or *nunc oblita mihi*—now my old courses are forgotten; or, as the apostle, I Peter 4:3, "The time past may suffice to have walked in the lusts of the flesh."—THOMAS MANTON.

CHAPTER 182

# IF SO — WHAT THEN?

*"If the righteous scarcely be saved, where shall the ungodly and the sinner appear?"* (I Peter 4:18).

"Scarcely saved" points out the difficulty of salvation.

Some think it easy to begin by believing; but the prophet cries, "Who hath believed?" and Jesus asks, "When the Son of man cometh, shall He find faith on the earth?"

It is no light thing to be saved: omnipotent grace is needed.

It is no trifling thing to be lost, but it can be done by neglect.

I. THE FACT: *"The righteous scarcely are saved."*

    1. From the connection we conclude that the righteous are saved with difficulty because of the strictness of divine rule. Good corn endures the sickle, the flail, the fan, the sieve, the mill, the oven.

       The great test of all is the omniscient judgment of the jealous God. What grace will be needed to pass that ordeal!

    2. From the experience of saints we come to the same conclusion. They find many saving acts to be hard, as for instance—

       To lay hold on Christ simply, and as sinners.

       To overcome the flesh from day to day.

       To resist the world with its blandishments, threats, and customs.

       To vanquish Satan and his horrible temptations.

II. THE INFERENCE FROM THE FACT: *"Where shall the ungodly and the sinner appear?"*

    1. If even the true coin is so severely tested, what will become of "Reprobate silver"?

    2. If saints scarcely reach heaven what of the ungodly?

       What can they do who have no God?

       What without diligence? When the tradesman, though careful, is losing all his capital, what of the spendthrift?

       What without truth? When the fire consumes houses strongly built, what must become of wood, hay, stubble?

    3. If saints are so sorely chastened, what will justice mete out to the openly defiant sinner?

III. ANOTHER INFERENCE. *Where will the mere professor appear?*

    If the truly godly have a hard fight for it—

       The formalist will find ceremonies a poor solace.

       The false professor will be ruined by his hypocrisy.

       The presumptuous will find his daring pride a poor help.

IV. ANOTHER INFERENCE. *Then the tempted soul may be saved.*
Uprising corruption makes us stagger.
A persecuting world tries us sorely.
Fierce temptations from without cause us perplexity.
Loss of inward joys bring us to a stand.
Failure in holy efforts tests our faith.
But in all this we have fellowship with the righteous of all ages.
They are saved, and so shall we be.

When the apostle uses the phrase—*"If the righteous scarcely be saved,"* he does not, assuredly, mean that there is any doubt about the absolute and infinite sufficiency of the ground of their salvation: or that there is any uncertainty in the result.

*His language refers to the difficulty in bringing them through* to their final salvation; to the necessity of employing the rod and furnace; the process, in many instances severe, of correction and purification.

If "fiery trial" be required, and His hatred of sin and His love to His children will not allow to withhold it, to purge out the remaining alloy of their holiness, what must His enemies have to look for from Him abhorrence of evil, in whom sin is not the mere alloy of a better material, *but all is sin together?*—DR. WARDLAW.

There is much ado to get Lot out of Sodom, to get Israel out of Egypt. It is no easy matter to get a man out of the state of corruption.—RICHARD SIBBES.

Of this I am assured, that no less devotion than that which carried the martyrs through the flames, will carry us unpolluted through this present world.—MRS. PALMER.

Where shall he appear, when to the end that he might not appear, he would be glad to be smothered under the weight of the hills and mountains, if they could shelter him from appearing?—ARCHBISHOP LEIGHTON.

# CHAPTER 183

## THE LORD'S KNOWLEDGE OUR SAFEGUARD

*"The Lord knoweth how to deliver the godly out of temptations, and to reserve the unjust unto the day of judgment to be punished"* (II Peter 2:9).

"The Lord knoweth." Our faith in the superior knowledge of God is a great source of comfort to us—

In reference to perplexing doctrines.
In reference to puzzling prophecies.
In reference to amazing promises.
In reference to distressing providences.
In reference to grievous temptations.

I. THE LORD'S KNOWLEDGE IN REFERENCE TO CHARACTER.
1. He knows the godly—
Under trial, when they are not known to others.
Under temptation, when scarcely known to themselves.
2. He knows the unjust—
Though they make loud professions of piety.
Though they may be honored for their great possessions.
No error either as to partiality or severity is made by God.

II. THE LORD'S KNOWLEDGE IN REFERENCE TO THE GODLY.
1. His knowledge of their case is perfect. Before, in, and after
temptation He knows their sorrows.
2. He knows in every case how to deliver them.
3. He knows the way which will be most glorifying to Himself.
4. His knowledge should cause them to trust in Him with holy
confidence, and never to sin in order to escape.

III. THE LORD'S KNOWLEDGE IN REFERENCE TO THE UNJUST.
The Lord knows best—
1. How to reserve them under restraints. He makes it possible
to reprieve them, and yet to maintain law and order.
2. How and when to strike them down when their iniquities are
full.
3. How to deal with them in judgment, and throughout the future
state. The mysteries of eternal doom are safe in His hand.
Two fine illustrations of the Lord's dealings with the righteous
and the wicked may be found in Acts 12, in connection with Peter's
life.
Peter in prison was unexpectedly set free.
Herod on the throne was eaten of worms.
On the headstone of a little grave containing a little child which
was washed ashore during the gales, without any clue to birth, name,
or parentage, was placed the epitaph: "God knows."—*Leisure Hour*.
In the *Life and Letters of G. Ticknor*, a remark is made to the
effect, that when in Brussels, and conversing with some of the *elite*
of society there, he could not avoid constantly remembering that two
of the high-minded intellectual persons with whom he was sitting
were under sentence of death if found within the grasp of Austria.
We cannot forget that many around us are now "under condemnation,"
and are "reserved until the day of judgment."

## CHAPTER 184
## BY-AND-BY

*"It doth not yet appear what we shall be: but we know that when He shall appear, we shall be like Him; for we shall see Him as He is"* (I John 3:2).

I. "IT DOTH NOT YET APPEAR WHAT WE SHALL BE."

At present we are veiled, and travel through the world *incognito*.

1. Our Master was not made manifest here below.
   His glory was veiled in flesh.
   His Deity was concealed in infirmity.
   His power was hidden under sorrow and weakness.
   His riches were buried under poverty and shame.
   The world knew Him not, for He was made flesh.
2. We must needs have an evening before our morning, a schooling before our college, a tuning before the music is ready.
3. This is not the time in which to appear in our glory.
   The winter prepares flowers, but does not call them forth.
   The ebb-tide reveals the secrets of the sea, but many of our rivers no gallant ship can then sail.
   To everything there is a season, and this is not the time of glory.

II. "BUT WE KNOW THAT WHEN HE SHALL APPEAR."

1. We speak of our Lord's manifestation without doubt. "We know."
2. Our faith is so assured that it becomes knowledge.
   He will be manifest upon this earth in person.

III. "WE SHALL BE LIKE HIM."

1. Having a body like His body.
   Sinless, incorruptible, painless, spiritual, clothed with beauty and power, and yet most real and true.
2. Having a soul like His soul.
   Perfect, holy, instructed, developed, strengthened, active, delivered from temptation, conflict, and suffering.
3. Having such dignities and glories as He wears.
   Kings, priests, conquerors, judges, sons of God.

IV. "WE SHALL SEE HIM AS HE IS."

1. This glorious sight will perfect our likeness.
2. This will be the result of our being like Him.
3. This will be evidence of our being like Him, since none but the pure in heart can see God.
   The sight will be ravishing.
   The sight will be transforming and transfiguring.
   The sight will be abiding, and a source of bliss forever.

God showed *power* in making us creatures, but *love* in making us sons. Plato gave God thanks that He had made him a man, and not a beast; but what cause have they to adore God's love, Who hath made them children! The apostle puts an *ecce* to it, *Behold!*—THOMAS WATSON.

Such divine, God-given glimpses into the future reveal to us more than all our thinking. What intense truth, what divine meaning there is in God's creative word: "Let us make man in our image, after our likeness!" To show forth the likeness of the Invisible, to be partaker of the divine nature, to share with God His rule of the universe, is man's destiny. His place is indeed one of unspeakable glory.

Standing between two eternities, the eternal purpose in which we were predestinated to be conformed to the image of the first-born Son, and the eternal realization of that purpose, when we shall be like Him in His glory. We hear the voice from every side: O ye image-bearers of God! on the way to share the glory of God and of Christ, live a God-like, live a Christlike life!—ANDREW MURRAY.

A converted blind man once said, "Jesus Christ will be the first person I shall ever see, for my eyes will be opened in heaven."

"You are going to be with Jesus, and to see Him as He is," said a friend to Rowland Hill on his death-bed. "Yes," replied Mr. Hill, with emphasis, "and I shall be *like* Him; *that* is the crowning point."

## CHAPTER 185

## LIFE PROVED BY LOVE

*"We know that we have passed from death unto life, because we love the brethren"* (I John 3:14).

I  WE KNOW THAT WE WERE DEAD.

1. We were without feeling when law and gospel were addressing us.
2. Without hunger and thirst after righteousness.
3. Without power of movement towards God in repentance.
4. Without the breath of prayer, or pulse of desire.

II.  WE KNOW THAT WE HAVE UNDERGONE A SINGULAR CHANGE.

1. The reverse of the natural change from life to death.
2. No more easy to describe than the death change would be.
3. This change varies in each case as to its outward phenomena, but it is essentially the same in all.

4. As a general rule its course is as follows—
   It commences with painful sensations.
   It leads to a sad discovery of our natural weakness.
   It is made manifest by personal faith in Jesus.
   It operates on the man by repentance and purification.
   It is continued by perseverance in sanctification.
   It is completed in joy, infinite, eternal.
5. The period of this change is an era to be looked back upon in time and through eternity with grateful praise.

## III. We Know That We Live.

1. We know that faith has given us new senses, grasping a new world, enjoying a realm of spiritual things.
2. We know that we have new hopes, fears, desires, delights, etc.
3. We know that we have new needs; such as heavenly breath, food, instruction, correction, etc.

## IV. We Know That We Live, Because We Love. "We love the brethren."

1. We love them for Christ's sake.
2. We love them for the truth's sake.
3. We love them for their own sake.
4. We love them when the world hates them.
5. We love their company, their example, their exhortations.
6. We love them despite the drawbacks of infirmity, inferiority, etc.

Just as in the gospel he rescues the word *logos* from antichristian uses, so in this Epistle he rescues the word *"know"* and aims at making his "little children" Gnostics in the divine sense. Knowledge is excellent, but the path to it is not through intellectual speculation, however keen and subtle, but through faith in Jesus Christ and subjection to Him, according to those most Johannine words in the Gospel of Matthew: "Neither knoweth any man the Father save the Son, and He to whomsoever the Son will reveal Him."—Dr. Culross.

The world always loves to believe that it is impossible to know that we are converted. If you ask them, they will say, "I am not sure; I cannot tell"; but the whole Bible declares we may receive, and know that we have received, the forgiveness of sins.—R. M. McCheyne.

In the early days of Christianity, when it triumphed over the old heathenism of the Roman world, it founded a new society bound together by this holy mutual love. The catacombs of Rome bear remarkable testimony to this gracious brotherhood. There were laid the bodies of members of the highest Roman aristocracy, some even of the family of the Cæsars, side by side with the remains of obscure slaves and laborers.

And in the case of the earliest graves the inscriptions are without a single allusion to the position in society of him who was buried there: they did not trouble themselves whether he had been a consul or a slave, a tribune of the legion or a common soldier, a patrician or an artisan. It sufficed that they knew him to have been a believer in Christ, a man who feared God. They cared not to perpetuate in death the vain distinctions of the world; they had mastered the glorious teaching of the Lord, "One is your master, even Christ, and all ye are brethren."—E. DE PRESSENSE.

## CHAPTER 186

## VICTORIOUS FAITH

*"For whatsoever is born of God overcometh the world: and this is the victory that overcometh the world, even our faith"* (I John 5:4).

I. THE CONQUEST ITSELF: "Overcometh the world."
  1. We break loose from the world's customs.
  2. We maintain our freedom to obey a higher Master in all things. We are not enslaved by dread of poverty, greed of riches, official command, personal ambition, love of honor, fear of shame, or force of numbers.
  3. We are above the world's authority. Its ancient customs or novel edicts are for its own children: we do not own it as a ruler, or as a judge.
  4. We are above its religion. We gather our religion from God and His Word, not from human sources.

As one in whom this conquest was seen, read the story of Abraham. Think of him in connection with his quitting home, his lonely wanderings, his conduct towards Lot, Sodom and her king, Isaac, etc.

II. THE CONQUERING NATURE. "Whatsoever is born of God."
  1. This nature alone will undertake the contest with the world.
  2. This nature alone can continue it. All else wearies in the fray. This nature is born to conquer. God is the Lord, and that which is born of him is royal and ruling.

III. THE CONQUERING WEAPON. "Even our faith."
We are enabled to be conquerors through regarding—
  1. The unseen reward which awaits us.
  2. The unseen presence which surrounds us. God and a cloud of witnesses hold us in full survey.

3. The mystic union to Christ which grace has wrought in us. Resting in Jesus we overcome the world.

IV. THE SPECIALTY OF IT—"This is *the* victory."
1. For salvation, finding the rest of faith.
2. For imitation, finding the wisdom of Jesus, the Son of God.
3. For consolation, seeing victory secured to us in Jesus.
   Behold your conflict—born to battle.
   Behold your triumph—bound to conquer.

When a traveller was asked whether he did not admire the admirable structure of some stately building, "No," said he, *"for I have been at Rome, where better are to be seen every day."* O believer, if the world tempt thee with rare sights and curious prospects, thou mayest well scorn them, having been, by contemplation, in heaven, and being able, by faith, to see infinitely better delights every hour of the day! "This is the victory that overcometh the world, even our faith."—*Feathers for Arrows.*

The believer not only overcomes the world in its deformities, but in its seeming excellencies. Not in the way that Alexander and other conquerors overcame it, but in a much nobler way; for they, so far from overcoming the world, were slaves to the world. The man who puts ten thousand other men to death, does not overcome the world.

The true conqueror is he who can say, with Paul, "Thanks be to God, Who giveth us the victory through our Lord Jesus Christ," and, "Who shall separate us from the love of Christ? Shall tribulation?" etc. "Nay, in all these things we are more than conquerors, through him that loved us." Such an one has recourse, by faith, to an infallible standard—the Word of God: indeed, there is no other. He detects the world, and will not be imposed upon by it. When he is tempted to take the world's good things as his portion, he rejects them; because he has something better in hand.

Thus, faith in Christ overcometh the corrupt influence, the inordinate love, the slavish fear, the idolatry, the friendship, the false wisdom, and the maxims of the world: it overcometh not only the folly, but the very religion of the world, as far as it is a false religion.—RICHARD CECIL.

It is asserted of this elegant creature (the Bird of Paradise) that it always flies against the wind; as, otherwise, its beautiful, but delicate plumage would be ruffled and spoiled. Those only are the Birds of Paradise, in a spiritual sense, who make good their way against the wind of worldliness; a wind always blowing in an opposite direction to that of heaven.—J. D. HULL.

## CHAPTER 187

# FOR THE TRUTH'S SAKE

*"For the truth's sake, which dwelleth in us, and shall be with us forever"* (II John 2).

## I. THE TRUTH IS A CHRISTIAN NECESSITY.

Once let the truth of God obtain an entrance into the human heart and subdue the whole man unto itself, no power human or infernal can dislodge it.

1. We entertain the Truth not as a guest but as the master of the house. He is not a Christian who does not thus believe. Those who feel the vital power of the gospel, and know the might of the Holy Ghost as He opens, applies and seals the Lord's Word, would sooner be torn to pieces than be rent away from the Gospel of their salvation.

2. The Truth will be our living support, our dying comfort, our rising song, our eternal glory.

## II. THE TRUTH IS A CHRISTIAN PRIVILEGE.

1. Without it our faith were little worth. Some truths we outgrow and leave behind, for they are but rudiments and lessons for beginners, but we cannot thus deal with Divine truth. Though it is sweet food for babes it is in the highest sense strong meat for men.

2. With it we learn much. The truth that we are sinners is painfully with us to humble and make us watchful. The more blessed truth that whosoever believeth on the Lord Jesus shall be saved, abides with us as our hope and joy.

## III. THE TRUTH MAKES US EXERCISE OUR LOVE.

No narrow circle can contain our gracious sympathies. As wide as the election of grace must be our communion of heart.

Much of error may be mingled with truth received. Let us war with the error but still love the brother for the measure of truth which we see in him; above all let us love and spread the truth ourselves.

## CHAPTER 188

## SOUL-HEALTH

*"Beloved, I wish above all things that thou mayest prosper and be in health, even as thy soul prospereth"* (III John 2).

### I. WE WILL EXAMINE THE WORDS OF THE TEXT.

1. "I wish"; more correctly, as in the margin, "I pray." Prayer is a wish sanctified. Turn your wishes into prayers.
2. "That thou mayest prosper." We may ask for prosperity for our friends; especially if, like Gaius, they serve God and His cause with their substance.
3. "And be in health." This is necessary to the enjoyment of prosperity. What would all else be without it?
4. "Even as thy soul prospereth." We are startled at this wish: the spiritual health of Gaius is made the standard of his outward prosperity! Dare we pray thus for many of our friends?

### II. WE WILL MENTION THE SYMPTOMS OF ILL-HEALTH.

1. A low temperature.
   Lukewarmness is an ill sign. In business, such a man will make but little way; in religion, none at all.
   This is terrible in the case of a minister.
   This is dangerous in the case of a hearer.
2. A contracted heart.
   While some are latitudinarian, others are intolerant, and cut off all who do not utter their Shibboleth.
   If we do not love the brethren, there is something wrong with us.
3. A failing appetite as to spiritual food.
4. A difficulty in breathing.
   When prayer is an irksome duty, everything is wrong with us.

### III. WE WILL SUGGEST MEANS OF RECOVERY.

1. Seek good food. Hear a gospel preacher. Study the Word.
2. Breathe freely. Do not restrain prayer.
3. Exercise yourself unto godliness. Labor for God.
4. Return to your native air: breathe the atmosphere of Calvary.
5. Live by the sea. Dwell near to God's all-sufficiency.
6. If these things fail, here is an old prescription: *"carnis et Sanguinis Christi."* This taken several times a day in a draught of the tears of repentance, is a sure cure.

Sin is called in Scripture by the names of diseases. It is called the plague of the heart (I Kings 8:38). There are as many diseases of the soul as there are of the body. Drunkenness is a spiritual dropsy; security is a spiritual lethargy; envy is a spiritual canker; lust is a spiritual fever (Hos. 7:4). Apostasy or backsliding is the spiritual falling sickness; hardness of heart is the spiritual stone; searedness of conscience is a spiritual apoplexy; unsettledness of judgment is a spiritual palsy; pride is a spiritual tumor; vainglory is a spiritual itch. There is not any sickness of the body but there is some distemper of the soul that might be paralleled with it, and bear the name of it.—RALPH ROBINSON.

If a portrait were taken of a person in strong, vigorous health, and another was taken of the same man after a severe illness, or when he had been almost starved to death, or weakened by confinement, we should scarcely recognize them as the likeness of the same man, the dear old friend we loved! Still greater would be the change could we draw the *spiritual* portrait of many a once hearty, vigorous saint of God, whose soul has been starved for want of the proper spiritual nourishment, or by feeding upon "ashes" instead of bread. —G. S. BOWES.

## CHAPTER 189

## JUDE'S DOXOLOGY

*"Now unto Him that is able to keep you from falling and to present you faultless before the presence of His glory with exceeding joy,*
*To the only wise God our Saviour, be glory and majesty, dominion and power, both now and ever. Amen"* (Jude 24, 25).

I. LET US ADORE HIM WHO CAN KEEP US FROM FALLING.

1. We need keeping from falling, in the sense of preservation from—
Error of doctrine; which is rife enough in this age.
Error of spirit: such as want of love, or want of discernment, or unbelief, or credulity, or fanaticism, or conceit.
Outward sin. Alas, how low may the best fall!

2. None but the Lord can keep us from falling.
We cannot keep ourselves without Him.
No place guarantees security: the church, the closet, the communion-table—all are invaded by temptation.
No rules and regulations will secure us from stumbling. Stereotyped habits may only conceal deadly sins.

3. The Lord can do it. He is "able to keep," and He is "the only wise God, our Saviour." His wisdom is part of His ability.

By warning us: this may be done by our noting the falls of others, or by inward monitions, or by the Word.

By providence, affliction, etc., which remove occasions of sinning.

By a bitter sense of sin, which makes us dread it as a burnt child dreads the fire.

By His Holy Spirit, renewing in us desires after holiness.

II. LET US ADORE HIM WHO WILL PRESENT US IN HIS COURTS FAULTLESS.

1. None can stand in those courts who are covered with fault.
2. None can deliver us from former guilt, or keep us from daily faultiness in the future, but the Saviour Himself.
3. He will do it. We should not be exhorted to praise Him for an ability which He would not use.
4. He will do it "with exceeding joy," both to Himself and to us.

III. LET US ADORE HIM WITH HIGHEST ASCRIPTIONS OF PRAISE.

1. Wishing Him glory, majesty, dominion and power.
2. Ascribing these to Him as to the past, for He is "before all time." (R. V.)
3. Ascribing them to Him "now."
4. Ascribing them to Him "forever."

We cannot stand a moment longer than God upholdeth us; we are as a staff in the hand of a man; take away the hand, the staff falleth to the ground: or rather, as a little infant in the nurse's hand (Hosea 11:3); if we are left to our own feet, we shall soon fall. Created grace will never hold out against so many difficulties.

Philip Dickerson, an aged Baptist minister, who died October 22nd, 1882, just before his death, said, "Seventy years ago the Lord took me into His service without a character. He gave me a good character, and by His grace I have kept it."

## CHAPTER 190

## THE COMING WITH CLOUDS

*"Behold, He cometh with clouds; and every eye shall see Him, and they also which pierced Him: and all kindreds of the earth shall wail because of Him. Even so, Amen"* (Rev. 1:7).

I. OUR LORD JESUS COMES.

1. This fact is worthy of a note of admiration—"Behold!"
2. It should be vividly realized till we cry, "Behold, He cometh!"

3. It should be zealously proclaimed. We should use the herald's cry, "Behold!"

4. It is to be unquestioningly asserted as true. Assuredly He cometh.

It has been long foretold. Enoch. Jude 14.

He has Himself warned us of it. "Behold, I come quickly!"

He has made the sacred supper a token of it. "Till He come."

5. It is to be viewed with immediate interest.

"Behold!" for this is the grandest of all events.

"He cometh," the event is at the door.

"He," Who is your Lord and Bridegroom comes.

6. It is to be attended with a peculiar sign—"with clouds."

The clouds are the distinctive tokens of His Second Advent.

The tokens of the divine presence. "The dust of His feet."

The pillar of cloud was such in the wilderness.

The emblems of His majesty.

The ensigns of His power.

The warnings of His judgment. Charged with darkness and tempest are these gathered clouds.

II. OUR LORD'S COMING WILL BE SEEN OF ALL.

1. It will be a literal appearance. Not merely every mind shall think of Him, but "Every eye shall see Him."

2. It will be beheld by all sorts and kinds of living men.

3. It will be seen by those long dead.

4. It will be seen by His actual murderers, and others like them.

5. It will be manifest to those who desire not to see the Lord.

6. It will be a sight in which *you* will have a share.

III. HIS COMING WILL CAUSE SORROW. "All kindreds of the earth shall wail because of Him."

1. The sorrow will be very general. "All kindreds of the earth."

2. The sorrow will be very bitter. "Wail."

3. The sorrow proves that men will not be universally converted.

4. The sorrow also shows that men will not expect from Christ's coming a great deliverance.

They will not look to escape from punishment.

They will not look for Annihilation.

They will not look for Restoration.

If they did so, His coming would not cause them to wail.

5. The sorrow will, in a measure, arise out of His glory, seeing they rejected and resisted Him. That glory will be against them.

Even so, Lord Jesus, come quickly! In the meanwhile, it is not heaven that can keep Thee from me; it is not earth that can keep me from Thee; raise Thou up my soul to a life of faith with Thee: let me even enjoy Thy conversation, whilst I expect Thy return.— BISHOP HALL.

"*Every eye shall see Him.*" Every eye; the eye of every living man, whoever he is. None will be able to prevent it. The voice of the trumpet, the brightness of the flame, shall direct all eyes to HIM, shall fix all eyes upon Him. Be it ever so busy an eye, or ever so vain an eye, whatever employment, whatever amusement it had the moment before, will then no longer be able to employ it, or to amuse it. The eye will be lifted up to Christ, and will no more look down upon money, upon books, upon land, upon houses, upon gardens.

Your eyes and mine. O awful thought! Blessed Jesus! May we not see Thee as through tears; may we not then tremble at the sight! —DR. DODDRIDGE.

"And the Lord turned and looked upon Peter. . . . And Peter went out and wept bitterly." So shall it be, but in a different sense, with sinners at the day of judgment. The eye of Jesus as their judge shall be fixed upon them, and the look shall awake their sleeping memories, and reveal their burdens of sin and shame—countless and cursed crimes, denials worse than Peter's, since life-long and unrepented of, scoffings at love that wooed them, and despisings of mercy that called them—all these shall pierce their hearts as they behold the look of Jesus.

And they shall go out and flee from the presence of the Lord—go out never to return, flee even into the outer darkness, if so be they may hide them from that terrible gaze. And they shall weep bitterly —weep as they never wept before, burning, scalding tears, such as earth's sorrow never drew—weep never to be comforted, tears never to be wiped away. Their eyes shall be fountains of tears, not penitential and healing, but bitter and remorseful—tears of blood—tears that shall rend the heart in twain, and deluge the soul in fathomless woe.—ANON.

## CHAPTER 191

## THE REPENTANCE WHICH GLORIFIES GOD

*"And the fourth angel poured out his vial upon the sun; and power was given unto him to scorch men with fire.*
*"And men were scorched with great heat, and blasphemed the name of God, which hath power over these plagues; and they repented not to give Him glory"* (Rev. 16:8, 9).

The judgments of God do not of themselves produce true repentance; for these men "repented not to give Him glory."

## I. THEY MAY PRODUCE A REPENTANCE.

1. A carnal repentance, caused by fear of punishment. Cain.
2. A transient repentance, which subsides with the judgment. Pharaoh.
3. A superficial repentance, which retains the sin. Herod.
4. A despairing repentance, which ends in death. Judas.

In the case before us in the chapter, the men under the plague went from bad to worse, from impenitence to blasphemy; but where there is godly sorrow, sin is forsaken.

## II. THEY INVOLVE MEN IN GREATER SIN WHEN THEY DO NOT SOFTEN.

1. Their sin becomes more a sin of knowledge.
2. Their sin becomes more a sin of defiance.
3. Their sin becomes a sin of falsehood before God.
   Vows broken, resolutions forgotten; all this is lying unto the Holy Ghost.
4. Their sin becomes a sin of hate towards God.
   They even sacrifice themselves to spite their God.
5. Their sin becomes more and more deliberate, costly, and stubborn.
6. Their sin is thus proven to be engrained in their nature.

## III. THEY ARE TO BE LOOKED UPON WITH DISCRETION.

1. Used by the grace of God, they tend to arouse, impress, subdue, humble, and lead to repentance.
2. They may not be regarded as of themselves beneficial.
   Satan is not bettered by his misery.
   The lost in hell grow more obdurate through their pains.
   Many wicked men are the worse for their poverty.
   Many sick are not really penitent, but are hypocritical.
3. When we are not under judgment and terror, we should repent.
   Because we shall find it sweeter and nobler to be drawn than to be like "dumb driven cattle."
   Be it our one aim "to give HIM glory."

Trees may blossom fairly in the spring, on which no fruit is to be found in the harvest; and some have sharp soul exercises which are nothing but foretastes of hell.—BOSTON.

I believe it will be found that the repentance of most men is not so much sorrow for sin as sin, or real hatred of it, as sullen sorrow that they are not allowed to sin.—ADAM'S *Private Thoughts.*

There is no repentance in hell. They are scorched with heat, and blaspheme God's name, but repent not to give Him glory. They curse Him for their pains and sores, but repent not of their deeds. True repentance ariseth from faith and hope; but there can be no faith of releasement where is certain knowledge of eternal punishment;

knowledge and sense exclude faith. There can be no hope of termination where be chains of desperation. There shall be a desperate sorrow for pain, no penitent sorrow for sin.

None are now saved but by the blood of the Lamb; but when the world is ended, that fountain is dried up. The worm of conscience shall gnaw them with this remorse, bringing to their minds the cause of their present calamities: how often they have been invited to heaven, how easily they might have escaped hell. They shall weep for the loss of the one and again of the other, not for the cause of either, which were repentance. . . . They suffer, and they blaspheme. —THOMAS ADAMS.

How awful to read, "men blasphemed God because of the plague of the hail!" How true it is that affliction makes good men better, and bad men worse! Wrath converts no man. It is grace that saves. The chastisement that does not soften hardens. Judgments lead men to blaspheme, and the greater the plague, the more they blaspheme. What a solemn, but truthful, representation of the consequence of oft-neglected warnings! See the employment of man in the future state—in heaven, to praise; in hell, to blaspheme.—GEORGE ROGERS.

## CHAPTER 192

## THE MARRIAGE SUPPER OF THE LAMB

*"And he saith unto me, Blessed are they which are called unto the marriage supper of the Lamb"* (Rev. 19:9).

I. THE DESCRIPTION OF THE BRIDEGROOM.

The inspired apostle speaks of Him as "the Lamb."

This is John's special name for his Lord. Perhaps he learned it from hearing the Baptist cry, by the Jordan, "Behold the Lamb."

1. As the Lamb He is the one everlasting sacrifice for sin: He will not be other than this in His glory.
2. As the Lamb, suffering for sin, He is specially glorious in the eyes of the angels and all other holy intelligences; and so in His joyous day He wears that character.
3. As the Lamb He most fully displays His love to His church; and so He appears in this form on the day of His love's triumph.
4. As the Lamb He is the best loved of our souls.
   Behold, how He loved us even to the death!

II. The Meaning of the Marriage Supper.

1. The completion and perfection of the church. "His bride hath made herself ready."
2. The rising of the church into the nearest and happiest communion with Christ in His glory.
3. The commencement of an eternally unbroken rest. "He shall rest in His love." The church, like Ruth, shall find rest in the house of her husband.

III. The Persons Who Are Called To It.

1. Those who are so called as to accept the invitation.
2. Those who now possess the faith which is the token of admission.
3. Those who love the Bridegroom and bride.
4. Those who have on the wedding garment of sanctification.
5. Those who watch with lamps burning.

IV. The Blessedness Which Is Ascribed To Them.

1. They will be blessed indeed when at that feast, for—
Those who are called will be admitted.
Those who are admitted will be married.
Those who are married to Jesus will be endlessly happy. How many a marriage leads to misery! but it is not so in this case.
Alas, some are not thus blessed!
To be unblest is to be accursed.

He Who once hung so sad upon the cross for every one, will look around that bright company, and in every white robe, and in every lighted countenance, He will behold the fruit of His sufferings. He will "see of the travail of His soul, and will be satisfied." It will be the eternal union of God fulfilled in its deepest counsel—a people given to Christ from before all worlds; and that they are, that day, all chosen—all gathered—all washed—all saved—and not one of them is lost?—James Vaughan.

We dare not say that our Lord will love us more than He loves us now, but He will indulge His love for us more; He will manifest it more, we shall see more of it, we shall understand it better; it will appear to us as though He loved us more. He will lay open His whole heart and soul to us, with all its feelings, and secrets, and purposes, and allow us to know them, as far at least as we can understand them, and it will conduce to our happiness to know them. The love of this hour will be the perfection of love. This marriage-feast will be the feast, the triumph, of love—the exalted Saviour showing to the whole universe that He loves us to the utmost bound love can go, and we loving Him with a fervor, a gratitude and adoration, a delight, that are new even in heaven.

CHAPTER 193

# THE SCRIPTURES DIVINELY TRUE

*"And he saith unto me, These are the true sayings of God"* (Rev. 19:9).

These words relate to that which immediately precedes them.

The judgment of the harlot church. (Verse 2).

The glorious and universal reign of Christ. (Verse 6).

The sure reward and glory of Christ with His saved one in the glorious period at the last. (verses 7, 8).

## I. A RIGHT ESTIMATE OF HOLY SCRIPTURE.

1. These words which we find in the Old and New Testaments are true. Free from error, certain, enduring, infallible.
2. These words are thus true and divine in opposition to—
   Words of man. These may or may not be true.
   Pretended words of God. False prophets and men with addled intellects profess to speak in the name of God; but they lie.
3. These words are all of them truly divine.
   "These are the true sayings of God."
   Neither too severe to be true, nor too terrible to be uttered by a God of love, as some dare to say.
   Nor too good to be true, as tremblers fear.
   Nor too old to be true, as novelty-hunters affirm.
   Nor too simple to be truly divine, as the worldly-wise insinuate.

## II. THE RESULT OF FORMING SUCH AN ESTIMATE.

If you believe that "these are the true sayings of God."

1. You will listen to them with attention and judge what you hear from preachers by this infallible standard.
2. You will receive these words with assurance.
   This will produce confidence of understanding.
   This will produce rest of heart.
3. You will submit with reverence to these words, obey their precepts, believe their teachings, and value their prophesies.
4. You will expect fulfillment of divine promises under difficulties.
5. You will cling to revealed truth with pertinacity.
6. You will proclaim it with boldness.

## III. OUR JUSTIFICATION FOR FORMING SUCH AN ESTIMATE.

In these days we may be accused of bibliolatry, and other new crimes; but we shall hold to our belief in inspiration, for—

1. The scriptures are what they profess to be—the word of God.
2. There is a singular majesty and power in them; and we see this when the truth of God is preached.

3. There is a marvelous omniscience in Scripture, which is perceived by us when it unveils our inmost souls.

4. They have proven themselves true to us.
   They warned us of the bitter fruit of sin, and we have tasted it.

5. The witness of the Holy Spirit in our hearts confirms our faith in Holy Scripture. We believe, and are saved from sin by believing. Those words must be truly divine which have wrought in us such gracious results.

> Whence but from heaven could men unskill'd in arts,
> In several ages born, in several parts,
> Weave such agreeing truths? or how, or why
> Should all conspire to cheat us with a lie?
> Unasked their pains, ungrateful their advice,
> Starving their gain, and martyrdom their price.
> —DRYDEN.

Of most things it may be said, "Vanity of vanities, all is vanity"; but of the Bible it may be truly said, "Verity of verity, all is verity."—ARROWSMITH.